971.82
Fouilla
Gatheri
finding
245479

M000170079

Gathering
Voices

KL DEC 1998
OS MAY 1999
RU MAR 1996

Mamunitau
Staianimuanu

Gathering Voices

Finding Strength to
Help Our Children

Innu Nation and
Mushuau Innu Band Council

Foreword by Katie (Kiti) Rich
Edited by Camille Fouillard

Mamunitau Staianimuanu

Ntuapatetau Tshetshi
Uitshiakuts Stuassiminuts

Innu Tasheutshimau mak
Innut Utshimauts

Nistam peta tshitapata Kiti Rich utipatshimun
Camille Fouillard mamustapan innua utipatshimunua

Douglas & McIntyre
Vancouver / Toronto

OKANAGAN REGIONAL LIBRARY
1430 KLO ROAD, KELOWNA, B.C. V1W 3P6

Copyright © 1995 by the Innu Nation
Photographs © 1995 by photographers credited

95 96 97 98 99   5 4 3 2 1

All rights reserved. No part of this book may be reproduced, stored in a
retrieval system or transmitted in any form or by any means, without the prior
permission of the publisher or, in the case of photocopying or other repro-
graphic copying, a licence from CANCOPY (Canadian Reprography Collective),
Toronto, Ontario.

Douglas & McIntyre Ltd.
1615 Venables Street
Vancouver, British Columbia
V5L 2H1

Canadian Cataloguing in Publication Data

Main entry under title
Gathering Voices
    Text in English and Innu aimun.
ISBN 1-55054-421-7

1. Montagnais Indians—Social conditions. 2. Naskapi Indians—Social
conditions. 3. Indians of North America—Newfoundland—Labrador—
Social conditions. 4. Indians of North America—Quebec (Province)—
Social conditions. I. Naskapi Montagnais Innu Association. II. Mushuau
Innu Band Council. III. Title: Mamunitau staianimuanu.
E99.E7G25 1995   971.8'2004973   C95-910059-8

Editing by Barbara Pulling
Cover and text design by DesignGeist
Front cover photographs by Camille Fouillard: Abandoned sweat tent;
    Sam Napeu (left); and Brentas and Shunin (right)
Back cover illustration by Christine (Kistinis) Poker
Printed and bound in Canada by D. W. Friesen & Sons Ltd.
Printed on acid-free paper

The publisher gratefully acknowledges the assistance of the Canada Council
and of the British Columbia Ministry of Tourism, Small Business and Culture
for its publishing programs.

The extracts from the Royal Commission on Aboriginal Peoples report
Gathering Voices: Discovering Our Past, Present and Future that appear in
this book appear with the permission of the Royal Commission on Aboriginal
Peoples. The full report is available from the Innu Nation, P.O. Box 119,
Sheshatshiu, Labrador A0P 1M0. Telephone: 709-497-8399.

Tshetshi mushinau tshesituakuts
Matnin, Manishan, Uenti, Jeremiah, Tanien, Tshakapesh
mak kutakuts

To the memory of
Manishan, Matnin, Uenti, Jeremiah, Tanien, Tshakapesh
and the others

MATNIN — MANISHAN

Matnin mak Manishan
Tshitshue tshimitatikuts
Tshutaun mak tshikaun.

Mushinau tshasitakuts
esinakatatau
ute iniun.

Apu tshekuan etutamats
Emamitenetamats
Tshinuau kaniseshits

Mushinau Muestata mets,
Kauitsheuekuets kauitsheuekuets
Innu auasits.

Tshinuau menuentamek
Euepatamke tshementun
utessits.

Kanisets tshekuan
uishinikashinat muestatamuts
ne auasits.

Nikamun Sheskun

MADELINE — MARY JANE

Madeline and Mary Jane,
Your mother and father miss you.
They will always remember you,
ever since you left them.

There is nothing we can do,
but remember you as the twins.
All your friends are sad,
your friends, your friends, the Innu children.

You will find happiness
in God's paradise.
You, our twins, why did you leave us?
Our children are lonely.

*Song written and recorded by
Sheskun*

Camille Fouillard Photo

KANIUEKUTAT

Mushuau Innu Utshimau

Upuamun kie inikamun
Apatshitapan tshetshi ish
pimutat Utinima.

Epipamutet Nte Stesinat
Uin mishiue senitam
Eshinakunits.

Aueshisha minu nakatuenimepan
Kie senitamupan tshetshi ish
Naskumat kaish
Ishimukut.

Utaimun miste espitenitakunu
Nukunipan espish
Uitshinikununtshi
Utinima.

Apu nita shakuenimupan
Kie apu nita unikuatak
Uine tante tshitshue
Innu.

KANIUEKUTAT

Kaniuekutat was a much-loved elder in the community of Utshimassit. We mourn his passing on October 1, 1994, and keep his spirit alive in our struggle.

For many generations, his people walked softly and gently on their land; he has done the same.

Through their visions, dreams and singing, his people have been able to lead their own; he has done the same.

His people have cared for Mother Earth, the animals she provided, knew the rituals and ceremonies to give thanks; he has done the same.

His people have spoken wise words, for they knew these words would strengthen their own; he has done the same.

His people have known hardships and they have taught one another to survive; he has done the same.

Because he, with his people, chose a path of pride and dignity, he is a true Innu of our time.

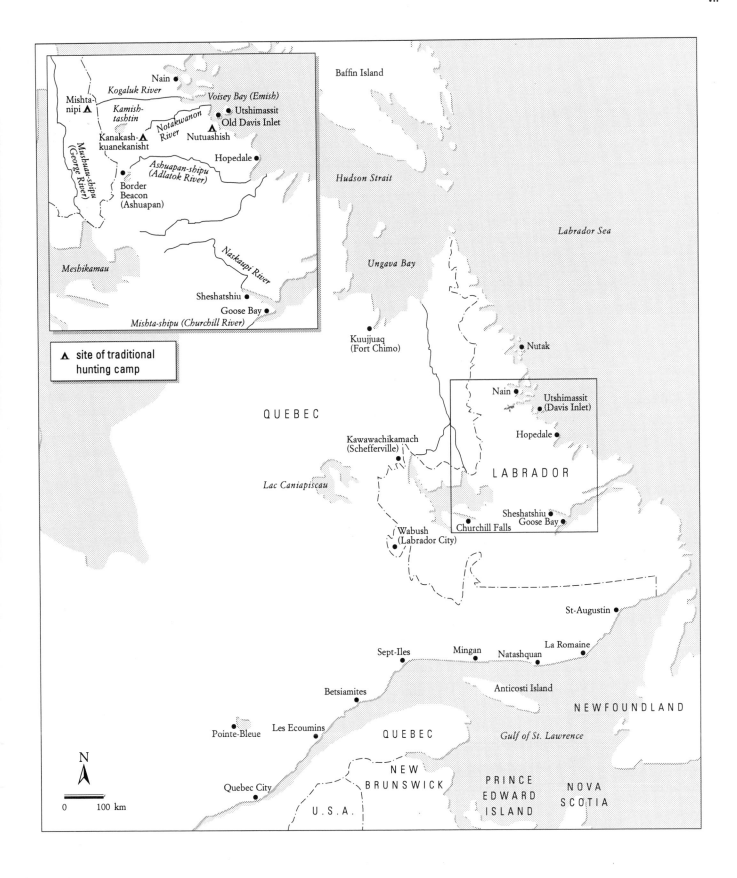

Inset map (upper left):

Nain

Kogaluk River

Mishta-nipi ▲

Kamish-tashtin

Voisey Bay (Emish)

Notakwanon River

Utshimassit
Old Davis Inlet

Kanakash-▲ kuanekanisht

Nutuashish ▲

Hopedale

Mushuau-shipu (George River)

Ashuapan-shipu (Adlatok River)

Border Beacon (Ashuapan)

Meshikamau

Naskaupi River

Sheshatshiu

Goose Bay

Mishta-shipu (Churchill River)

▲ site of traditional hunting camp

Main map:

Baffin Island

Hudson Strait

Labrador Sea

Ungava Bay

Kuujjuaq (Fort Chimo)

Nutak

Nain

Utshimassit (Davis Inlet)

Hopedale

QUEBEC

Kawawachikamach (Schefferville)

LABRADOR

Lac Caniapiscau

Sheshatshiu
Goose Bay

Churchill Falls

Wabush (Labrador City)

St-Augustin

Sept-Iles

Mingan

Natashquan

La Romaine

Betsiamites

Anticosti Island

NEWFOUNDLAND

Pointe-Bleue

Les Ecoumins

QUEBEC

Gulf of St. Lawrence

N

PRINCE EDWARD ISLAND

NOVA SCOTIA

Quebec City

NEW BRUNSWICK

U.S.A.

0   100 km

ESHINAKUATS TIPATSHIMUN

CONTENTS

TSHINASKUMITINAU

Tshitshue naskumauts kanutshikats emamuinamau aia-munueuni: tshenuts, auashits kaemakanits kauita-matauts tshekuanu. Naskumakanu Camille kamiste atuset kie kauitshiat Shuash, Manteskueu, Epa mak Etien.

Kie naskumakanuts ents ka uitshinuets tshetshi Innus-tents mishinanikanu - Kashetan, Shustin, Shuash, Ipuan, Tshatsh, Penash, Penute, Anishen, Mata Penetet mak Tun.

Kanakatuapashets - Penute, Kiti, Tepit, Uinipapeu, Ketshastipineu, mak Tanien.

Sheskun kanikamuts kie Kistinish kamishinantshet kie kaunishinatantshet.

Kie kaminuets akunikea - Peter Sibbald, Camille, Kiti, Jamie Lewis, Nigel Markham, Field Museum of Chicago, Smithsonian Institute mak Ray Webber.

Kie kauitshinuets enu mishinanikanu - Sandy Williamson, Oxfam-St. John's, Geoff Carre, Kuekuat-sheu mak Marie Wadden.

Kie tshetshi passe apitshitaiats kutak mishinanikan kaushitakants ents Royal Commission kantuenitas tshetshi ushitakanits en mishinanikan ishinikateu Kamamuetimak: Tshentusentimak Nte Steniunu Utat, Nitshish, Kie Nte Nikan kie naskumakanuts kauit-shinuets eushitakanits mishinanikanu Shimun, Tshan, Tshenish, Tumas, Ipuan, Shunin, Manteskueu, Patinik, Nanishi kie Camille.

Kie Peter Penashue, Innu Nation.

Eku Masten Tom Siddon katshi mintak tshetshi tshi-nai tutamuak.

Nitenitenan en e mamunamats nitaianimuanan tshet-shi eka minuats unikuatakanits Innuts. Kie nitenitenan tshetshi etu shutshinash kie shapinash kie miskemash nte uantuteash.

Tepit Nui
Innu Nation

Kiti Rich
Mushuau Innu Utshimauts

Tshenish Pasteen
Tshenu

ACKNOWLEDGEMENTS

Many thanks go out for this Gathering of Voices:

to the elders, children and all the participants who shared with us;

to those who worked on this project—Camille Fouillard for her tremendous effort, as well as the commissioners, George (Shuash) Gregoire, Marie Georgette (Manteskueu) Mistenapeu, Nympha (Epa) Byrne and Etien Pastiwet;

to those who helped with the translation and peer review: Cajetan (Kashetan) and Justine (Shustin) Rich, George (Shuash) Gregoire, Yvonne (Ipuan) Asta, George (Tshatsh) and Penash Rich, Prote (Penute) Poker, Angela (Aneshe) Pasteen, Martha (Mata) Piwas, Bernadette (Penatet) Nui and Tun Rich;

to the committee members: Penute Poker, Kiti Rich, David (Tepit) Nui, Joseph Mark (Uinipapeu) Rich, Mary Jane (Ketastipeneu) Nui and Daniel (Tanien) Poker;

to the Sheskun band for their song, and Christine (Kistinis) Poker for her poem and cover artwork;

to those who provided photos—Peter Sibbald, Ray Webber, Camille Fouillard, Nigel Markham, Jamie Lewis, the Field Museum of Chicago and the Smithsonian Institution; to those who helped put the original final report together: Sandy Williamson, St. John's Oxfam, Geoff Carre, Peter Armitage and Marie Wadden;

to the Royal Commission on Aboriginal Peoples for funding a community-based research project in 1993 entitled *Kamamuetimak Tshentusentimak nte Steniunu Utat, Nistish, kie nte Nikan*—a second gathering of voices—and allowing us to use extracts from the research report for our epilogue in this book; and to the team who worked on that project: Simon (Shimun) Poker, John (Tshan) Nui, Tshenish Pasteen, Joseph Raymond Mark (Tumas) Rich, Yvonne (Ipuan) Asta, Julianna (Shunin) Saunders, Manteskueu Mistenapeu, Patrick (Patinik) Rich, Nancy (Nanishi) Jack and Camille Fouillard;

to Peter Penashue, president of the Innu Nation;

and finally to Tom Siddon for giving us the opportunity in 1992 to do it on our own.

We hope this gathering of voices has broken the silence of a forgotten people. We hope also that it will continue to help us to find our true spirit and strength, as well as dignity to plan our future.

David (Tepit) Nui, Innu Nation
Katie (Kiti) Rich, Mushuau Innu Band Council
Tshenish Pasteen, Elder

ENKUN USSI UTAPATSHEMUN

Epishiminiskueu peikunu ashu neu eukun nta
tshishuk manakant shatshiakantshi auen tshekuanu
kie minakanu kanuna. Muk tshishuk epishiminiskueu
peik unu ashu neu mauats tshika unikuatumuts Utshimassiu Innuts. Ekun tshishuk kaueakanits ashutash
auasits. Nas apu tshekuan tshitutamas tshetshi nutshi-
akants niskueut, muk nakatuapatenan. Miseni-
makanuts auentshi etats nte mitshuapits, eku napeuts
ntuapameuts auasa nte mishiue mitshuapits. Unap-
atsh, uiapatamats nte etauakue auasits. Mishiue Innuts
uauapatamutsh enu neskuatents, eku minatsh.

Tshash nist pun epish kaniskuatets mitshiuap, esk
nimamitinenimaaets ntshe auasits. Nipekupitikunan,
eku nimamitunenimaiats nituasiminaits kie tshekuan
tshetutamas. Minishinakuen tshetshi ish Inniuts nituasiminaiats. Kie uinuau nituasiminaiats ui minu inniuts.
Kie nitshitapimushunan tan pan tshi uitshaiats. Eukun
uish tutamas mishinanikan kie mishiue Innuts uitamuts
enu espish eka minupuniakanits Innuts. Nakatuapa-
makanipan tsheutshimau espish piuenimat Innua.

Mauats minuats. Mishinanikan katshi tutamats
ninan nisenitenan tshetiats. Tshika uapatenau eish
tutamash uauitshinishunatsh pase kauitas Innu tshetu-
takanits. Pise niminupunan. Mak pise apu min-
upunats, tante tsheutshimauts apu uiuitshinimish.

Tshepishum 1993, akunakanuts auasits esi uakani-
uts. Nukakanuts auasits espish eka minuenitas. Eku
etutakanits ntshe kashetshimakanits nte uauiu. Kie
shakuenimunuku tsheutshimau espish piuenimat
Innua. Mishue nukushuts mak nte kamisis nukun
mishiue, tapue nishinakunishipan nte nussits. 1988
ashutash niskuesits uinipanushupants, mitshipants
ntukuna. Petakunipan nte tipa tshimushinanikan muk
tsheutshimau ishishuepan "apu tapuants." Eku nush
katshi nukushits auasits tshitshue mitshetuts tsheutshimau kakuseshima, kakutsheshits kie kauapukushits
mishikauts uauapatas eshinakunits Utshimassit.

Shuka kie ninan niui uitshinushunan kie shuka
niuinukutanan eshinakunikuiats. Eku etutamats mishinanikan tan pa uish uitshinushunan. Tapue pise tash
tshishipinua ne tshastishauakanit auasits mak nina
tshashipinitais tshetshi uitshiakanits Innut. Muk
esk mamishaua tshekuana esk eka tapuetakants. Ne
tshetshi uauitakants assin mak kauiatukuants. Kie
kamakunueshits.

Ninan niuisenitenan tan pa tshitutenan tsheish atini-
mats tshekuan eka minupants nte kamakunueshits kie
ueueshakantshi Innu. Nistam nta tshishipinipan, nish
pushuts Innuts uakamakunueshiuts. R.C.M.P. ekunts
tapants ni uta Utshimassits, eku kue tshetshimatshish
tsheutshimau tshetshi nistuapamats enu Innu
kamakunueshintshi kie tshetshi ashutat tutameastakan
uitshitusemituts. Apu tapuetak tsheutshimau. Atueni-
tamupan nte skutimashuntshi enua auasa, kie
uimamishimepan enu ekamakun ueshiuntshi. Apu
apitenimitshish. Ninan nistuapamaets enu
kamakunueshiuts. Tshitshipinuts eatusets, minuats
nist kutakuts pushuts kie tshishitauts ekamakunueshi-
uts. Tshitshue tapue tsheutshimau uitapueu
uatipenimitau muk mushinau nikukue tshimanan, apu
tapuet, tante apu nita mishinaushut Innu, tshetshi
tapuetak tsheutshimaua tipenimukut.

Pishimus peikunu ashu ashutas, tapue nukunu Innu
nist uauitshinushut. Ueuespimitakanuts tshekamakunuest kie kamakunueshits. Ntisishuenan apu
minuats esh ueueshakanits Innuts kie esh makunakan-
its. Uinuau Innuts tshika senitamuts enu tsheish uitshiakanits ents ketutamutshi tshekuanu. Katshi
petakuak enu etutuakants katipenimat tshekamakunueshintshi isishueu "auen kaueuespimitat
tshekamakunueshintshi tshika tshishikashuts." Eku
Innu Utshimauts kie uinuau mamishimeuts enua
mishiue tepemimukuts tshekamakunuesits. Muk katshi nish meastakanuts tsheutshimau mamishimeu nist
niskueua Kiti, Epa, mak Shustinish tshika ueueshakanuts. Nistam pita tshika ueueshakanuts iskueuts,
ishishueuts, patush tshetshi-tshi- tapatamats Innu
Utshimaua umishinanikanu. Enkunu tshe ueueshi-
akanits uiniskupishum. Ume issishuanuipen tshetshi
ueueshikunat 13 Uiniskupishum, muk menui itutean.
Niuitamakutan tshetshi makunikuiat kie tshetshi
nataukuiat muk menita ene takun.

Napinits 1994, tsheutshimau Ed Roberts uitutam
nishuau tshetshi pitekat tshekamakunueshintshi kie
kamakunueshintshi. Kie tapuetuakanu tshetshi apit-
shat ashimakanisha mak kauauastatsheshintshi. Peik-
mitashumitunu kamakunueshits mak ashimakanishits
uimishikapants. Mak eiapits tshipauepan kapiminashintshi tshetshi tueuntshi, eku neka nte tueuts kapiminashits. Uiapatas Innu etutak tsheutshimau, eku

FOREWORD

February 14 is usually a day when one gives a loved one a Valentine's present, message or card. But February 14, 1992, is a day the Innu of Utshimassit (Davis Inlet) will never forget. It marks the death of six innocent children in a house fire. Helplessly the community stood and watched the house burn to the ground.

There was no water to put the fire out. Confused about whether or not there was anyone in the house, men went from one house to another to look for the children. Daylight came, and we saw the bones. All day elders, women and children came and examined the ashes, stood around in the freezing cold and cried.

Three years after that horrible day, we remember. We think about those children. That day woke us up, made us think about our children and what needs to be done. Our children don't have to live like this. They have the same hopes and dreams as any other child. We also knew we had to examine ourselves to be able to help them. We had to be honest with ourselves. This is why we held a People's Inquiry and gathered voices. The whole community became involved, and we truly spoke from our hearts about how various outside agencies have played a role in our near-destruction, about how we stood by and watched them do it.

But not any more. The fire, then the inquiry, stirred us to action. Since this report was first released in June of 1992, we have worked hard to regain control of our lives. Our efforts have paid off, as you will read in the epilogue to this book. We have some success stories. But some of our attempts to combat the social problems we face have failed, mostly because the governments of Newfoundland and Canada continue to squash us rather than trying to provide us with the support and help we need.

Tragedy, especially involving our young people, has not ended. In January 1993, armed with a video camera, we tried to capture the hopelessness of our youth and how they are coping with their despair. We hoped these images would alert the world to our reality and shame the governments into helping us. The images we videotaped of six youths wanting to die from sniffing gas were shown around the world and made Utshimassit a symbol of the poverty that exists among First Nations in Canada. This was not the first such suicide pact. In 1988, six girls in our community quietly collected pills they said would help them end their lives. It made the front page of a newspaper, and the government's response was that "there was no substance to the story." But this time planeloads of government officials, reporters of all shapes and sizes, preachers and others descended on our community to get a first-hand look.

We weren't going to let our children or the issue die. We held meetings and prepared a seven-point plan, "Hearing the Voices," explaining steps needed to correct the situation. Some of these have been implemented, such as sending the children to an Alberta treatment centre and holding our own treatment program in *nutshimit* (the country). But other important issues, such as land rights, relocation and policing, are still outstanding.

This last issue, policing and the justice system, is one clear area where governments should have celebrated our efforts but instead stubbornly blocked us all the way. We were forced to take matters relating to policing and the courts into our own hands. The whole thing started in 1992 when two of our young people took the initiative to travel to the First Nations Tribal Police Institute in British Columbia to train as peacekeepers. The community was being policed by R.C.M.P. at the time of their return, and we approached the provincial government for recognition of our peacekeepers and six weeks of on-the-job training for them, an arrangement that has been made in other places in Canada. The province refused. They wouldn't recognize the credentials of the school (although Micmac constables in Conne River on the Island have been trained at the same school) and threatened to charge our peacekeepers with impersonating a police officer. But we didn't care if the governments recognized our peacekeepers or not. The two peacekeepers, under the direction of the Band Council, started their duties. Three more of our young people went for training. The government's refusal to co-operate led us to really question the jurisdiction of both governments over our lives, since Innu people have never signed any agreements or treaties.

On December 16, 1993, we took another important step in asserting control over the justice system. We evicted the judge and his court from the community. We were saying that the whole justice system does not

Innuts uinuau tshipamuts kapiminashitshi kateuntshi. Mishiue Innuts uinuau tshipamuts kapiminashitshi kateuntshi. Mishiue Innuts uitshinueuts kie uauitamuts tshetits. Kapipamaskuanikanitshi ushitapants. Uepastashuna tsheutshimau uteia, aiatshimutakanua, tante apu minuenitas Innuts etutuakanits.

Unapatak Innua euinuuinukut, tsheutshimau kuet punt tshetshi papeiat kamakunueshintshi. Nispanishapan nte Ottawa, kie tutueu tsheutshimaua tshetshi mishiue tshipas enu assinu kauauitakanits mak kauiatukuanits kie tshipam enu uauitakanits tshetshi Innuts pimpinushuts. Ishishueu tsheutshimau, nistam pita Innuts tshika issishueuts ninanu tipenimukuan tsheutshimau, mak tshika tapuetueuts tshekamakunueshintshi tshetshi ueueshinuentshi uta Utshimassits. Masten tshika tapetuakanuts kamakunueshits tshetshipitshets minuats uta Utshimassits, kie tshikaui-issishuenan menui-ust-tutean auk-essi mishinaushunat mishinike tshetshi minuat pitshet kamakunueshit ute utenat. Eku kutak tshekuan tsheui tapuetaken tshetshi minuat kaupimpints kaueuestan kie tshetshi kie ninan takuak tshetshi issishueiat uen tshemakunakan kie uen tsheka makunakan muk-e-ishinakuak tshetshi uitshikunak ume tshi-issishueian menui-ust-tuten, nika issishuen kie nika-tuten.

Muk eukun ume mitshenipani mishinanikea ueshitakantshi tshetshi etu uitshinikuts kie tshetshi etu nukutakanits espish peuenimakanits Innuts. Peik tapan kakeshau Donald McRae ishinikashupan. Kuekuetshimepan tshenua uta Utshimassits etutuakanits Innuts uipats. Eku katshi tipatshimuts Innuts, mamustau ne kakeshau, eku isishueu. Uin ne tsheutshimau pikunam enu tshipa ish uitshepen Innua. Ishishueu, Innuts uta Ntessinan nastesh mikastina-

muts enu esi minakanitshi kutakua Innua nte Kanata. Uipats une itishumakanishapan tsheutshimau (Newfoundland) tshetshi uin nakatuapamitak, eku minuenitam enu kutukua tsheutshimaua (Kanata) uauinakanitshi. Isishuemikan mishinanikan, enishits tsheutshimauts uinuau tutueuts Innua tshetshi teats uta ministikuts. Katshi tshitapatak tsheutshimau (Kanata) enu mishinanikanu, eku pepikushum katshi takanikanits. Eku mushinau nikuekuetshimanan anutshish tsheutshimau tshetshi tshitapatak enu mishinanikanu muk esk minita uitam etenitak. Eku esk ishinuakanu.

Eku mitshetuts kakeshauts mishikauts, tshetshi uapatats eshiniuntshi Innua kie mishinatamuts etutakanits, muk ume mishinanikan ninan nitipatshimunan. Tshika uapatenau esk nititenan nitainimuanan, atikunkaiets kie esk ntitetenan iesh inniuiats. Shuka kie nanan niuitutenan ne etishimushunats, tante tsheutshimau apu minuanits enu uatutunimits. Eku shuka niuipikunamuanan enu uatutunimist, esk eka pikunimit.

Niuapamushunan espish shutshinas kie uauitshitshish nituasiminaets. Mishue nipetakushinan uta Kanata mak nte kamisis. Eshukun tshishik, niuapamaiats nitshininaits uauitshinushuts. Kie ninan niutinenan tan pan katinan. Nikukuetshimaiats tshenuts tshetshi uauitshinuets. Nika ushitanan tshetshi minuenitas auasits eniuts. Ntutakunaits auassits tshetshi etu tshishepeniats e uauitshinushunats.

Nin
Mushuau Innu Iskueu
Kiti Rich
Shiship-pishum, 1995

work for the Innu and does not meet our needs to heal. We should be the ones to judge our own people. We should be able to have our own law enforcement and our own laws. We want to deal with the root causes of problems through healing circles and treatment programs. Punishing people is not the answer. A couple of days after our action on December 16, Chief Judge Donald Luther issued a statement saying that those involved would have to pay. The Band Council responded by filing a complaint with the Judicial Council of Newfoundland against Luther and the judge who was evicted. Two weeks later, charges were laid against three women involved in the incident, namely me, Nympha (Epa) Byrne and Constable Justine (Shustinis) Noah. The Judicial Council said it would deal with our complaint after our trial, set for March 13, 1995, but we refused to appear. Warrants were issued for our arrests but have never been executed.

In the summer of 1994, Newfoundland Justice Minister Ed Roberts attempted to bring the court back to the community. On two occasions, he ordered R.C.M.P. in full riot gear to escort Chief Judge Luther into the community to hold court. Roberts also received permission from the minister of national defence to access helicopters so that 100 R.C.M.P. and military could enter the community. He ordered the Department of Transportation to close the airstrip at Utshimassit and to stop all traffic from coming within seven miles of the community. We held strategy sessions. We decided no planes would land in the community at all, including military planes, so we barricaded the airstrip with oil drums, lumber and trucks. The whole community participated, giving ideas and making placards with our messages to the outside world. Both Canadian and Newfoundland flags were hung upside down. We considered the actions of the governments a military invasion. Youth vandalized the R.C.M.P. patrol cabin in anger, saying, "So what? We are going to die tomorrow anyway." Seeing the resistance of the Innu, the minister abandoned his plans for an invasion. He had other plans. He travelled to Ottawa and convinced the federal government to suspend all talks with the Innu. Negotiations on land rights, relocation and the devolution of social programs as of today are still suspended. Before these negotiations can resume, governments are saying we will have to acknowledge that we are Canadian citizens. We will have to allow the court back into the community and apologize. We have finally signed a policing agreement with the province. Next they will have to agree to a court system where we have say over who goes to jail. If an apology from me can help us get this, I will do it.

But this is a human rights issue. In 1993, Dean Donald McRae, special investigator to the Canadian Human Rights Commission, examined our case. His conclusion was that Canada has continuously violated our rights. The federal government broke its own law by illegally transferring responsibility for the Innu to the Newfoundland government when Newfoundland joined Confederation in 1949. As a result, we have never received the funding or services that other First Nations get. Who is not respecting the law of Canada here? McRae also said that when the two governments moved us off our traditional land to settle us on this island, they were violating a special trust obligation. The provincial government read McRae's report and was glad to pass the buck. The federal Conservatives shredded the report (literally) after the last election. We had to send another copy to the new Liberal government. We have requested a formal response from Canada on this report countless times, but to this day we have not received one. We feel our basic human rights have been violated from day one, and this is how we have come to this place of despair where our children want to die.

Many people have come to study us, written books about us and reported on us, but this book is our own story. As you read it, you will know we have our own language, culture, traditions, legends and values. You will know that our path is far different from the one mapped out for us by governments. You will know that we are fiercely determined to break the policies of the governments before they break us.

As we become stronger and Utshimassit becomes a better place to live for our children, we are making our voices heard across Canada and around the world. Each day, we see more of our people healing. We are making choices and decisions. We are seeking out elders to help us. We will be a nation that our children will be proud of. In the meantime, the death of our children and the story you will read in this book remind us that we need to struggle forward.

Katie (Kiti) Rich
April 1995

ENISHINAKUASH

"Anutsh nas-tshika-ui shapinan emamunamak staian-imuanu." *Pitshuiantshuapit eianimuants nete Nutu-ashish*

Utshimassit, einu-nikatet Davis Inlet, nte nenemeu takun ntessinat—ume eiapastaiak einueimiak Ntassinan. Ninan ekute ute ntatanikutan ute ministikut Ilukuiak ministuk ishinikateu ute etaiat, nene 1967 estistet atshitashun ute nitispish taian. Utshimassit, 500 muk Innut, kie ekuta nta uets shitshiniat Innu Nation. Ninan mamu eniunats 13,000 nitishinan, 13

Innu utenu etats Innut, ute Labrador mak Quebec ute Ntassinats. Ume nas-pessish etakuak Innu utenu ute-takun Sheshatshit. Uaiu kakeshauts nitishinikatikunan "Montagnais" mak "Naskapi," muk ninan u-Innuts. Ute Utshimassit Innuts ishinikashut Mushuau-Innu. Kie mak Mushuat Innut ume uipats uets apastaiat assi ute tetshe nenemeu Ntassinat, at-kepue passe Innut itutepant nete tetshe Sheshatshit mak Uashat.

Utshimassit, ume eimun itenitakun miam utshimau assin. Eukun ne-ishinikatepan uipats Utshimassit, nenu katshi-tshimitat utshimaut (Hudson's Bay Com-

Uinipapeu, Tepit and Tamene at Nutuashish Gathering workshop / Uinipapeu, Tepit mak Tamene nte Nutuashish kamamuitunants, 1992

CAMILLE FOUILLARD PHOTO

INTRODUCTION

"Now we must be strong in gathering voices."
Tent meeting, Nutuashish Gathering

Utshimassit (pronounced Oot-she-mah-seet) is the Innu name for the community of Davis Inlet, situated on the northeast coast of Ntesinan, the word we use for our land. We were settled in this village on the island of Iluikoyak in 1967. Utshimassit now has a population of about 500 people. We are part of the Innu Nation. Our people number about 13,000 and live in thirteen communities on the Labrador and Quebec sides of Ntesinan. Our sister community in Labrador is Sheshatshiu. Europeans called us Montagnais and Naskapi, but we are the Innu. Innu from Utshimassit are called the Mushuau Innu, or Innu of the Barrens. Our traditional territory is the north of Ntesinan, although some of us travelled to the south as well.

Utshimassit means "place of the boss." It was the name we gave to old Davis Inlet, a Hudson's Bay post set up in 1869. Old Davis Inlet is about five miles southwest of the present one. We don't know who Davis was, or how Davis Inlet got its name. We never lived in old Davis Inlet for long. We would only go there to trade with the post and to see the priest, and then go back to the barrens. There were only two houses ever built there.

Utshimassit has always been the place of the boss for us. We never had much say in being settled here. It was a bad decision, and we need to move. We have chosen Nutuashish as the site for relocation. Nutuashish is a traditional gathering place for us, about seven miles west of Utshimassit on the mainland. This place has plenty of fresh water, space for expansion for our growing population and a trail to our hunting territory.

Why We Gathered Voices

In February 1992, our community of Utshimassit lost six children in a house fire. This is still a very painful time for us. This is not the first time that our community has been struck by tragedy. Everyone here has been touched by tragedy in our lives. Since 1973, we have lost 47 people in our community through alcohol-related deaths. In March 1992, the Innu Nation and the Mushuau Innu Band Council decided to hold a People's Inquiry to gather information on why we have had so many tragedies in Utshimassit. We decided it was time we stopped and looked at why these accidents and violent deaths are happening to our people before it happens again. Too many people have died.

The Innu Nation asked the federal minister of Indian Affairs, Tom Siddon, to call for a public inquiry into this fire. The minister said no, so we decided to do it ourselves.

We decided to call this inquiry *Mamunitau Staianimuanu: Ntuapatetau Tshetshi Uitshiakuts Stuassiminuts* or *Gathering Voices: Finding Strength to Help Our Children.* We wanted to hold this gathering of voices:

1. To look at what has happened to us in the last thirty years and why these tragedies are happening in our community. To encourage people in our community to talk about these things in order to help them understand what is happening. To examine how the various outside agencies and institutions have impacted on our lives;

2. To look at alcohol problems in the community: why people drink, the problems caused when they do, and what is being done or not done to deal with these problems;

3. To provide means for people to talk about their

pany) utetautshiuapuau 1869 etisten atshitashunu. Ninan mentshessenimanan uen. E-Davis ishinakushukupen. Kie nastesh metshessenitenan tante uets tshi-ishinikatet Utshimassit Davis Inlet. Menita nte shuka tapants Innut nte uipats Utshimassit. Muk nanikutini ua-itauatshetau umaniunuau mak kaua-pukueshin ua-uapamatau ekunu muk itutepan Utshimassit eku kau ni-kuet tshiuets nutshimit nte mushuat. Kie muk nishinipan mestikushiutshiuapa nte uipats-Utshimassits.

Utshimassits eukun nantim nitishinikatetan utshimau assi. Nas, apu uts-takuak tshekuan tshetshi issishueiat, nene iatukeikuiat. Nastesh memenuapen nene eshutineken tshekuan ute ua-atukan-eku anutsh niui-atutshenan ninan nitshissenitenan nte tsheiatutsheiat Natuashit. Natuashit mushinau nte mamu tapents Innuts, muk 7 tatupaskuniau nte tetshe tshistakamukuts. Ume assi tshitshue nta meshau nipin eminuakamits, kie mishau nte assi tshetshi mamu tanuts, at-etu mitshetinanut nte esk aiskat, kie eukun ne-tetshe espeitunanut ua-itutanut nte nintuiussinat.

Tshekuan Uish Mamunimau STaianimuanu

Epishiminiskueu 1992, ashutash ueiakanipants auashits nete neskuatetsh mitshuap. Tshishue animin tshetshi anumeatimash. Ekun meieu muku nakunikunash eshinakushinash. Mishetuts nakunikut. Nispish 1973, 47 neunu-ashu-nishu-ashutat inuts niputs shitakunapunu etutakuts. Uiniskupishum 1992, Innu Utshimauts tutamuts tshetshi mamuinats tipatshimunu tshekuanu uishi uishinakushinak uta Utshimassits. Tutamuts tshetshi nitshikaputs kie tshetshi tshita patats tshekuanu uishi nishinakushinak kie tsheka minuats nishinakushinau Usham mishetuts nepits Innuts.

Innu Utshimau kutshimeu tsheutshimatu tshetshi ntusenitamintshi tshekuan uishi niskuatets. Tsheutshimau mauats itukuts, tshishueu eku nishats etutakamits.

Ekun eshimkatikants ume katushenitakants *Mamunitau Staianumanu: Ntuapatetau Tshetshi Uitshiakuts Stuassiminuts.* Nuui ntuapatenan ume tshe manuinimats aianuman:

1. Tshetshi uapatamats eshinakushinak nispish nistunuepuna kie tshekuan uishi ishinakushinats tshetshi tutuutshish Innuts tshetshi aianumeuts tshetshi shenitats tan tshenesh uitshiakanits tshetshi ntuseni-

makanits uaieu ueshipanit uentshi eshi-ustupinimits;

2. Tshetshi tshitapatamat shitakunapun eka menupanikuiak, kie tshekuanu uets miniats, mitshen tshekuan eka menupanits meniats kie tshekuan etutakan kie ama kutshitanu tshetshi minupanitakan;

3. Tshetshi Innu uauitak kamenupinit kie uin uitshinukut;

4. Tshetshi ntusenitakantsh tshekuan tshetutakant tshi minustakant kamenupinak kie tshetshi eka minuats nishinakushinak kie tshetshi ntusenitakant tante tsheutshimau tshetshi ashipent;

5. Tshetshi miskamats tshishats tipatshimun kie tshetinak atutsheatsh.

> "Ekun uishuui ntusenitamau kaniskuatetsh mitshiuap epishiminiskueu. Tshishue ntakunikunaapin uta utenats. Ekun etenitamats tshetshi miskamau tshetshi tshitapimushunau tshetshi eka minuats nishinakushinau." *Kiti*

Tapitunean mishiue enishishuet put kie eshi tipatshimut. Eshinakushinak ekun stinishiuitamakunaapin nutauinaets kie nimushuminaets. Ume kamamuinimak staianimuanu ekun esh uitamakunau uipats eshinakushinak. Ekun tshishue uishi uitshinikunak etapitunumak staianimuanu tshetshi miskimak kamenupinak. Ekun tshetshi senitamak tshetshi nakituenimushunak kie tshetshi utshimamitashunak. Ekunu tsheutshimau uatimuak tshekuan uanishinakushinak. Ume kie tipatshimun uauinakanu kaskutimasheutshiuap, emeutshiuap, mitshimitshimau, kamakunueshits, ataueutshiuap kie ntukutshuap tshekuan eshi ntuenitamau. Uauitakanu kie tshekuan tshetshinue tshipa tshishipinanu put kie eskute tshipa ishi-uitshikunan nte anutsh kie aiskat.

> "Nuuitamuauts tsheutshimau tshetshi tshishikashuts umenu mishinanikanu eku mauats ntukunai. Ninan nikantusenitenan. Ekun ninan etutamats. Innuts kaatuskatats umenu mishinanikanu minuanu utatushenuau. Nikustenapin tshetshi eka minupint. Tshash niuapateu menupinit tshitshistutakantshe mishiue tshika uapatikanu mishinanikan. Tshika petum katipuatshimushits. Tshika Innuts minakanuts umenu mishinanikanu. Innuts tshika senitamuts tshekuanu kamenupinau uta utenats. Tshiats tshipa ushitanan meskeau tshetutets stuashiminuts kie tshetshi senimitauts etuteuak." *Tepit*

problems, which would be a healing process for the community;

4. To identify steps and actions the community could take to address problems and put an end to these tragedies, as well as to make recommendations for changes needed from government and its agencies;

5. To gather information we need for our plans to relocate the community.

> "We are having this inquiry because of the fire which struck our community in February. This is the saddest thing that has ever happened in our community. We thought this inquiry was the only way to begin to look at how to prevent these things from happening again." *Kiti, workshop at the Nutuashish Gathering*

We have put together this report from the words and stories we gathered. Our history has always been told to us through stories from our parents and grandparents. This gathering of voices tells the history of our people at this point in time. We see this report, *Gathering Voices,* as a tool to help us to solve our problems on our road to recovery. It will serve as an important building block in our future discussions towards self-government. The report states clearly to governments what we want. The report also tells the various institutions—the school, the church, social services, the police, the store and health services—the things we need to tell them. It provides recommendations for both short-term and long-term changes we feel are required.

> "We asked Indian Affairs for funding for this inquiry. They turned us down. They said they were doing an engineering study. This would be their inquiry. We decided to do our own inquiry. The people who are working on the inquiry are doing a good job. I was afraid this inquiry would not work. I see that it is working. After the report is done, it will be all across Canada. The media will hear about this too. It will be a report that we will hand back to the people. People will know what our problems are in the community. We have to make a road for our children so they will know where we are heading."
> *Tepit, workshop at the Nutuashish Gathering*

How We Gathered Voices

The Innu Nation and the Band Council held a meeting of elders and a public meeting during the first week of Gathering Voices to get input from elders and the community on how the inquiry should be carried out. All Innu in the community were invited to participate in the public meeting and in the inquiry through the community newsletter and posters. Input into the early planning was also received from an interagency meeting held on March 30.

At the public meeting, a committee was formed to direct Gathering Voices. It was made up of two people from the Innu Nation Board, David (Tepit) Nui and Joseph Mark (Uinipapeu) Rich; two people from the Mushuau Innu Band Council, Katie (Kiti) Rich and Prote (Penute) Poker; and two other people from the community, Mary Jane (Ketshastipeneu) Nui and Daniel (Tanien) Poker. Four commissioners were appointed by the committee. These commissioners were Marie Georgette (Manteskueu) Mistenapeo, George (Shuash) Gregoire, Nympha (Epa) Byrne and Etien Pastiwet. An effort was made to have a committee and a team of commissioners who would represent the various families or clans in the community. The committee and commissioners worked together in developing the agenda and the schedule and in planning the work of the inquiry. Commissioners recorded the contents of the various events and forums of the inquiry. Camille Fouillard worked with the committee and commissioners. She facilitated the planning of the inquiry, trained commissioners and compiled the voices for the final report.

> "We were hired as commissioners. This inquiry is very important to our people. Everything has to be discussed, past and present problems. We cannot have any cover-ups. Everything has to be out in the open. We will interview anybody who wants to talk to us. If there is anyone who wants to see us privately, we are willing to see them in their homes. If people can't talk about things today, they can see me, Epa or Manteskueu later." *Shuash, workshop at the Nutuashish Gathering*

We gathered voices for six weeks. We offered a number of different ways for people to participate in Gathering Voices. We wanted to talk to as many people as possible. They could choose to participate in the way they felt most comfortable. We produced a question-

Tan Eshi Mamunamat Aianimuan

Innu Nation mak Innu Utshimaut, aianimu-epan mamu tshenu mak kassinu Innu usket ne-minastakan tshatshipinant emamunikan aianimuan, kie tshenut kie Innuts uitamuakanuts tan tsheishinakutakan ne-emamunikan aianimuan. Mishiue Innuts ute Utshimassit uishamakanut nte eianimuanits kie kassinu tshekuan uapatakanu nte tipatshimushineikinits kie akunikan. Ume uaishinakutakan mishineiken eiapits nte uauitakenipan nene kaianimuants nistunu 30 etshistauakan uiniskupishum.

Nene-eianimuants utinakanipants ntshen tshe ueuetishutak umenu ua-mamunikanits aianimuanu. Nish nte utinakanuts uts Innu Nation, Tepit Nui mak Uinipapeu, mak nish nte uts Innu Utshimau Kiti Rich mak Penute Pukue, mak nte nish Innut nte ut Utshimassit Ketshastipeneu mak Tanien Pukue. Eku neuts uetinakanits ntshen tsheituskatak, Manteskueu Mistinapeu, Shuash Kenikue, Epa Byrnes mak Etien Pastiuet. Utshen niakatuapatak mak ntshen etuskatak eukun ents tsheuapamats Innu ute Utshimassits. Kie ntshen niakatuapatak mak ntshen etuskatak, mamu nenu nutshikamut tshekuanu tshekukuetshimakanits Innuts, kie nte tsheishi-tshitshipinants ume ua-ntussenitakan tshekuan utshents etuskatak kassinu mishinamuts eitinanunts kie mishineike etutak Camille Fouillard (Kuekuatsheskueu) mamu nenu uitshitussemeu niakatuapatamen kie nenu etuskatimin mishineikenu. Uin nenu pimpintau tshipa ishi-tshitshipinanunu. Kie etshiskutamuat nenu etuskatamen mishineikenu, kie tshetshi nas minunakunits nete tshistakanits mishinikan.

"Ninan niutinikunan tshetshi atuskatamat ume atusseun. Ume netussenitakan tshekuan tshitshue miste itenitakun tshetshi uitshinikuts stiniminuts mishiue tshekuan tshika uauitakanu, anutsh kie uipats tshekuan eka menupinikunak. Eka uin katak tshekuan mishiue tshekuan tshika-ui-mushestanan. Muk eshinakust uenua-nika eimianan uen-ua-eimimits tatshe nte uen uapamimits nte uitshits nika uitamakunan kie nika natanan nte uitshit. Anutsh ume eianimuenak etakue ute uen kakatshi issishuet tshekuanu, nipa minuentamuan uapamit nte epeikussuk kie mak Manteskueu, kie mak Epa ui-uapamat nipa uapamukunan tshi-aianimuantshi." *Shuash, Kaianimuants nete natuashish kamamuinants*

Nimamunenan aianimuan issi ashutat tatuminastakan mitshetuit nte nitishi kutshitan tshipa-ut-tshi takushinuts Innut ume miamunikan aianimuan. Muk essi uapamitshit uentshi nika uapamaiants. Uinuau tshika tshissenitamut nte uaishi-uapamukushit, nte eshi-minu-enimuts. Nituteian eiapits mishineikea eku etishamat nte mitshuapits passe Innuts tutamuts umenu mishineikea eku kau pietisheimuimits. Kie mitshetuau nitaianimuenan. Auassit 5 mak 8 etisten umishineikenuau mak 9 mak 12 etipits eiapits niuapamatan. Kie auassit uitamuakanipan tshetshi unishinateik menuan kie eka menuan tshekuanu etutakut auassit ute Utshimassit, kie nenu tshekuan maskutshipinits tshessenitak anutsh, mak at-nete uikanishuau ishina-kushinikupen ueskat esk euassiun, kie utshen uenishinateitshet auassit takunu ute mishineikan. Kie kukuetshi makanut auassit tshetshi uitak tshekuanu ua-uapatak ute Utshimassit tshetshi etu minupinits kie tshetshi etu uitshinikut.

Kie ustinitshut kemesteitistenui umishineikenuau eiapit unishinateitsheut kie uitamut etenitak nte mishineikinits, nene eianimuanits. Kie eiapits uapamakanipants Innu katshiskutamatshet kie kastipets. Kie nene eianimuenats niuapatinu-etan kaishetshimakanits, uipats akunikenits esk eka ute etaiat ume ussi-Utshimassit kie usket iatutsheiat ute Utshimassit. Kie utshen kaishetshimakanit niuapatinanan tshenut esk eka eimitshit.

Kie mamu animuanuipan nte natuashish, Francine Jourdain, Innu tshekat ntukunish itenitakushu eketshessimat uenu tshi-atusseshipan nte apishipeutshuapit kie uitam nenu eshinakunit utatusseun kie eshitshissenitak nete miamuitunanunts uitam, kie uauitam etenitakunit Innu assi nete tetshe Quebec (Uepistikuiat) Ntassinat. Eku Innut katipan nte uapamitut, nenu uauitamut, masten nishinua nenu tshekuana uiauitak. Nene miamuitunat nitshissituaiants nekan auassit kaiskuashut, nene epishiminiskueu, kie nekan kutakut Innuts kanipits nte pets utats. Kie nikukuetshimanan Innut nas tshetshi minu nitutatut kie tshetshi nas ispitenimitut, kie tshetshi eka uauintuts.

Enkunu enish uitamutshitsh Innuts uenapimitshikaui:

1. Tan eshi taiak Utshimassits? Auen etutak? Tan eshinakushinak katshi taiak ute?

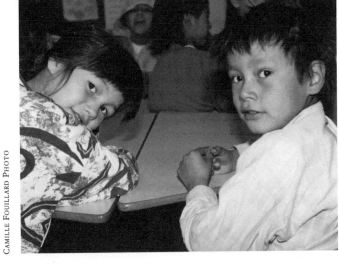

CAMILLE FOUILLARD PHOTO

Children at school workshop / Auasits nte kaskutimat-sheutshiuapits, 1993

naire and distributed it to each home. People filled these out and returned them to us. A number of workshops were held. There was a workshop with children from grades 5 to 8 and another for grades 9 to 12. Children were asked to do drawings which showed the good and the bad things for children in our community, and how they thought things had changed since their parents were children. These drawings are found throughout this report. They were also asked to name what they would like to see in this community which would make life better for them.

High school students did drawings and filled out questionnaires during their workshop. Workshops were also held with the Innu teachers and the workers of the Alcohol Program. During these workshops we showed slides of the old days before we were settled in Utshimassit and during our early days of settlement. These slides were also shown to a number of elders before we interviewed them.

A public workshop was held at the gathering at Nutuashish. Francine Jourdain, an Innu psychologist who works in alcohol treatment, facilitated the workshop at the gathering. She talked about her work in Innu communities on the Quebec side of Ntesinan. People in small groups then discussed the first two and the last two questions of the questionnaire. In our meetings and workshops, we began by remembering the children who died in February, and all the others who have died tragically over the years. We also asked people to listen to each other, to respect confidentiality and to avoid gossip.

These are the questions we asked in the questionnaire and through our interviews and workshops:

1. How were we settled in Utshimassit? Who decided? What has happened to us since we came here?
2. How have the Roman Catholic Church, the school, social services, the store, the clinic, the police and the government changed our lives since we were settled in Utshimassit?
3. Why have so many tragedies, like the fire in February, happened in our community?
4. What is happening to our children in the community these days?
5. What do we need to do to stop these tragedies from happening?
6. What do we need to do to regain control of our lives?
7. How do we make sure we don't bring our problems with us when we move to the new location?

Commissioners carried out a number of detailed individual interviews with elders as well as with other adults in the community. Group interviews were held through kitchen meetings in the community or through tent meetings at the Nutuashish Gathering and at camps in Sango Bay or Etamaput. A number of group interviews were held with different organizations or groups in the community: the Band Council, Band Council employees, the Innu Nation Board and employees, the Family Violence Project, the Youth Council, and Innu workers with Social Services, the clinic and the store. Commissioners also gathered voices at the Band Council and Innu Nation meetings held at the gathering. The meetings addressed some of the issues and questions of the inquiry.

Another public workshop was held in the community during the last week of Gathering Voices to discuss recommendations on what we need to do to stop these tragedies and regain control of our lives. A working paper prepared for this workshop outlined the recommendations and strategies people had already mentioned through our workshops and interviews. Those who attended were asked for further suggestions and to build on those ideas already presented.

Our community band, Sheskun, along with a group of kids, wrote a song about the children who were lost in the fire in February. The words to this song are included in this report. As well, our children at school staged a play called *The Boneman (Kaiatshits)*, which tells the story of our people since the 1920s. The story

2. Tan etutakuiak, emeutshiuap, kaskutimasheutshiuap, mitshimutshimau ataueutshiuap, ntukutshuap, kamakunuest kie tsheutshimau stiniunaanu esi tapituuiiuak uta Utshimassits?

3. Tshekuan mushinau eshinakushinak kaniskuatet epishiminiskueu pishum uta utenats.

4. Tan etits eku auassits uta Utshimassits anuts?

5. Tan tshipa tutenan tshetshi eka mi-nuats nishinakushinak?

6. Tan tshipa tinan tshetshi kastininamak kau stiniunu?

7. Tante tshetutamak tshetshi eka ntus-taiak kamenupinikunak nete atutsheakue?

Utshen etuskatat mitshen tshekuan uatamakut tshenu eiemiat kie kutaka Innu ute Utshimassit. Kie kutakut mamuiut nte uitshuat eimiakanit kie nte pitshuiatshuapit, nete miamuitunants nete natuashit kie nete shankut kie nete etamaputs. Mitshetut uentshi uiapamakanit ueutshimaushit ute Utshimassit, Innu Utshimaut kie nenu ukakusseshimuau, kie Innu Nation kanakatuapatshet, kie kaitusset, iskueut kauauitshi-aushit, ustinitshut, Innu mitshimitshimaut, nitukunitshuapit kaitusset, atau tshiuapit. Kie utshen etuskatat mishineikenu eiapits utinamuts nte eianimuen Innu Nation mak Innu Utshimau nete natuiashit miamutunanunts. Nete miamuitunants uauitakanu passe ne-mishineiken ua-ushitakan.

Minuat eianimuan nte Utshimassit esk enishuminastaniat tsheissi tshistakan ne-mishiniken mamunetau staianimuanu uauitakenipan tan tshipa tutenan tshetshi eka minuat ishinakushinak ne-essi eka minupaniak kie tan tshipa tutenan tshinan tshetshi uitshinushunak. Tutakenipan mishineikan tan tshipa ishi-uitshinushunan nene kaissishuanut tshetshi tutaken ua-minupintaken tshekuan nte kapets eissishuet Innuts euitak etenitak kie mushineikea etutanikau kie itishimuakanut nte kapets issishuanut eianimuantshi. Utshen tekushinits eianimuanun, kukuetshimakanuts tshetshi issishuet tshekuanu tekunikue kutakanu tshekuanu etenitak tshetshi etu misheiken ne-mishineiken.

Nikatauapekeitsheshiminan Sheshkun mak nenu mamu uituassuau, tutamut nikamunu enikamutuat auassa kaiskuashun nene epishiminiskueu. Ume nikamun uitakanu ute mishineiken. Kie eiapit nituassiminan metuepan nte katshiskutamatsheutshiuapits, *Kaiatshits*, ishinikashut, eukunu nenu tipatshimunu,

tshipa ishinakushut Innuts utat nte 1920's. Ume tipatshimun tshekat miam kuetenitakuats ume mishinikan etutamats miamunamats aianimuan kie nenu auassit mietuet akunakanut ute mishinanikenits.

Niuitshitussemaiants kastipets tshetshimamu aianimueutshit nte kaskutimatsheutshiuapits kie nete miamuitunanunts. Utshen kastipet niminikunants mishineikenu essi-eka minupuninuent shitakenapunu kie etishit uentshi nepanikuts shitakenapunu essi tanut ute Utshimassit. Tshen ntuuapatamek nte masten mishinanikenish (Mishinanekan etistets B).

Essi ashutat tatuminastakan essi mamunikan aianimuan, nistina tipatshi-mushineikea etutanikau kie itishimuakanut kassinu uentshi. Kie utshen uiauitamuat Innu umenu eshitussanun, ume miamunikan aianimuan kie tshetshi uitamuat uenu nte tsheietitussanun. Kie passe nenu nimishinamuanan nenu eissishuet Innut, passe muk uinakanut eshinikashut kie nte eianimuants essishuanuts, etu tshetshi shapenitats eianimuet kie etu tshetshi uauitshiaushit.

Peiku mitashumitunu ashu-ashut tatunu ashu-ninianeu (168) Innuts teshut Utshimassit eku 102 teshut ntshen kaniputs eimitshit mak 13 teshut tshenut. Eku 42 teshut auassit etat nte katshiskutamatsheutshiuapit tekushinit eianimuanits. Eku mamu 144 teshut uentshi eimimits. Ume mishinikan kassinu mishinamut utshen etuskatat nenu eissishuanun nte eianimuantshi kie miam uiapamatau uenu. Mitshen tshitshue pes-nte meshinamutshit Innu eissishuet muk apu uintshit nte eshinikashut passe muk niuinanan eshinikashut eku passe apu uintshit tante nikaui ispitenimanan, tante passe apu tapuetet tshetshi apastakanit eshinikashut. Ute mishinaniken kassinu tshekuan niuitenan miam kaissishuanut kie essishuet uen eimiakan, miam nenu kaissishuet ekun etistautshit. Ume uet tutamat, nas tshetshi tapuanuts kie tshetshi tapuemikak ume mishineiken uinuau nenu essishuet uentshi ekun miam etatshimutshit nas tshetshi tshissenitakuak eshinakushiak petsiniuiak.

"Tsheutshimau ute nitanikunan menistikut eku muk tshatapimimit niekatshiutshit. Anutsh nimamunenan nitaianimuanan kassinu etashiat ute Utshimassit. Eku eukunu put tshepetuimits tsheutshimau kie tshenitutuimit. Eku eka petuimit, minuat tshika mamunikenua aianimuana ute Kanata kie nte eiatissit, eku nikaui petakunan tsheutshimau put." *Kaniuekutat*

in this play was very much the same as the stories we were gathering in the inquiry. Pictures of the play are included in this report.

We worked with the Alcohol Program in the planning of the school workshops and the workshop at the gathering. The Alcohol Program also provided statistics for us on alcohol problems in the community and the number of alcohol-related deaths since we were settled in Utshimassit. These are found in Appendix B.

During the six weeks of Gathering Voices, three newsletters were circulated to all the homes in the community. These served to inform people about the work of the Mamunitau Staianimuanu and to let them know about upcoming events. We quoted some of the words and stories we had gathered in our interviews and workshops to get people talking and interested in participating.

Of the 168 adults in the community, we gathered the voices of 102 adults. Thirteen of these were elders. We also reached 42 children in our school workshops. In all, 144 people spoke to us. This report was written from the transcripts of notes recorded by the four commissioners in meetings, workshops and interviews. We have used many direct quotes from people in this report. (In some cases, we did not use names to respect confidentiality and because people requested we not use their names.) In the rest of the text, we also used many direct words and phrases from the transcripts of interviews, workshops and questionnaires. We did this in order to remain as true as possible to the voices of the participants, to the way we tell our stories and define our lives.

> "The government put us on this island and they have stood and watched us suffer. Now, we are gathering the voices of all the people in the community.
>
> "I hope the government will hear us and listen to us. If not, more voices will gather from across Canada and from other countries. The government will have to listen." *Kaniuekutat, Innu elder*

Snowmobiling through winter, Utshimassit / Papatunanu pepush, 1993

PETER SIBBALD PHOTO

PEIK ETSHITAPATEKEN

TSHEKUAN UISHINISHINAKUASH TSHEKUAN?

Tshishue tapue miskuau tshetshi uauitamak ne
kaniskuatets mitshuap nta epishiminiskue nush
kapuna. Ekunu tshishue metshetakuash katshi nishinakuats stasinas na stuassiminuts kaueiauts nete
niskutesh tshatashamakunuts tshekuanu tshetshi uitshauts. Nastesh matshanatutuaiets stuassiminuts. Eku
tshika-kutshitanan tshetshi natutuauts, tshinan kama-
muitunak stainimuanu uta stassinats tshetshi Miskamau shutshiun tshetshi uitshiauts stuassiminuts.

Tshishue tapue mitshetuts Innuts nepits uipats,
ekunu pisse shitakunapunu etutakuts mishiue tapue
tshimiskatenitenan katshi nashanakuashi tshekuan.
Ekus tsheuissi miskamau tshekuan. Uissi-
nashanakushiau, tshinan nta tshikaianimuatenan
estakunau shitakunapun, tshinan nta tshika nistutenan
tshekuan shitakunapun shuka kamatshapanua uta
stassinats.

"Epishiminiskueu neushap etshistanikant. Na auassits tshitshue na mitshima uui kanishituauts,
tshishue nimitshenitenan nastesh manakuatu tutenan tshemitun muk senitam uis nishinakunits,
mushinau katshis-situauts." *Shustinis*

"Mishetuau tshishue niuapaten tshekuan eshinakuashi, esk ekaniskua tets mi-tshuap. Mushinau
Innu nepitsh muk shitakunapunu tutaku. Shitakunapu tshishue metshapants. Mak takun
nepanushunants, kaushikunushunants kani-patu-
nants. Mak tshenuts miste minuts, tante nastesh
kastapitenimaitshi mak nastesh matshanatutuaiets.
Matshapetuaiets tate muk tshamanan shitakunapun,
nastesh eiapits mastapitenamaiats stuassiminuts
mishiuetshekuan tshikan ashanakun." *Epa*

"Uenua tshekuaia kameniputshi anush enua mussipi-
nua. Nte etaiku nushimits, matshanita mitshipan-
ian. Mitshetuts Innuts nepanikuts shitakunapunu

essieatukuants uta Utshimassits, uue nu utatusseun?
Tsheutshimau uta stanikunu uta ministikush, eku
muk tshanakatuapamu kunu eshinakushuak,
mushinau nuapamauts Innuts nepitaui nte nushimits
muk mana panikuts enu shitakunapunu."
Kaniuekutat

"Innuts uinuau nipanushuts nta ussipinu shitakuna-
puts." *Miste-Nita*

"Mushinau nuapaten eshinakuatshi tshekuan uta
stassi-nants, uipats, mate manita nishinakunipan
Innuts mushinau nakatuenimushupants, ne epishiminiskueu nastesh matshenkuan tutakanu tshetshi
nani kanikants, tshishue tapue miskatenitakun stuassiminuts katshi niskuashuts. Uipats Innuts manista
minipats nush kitutshi, tshishue mishau tapue shitakunapun nush. Mishiue tshekuan nishinakun
nipun mak nepanu-shunants, utamuauts mak ukua-
mauts shuka tshikau iminu tshitapameuts utuas-
siminuaua." *Tuamish*

"Uipats Innuts mushinau mitupants mitshaminu,
eku nush tshishue mistuitshituts. Nta shitakuna-
push. Nastesh mamanauau, eshinakuash mushinau
nipu auen mak nipanushu auen uta stassinats uassits
tshitapameuts ukuauaua mak utaua-ua, manan nush
tshishue kaketshestanuapin tuassim." *Innu Utshimauts*

"Shitakunapun tshi-shue stakunikunu. Ama naman
nin muk unapamatshi Innu metshi, tshishue
takunuk. Innuts muitamakuts tshetshi nishinipinan
kenin eshinipits. Nastesh manuinishinipan nta shi-
taunapush." *Kaniuekutat*

"Ama naman nin, muk menantshi tshishue mana-
shapeniten. Ekun kuestatshian eshi minits Innuts
uta stassinats, kie nteieskushin." *Innu Katsheniut*

CHAPTER ONE

WHY DO THESE TRAGEDIES HAPPEN?

It is very hard for us to talk about the fire in February of this year. This is one of the saddest things that has ever happened in our community. Our children that were lost in the fire are sending out a message to us for help. We are not listening to our children. We must begin to listen to them. We are gathering voices in this community to help us to find the strength to help our children.

People die in our community and over the last few years many of these deaths have been alcohol-related. We have all been touched closely by these tragedies. This inquiry is to find out why these tragedies are happening. We must talk about our alcohol problems. We must try to understand why alcohol is such a big problem in our community.

"February 14, 1992. Those children were my close relatives, and I'm very sad. I couldn't do anything. We all couldn't do anything for them. God knows why it happened, but we will always remember them." *Shustinis*

"I have seen so many tragedies before we lost the children in the fire. Every time a person dies, it is from alcohol. Alcohol is a big problem. There are suicides, accidents and murders. Our elders drink too much also because we don't care and we don't listen to them. We don't hear them because we drink too much, and we don't look after our children. Anything can happen to anybody at any time. This could have happened to any of us." *Epa*

"These kinds of problems are very new to us. When we were in the country, we never had these problems. Many Innu have died from alcohol since we moved to this community. Whose fault is that? The government put us on this island and they have stood and watched us suffer. I have seen people die in the country but they did not die from alcohol." *Kaniuekutat, elder*

"People are killing themselves from alcohol." *Miste-Nita*

"I have seen many tragedies happen in this community. In the past, these things never happened. People always took care of themselves. In February, there was nothing people could do to stop it. It is too much to see our children dying. In the old days, people didn't used to drink like they do now. There is too much alcohol abuse now. Bad things happen like deaths and suicides. All parents should keep an eye on their children." *Tuamish, elder*

"Long ago, people used to share food, now they share home brew. This is not right. Like many other deaths and suicides in the community, the fire was alcohol-related. Parents drink and the children drink too. Children see so much from their parents. It is a cycle. If I start drinking, there is a good chance that my children will drink too." *Band Council*

"Alcohol is really hurting us. I don't drink myself, but when I see a person drink, it affects me too. People tell me I will die just the same, but I don't want to die from alcohol." *Kaniuekutat, elder*

"I don't drink, but when there is drinking in the community I feel tired. Is it from being scared about how the drinking is affecting the community?" *Elder*

We really miss the children who died and so many others we have lost through tragedies in this community. It is hard to talk about these things but we never forget, and we live with the memories for the rest of our lives.

We Couldn't Stop The Fire

There were other reasons for this fire, too. There was nothing we could do to stop the fire. We have no fire hoses, no fire equipment. Even if we had this equip-

Tshishue mitatakanuts auassits kanipits, mak mishetuts kutakats kanipanikuts uta stassinats. Tshishue tapue miskuau tshetshi uauitamau muk tshakatshinita unikuataan. Mushinau tshika takun tshistukuanats essi-iniunakue.

Tshetshi Astueimak Niskuat Etshe

Takun nte tshekuan uishinasha nakuash ne kaniskuatets mitshuap nastesh matshe kuan stitinan tshetshi nanikamak niskuteu, mistititenan enua nipin nta kuishueuepinua. Mak nte tshekuan tsheapitshitakan neskuatetshi mitshuap, mak tatamaikue enua tshekuaia tshakassiapits itakunipan nipin uta stassinats, takuatshe mane nipin tshakatshiput tutakanipan tshetshi nanikanikants mitshuap kaniskuatets. Enua tshitshanua tshe takaua ekun uish apatshitaiau katshatepu tshi, tshitshushunau. Kutakuts Innuts apatsheuts enu pimina kapunakantshi uakutuetaui. Thishue kustikun tshetshi tiak. Ekun tshishue tsheshipants niskuteu put mak ke uastepimakepisha matshi miam tukamutakanitsheni. Nema nispish 25 tatupuna muk piekuau atimutakanipini uastepimake pisha. Kutaka mitshuapa tshikutuai ne kaniskuatets mitshuap, tshen mistinutin mak piekutshimiteu mitshuap.

"Tauts uta kaniskutueshits muk tapue nastesh matakuna tsheapatshitats. Tshiskuenan tapue. Etatsh kaniskutueshits nastesh kaetukunits tshekuana tsheapitshitats, mak nipin katakunuau, kaueiakuts auassits ashutash katatishits nastesh amu tapue nikuatu tutamuts kaniskutueshits." *Ataueutshiuapits Kaitusets*

"Takuashakuenimate katshiteputshi nte mitshuapits, tshakantshiput nita apitshitakanipinin enu kantshiteputshi nte mitshuapits. Put tshakantshinisku atepan mitshuap." *Shuash*

Kanishinakuats tshekuan tshipa minuats nishinakun nete eka minants put kie eminants. Ama tshishenitenan tshekuan uanishinakuatshi. Tshishe manitut muku shenitam uaishinakunitshi kie nastesh ama tshishenitenan tshekuan uish nishinakuats. Tshishenitenan muku uta Utshimassits usham tshimiste ueauts Innuts tante shitakunapun. Stenitenan shitakunuapun stutakunan uish ueauts tshikanishinuts kie stuasiminuts. Stuasiminuts tshuui uitamakunuts tshekuanu eunishinatatshet nenu kame-nupinits tante shitakunapun takun. Mitshipininueu.

Natutuatauetshi Uassits

"Uta essitaiau Utshimassits, etu Innuts minuts, mak etu nipanushuts, niputs Innuts." *Kaskutimashuts*

"Ekun muk tshkuan metshenitaman uta Utshimassits tshe mishau shitakunapun mak kaminatiskueshits tauts eiapits." *Kaskutimashuts.*

"Kaminatiskuants mak shitaunapun tshe mitshipinu uta Utshimassits, mak auassits tshetshanue minuts shitakunapunu esk ekatatupineshits auassits minuts, pase uassits akushiskakuts tshash, mak enu eminatiskuets, tshitishimuts ni nte uitshuash kuet minatskuets nastesh manatutueuts utauaua mak ukuauaua, netshi ukumuau mak utamuau nastesh manakatuenimeuts utuassima, eku ni metuatsheuts ni kutuakeia ekun eiapits uish niskuatets ni, nteme nutshimis Innuts uauitshitupants ekuta essitaiak Utshimassit tapue tshamatshenimitunai." *Kaskutimashut auas*

"Ekune epishiminiskueu kaniskuatets mak uassits kaniskuashuts, Innuts muk uaskakapuuts nta mitshuapinu eskuatetsh, shitakunapun mushinau uestutueu Innua, makush katukuash shitakunapun uta Utshimassits, tshekuan mitshe uish katapuetatau tsheutshimau uaatutsheuau. Nastesh katshimamitinenitenanaua." *Auas kaskutimashut*

"Eshitshitapataman nin petsh uassiunan, mushinau namanatiskuen, ekun uesh minatiskueian Nastesh matua uen tshenakatuenimit, mak nikaun mak nutaun tutepamuts." *Auas kaskutimashut*

"Mushinau minuts Innuts eshikum tshishikaua minuts nastesh mapitenimeuts. Utuassimuaua, nastesh en mishenimuets nakuats, muk minuts, minuts." *Kaskutimashut auas*

"Uassits menatiskuetaui nishinimuts. Kie eatapa ntenimuts. Mak Innuts nanikutini miskeauts ematentats nipauts. Ekun tshe put uistits nte nutshimits etaiantshi, minishinakun, manita tshuapinanu; muk atuskanu. Kataianua Utshimassits mushinau tshuapatenan metshit tshekuan eshinakuash, mak mushinau takun tshekuan etutakantshi, kuskanu, eute tshika tinanu mustinau mak etuiuna. Tshipatinan tshetshi tshimanisheau mak tshetshi ni kuteiau." *Auas Kaskutimashut*

"Menatiskuetaui uassits nishinimuts ni, mitshinu etutussets. Pimin tutakunan tshetshi papushish. Shi-

ment, we have no water in the community. If we had water, we might have been able to stop the fire. Our houses are cold and we use hot plates to warm them. Some people use diesel oil to start their fires. These are dangerous things to do. The type of houses we have catch fire very easily. Maybe the electrical wiring in the houses is not done properly and is not safe. In the last twenty-five years, only once was the wiring changed in the houses. Other houses have started on fire, but people managed to put out the fire before it spread through the whole house. The night of the fire, there were high winds and the house stood alone.

"We have firefighters in the community but they don't have anything to use for fire equipment. This is crazy, having firefighters with no equipment and no water. When we lost those 6 children, there was nothing the firefighters could do." *Store workers*

"If there had been heating in this house, the hot plate would not have been used. The fire never would have started." *Shuash*

These tragedies happen everywhere, in both non-drinking communities and alcoholic communities. We cannot predict these things. Some of us say only God knows why it happened and sometimes there is no reason for these things to happen. But we know here in Utshimassit that we have lost too many of our people because of alcohol. Many of us believe alcohol is the main reason we are losing so many of our relatives and children. Our children's voices and drawings tell us about the problems we have because of alcohol.

Listen to the Children

"Since we were settled in Utshimassit, more people drink, there are more suicides and more people have died." *High school student*

"The thing we hate the most in our community is too much alcohol and gas sniffing." *School child*

"Gas sniffing and alcohol are big problems. Young people start drinking at a very early age. Some children are sick from alcohol and gas sniffing. Children don't like to be at home. They run away from home and they do some gas sniffing. They don't listen to their parents. When the parents are drinking, they don't take care of their children. When kids are left alone, they might play with matches; this is how fires start. In the country, the people used to help each

Child's drawing at school workshop / Auasits kaunishi-natatshet, kaskutimatsheupits kaianumats, 1992

other. When we are in the community, we hate each other." *School child*

"In February, there was a fire in Utshimassit and all the kids burned up. The people stood around and watched. Alcohol always does something wrong to the people. I wish the alcohol was not in this community. How come the government doesn't want to let us move to a new location? We have been thinking about this." *School child*

"When I look back when I was a child, I was usually sniffing, and the reason is that nobody cares because my parents were out drinking." *High school student*

"Some people drink every day and don't care about their children. They don't know that they are hurting them. All they do is drink and drink." *School child*

"When the children do the gas sniffing, they feel strange and see things. Some adults are often found on the road sleeping because of drinking. In the country, there are a lot of different people living in peace, no arguments, and working together. When we are in the community, we see a lot of bad things happening. When we are in the country, we always find something to do, like fishing. This is the way we should live. When we are not hunting, we can cut and haul wood. This is the life." *School child*

"Gas sniffing makes children see things. It is bad for

takunapun mitshin uta Utshimassits, menakantshi shitaunapunu Innu tshitshue mitshin, makatakuash shitaunapun ekush." *Kaskutimashut auas*

"Tshishue mitshen tshekuan eshinakuash essi atukuantsh uta Utshimassit. Mak tshe mistiminanu kuet nikatakantnits auassits. Menantshi, mak netsh uassits tshash minuts kuet nutshikashuts ni, kuet eiapits auassits minatiskuets." *Auas Kaskutimashut*

"Katshi taiau uta Utshimassits tshe mishau tshekuan eka minupininukunau ne tshekuan uish tutakunau shitakunapun. Tshemitshetuts kauishepeshits. Nakateuts ni utuassimunaua nepataui, mak uamintaui manu nistam etuapamats kakeuasheshitshi." *Auas Kaskutimashut*

"Tshemishau shitakunapun uta Utshimassits mak tshe mushinau petautakanu niskuteuapun uta stesinats." *Auas Kaskutimashut*

Uin Utapatshemun

"Esitaiash ute Utshimassits, nikaun mak nutaun tshishipinipatsh tshetshi minitsh, nastesh miminuau. Akuepatsh utuasimuaua. Nimitsh mak nin tshishipinai tshetshi minash tshishue mishau tshuapun. Eku etaiashi nte nutshimish nitutuanants nikaun mak nutaun etishemukunashi, eku uta Utshimassit natesh minetuteia.

"Nikaun mak nutaun tshishipinipatsh tshetshi minits, tate metukun tshekuan tshetitsh aputikuanitsh atuseun ute Utshimassit. Eskune ntuasiun etaiash nte nutshimish, kuet taiash nte Utshimassit nutaun atusepan nte kapukueshitshi, atuskatimu mitshuapa, enkun une minuapan etaiashi ute Utshimassit. Mushinau auen Innuts uauitshitupatsh, napeuts tuiuipants eiapits aishinapatsh mak uapanekanu shepantsh. Niskeuts uinau uauitshitupatsh keuinuau eka uishitataui shitaunapunu. Mushinau Innuts uitshimitupatsh, niskueuts miste piminuapitsh. Innuts inemashupantsh mitshiminu. Tikunipan eiapits nipushnapan etatutikanipan mastetuskan mak meistakan, eka skutimashunatshi.

"Etnitautshinan, menuapate tshetshi tinatsh minuatsh etu minanu. Eku nush niskueuts nutshikatuts. Ukuamuauts tsheuauitamupantsh utanishuiaua tshekatshititshi tshekuanu. Eku nush nastesh mapitenitamutsh tshekuanu. Mitshetuts niskueuts uitshiminemeuts unapuemuau euashiunan, nutaun

minipan muk, nikaun mishin tapan nte etautshish, eku mametshi tshishue mitshinipan, nekatukunaipan, ninan nakatue nimeshunaipan. Tshine tshepapashi nueshamikuamunan uaskutimashunashi, metukun tshekuan tshemittshinatsh. Uipatsh tshetshepapitshi ntutepamupatsh.

"Tauniskuts tshishue nikaun mak nutaun metaui, mushinau tenimapatsh natesh, metshinakatuenimuk natesh metshishatshinikutshetshi tenimauts, metuaui tshitaskunapunu.

"Nutshimish etaishi, katshinitautshinan etu eiapits menipatsh nte nushimish. Tsheshe nitimatshi uatuteashi nte nutshimish, tshitashumunai, tante niseniteia tshemiste teskanikunas natesh menuitai, menatshi, tate nash uapetumutsh ni.

"Nikutshitaia tshetshi minuenitash, tsheshuenimistustui tsheka minits. Punitauts nanikutini, eku netututsh shni. Nipiminuai tepiskatshi pinekupituaui etutepatuaia, nimitshenai nakatuapumukuan.

"Nikauinai tenimaia, napamanutekunai, eiapits uapekatsheu. Nutamakunai nutaun nash tsheshuapitshi, kutak nimesh muskuestuepan nutauna mak nikauna uinuepan.

"Teshemukunaist tshetshi kuapitsheutshish tshetshi ushitash utashiuau, eipats nushituauts, nau enu tsheskutimashunashi tenitakun. Muk tshetshi minenitatsh kuen tapuetamash. Minuitaia nitshinash menatshi, nte nitustuts uitshuast titaia, kuet nist tshishipinatsh tshetshiminatsh, minaskutimashunan, nutatauaia pimin, natesh mitukunshekuan tshetinatsh ute Utshimassit, etuish shatshitauts unipimuau nikaun mak nutaun tenimauts." *Utshimassiu iskueu*

Tshekuan Uish Nispiniunak Nte Shitakunapush

Uenua tshekuaia uish nishinakuashiu shitakunapun tutam. Uenua tshekuaia nishinakunukunau nastesh mashanakaatueni mushunan. Tshe Mishen tshekuan eka minu puninukunau tshe tapue tshamiskutshipinau. Tshe tshueiats tshuitshekakanuts mak tshikanishinuts, nastesh mitshishenitenan Innuts Nepitaui. Nastesh mitshinakatueniten ne uipats kanitiak, ekunu aueshishits tshatashamakunuuts tshekuanu tsheshuapitaui.

"Utshimassits nush, tshishue mishen tshekuanu eka minupants, nastesh ne kanashanakunua ne uipats kanashanakuash, mishiue Innua minu nakatieni-

them. Gas makes us laugh. Alcohol is bad for the children and the community. Giving alcohol to others is really bad. We need to be free of alcohol." *High school students*

"Many things have happened since we moved here. There is heavy drinking going on and the children are left alone. Young adults start to drink heavily and start beating other people. On the other hand, children are vandalizing the homes and sniffing all kinds of solvents." *School child*

"When we were moved to Utshimassit, we got a big problem. The problem is alcohol. There are a lot of alcoholics, parents drinking. They leave their kids when they go to bed. Something can happen to them. If the parents want to drink, the first thing they should do is find a babysitter." *School child*

"There is a lot of home brew in our community. Also there is too much alcohol brought into Utshimassit." *School child*

A personal story

"When we came to live in the community, my parents started drinking. It was really bad. It hurt everybody in the family. My sisters and I started drinking too. There was a lot of violence. When we were in the country, we used to listen to my parents all the time when they wanted us to do something. But in the community, we never listened to them.

"My parents started drinking because there was nothing to do; there were no jobs. But when I was really young, we would be out in the country and come back to the community. My father had a job with the priest, working on the houses. Those days were good even if we were in the community. A lot of people were always helping one another. Men would be out hunting together. They would be playing checkers or cards all night. Women used to do things together too to help one another. Instead of going to home brew, people were always having meals together. The women would make a big pot of food, people would help themselves. There would be a big pot of tea. This would happen on the weekends, rather than when we were in school.

"As I got older, I didn't see this happening much. There was more drinking. Now, women are fighting one another. Women used to tell their girls not to do

Children drawing at school workshop / Unishinatant-sheuts auasits kaskutimatsheutshiuapits, 1992

CAMILLE FOUILLARD PHOTO

stuff, but now they just let things go. A lot of women are drinking with their husbands too. When I was young, my dad would drink but my mother was always with us. When she started drinking it got really bad. We were left by ourselves, we had to look after ourselves. In the mornings when it was school, we would sleep in. There would be no meals on for us. They would be drinking very early.

"My parents' drinking would really hurt me. I always felt like my parents didn't want me. I felt like they didn't love us when they turned to booze. It still hurts.

"When they were in the country when we were getting older, they used to drink in the country too. When we knew we were getting ready to go, we would run away. We didn't want to go because of the booze. We would walk back to the community. We would have to do all the work they would tell us. I didn't want to be around them when they were drinking. They would stay up all night.

"We always had to try to make them happy and we thought they would stop drinking if we listened. But even when we listened to them they wouldn't stop drinking. We would have to cook the meals. They would get us up in the middle of the night telling us to cook meals. When my parents would be out drinking, my older sister looked after us. She was like a mother. She would cook meals and do the laundry. My dad used to hit us when he would get really mad. My other sister was the hard case, and she would fight my parents.

"They would want us to get water to make their home brew. We used to help them. They would show

tamupan tshekuanu nepatatshi. Mishiue uueshish miskatenitakushu, mak ne ustikuan aueshish kutakanu nta mistikush, nush etatupuneshinan, tshe mushinau nu a paten atik uskea. Nite ueuetasmish, atumuts enua ni mitshuts, tshetakunukun unapataman. Mushinau nimanakatueniten nin tshekuan ueshipantshi nta ueshish, ekun nitshe tshekuan metshits mushinau eshinakuash katamenitetau shitakunapun, tshinanu tamenimushutau, Nastesh kamenunanakatueni tamak atik uskeaa." *Tshenish*

"Nastesh mitshimintutenan aueshishits kamintushits uskanuaua. Atikuts nastesh puminukakanitshi, kumin-tushits. Tshi nakatuenimukunuts ishinakatuapamukunuts tshishue tshinan tshitshuaiaits aueshishits umintu-shimuaua tshiunitaia kainitinau

Child's drawing at school workshop / Auashits kaunishinatatshet, kaskutimatsheupits kaianumats, 1992

uipats. Stuassiminuts kauniakuts nete niskutesh tshuiuitamakunuts tshetsh uitshiakuts, nastesh, punitutuakuts stuassiminuts. Tshinan tshikanantuapatenan uipats kaianitinants tshika utinenan." *Kastipetsh*

"Innuts tshishue mistaminuts shitakunapunu tante apu tshiuitats enu eshkaminupanits. Ishekuan takunithe pitikamish stiniunash naspusenamak auen tshikau emaik." *Mitshimitshimaskueu Katusehits*

Tshiuinikatenan kamenapuninakunak tshekuan menau. Nastesh putshitapatamak put kie tshetshi kutshitaiak tshetshi minupanitaiak. Tshikutshitanan tshetshi unikuatimak, minatenitameaku. Eku napeshipe aku eskutakamenupuninakunau, eskuta tukun. Tshinan te stititenan, tshishue tshimistimestinenan tshuniaminu nta niskuteuapush. Tshiminan mak statusenan, kuet pikupininukunak.

"Pase esishueuts ne uipats kanipinits Innuts tante tshishue mishau tshekuan uta stassinash. Uitshiuakean mitshenimeu utshiuakea muk papiuenuuts. Muk utshiua-kea nutshikashuntshi." *Misteshishin*

Innuts nte nispaniuts te shitakunapunu etakunits kamenupanits. akushum mak stimauts, puminautshi mitshuapa, make aupu takuak nipin, mak mitshan pusikua apuminuatshi, apu takuaki atuseuna kie apu tshituiunushinak. Innuts katsheniutsh nas apu shapenitakau.

Auen Tsheatamenimak?

Auen etameimakant pase tshinan statameniman kakeshau ne steiniunana kamenipunitshi, mak pase stenitenan tshinan tshikanakaatuenimushunan mak mishue stitapenamushunan.

"Uipats ute minupanipan tante auassits nastesh ama minipats, kuet auassits mishetuts menits kuet nastesh apuminupaniak. Nete kauishatukuants pase kanipushits minuts, apu eshukum tshiskaua minits. Tshishue tante kuseuts utuassimuana tshishue uitshinikuts. Innuts ite nitamuts tshekuani tshe uets nitutuats kakeshaua. Nitshisiten uipats apu auassits uapamakau tshetshi ntuapatats shitakunapunu nate mitshuapits ekutete emasha uipats Kauapukuest kustineu utshimaua tshetshi atauatshentshi shiustimakana. Nastesh tshekuan eash itentakuak. Esk minanu esk Innuts nimatanueuts shiustimakea." *Katsheniut*

us how and we used to make it for them. It's like enabling, that's what my sisters and I were doing. To make them happy, we had to do it. When my parents were drinking, we didn't want to stay home. We would go to my aunt's house and spend time there. Then we started to act up. We were drinking; we missed a lot of school. We started sniffing gas. There was nothing for us to do in the community. The home brew bucket was more important to my parents than the children." *Utshimassiu woman*

Why We Turn to Alcohol

These tragedies happen because of alcohol. But the alcohol is a symptom of other problems. These things happen to us because we don't look after ourselves. We have too many personal problems. We don't care about ourselves any more. We have changed too much. There are too many divisions in the community. We lose family and friends from alcohol, and suffer. We don't know how to deal with their deaths. We no longer practise our culture and spiritual beliefs. The animal spirits are sending us signals that they are upset.

"In Davis Inlet today, there are all kinds of problems. It's not like life in the past. All the people used to respect the animals. Every part of the animal is important. The skull has to be hung on the tree. At my age now, I have seen so many caribou bones being thrown away outside the house. The dogs eat the bones. It really hurts me to see these things happen. I myself have always respected everything that comes from the animals. This is how so many bad things happen to us. We can't blame all our problems on alcohol. We have to blame ourselves too, for not taking care of the caribou bones." *Tshenish, elder*

"We don't respect the animal spirits. The bones of the caribou are not properly taken care of. The spirits are looking after us, keeping an eye on us, and we are making the animal spirits angry. We are losing our traditions. Our children that were lost in the fire are calling out a message to us for help. We should get our culture and traditions back." *Alcohol Program workers*

"People drink so much alcohol because they can't talk about their problems. The stuff is bottled up inside of us and we don't know who to talk to." *Social Services workers*

We try to get away from our problems when we drink. We don't look at them or try to solve them. We try to forget them when we are drunk. But when we sober up, our problems are still there. We keep them bottled up inside of us. We spend too much money on booze. Then when we work and drink at the same time, people have no choice but to fire us.

"Some are saying that these deaths occurred because there is too much division in the community. Friends hate friends, and enemies just sit back with a big smile on their faces when their friends are struggling." *Gathering Voices participant*

People turn to alcohol also because of community problems. There are health problems and poor living conditions, poor housing, no water or sewage systems, no jobs, poverty, no recreational facilities and isolation from the mainland so we can't go hunting for a good part of the year. Elders are sick from the stress.

Who Is to Blame?

Some of us blame white society for the way our lives have changed. Some of us think we need to take responsibility ourselves. Others think there is blame on both sides.

"When we were first settled, everything seemed to be okay because the young people were not drinking. When Hopedale began to sell beer, young people here began to drink more and we have had all kinds of problems. In old Davis Inlet, most people who drank were married and they did not drink every day. They were too busy fishing, and their girls and boys were helping them. As the years went by, the Innu realized that they should never have listened to their white advisors. I remember when I was still drinking. I didn't see any young people looking for home brew from one tent to the next. That was in Emish [Voisey Bay]. The former priest had asked the store manager to stop selling yeast in the store. But it didn't change anything. The drinking still went on. People still ordered yeast from the outside." *Elder*

"If those people [white agencies] had left us alone, maybe our lives would have been much better. Our

"Kakeshauts kauapamakuentshi tshika minupunaiapen put. Tshutauinuts mak tshikauinuts kuet minits, nastesh punakatuenimats utuassimuaua. Aiamieutshiuap kie tutam. Nas kaeshauts tshiuitenitakunnan. Enkun kishunikuatimau uetuassimiau mak staitusennu make uipats kainitinanuts espish aiat ministukushish, tshisue mshau tshekuan kamenupuninakunau, tshitshueninuikunan?" *Akatis*

"Statamenimaiats kakeshauts kamenupaniak. Tshinan tshika tapenimushunan mauats kakeshauts. Kakeshauts mipetustatus ute etauak shitakunapunu. Tshinan tshinatenan shitakunapun." *Kaianumeatikantshi tshekuan tshetinants*

"Mentshi auen, nakateu utuasima nte uitshuats. Nantuapatashi shitakunapunu nte mitshuapits. Utshimassits ute tshishue mishau shitakunapun. Muk misitamenimitunan tshemintum tshinakatuenimukunu etutamau tshekuanu. Mitshisenimanu etenitau tshementun." *Shapatesh*

"Nishinakun tshetshi atamenimushunau kie tshinau. Mushinau tshkiminauu stuasiminuts tshineas pitakunuts menuau. Miste auasuits tshashipanits eka nutshikas shitakunapunu, eku etauts ni tshiminau ketshinuau enkun uish minas tenitakushinan euasiunants katshi atukuantsh, eku tshashipinants tshishue eminants, kie auasits tshishipanuts eminits." *Miste-Pinip*

"An uetsh niskuatets mitshuap shitakunapun. Kauapishit tshutinenan tsheminak, tshiskutamakunu tshenish ushitanak shitakunapunu. Mishiue nishinakum tshetshi atamenimushunak ne eshinakuats, mitshi minu nakatuenimanuts stuasiminuts. Muk eminiak enkun muk nakatuenitamak. Tsheutshimau ama tshikasi tapuetum tshetshi petautakanits Niskuteuapunu. Nipunant tshe utshimau tshipa tshi tutam tshetshi kustishet niskuteuapun tshetshi petautakanits." *Shuash*

Tan Etits Eku Stuasiminuts?

Kaniskuatets ne stutakunan tshetshi mamuunenimauts tan etits eku stuasiminuts. Uipats nte matukunipan tshekuanu tshipa mitshipininukuts stuasiminuts. Minista uapamapants auasits tshetshi minamats pimina. Katshi atukuanits eku eash etenitakushits auasits. Auasits etu akuakanuts atisi akuakant Innut. Uapatamuts auasit esi nenekatshinukunak shitakunapunu.

Tshuapamanuts auasits tshishue mishimenitamuts muestatumuts, mak passe ntenitamuts. Mintapatenimukunan uapatamuts kamenipunuentsh tshekuanu enkunu nenu uestuentaminikuts. Auasits uta uinakatuenimukushuits mak uishatshinukushiuts tshetshi minuenitats. Katukunitaue nua tshekuanu auasits. Akushikakuts nte tamits eku apu minupanikuts. Miste mishanu tshekuanu auasits uestuentaminikuts. Tshuitutakunuts tshetshi uapamants mak tshetshi uitshauts. Uiuitshinukushiuts stuasiminuts mak tshinan tshipa uiuitshaiuts. Tshipa shatshiaeuts

Auasits nakatakanuts nete uitshuats entantaui kutaka auasa kassinu tshikuanu metuatsheuts kaetantaui unitshinikuaua. Nastesh mapitenitamuts tshekuanu mitanua tante utauaua mak ukauaua. Passe auasits nitamuk enitauts tepiskantshi. Tshekuanu etuapatats? Nantumiskamuts tshekuanu tshetutats menitaui unitshi-nikauaua. Passe nte tauts nitamuk mitshuapits. Menitaui ukuauaua mak utauaua. Utamuauts mak ukuamuauts mapitenimeuts utuasimuaua nepantshi mak tshe mitshintshi, tshekuanu. Auasit kustatshuts tshetshi tshiuets menanitshi nte uitshuats. Miminuenitamuts nenu auasits. Usham mapitenimakanuts auasits. Kauishatukuants nte, nastesh minita tapuetuakanipants auasits tshetshi miste papmutets tepiskantshi. Muestatenitamuts auasits. Auasits muk tshiueuts kamenitaui unitshinukuaua.

Stuasiminuts eskushiuinikuts shitakunapunu euapatats kamenupuninuents. Passe Innuts nteuts auasa tshishue tshiskueapatmuts. Minitutueuts ukuauaua mak utauaua kie nenua katsheniuntshi Innua. Eapits kuestinakantaui tshetshi tshitutets tepiskantshi nastesh minitutamuts auasits nas ama utueuts ukauaua mak utauaua. Ukuamuauts mak utamuauts minutueuts kie uinuau utuasimuaua. Passe ukuamuauts mak utamuauts nisishueuts minisenitamuanan tshekuanu etuenitats. Auasits tshuaputs usham tshi miste nutshikenan shitakunapun usham auasits miste uapatamuts enutshikatunanits nte uitshuats nenu auasits uish ntenitakushits tshuiuapatinukunuts enu tshetshi uapamauts pakuas Mitshuapa, shipuastenitakea, ketshemutits kie pasetsh mitshuapu kaetanitshi auasits keapishishutshi pimpinitaut utapanisa nishinakunu tshetshi ushukunukuts.

"Auasit neaspitueuts unitshinukuaua mak nenua Innua shinatshats mushinau menitaui pakunamentshi tshe-kuanu." *Auas Kaskutimashut*

Child's drawing at school workshop / Auasits kaunishi-natatshet, kaskutimatsheupits kaianumats, 1992

parents started to drink and neglect the children. The church had a lot to do with this. We act like white people. This is how we forget about our responsibilities as parents, our work, traditions and culture. Ever since we are on this island, terrible things have happened to us. Are we being punished?" *Akatis*

"We blame the white man for our troubles. But we are the ones to blame not the white man. The white man doesn't bring alcohol to us. We go to alcohol." *Workshop discussion recommendations*

"When a person drinks, he or she leaves the children alone in the house, while he or she looks for some home brew in the community. Davis Inlet is filled with alcohol. Anyway, we can't blame anyone. God is responsible for every one of us, and for everything. We don't know what he thinks." *Shapates*

"I think we have to blame ourselves. We have been drinking a lot and our children follow our ways. They start drinking at a very early age. When we try to tell them they shouldn't drink, they say to us that we are drinking and that is why they drink. In my days, we were different from the kids today. After moving here, we started drinking more, and the children started drinking too." *Miste-Pinip, elder*

"Part of the reason for the fire is alcohol. White people brought alcohol, taught us how to make home brew. We are partly to blame for what happened, because we don't look after our kids because of alcohol. The government should not allow hard liquor to be flown in. The Newfoundland government has the power to do that." *Shuash*

RAY WEBBER PHOTO

*Girls picking boughs for floor of tent / Niskuesits
meashiteuts, 1963*

Auassits kanutshikatuts enkun ne uapameuts Innua
kaminitshi kanutshikatuntshi. Auassits tshikatshes-tin-
uapamkunuts. Tutamuts enituau. Nastesh minaki-
tuenimeuts utauaua mak ukauaua tshash tshishipinuts
eminits mak minatiskueuts mak tshishue tshetshinue
pituauts mak tshiuapimananits stuassiminuts uani-
panushuts enua tukuna, mak uapekanikeapunu, mak
pimina minameuts, auassits uishtutats tante masenitamuts tshetshiminupaninushuts.

Auassits natesh pase matukunu mitshiminu tshemit-
shuts enkunuenu uish eakushits.

Auassits nas pushapenitas auassits esikuets uenue
enu etitshits. Tshekuan tshikatutenan tshetshit kami-
nustaiak kamenupuninukuak nete atikuantshe.

"Ntenitenan etu tshika mitshipinan mak tshekuan
tshika timikan, ene kanaishinakuak tshash nishu
pishimueau. Enkunu Innuts esishuet. Innuts pase
kauiatipits. Esishuet tshikapimpinua nipina Enkun
tshikaueshiuts uishitataue shitkunapunu."
Kaskutimashust

"Nin etenataman. Atutshiakue tshika mitshetuts
tshishue Innuts menits. Tshika tshishue misteni-
panushuts." *Kaskutimashust*

"Kamenupuninukuiak tshekuan nas mushinau
tshika tukun at nikataikue put mak uauitime auen
tshisenimit." *Kaskutimashust*

Enkunu enu auassits uishiuinikatets uta Utshimas-

What Is Happening to Our Children?

This tragedy has made us ask ourselves what is happening to our children these days. In the past our children were not having these problems. We never saw children doing things like sniffing gas. After moving here, children started to change. Children are more likely to be hurt than anyone else. They have witnessed most of these tragedies. We are seeing the children in this community are upset, sad and lonely, and many feel neglected all the time. They see and are affected by all the problems in our community. Children here need to be loved, cared for and happy. Without these things, children are crying within their hearts and slowly losing confidence and pride in themselves. Our children are having a lot of problems. They need our attention and our help. We need our children and they need us.

Children are left alone at night with other children in the house. They play with everything because their mother and father are not home. They don't care because their parents are gone. Other children are staying all over the place at night. What are they looking for? They try to find a way to occupy themselves around the community while their parents are out partying every night. Some of them are staying in other homes when their parents are drinking. Some sleep from house to house. They are afraid to go home and see them drinking. Drinking parents don't care where their children sleep and eat. This is too hard on the kids. There is too much neglect. In old Davis Inlet, the children were not allowed to stay out late at night. The children are unhappy. These kids only go home when their parents are sober.

Our kids are tired of seeing the alcohol problems in our community. Some people say our children are getting really wild. They are not listening to their parents and elders. Even when they are grounded they keep doing things over and over. Children don't respect their parents. Parents don't respect their children. Some parents say they don't know what their children want. Our children are upset with us because we are drinking too much. They are seeing too much in their homes—fighting and physical abuse. They are doing things to make us see them, always getting into trouble, like vandalizing buildings, breaking windows, stealing and break and entry. Little children are driving skidoos and they could really hurt themselves.

"The children are learning from the parents or other people close to them who are on alcohol and who break the laws." *School child*

Children are fighting because they are seeing drinking people fighting. Our children learn from us. They do what we do. Parents don't care about their children. Children don't care about their parents. They are starting to drink and sniff and smoke at a very early age. We have seen some of our children trying to kill themselves with pills, Javex and gas sniffing. Children are doing these things because they don't know how to deal with their problems.

Some of our children are not getting enough food to eat. That is why some of them are getting sick and getting skin infections and rashes.

Some of our children don't care any more. They are losing hope. These are some of the things they said when we asked them what we need to do so we don't bring our problems with us when we relocate:

"I think when we move, there will be more problems and tragedies, like the one that happened two months ago. That's what people from other places say. When the people move to another place, they say they are going to have running water, and it's going to be easier and faster to make home brew." *High school student*

"In my opinion, when we move more people will drink and there will be more suicides." *High school student*

"The problems that we have will always exist no matter where you want to go or whether you talk about it with a person you know." *High school student*

All of these are reasons why our children want to be sent out from Utshimassit. The children who are sent to the Sheshatshiu group home are well-dressed and have enough food to eat. When they are home their parents don't have these things for them. This is not only because of alcohol. People are poor. At the group home, children can do what they want and see many things. Also when children come back to the community, they tell other children about their experiences. They tell them that they are well taken care of. Then the other kids start acting up and getting into trouble, like breaking windows and stealing, breaking and entering. They don't care any more. Also, some of our parents have gone to the social worker and asked them to take away their child. Some parents are out of

sits, auassits kakeuenimakanits uete Sheshatshit tshishue minuaspishuts mak mushinau Mitshuts. Eku etataui nte utuuaua mak ukauaua. Nastesh mitakunu tshekuanu. Mieu namuk shitakunapu Innuts pase nas putitats tshekuana nete kakeuenimakanits auassits muk uainitits mak uauapatats tshekuanu tshika uapatamuts. Kie uitamuets kutaka auassa, uitamuets nas menupanits, kuetaka auassa pipikueimintshi shipuastenitakea mak katshemitunua. Pitshenua mitshuapits Innuts etateuts nete mitshimitshamaskuena uitamuets tshetshi utinantshi utauasimuaua Innuts tshuaputs. Auassits kakeuenimakanits nas puitshaiats aussits aiask puminupiaiats.

Auassits mitshetuts etishaauakanits nete Sheshatshits. Mistapitshitkanu tshishue shuneanu peik puna. Enkun tshikaiapitshitakanipan uta tshetshi minupanits uta, esk eka utinants mitshimitshamaskueu auassa. Innuts pase esishueuts tshinan tshika natenan kakeuenimakanits auassits. Tshitkatshi utishauakanuts nete Sheshatshit.

Kutak tshekuan takun niskuesits auassiuts uetuasimits, tshika uitimunants stuassiminuts enu kamistutakanits mak kaututuasiminanits tshikauinats punta uitamatakuts kamistutikanits mak kautuasiminanits tshika uitshiananits stuassiminuts tshetshi kautuasimits euasiats. Tshika uitamuanants kimistutakanits tshetshi katutas. Ama shentamuts tshipatshi uitamuets kamenuats eku put ama tshikishi tutamuts.

Tshika minunakatuenimanaits stuassiminuts minuats nte tshitshinash mak pipinits nipinu tshika minuenitamuts. Nas putakunits stuassiminuts tshika tutuananits uta stassinash. Pukuetamuts tshetshi tutas tshekuan tshetshi minuenitats. Kaituseshits nte katshiskauakanitshi uitshieuts auassa, nuteimuts tepiskantshi katshiskauakantshi mak katuaianits nta masteutiskanu mak miastakanu. Uipats enu takunapan auassits kametuets. Auassits apu nita takunits tshekuanu tshetshi kaminupanits tante takunu auassits tshemetauets mamu.

Passe uassits nastesh ama senitamuts tshekuanu ne uipats kaenitinanits, kashe tshimakanitshi enua maskutinikutsh uasits. Ekunu ues unitatau uipats kaenitinanitsh. Nash enu tenitamuts nta kashetshimakanitshi unapamatui ekunu eiapits uesh tshissinu uapamat. Mak auasits uinuau ni utinamuts tshekuan nte kaskutimatsheutshiuapits. Nte uishassenitamuts tshatapatahaui mishinanikea, mak petueuts kakeshaua.

Pashe auassits tshe nitau tuiuts muk tapue manakatuetamuts tshekuanu nepatataui, mak pashe uassits tenitamuts unashunt ne katuiunanua. Mak pashe auassits tenitamuts tshe mishau eniskiuet katsheniuts, manastutamuts enu essiuanits.

Mitshetuts auasits menuenitats nte nutshimits, uapatumuk nenu etenitakumits nte nutshimit, mak uta Utshimassits.

"Nutshimits nte inutshuapa apatshitauts Innuts. Shitits apatshiakanuts nta pipitshitukuts. Mamu mishue tauts auasits, mak mushinau takuea mita. Nutshimits etaiantshi tshishue minu mitshuts auasits. Mak mushinuau takunu mitshim tshe mitshits. Auasit uitsheuts kuauaua mak utauaua, natas ni nipinu. Etaiau nte nutshimits, tshishue minu inniunanu. Minuenitakun nte etaiantshi nutshimits muk eshinakust auen uitshakanu, etutashi tshekuanu. Auasit mushinau uiuitshaushuts enitinanitshi. Minuenitakun ume eshiniunantsh. Niminuenitenan inutshuapits etaiashi. Takunits nte Innuts nipinu uitshuats auasit tshipa minunakushuts atuts tshiuinakushuts. Uta Utshimassits nastesh mitakunu tshipa tutamuts auasits. Ataueutshuap minuau, mak nanikutini nutepanu tshekuan nte ataueutshuapits. An miste metshenitamats ute Utshimassits usham mishau shitakunapun, mak mitshetut auasit menamats pimina." *Auassits Kaskutshimashuts*

Tshipa nitutuaiuts stuasiminuts, esishuetaui tshekuanu. Tshisenimanuts uestuenitats nte tamits mak ke nantuapameuts auenua tshipa uitshinukuts. Katsheniuts ama miminuenitamuts unapamats usumuaua eshinakushintshi. Tshipa uiuitshaiuts stuasiminuts esk eka unitats mishue uipats kaishiniunanuts. Nishinakunu tshetshi natutuauts stuasiminuts. Uitshatusemauts mak emiauts, kie uitshinushunau punitaiak eminak, tshipa nitutakunuts. Tshishatshianuts stuasiminuts mak uinuau tshi shatshinukunuts. Tshishue stuasiminuts tshika miste espitentakushuts eskuntetshi shinitautshitaue.

Tshipa Uintumeskenan Tshetshi Uitshinushunak

"Shitakunapun ueuetishutam stiniunanu tshishue shutshimikan shitakunapun. Auen ment shitakunapunu nastesh matshi uuetishimushu, shitakunapunu ueueti-shumukuts. Tshisenitenan tshipa tshi uitshinushunan—uiuitshinushunak. Mauats tshikatshi aiatinimuanu tshementun etishumitak muk tapue stap-

CAMILLE FOUILLARD PHOTO

*Nesha, Brentas and Shunin / Nesha, Brentas mak
Shunin, 1992*

control. And group homes are not helping our
children. They are only making things worse.

About 75 per cent of the children being placed in the
group home in Sheshatshiu since it opened are from
Utshimassit. It has a budget of $350,000 a year. This is
funding that could be used here to try and stop the
problems before Social Services or the courts take away
our children. Some of us are saying we should have our
own group home instead of sending all these children
to Sheshatshiu.

Another problem we have is young girls are getting
pregnant. We should talk to our children about sex and
pregnancy. When we were young, some of our mothers
never told us about sex, and some of us got pregnant.
We should try to prevent our kids from getting pregnant at an early age. They don't know. We have to talk
to them about sex and then maybe we can prevent this
from happening.

We should look after our children. If our children
lived in clean homes with running water, they would be
happier. There is nothing to do for the children in this
community. They need recreational activities. The
Youth Council is helping with this because they open
the hall at nights and the gym on weekends. Years back

there was a playground and children never got into
trouble because they had a place to play together.

Some of our children don't know their own culture
and history. Television is changing our children. It is
making them lose their culture. They believe what they
see on T.V. That is how some of the trouble starts. Children also get some of their ideas from school. They
learn a lot of things from books, see and hear a lot
from white people. Some of our young people are good
hunters, but they don't follow our ways. They don't
respect the animals. Some children think it is a big joke
when the elders speak. Also our children sometimes
can't understand when the elders are speaking. The
language is hard for them.

But many of our children love the country, and see
the difference between life in the country and life in
the community.

"In the country, people live in tents. The floor is covered with boughs. All the children are in the tent,
and there is always enough wood. In the country,
children eat good food and there is always enough
food. The children help their parents, like fetching
water. When we are in the country, we feel healthy.
We love to be in the country where we always help

inan, naiani-mueak mak tshetshi uauitshinushunak."
Shustinish

Ntukuniskuesits tshuitamakumuts shitakunapun staushiskakunan tshisenitenan nakushiskunak. Passe Innuts matshi punitauts eminits shash tante miste akushuts.

Mitshetut Innuts eshishuets uaminaui, nistam tshipa tshitapimanuts stuasiminuts, mauat tshika tshitashimukunan shitakunapun. Mushinau ne shitakunapun tshika takun ute etaiak. Tshipa uitamashunan tshekuan nistam tshipa tutenanan, uaminau shitakunapun, put kie stausiminuts? Miste ispitentakushuts stuasiminuts, enkumtsh auasits tsheutshimaminak eskunte. Tshipa skutamuanuts auasits uipats kaishinunanuts. Tshipa uitamuaiut nenu metshipinuent shitakunapunu. Auasit tshikatshi nita unikuatamut ne kaniskuatents mitshuapinu nta epishiminiskueu pishuma mushinau tshika atamenimukunuts, esk eka nishinakuash ne tshipa uiuitshanuts stuasiminuts. Kauipuinitaiue shitakunapun enunau, stuasiminuts tshishue tshika nutshikamuts kie utuassimuau shitakunapunu. Atuts eshi minuau.

> "Mitshetau nu uitamuau tsheutshimau mieute nte uetsh nitautshinan. Akaneshau, apu tshi ishiniuian nte akaneshau, pase innuauasitsh uiishiniutsh akaneshaua, ama senitamuts tshetshi eka nita akaneshauts. Innu auasits tshetshi skutamashuts uipatsh Innua eishiniutshi. Tshetshi tatsh nete nutshimitsh tshetshi skutamashutsh nenu uipatsh innutsh kaititsh nu uiuapamantsh nituasiminants tshe tshe eishiniutsh innua." *Tshenish*

Nisenitenan shitakunapun metshipanikunash kie metshepauiat ntessinau mitshetuts Innuts nepanikuts shita kunapunu, uipatsh nete nisenitenan kamenupaniatsh muk ama nisenitenan tshetutamats tshekuan. Kie tshash nimiskenan tsheish uitshituiats.

Nemishetinan eshishueatsh tshetshi eka punatsh

enatututshitsh nitsheniminantsh, tshetshi etu minupaniatsh. Tshetshi mintutushits aueshishets kie tshetshi skutimashuiats tshetshi mentututshits kie uinuau. Upatsh nete tshetshi kastinamatsh kaish niunanutsh. Nu uiskutimakuunan nte uts katsheniutsh.

"Tsheutshimau senitam ume kamenupanikuiats tshekuan muk esk uikatueu nenua Innua senitam uin tshekuanu kamenuanits. Uin tshikasenitam tshetutak. Uin ishinakushu tshetshi uitshintak."
Manteskueu

"Nitenimau auen puntshi emint utuasimau miste minu iniiunua. Ume kapunan eiminan ntuassiminants tshitshue eash ntenitakushuts nimintutakutsh kie nin nimintutuautsh esk menian etu ntuassimitsh miste mishemenitamutsh kie nete uipatsh kaitain nimiste akunikun esk eapitsh eka minian mauitsheuautsh ntuassimitsh misheue etuteant muuiuapamauts ntuassimits tshetshi tshiam Iniuits."
Shushepmak

"Niteniten peik kutshishukaua mishinanikan. Ume kauitshipet minishineikan A.A. kaishinikatet. Ueskatsh tshitshiue nta nimeniten eku anutsh niseniten. Kie nu uitshinikun ume tshekuan uiatikants ute mishinanikanish tshekate kuetenitakuats nete eishiniuiatsh. Uauitakanu tshekuan tshenutsh uiatimunimis neu kantuiunanuts mak kauitshiitunanuts. Ume mishinanikan uitakanu tshekuan tshetshi minu nistutamash uipatsh eishiniuiatsh. Nuuitshinukun tshetshi minu Senimushunan tshetshi uitshinushunan." *Penute*

Mista animan tshetshi eka nimishetinan ntapuetenan punitats Innuts Shitakunapunu. Tshekuan put eash tshi katshi nispanu put kie pusk 50% Innutsh kamenitsh tshipa tutakanu tshekuan puk kie kutakutsh innutsh tshipa uipunutsh eminitsh put kie tshipa tutakanu tshetshi pipinitaiak tshi kaskutimatsheutshiuapinu kie nenua kapimpinitat tshe utshiniau neu kaskutimatsheutshiuap, kie katsheutshimaatushet kie nitu kuntshuap.

each other. There the children always want to help the elders. This is a wonderful way to live. We like to live in tents better. If people had water and sewage in the houses, the children would always be clean. In Davis Inlet, there is no place for recreation. The kids have nothing to do. The store is not bad, but it is always running out of food. The thing we hate the most in the community is too much drinking and gas sniffing." *Group of children talking at school workshop*

We should listen to our children, what they have to say. We know that they are hurting inside and they need someone to care for them. Elders suffer the most because they see their grandchildren are not living like they used to. We have to do something before it is too late. We have a responsibility to listen to our children. If we work with them and talk to them, if we help ourselves and stay sober, they will listen to us. We love our children and they love us too. Our children are so important for our future.

We Must Find a Way to Help Ourselves

"Alcohol controls our bodies and it is a strong medicine. No man who is an alcoholic can control himself over the alcohol. We all know things that we can do to change our lives, but we cannot change the power of God and our culture. All we can do is sit and talk about trying to get over it and help each other." *Gathering Voices participant*

Some of the nurses and doctors are telling us the alcohol is making us sick and we know this. But some people can't stop drinking because they are too sick.

Many of us say if people want to drink, we must first look after our children, because alcohol will not run away from us. It's going to be there all the time. We must ask ourselves which we will take first, alcohol or our children? Our children are more important, because they are our future leaders. We must teach our children about our culture. We must warn them about alcohol. The children will never forget what happened last February. They will blame us for everything. Before that happens, we must find a way to help our children. If we don't stop drinking now, our children will drink more than we do now.

"How many times have I told the government I did

not grow up from white people? I can never live like white people. Now some of the children want to live like white people. They don't know they can never be white people. Innu children have to learn our traditional way of life. They have to be in the country to learn about our culture. I want to see our children live as Innu." *Tshenish, elder*

We all know alcohol is destroying our lives, and it destroyed our community. We have seen many people die of alcohol. In the past, we did know we had a problem but we didn't know what to do. Now we must find a way to help ourselves.

Many of us say that if we had not stopped listening to our elders, things would be a lot better for us. We must respect the animals and learn how to take care of them again. The old ways have to come back. We need to learn these things from the elders.

"The government knows about our problems, but he is trying to hide from them. He knows these problems will have to be dealt with. He is responsible for helping us." *Manteskueu*

"I think when a person stops drinking, his children feel free. When I quit drinking, I find my children are very different. They respect me and I respect them. When I was drinking, it was my children who suffered the most. My past has really hurt me. Since I stopped drinking, I bring my children wherever I go. I would like to see my children live in peace." *Shushepmak*

"I have been reading the Twenty-four Hours book. This is an A.A. book. At first I found it very hard, but now I understand it. It helps me. There are things in this book which is like our culture. It talks about things that our elders tell us, like about hunting and sharing. The book talks about things that are familiar to us in our culture. It helps me with my spirituality." *Penute*

It will be very hard to stop these tragedies in our community. But many of us believe that if people could stay sober, things would look much better. Even if we have 50 per cent of our people sober, we can do things. Other people will want to stop drinking. And the best way to do this would be for us to run our own school, and the government agencies like the store, Social Services and the clinic.

NISH ETSHITAPATEKEN

TANTE UENTSHI TANAK UTE UTSHIMASSIT?

"Ashimakanishuut tukushipinipin Utshimassits his-
tunuepunitshe tshishiue mitshea uepastashuuna.
Kauapukuest kie Innuts uetaspishuuts ntukuunan
tau-uta tshe utshimau ntukuunan kie uiuapameu
Innua ntukuunan. Ntukuunan tshe utshimaskues
ukupaneshima amanisenimaunin. Kauapukuest tshi-
utunikakunan katshiaanimuet niuitamakuunan eni-
sishuet. Ntukunau esk eka mishikat tshishue Innuts
mishiue titamuts tshekuanu miniuanua uitshuaua
pimpinu unipimuau. Katshi uapataman amatapuani-
shipin ntukunan. Tshitshiuepinae nkuui tamuau
tsheutshimaskues eshuapataman Innuts innutshuapits etats. Innu Utshimau itak Innuts tshishue
stimauts kie tshishue takanua nuutshiuapa."
Kaniuekutat

Anuts ntenitenan amaeuninan etutamats etats Innuts
Utshimassits. Tsheutshimau ntutakunan kie kauapukuest miste kink enkuepeik tshe utshimau ukupaes-
tima. Enkuta etat utinu tekushipinits esk une utshimaut miste Smallwood Shushepis enkue utshimauipin
natukuanits. Kauapukuest utineu tshetshi utshi-
mauntshi uin eiapits ueuestapin. Katshi nistunuepuats
ama nisenitenan enitinants nimishetinan etenitamats
anuts kamenupunats kaueshimukunat.

"Innuts Utshimassits amaenu uinuau etishumushuts
tshe utshimau stishumukunu uish tapitutauak.
Tshenuuts tshipaueuetishuepints tante uinuau senitamuts eshiniuak mushinaunte nutshimits tauts. Put
stitinaatshe enitinau eka nastesh mamitenenitaman
tsheutshimau senitamutshe etshipistinak shuneanu
amanisenitenan tapitu etanau. Tshipantusenitenante
mishinanikanish." *Kaskutimashushits*

"Ueskat uetimakuiat tshetshi itishinikuiat nte ministikut putut minuuatiman nantem nitente tshetshi
itishinikuiat nte estekamikut muk put tut esishuet

tshekuanu auen. Kuet atutshe iat." *Tshenish*
Tshenuuts mushinau tipatshimupints uipits eshinakunits. Kie tapitu etshitauak uta Utshimassits.

Eshinakushinak Esk Tapitu Katananut

"Euasiuinan mushinau ntitanapin Mushuau-Shipits.
Mitshim nutshimits etshiniunan enkun uisheka min-
uenitaman mitshim ataueutshiuapits. Maniunu
kaeats aetustueuts Innua nutshimits tante Innua
kusteuts tshetshi atamantshi umaniunu kutika.
Uaskanikanish nistea pikitakea tshitshue mamishap-
ini inuuta napitshitakantshi Innu umaniunu kinasti-
nashi mitshiminuni ntuenitam. Ama apitenitamuts
matshitaui nutshimits mitshiminu nanikutini ama
titamuts nipisha kie stemaua etitamintshi tshekuanu
Innua mushinau minukuuts ni etuenitataui."
Tshenish

Anuts tshuapa anuts uskauaenua uipits Innuts nete
tapits tipi inuutshiuapa tetauts nta kutuanipin. Atikuts
umistikuaua apitshakanipants kie tshishue miskuapin
eku mapitenitamuts tante eku uishiniunants. Tshemi-
nuanipini uitshuaua nastesh amanimishimenitenan
niskueu. Kutukuts Innuts nipapints ueuetimits
nanikutini nistutshishikaua ekun etaiats uemistukut-
shiuapits eku nimishimenitaminukunan niskuteu.

Tshemiskuapin uipits apitshitakintshi inutshuap
eskua eka tshimitakants inutshuap nistam pita ntuap-
atakanu ashinin ekuta nta uatshinats ashinin etukuats
ishishue miskuau pepushi tshetshi miskakints ashinin.
Nishuashutats apitshakanuts mistikueets, neu nashuk
eku nist nispimits nukuminaets tshimitauts inutshi-
uapa. Tsheueshinukuuts ni kie misteatuseuts.

Pitikimits inutshuapits neush uataantsh petshikuan
ushitakunu kie muetshin ushitakani stinikanu
unashits. Kie tshishue miskuau tshetshi mamaku-

CHAPTER TWO

HOW DID WE END UP IN DAVIS INLET?

"A military ship came to old Davis Inlet about thirty years ago. It had many different flags. A priest and other people were all dressed up. We were told that a government person was on the ship and he wanted to meet with the Innu people. We were told he was a representative of the Queen. I don't know who he was. The priest was the interpreter. After the man finished his speech, we were told what he said, whoever he was. He said that before he came here he was told that the Innu people had everything—good housing, water and sewage. Now he could see that this was not true. When he went back, he would tell the Queen what he had seen: that the Innu were still living in tents. The former chief told him that the Innu were very poor and that it was cold to live in tents." *Kaniuekutat, elder*

Today, most of us think that we never decided to settle here in Utshimassit ourselves. We believe it was the government and the priests who made the decisions in those days. Ross King was one of the government people. He was the person on the military ship. This was during the Smallwood government. Joe Rich was the chief at the time we were settled in the community. The priest, Father Edward O'Brien, chose him to be our chief. He was part of this decision. Now, thirty years later, it is not clear how these decisions were made. However, most people feel we did not have enough say in this decision that would change our lives forever.

"The people of Utshimassit didn't decide to move themselves. We were settled here by the government. The elders should have made the decision because they knew everything about our lives. They had moved from Quebec before coming to the barrens. Maybe we did what we were told without thinking about it. The government must have decided about

how much money they would spend. We don't really know how we were moved. We need history books." *High school students*

"When we were first told we would be moved to the island, I didn't like the idea. I always thought we should have been settled on the mainland. But no one said anything. We just moved." *Tshenish, elder*

Our elders tell us stories about what life was like before we were settled and how we ended up in Davis Inlet.

Life Before We Were Settled

"We would stay in nutshimit one full year when the food was plentiful. We would go to old Davis Inlet when the food ran out. We travelled to where the caribou was, places like Ashuapun [Border Beacon], Kakatshekatet, east of Ashuapun. We used to walk and haul our sleds from Miste-shipu [Churchill River] to Kaskakapununakamat. We would camp where we killed the caribou. We would meet other families and sometimes travel with them. Some would be travelling from Emish [Voisey Bay] and places like that. They usually came hungry and people would give them food." *Meneshkuesh, elder*

"In my younger days, I used to spend my time on the Mushuau-shipu [George River]. I survived only on country food. That's why I don't like the food from the store. Traders used to bring food for the Innu into the country. That is because they did not want the Innu to sell their furs to other traders. From Uaskanikanish [Fort Chimo], there are only three portages. People used very large canoes. When people would get a few furs, they would trade them for food. They didn't mind just eating wild foods. The only problem was when they ran out of tea or

atikantshi. Tshek tshishue amashapau, namesh eiapits pimikaanu naau atikuunashinu etutuakanshi. Pashikanuni unash eku tekuanikants pimin mukushan kimikuauani mina apitshitakanua.

Nutshimits Innuts kie tshishue minu iniuts kie shutshiuts tante mushinau mitshuuts. Napeu, utiskuema, utuasima tshishue mistutiseuts. Niskueu eiapits kuetshimistutisets. Napeua eskune amatauts atumuts. Niskueu tshishue mistuutapueu eku unapema ntuuiunua. Niskueu tshishue mistuutapeu kie utuasima, utapitshi taunuaua. Napeu uitamueuni utiskuema tante tshemantshet tshi tekushintshi napeu uitshuats tshash tshimitenu mi tshuapinu kie umitima tshitshue kushikunu niskueu uetapetshi muk-enu uin utapeu pepampitshitaui.

Unapema nipeenua atikua eku pinetutaantshi eku espinits mithiminu, eku tente tshipatauts kie pase tshipa astauts usimua umunumuaua. Tante nepakantshi atik minuanunte eiapits etats matsheshuuts. Nanikutini atikana miskuakanu nete nutshimits anuts. Kauk eiapits enk uastit. Pase inuts nipeeuts kakua nish kie neunua nanikutini, epupunits shisukuts tshi panipau amusk eka entinitamen. Peikuau napeu uapimepin amuskua kuuinipishinuani kie amanista nitshipinu enantuapamat esk eka miskuat.

Uipits Utshimassits ataueutshiuap api tshi takanipan mitshim tshetshi astets kie asikumana nete Innuts. Peik tshekuan ataueutshiuap uipits nikutshitanan tshetshi utinamats ntushumukuunan. Tshishue miskuau entuuiunants tshetshi kashustamats. Muk auen eshinakust Innu ntutepen ataue utshiuapits ama uimishinani tshe tinakanuuantutetshi nutshimits. Muk Innuts pase mishinantshetinakanuuts eteatauii umauniunnan. Kutukuts Innuts ushitauts Innu misina kie ashama etutauatshets eku tshisenitenaua eshiniunats.

"Ntitanaiapin nete nutshimits ntuasimits tshishue uimitshuuts eku etuapatamats nipimuten niuitsheuau sham kie etien. Tshishue uaiu nitutenan etuapamitshits atiuk. Nipimutenan nishunuashu nishuautash, tastipani kea tshishikau kie tipiskau. Peik tshatuteash tshinetshepapash eku ama ntshitshiuean. Katshi kue-steshe tshine tshepapash neunta tshishue papinits. Tshishue nishuenan eku tanta maste etuuiunan kie tshimikitauauts nutapaaskuts uanispitshinan Utshi-masits. Tsheapisisisu ntanish, eku niui tamuau etien kutshipinita tshitshi atumuts stinuutaatau. Pase atik niua pamanan. Kie amantiti-

tenan aueshishish katea-kanits. Atutshimuk tshiituten aueshishish kakeueni-makanits kie tshetshi nipiikuau etutak enu kakeeshau. Kie ama ntiteanants uishuautikuts, maetanishits kie pikakuaets. Tshishue niuskuuin ninistim pita nantua-paten mitshim, kie tshishue nimiste atusen. Ntuskuem kie ntuasimits ntishunuapamukuts tshetshi petutean kie tshetshie petustaan kametuats nistunupena tshash etshi itutenants nete Mistinipi kinishinikate nin muk ntiskuem, kie uskats ntuasim, tshepisisisu nikus kie pipami tatshimushu. Kie itshishue niuimiste atuskuate tshetshi na ntuapataman mitshim ,unash, eshiuapatamats." *Shenum*

Uipats nete, iat-ishiniuipan nituassiminan mak anutsh eshiniuits auassit. Uskat, passe auassit nutshimit nete iniuipan. Iskueu uaminushit, uinuau tshissenitamupan tsheishi-nikiat auassa. Animinipan einikiakant auas, iskueu uaminushit, nimitshetinan ute etaiat anutsh, nete nutshimit nitiniunan. Nanikutini kukuminashit inikeipan auasa. Kie uinuau nenu uitamuepan ukuamuau tsheishinikashun nenu auassa.

"Nikaun nte nutshimit inniunipan utuassim, peik ne nishim. Ntuss, nukum mak peik nikanish mak mamu uitsheuakanuau - inikepansh nishima. Ama nitshi nashipenan shakuak, miam pikupin miskumi eku nutshimit nte iniunu nikaun utuasima, tshitshue nipukuenitamuapan tshetshi Innu nikashut nishim. Usham nimiste minuatamuan, uiapamik nishim eniut nte nutshimit. Pitshuantshuapit nte nitiniunashipan ute Utshimassit, tshitshue tshipa minuapan nte nutshimit iniuianakue kie nin ninatau nikaun tshetshi tipatshimustut kie-niteiemiau essi-ui-petaman ne-kainiuian. Kutaka nte iskueua uitshinikushipan kie nin niuitshinikushipan eniuk." *Epa*

Mitshetut Innut mushinau tshessitak nene kaishinakushit esk pet euassiuits kie nantim tapan Innut nutshimit. Ukamuauts mak utamauts mamu utuassimuau nantim mitshima tapansh. Nantim mamu eshitussepan etutakau tshekuanu tshetshi uitshituts.

"Nantim niminuatetan nte nutshimit uipats, kie tshitshue minuapan. Ama shuka nita tanapan nte Utshimassit. Nantim nte nutshimit nitanapan, nukum Manishan niuitshimatit. Masten nte etaian nutshimit, nutau niuitshimatit, shash tsheniuipan nutaun, nin ninikanteiauts atamuts kie nin nitaiatinen nutapanan. Ama shuka nita uitshimapin nutau.

tobacco. Whatever the people had, they always shared it with others who needed it." *Tshenish, elder*

The kind of tents we have now are a new kind. In the past, Innu lived in *innutshuap* (teepees) with an open fire in the middle. The caribou hides were used to cover the teepees. It was hard times, but we didn't mind because it was part of our culture. We were safe in our teepees; we never had to worry about fires. Some Innu used to sleep outside for up to three days. Now we live in houses and we are always worried about fire.

Life was a lot of hard work when we were still using teepees. Before we could set up the teepee, we would have to find a rock. That's where we would camp. We would build our fire on the rock. It was very hard, especially in the winter when the rocks were covered in snow. It would take seven tanned deer skins to cover a small teepee, four on the bottom and three on the top. Our grandmothers would set up the teepees. It looked very easy for them but it was a lot of work.

Inside the teepee, we would prepare *pitshikuan* when we would be staying for a long time. We would stretch out the dry meat and tie it to a pole. Then we would pour a mixture from the caribou stomach and blood over the meat. Anything that was hard to chew, like the caribou ligament, that's how we would keep it and make it soft. Fish could also be made into *pimikuan* in the same way caribou meat was. We would dry the caribou meat, pound it and make it into a powder. The *pimin* from *mukushan* could also be mixed with red berries.

When people were in the country, we were always healthy and strong because we were eating country food. The man, his wife, the children would work very hard. A woman used to work as hard as a man. That was before we had dogs to pull the sleds. A woman would travel from one camp to another while her husband was doing the hunting. We could call it mobile hunting. The wife would travel with the small children, pulling the sled with all their belongings. The husband would tell the wife where to set up camp or where they would meet. By the time he would get there, the tent would be all set up with plenty of firewood. Can you imagine how heavy that load was? She herself would pull it from one camp to the next.

If her husband killed caribou and they thought they had enough food, they would stay in one place and he would do some trapping. Usually where the caribou is killed is a good place for foxes. Sometimes, the caribou was nowhere to be found in the country, like today. Porcupine was the main food then. Some people would kill two or four porcupines. If you were lucky you might kill a black bear during the winter. Once a man saw a sign where the black bear might have been. He never stopped looking until he found the bear's den.

The Hudson's Bay Company used to supply food and steel traps for the Innu. One thing the HBC did to us was to try to force us to only trap. It was very hard for us to trap and hunt at the same time. When someone wanted to go to the country, the Hudson's Bay Company would not give people any credit. The only people who would get credit were those who would get a lot of furs. Other people used to make moccasins or snowshoes to sell. This is how we survived.

"We were in the country. My children were starving when I went to pick up some supplies. We walked with Sam and Etien. We walked a long ways to hunt for caribou. We walked twenty-seven hours, day and night. We left at one o'clock in the morning and didn't get home until the next morning at four o'clock. We were very hungry. That's the last time we were going to hunt and then I was going to cut my komatik short to make it to Davis Inlet. I had a small daughter, so I told Etien to try to keep the dogs as long as they could. So we had luck with some caribou. I didn't have any farm I can depend on. I couldn't just go to the farm and kill what I wanted to,

Fort Chimo / Uaskanikanish, 1880

LUCIEN M. TURNER PHOTO

SMITHSONIAN INSTITUTION PHOTO

Mani with bow / Mani mak ukusk, 1928

WILLIAM DUNCAN STRONG PHOTO

Unkueu prepares the bones for the mukushan / Unkueu ashepan, 1927

Nukum mak nimushum nantim niuitshimatit. Kassinu nte nukum nut-tshisseniten, meu nte nikaun uet-tshiskutamashuian, tante nantim nikaun akushipan. Tatuau etaiat nutshimit, tepiskansh, nimushum nikustinikunan tshetshi eka ituteiat nte iatshimitshuapit." *Shanutis*

Et nete animinipan ueskat. Ukamuauts kie auassit iat-itenitakushipan, nanikutini auassit itenimepan uikanishuau kie tshenua, usham kenui-ueuetishi imukunanua, muk mak auassit nitutuepan uikanishuau uatamakutau tshekuanu.

"Nin nete pets euassiuian, ama nita ishitutakupants nikanishit etutuakanits anutsh auassit. Anutsh auassit eka mentutuantau, apu nakatuentak nenu kie apu nistutuat nenu uikanishuau. Nin nantim ninitutuatit nikanishit kie niuitshiatit nikanishit kie niuauitshiatit kutakut Innut eka mentutaman—niuitamakutit nikanishit tshetshi eka mitshenitakushian, miam uiapamitau tshekuanu ua-eituk, kie uatutamuk

tshekuanu. Apu nita-ut-eishi-tututs nin nikanishits anutsh etenitakushit ukaumuaut kie utaumuauts. Eku menupinian, nantim nte tapan nikanishit - tshetshi—uitshinits. Kie nitapuetuatit tshekuanu eshitaui." *Kaniuekutat*

"Nte pet euassiuian, ninitutuapan nikaun kie ama nita uaushinuau uen, nantim ninitutua nikaun tshekuanu - uatamut. Kie nin nantim nitispitenimapin uen kie nantim niuauitshiapin nukum kie nimushum kuiapukukau kie nekutukau." *Tshenish kie Meneshkuesh, katshiskutamatsheutshuapit eianimuants*

Innuts apitshitapints akupa mistikuea tshishiue nistimaunan. Kie ama takunte kamamishimituants muk ninan nipimpini-nushunan. Mishiue Innu sheshetshu. Mushi-nau ninan ntutashunan. Ninan muk ntitanan nitshinash. Nasteen amaniui ta makuunan isteastaiats ntisukumanaua kie etuuiunats Innu tshipauitutashu uaitutet kie uantutet.

like the white man. I didn't have any cows and sheep and chickens. I was having a hard time. I have to look for my food first; I had to work for it. My wife and children were waiting for me to come back to see if I got any game. Thirty years ago, I went to Miste-nipi at the Quebec border. There was only me, my wife, and I had my first child. He was only small and could only crawl. I had to work for my family for the wild meat that we depended on." *Shenum, elder*

The life of our children in those days was very different than it is today. First of all, children were born in nutshimit then. When the woman was in labour, they had their own way of doing it. It was hard work for the women to deliver the babies. Many of us living in the community now were born in the country. Sometimes, the elders were the midwives back then. Also, it was the elders who would give the child's name to the parents.

"My mother had her baby in the country—my brother. My aunt, my cousin and grandma and their friend were the midwives. We couldn't come back to the community; the ice was just breaking up, so my mother had my brother in the country. I always wanted my brother to have an Innu name. It was so beautiful to see my brother born out in the country. I was born in a tent in old Davis. It would have been nice if I had been born in the country too. I used to go to my mother and talk to her about it and wanted to know more about my birth. It was other women from the community that helped my mother with me too." *Epa*

Many people have very good memories of what it was like when they were small and Innu people were always in nutshimit. Parents and children used to be very close at one time. They were always doing things together.

"We always had good times in nutshimit in the old days. It was very good. I never spent time in the community. I was always in nutshimit with my grandmother Manishan. The last time we went to the country with my parents, my father was very old and I had to take the lead and control our dog sled. I didn't spend much time with my parents; I often stayed with my grandparents. Everything we learned about the culture was from our grandparents, not from our mother, because our mother was always sick. Every time we were in the country, our grandfather would tell us legends." *Shanut*

There was more discipline in those days. Parents and children used to behave differently. Sometimes children would feel like their parents or elders were trying to run their lives, but they would still listen to them.

"When I was young, my parents never treated me like parents treat children today. When children get abusive, they don't recognize or understand their parents. I always listened to my parents. I used to help my parents. I was very supportive of the people. When I was being mischievous, I was told by my parents not to get bad when they would see me trying to do something. My parents never treated me like parents today. My parents were always there when I had a hard time. I would just listen to them." *Kaniuekutat, elder*

"During my young days, we used to listen to our mother, and not make fun of someone. We always used to listen to what my mother said. I always treated people with respect and I always worked for my grandparents, like getting water and wood." *Tshenish and Meneskuesh, elders at school workshop*

People used to dress in caribou skins. We were very poor. There were no game laws. We used to travel wherever we wished. Everyone was free. We were always on our own. We were our own bosses. Nobody would tell us where we could trap or hunt. A family could choose to go wherever it wanted to.

"When I travel on the plane from Uashat [Seven Islands] or Schefferville, and think about how people used to travel from Fort Chimo to Seven Islands, I think about how long it would take for people to walk with little food. People were hungry and suffered, but they travelled wherever they wanted to. The government wants us to follow white man's way. People used to travel wherever they wanted to go. Now the government tells us what we should do or not do." *Akatis, Innu woman*

Mushuau Innu used to meet up with Innu from other territories like Uashat (Seven Islands) and Sheshatshiu. There was no boundary between Quebec and Labrador. The land belonged to the Innu. We were always very happy to meet. Those groups of Innu would have a lot of food, tea and tobacco. Sometimes we would meet settlers on the coast. They would give our children clothes to wear, like shoes.

"Once a person was sick in the country. I was the

"Nipushinapin kapiminast nete, Uashats eku nten-iten tanispish Innuts tshipa apitsheeuts kapiminash-intshi ete Uaskanikanish kie Uashats, nteniten tan tshetshi pimutet Innu epish etakunak mitshiminu. Inuts shiuenuuts kie ninikatenitamuts, eku eiapits pushuuts uapushitaui. Netema Sheshatshit kie uashat, ministanastesh tashine asin kie ama nista apin kie tshetshi minipan nimisina ekuete patush meshikaian. Tshe utshimau niui tamakuanan kakee-shaua etutimitshi tshetshi tu tam utshits Innuts apit-shitauts pushi taui muk uinuau uatu taaui. Ekuanuts tsheutshimau ntituanan etishuminimit kie uakatu-tam utshit." *Akatis*

Mushuau Innuts uapamepints Innua nete Uashat kie uaska nikanits, kie Sheshatshit. Metikunupen ne-kemeshinanikenua Quebec mak Labrador. Innu tipenitam utisin. Kie minuenitamuts tshetshi uapami-tuts uutshe Innuts kitautshi tshishue umitshimuts, nipishapun kie stemau. Nanikutini niui uapamats utish kakeeshauts. Kie auasits tshipamina-kanuuts misina.

"Peik Innu tshishue mistakushu nutshimits. Eku nipetutau uta utapaaskuts ntapitshinimaua atumua eku nepit katshitat uipits Utshimassits. Enkun tshekuan tshipaui tshiitunan mishiue anuts."
Tuamish

Mushinau tshipa uitshiitunan manuma Innua utu-asima nutepinu mitshiminu, eku kutakuts pase mamu nimatuuts mitshiminu. Anutshu, stitanan pepemau uipits Innu nastesh ama tshuuetishinukunan, eku anuts tsheutshimau tshiuiuuetishumukunan etshi aniu-nau. Tshi pa nas tapuetatunan mamu nistimaunaiapin eku niminuenitenan, muk tshishue niuishishekan etshiniuian.

"Ntitanapan nutshimits ntuasiun kie amantititenan mitshim. Nent niuiatuten. Ntepauanants Innu uts ute uashat, nimiskuanan atik nipeeshipints unapimi tshishi, eku pase unashinu uetinumutshistu eku kutak tshishukunu unapimitshis niui tamuanant enua atikua. Tshishue minueni tamuts unapiminits. Niuita makunaets miam stutenau uetinimek unash tante kie anuts niuapamitunan enkunuenu Innu uishuui uitshaat uitshinua tshinanu usteshimauts kie pepemau tshuushinan tshinanu mushinau innuuts."
Tuamish

Innuts mushinau kuspitshuuts nutshimits ama

nakituenitamuts eshinakishits. Kie nistim e tshaship-initat uetshimauuta eku eiapits mishiue tshikaituteuts. Atusi nakatuenitenan espishetinants eku eiapits tshipa utinuku uetshimautshi. Uue Innu ama utshimau muke kauiapitshat utinima tshipa uitamueu eshipimpintshi antanteshe mupimantshi nisishuete eku tshash utiship-ini tshesi stuteau eku mishiue nas tshipatapuetenan. Mushinau ntetau ueuetishuet nutshimits. Nanikutini mistapeu nutshimaminan uetinitshish. Ustinitshu nut-shimaminan eiapits nete uipits Utshimassits.

Nitutenan nete nutshimits kataiats uipits Utshimas-sits eku uataueats mitshim napishima, ntapitshi tan inuuta, eku pepushi nipimutean. Ama ntapitshananants atumuts, utapaaskuts ntapitshaaets niutapenan niuinatshi tauenan tshetshi minu iniuiats. Tshishue mishau shuneau etutauatsheash nimaniunan: masheshiueaets, ntshuk, nisukutsha euaets kie amusk kie atshikash kie kutakuts aueshishist. Maeanapan etutauatsheats ashinina, stemau pimin kashiuas kie unusk usua ets. Napeuts muk tshi eapints mitshima. Muk nete ninan ntitanan ntisinats apisis eku nete impaitutenan nutshimish tshetshi ntuuiunash nimesh, pineu kauk kie kutak miskimash metueun.

Kauapuskuet enkue nistim kauapukuest tekushint ete ntitananapin nete emish kinishinikateua niuita-makunan taunte kauapukuest Utshimassits nituku-unan kie niui tana nte pepunits kauapukust muk mishikau katshi peik pupunitshi muk nishu tshishikaua tau ni. Innuts ashimukuts kauapukuesh-intshi meshikan tshi. Kauapukuest niuitamakunan tshetshi takushinuutshish Utshimassits eku etuteutsh nutshimits. Pase nete ituteuts Mushuau-Shipits tante nisenimanan atiuk etutetshi shipits. Eku nteeskunenan mushinau niuitshina shipits eku nta shinuapamanan atik tante uetutet.

Uipits Utshimassits, tshishu amatshintutenan ataueu-tshiuapits shakuatshi kie nutshimits. Naniku-tini ntashi nuapatenan tshetshi kie nipaameunuts esk eka pimu-teats miskumits. Kie neush amamiskuutin nipis.

"Nipeten muestateni takushuts innuuts nete nut-shimits. Kie ama nispinuuts mitshiminu. Unapema uitamakune iskueue kie ukus tshika nikatamuts put mishue tshipa nipi pints uitshuash. Eku kutuk napeu tshishue uiui-tsheueu esk tshishuk ama uti-shipanu pimuteuts, napeu nasteesh ama tshipimuteu eku nekitats. Akanika takuentshi, mishiue tshipa

one who brought him up here although that was before we had dog teams. He died later in old Davis Inlet. This is how we used to help each other."
Tuamish, elder

We always used to help each other. If one family had a short supply of food, other families had to share the food. Today, we live very differently. In the past, people were free; now the government is controlling our lives. We used to respect each other. We were poor but we were always happy, proud of our culture and the way we lived.

"I was just young in the country one time, and we didn't have any food. We found caribou killed by Innu from Uashat and we took some meat before we saw them. The next day we saw them and we told them about the caribou. They were very happy to see us and they told us we did the right thing to take their caribou meat even if this was the first time we met each other. This is how we used to help each other. We were not strangers to each other. We were like brothers even though we came from different territories. We were all Innu." *Tuamish, elder*

People always travelled inland with anyone, no matter who they were. Whoever started first became the leader and eventually more families would follow. It would not matter how many families there were. They were accepted by the *utshimau* (leader). This person was not like a chief, just a person who led his people. He would tell them when to move, when they should have mukushan. When a leader said it was time to move, everyone had to respect his choice. There was always a leader in the country. When we canoed, the person who sat at the back was the leader. Sometimes a *kamiteut* (shaman) was chosen to be a leader. Ustinitshu was such a leader in the days of old Davis Inlet.

We used to travel from the country to old Davis Inlet to get groceries. In the summer, we would come by canoe, and in the winter we would come by foot. We didn't use to use dog teams. We pulled our sleds ourselves. We would get groceries with the animals we killed and trapped. This was the only way we could get the groceries we needed to survive. Back then, a lot of money was made selling furs: foxes, otter, muskrat, marten, weasel, squirrel and beaver. We would sell these furs to buy ammunition, tobacco, butter, sugar and flour. Many times, only the men would come in to get supplies. We only stayed in the village a short time. Then we would go back to the bush to hunt for food like fish, porcupine, partridge and any kind of game that could be found.

Father O'Brien, who people called Father Whitehead, was the first priest to come. We were in the Voisey Bay area that time. We were told the priest would be in Davis Inlet and we all had to be there. For years, the priest would only come once a year and stay for a few days. People would get relief from the priest when he came. The priest began to tell us when to come to Davis Inlet and when to go in the country. Some would go into the interior as far as the George River. We knew exactly when the caribou would cross the river. We had to be prepared at all times. We would get to the river and camp on the west side because we knew the caribou would arrive from the east.

In old Davis Inlet, it was very difficult to get to the store in the fall from the country. Sometimes we would have to wait until just before Christmas before we

Shimun and Shaiet Pokue erecting a teepee / Shimun mak Shaiet Pokue tshematas tshinaskutshiuapinu, 1963

RAY WEBBER PHOTO

nipipints amanukuetu tuuts eku kutak tshishuk utit-shipanu, uapameuts atikua. Napes peikusu muk, euasiut eku niskueu tsheniskueu utinum pasikanu eku pinasi tshet muk apisis tante apisisinua ukusa eku napes pinasuat atikua. Eku pitetash nepiat ama ituteu nete iskueu unapema, tante ukusa ama shapentakushinua kie amatshipimutenua. Muk ash-inuapameuts. Put pase Innuts tshipapi-muteuts kat-shi nishu tshishi kanits, Innuts petuteuts kie uita-muts etshi kuaitets." *Tshenish*

"Tshishue nimishetinan ninan ekuspitshinats. Ninan ute nastesh ama nuimitshiminan. Nititean atik muk minispinu, eku ninan etuteats Utshimassits natimats mitshim eku nastesh amatakun mitshim katshi ntuteats Utshimassits. Nastesh amaniskupinu mit-shim ata ueutshiuapits katshi taiats, muk nipishae kie stemau eku minuats tshaueats nutshimits. Tante amashuka nakituenitenan pase ninan nipasa uanishenan tante pase atik niuapamanatshe ute eta-iats katshishikats nutaun uapatepan atikua umeskeaminu. Ama shuka tshiuitum nte etutentshi ekuminuats uiapats eku unapamitshisn atikuts. Peik ninan nininashuanan, eku nastesh ama ninipanaets nimiskatenitakushinin tante kuesteshe nituten pase nipaauts atikuts. Katsheniut atik ninipau tante meskeape niui-tshinukunan. Nishuau katshi ituteats nutshimits nimupimenan mishiue atik kanipaatshish. Ntenimau meskea mishiueenua tshikanipeeu ntenimanan. Nastesh ama nipeeu put amatshitakunimut-she uskinima etishumushut enkunuenua atiuk utipenimukushima tsheshuapintshi enkunu nastesh amanipeeu atikua." *Tshenish*

Tshipatutenan

"Innuts uipits tapints ute eku patush kakeeshau pinetutet. Utshimassits ishini katakanu. Kakeeshau nishinikatum Innu mishiue enitau asits. Muk eshi-nakust innutau nutshimits, Eiesimeu (Inuit), Innu-uts (Cree). Kakeeshau petutepints kie minu uit-sheueuts inua." *Tuamish*

Katshitat Kauapuskuet kauapukuest eku kutak mist-ikauapukuest petuteuts. Enkue etat uta Utshimassits kauapukuest. Uskats pepunits, niuitamakunan tuku-nu nte tshetshi atusets Innuts katasipu takants kaishi-nikatets, eku patush auasits tshipa ushitakanu mit-shuapinu tshetshi skutimashuts. Innuts tshipaituteuts nutshimits, eku auasits tshipaskutimashuuts. Katshi

ushitakants kaskutimatsheutshiuap, auasits tshipa sku-timashuuts nete eiapits Shintshanish nas tshipaminu skutimashuuts. Pase tshipa petuteuts tshi-pauitshieuts inua. Pase katsheniuts nisishueuts tshipa ta pue tamuts tante ueskats unapatats tasuputakanu kie kaushitakanits, kaskutimatsheu tshi uapinu. Pase nisishueuts tshika utinakanuuts akaskutimashutaue, kie eshimukuunatshi pisis tshika ashimukunaumuk tsheniuts Innuts tapuetueuts mistekaua pukueshintshi esishuentshi, eku mushinau tsheiniuts tapuenane tante takun katshisuputakants uipits Utshimassits. Katshi, nishu putsh mistikauapukuest pushu eku ama takunu katshasiputakants.

Eku katshi puashit ashimakanishiut tikushipinu nimu pistakuunan uipits Utshimassits, tsheutshimau minueu pipi tshituka mishiue maminueu eku Innuts ueshitats uitshuaua apitsheeuts mistukua kaminakanits ekuntenispimits apakuanu apitshitauts tshishiue minu-aua eshinakuatshi etu minua innutshuap kie tshiteua. Kauapukuest apitshitau uastenipimakea uishipim-pinitshi eku tshe kumuat mitshuapits Innu Utshimau peikusumuk uatshit nete uipits Utshimassits.

Kauapukuest tshishue uuetishumueu Innua Utshi-mau. Kauapuskuet kauapukuest nuutinukunan, Shushepis, ama tauaakanu pase ninan ama niseni-manan uetshiutshimaut. Pase nisishueuts tante mit-shetuuts enkunuenu uishuutshimaut ueuetishuet. Nishinua uuitsha, eku kutuka Innua apinua innut-shuapish. Minakanu atuseunu manuet mitshiminu Innua kauapukuest. Pase Innuts miminuenitamuts.

"Uipits uune ninan ntutean uaituteats menuenita-mats. Uetshimaute mushinau enkue tshipa uuetishueu. Aiask etshimitshetinats Utshimassits, utshimaun amatakun. Mukune uetshimaunants kauapukuest utineu innua. Meunimuk ishetshi mit-shenimik numushum. Mimushum tshimaut tante kauapukueshintshi itushumuku." *Kiti*

Tshishikatshi, kauapukuest niutunikakunani meshikataui, tsheutshimau ukupaeshima meshikantshi. Kauapukuest tshishue mitshinita kushu tshashikantshi Innuts kusteuts tshetshi nutshikuats kauapukuesh-intshi nimitshetinan etenimitshish mishanu kamenuats etutak.

Katshi pushit mistikauapukuest, kutuk tau kaua-pukuest Miste-Pitis (Frank Peters) ishinikatakanu ue kausit kauapukuest uskanu etenita. Mishiue tsheutshi-mau ukupaneshima mamu miste Pitish tsheuapamat

could walk on the ice. It would take a long time for freeze-up in the rattle between the island and the mainland.

"Once I heard a sad story of people who were in the country. They were short of food. The husband told his wife and son they would have to leave or they would all die in that camp. Another man was anxious to go with them. After a day of walking, the man couldn't walk any more. They had to leave him behind. If they didn't leave him behind, they would all die there. They had no choice. The next day the husband could no longer walk and had to be left behind. A day later, they saw some caribou. The son was the only young fellow, so the old woman took his gun and put powder and flint into it, not too much powder, since he was only a young boy. With his first shot he killed a caribou. He got five caribou. They couldn't go back to the husband, because the son was too weak to walk any further. All they could do was wait. Maybe some people would come along. A few days later, people did come and were told the other people had starved to death." *Tshenish, elder*

"Once, a large group of us, our family, went into the country. Before we got there, we ran out of food. We got a few caribou but not enough. So we decided to go back to Davis Inlet for more food. There was no food left in the store when we got there, only tea and tobacco. We went back to the country anyway. We didn't worry too much. Some of us had dry meat. We knew the caribou would migrate our way soon. One day, my late father saw tracks which he thought were caribou tracks. He wasn't sure because it was too far to tell. The next day, we went hunting and we saw some caribou. One of us went after them, but he didn't get any. I was lucky I was on the other side. So I killed most of the caribou. An old shaman was with us. Twice on our way to the country, he had a mukushan with the whole caribou. He thought he would kill a lot of caribou as the shaman. But he didn't kill any. Maybe he didn't handle the bones in the proper way. That makes the caribou spirit angry. That's why he didn't get any caribou." *Tshenish*

The Decision to Move

"The Innu were here long before the white man came. There was no such name as Davis Inlet. White men gave this place its name. We Innu were every-

where on the land. All kinds of people lived in the country—Inuit, Cree. The white men came and were not nice to the Native people." *Tuamish*

After Father Whitehead, Father Joseph Cyr came. He was the first permanent priest in old Davis Inlet. His first year here, he told us there would be a sawmill where people could work, and a school would be built where children could go to school. Parents could go to the country, but children would have to stay for school. When the school was built, children would finish high school and would go to St. John's for a better education. Some would come back and help the Innu. Some elders now say that the elders at the time agreed with him because that was the first time they would see these things like a sawmill and school. Some say we were told our children would be taken from us if they didn't go to school, and our social assistance would be cut. Perhaps the elders thought if the Innu followed Father Cyr's advice, they would always live in peace. It was true there was a sawmill in old Davis Inlet. After two years, Father Cyr left and at the same time the sawmill was gone.

About a year after the military ship came to visit old Davis Inlet, the provincial government gave plywood to every Innu family. Each family built their own shack using the plywood on the floor and for the walls, with tent canvas for the roof. The shacks were better than the tents, a bit warmer. The priest used to have his own power generator, so he hooked up every tent. The chief was the only person who had a house in old Davis Inlet.

The priest had a lot of influence on the people and on the chief Father Whitehead had picked out for us— Joe Rich. He was not an elected chief. Some of us don't know why he became chief. Some say he was picked because he had a big family that he could influence. He was given a two-storey house while the other Innu were living in shacks. He was given the job of handing out food to the people for the priest. Some people didn't like this.

"In the old days, families used to travel inland wherever they liked. The leader always made the decision to move. As more families settled in Davis Inlet, the leadership disappeared. The only visible leadership was by the priest or his chosen people. Not that I dislike my grandfather. He was definitely a good leader, but he was taking orders from the priest." *Kiti, chief*

shushepisa. Uikanisha eiapits tanua—kauapukuest niutinu kuakunan.

"Tsheutshimau uku paneshima tepueuts tshetshi aianimuanits niui tamakunan tshash tshekat tshika atutshenau anutshu uipits Utshimassits uishamiats ashiniu, eku nte ama takun tshetshi ushitakan tshi mitshuapa, muk tshitshue mishau nipin. Muk amatshika tshitshi kumutakanua nipin mitshuapish enamiats ustunakun, stasiuau eamiats apishashi tshetshi uskats stasiuau. Tsheutshimau niui tamakunan kie nantuapa tamupan tshetshi atuseutshish. Innu Utshimau kie pitu utshimau (atuaueuts kauapukueshintshi) tshetshi ntuapatamintshi tsheutshimasits niui tamakuunan Innu ntenitamuts minuau, tshetshi uapamats tsheutshimaua nete shintshanishish eku nisishueuts minuaau tsheutshimau uauitshiat inua tante esk ama takunipin uemistiukutshiuapa. Nisishueuts tshetshi eie maats innua. Kie niuitamakunaents tsheatutsheek kie mitshima tshika tukun ataueutshiuap tshika takun ministukuts nituenitenan pushuunan kie kaskutima tsheutshiuap. Nishi shueuts kaskutimatsheutshiuap apishashu kie esk amamitshe tinanu. Katshinishutshishi kanits, tsheutshimau mupistamupan Utshimassits minuats eku tapuetitau uaatukani kani kuunak." *Miste-Pinip*

Peikuau tsheutshimau ui-kutshitapan tshetshi ui-aiatinimit, ninan emushuaniutshit niui-tutakunan tshetshi taushit nete ustetshe nain, Nutak ishinikateu, shash petetat tatunuepunutshe ume eitutakuiat.

"Tsheutshimau, nitikunan Nutak tshika itaunikunau tante tshika tshipanikanu utshimaut utatautshiuapuau. Eku piapinit ut-meshat, eukun pushiat, eku katshi petaunikuiat nte Nutak, eku minikuiat mitshim. Tapan nte peik kakeshau miste puntshe ishinikashupan, eukun ne-manuet mitshiminu. Tapansh nete isimeuts nete Nutak, mitshetipansh issimeut—ama shuka mitshetuts kakeshauts. Akamits nete nist—taut, kie ute akamits nitanan, eku tshek nutaun uatshiuet. Eku kauapukuest iteu nutauna, tshetshiuein kau iteu eku kassinu Innut uatshiuets. Tekuatshinit peik nte nishim nipaniku nipinu, pekestuepinu, shakuatsh eku kau—tshauepitshiats nte uipats Utshimassit ama nisseniten tshekuanitshe uet-itaunimits tsheutshimau nete Nutak. Muk nete ashamitshepansh Innuts." *Meneshkuesh*

Pase tshenuts niui tamakunants miste kink, peik tsheutshimau ukupanema, uitsheepin atauautshiapits utshimaua Miste Aush, kauapukuest kie Innu Utshimau Shushepis, uinau utinumuts asinu tshetshi atukuanits menuats. Uinuau utinamuts tsheutshimau ministukunu Utshimassits kaishinikatets. Put tsheutshimau ama tshinispinitshe shuneanu uish eka minuats etauatak asinu, enkunu enu uisheka utinak asinu kamenistukuunts. Nisishueuts asits minuau ueshitakantshi mitshuapa tante nipin timiu uish papintshi uta.

Pukunepitauts nipinu asits eku etukunits nipinu ntukunaets takun nipin mishiue auen tshika nispinu. Kie niuitamakuunan mishiue mitshuapa tshika tukun nipin kie kapimpitshi kastapistesi kie tshitempunuani niuitama kunaents eamiats mistunitin uipits Utshimassits mishiue nte nakatuenitenan kie tshika takun kapiminashits katueuts.

"Nipetenan tsheutshimau ntishumeu Innua tshetshi atutshentshi. Utishipinu inuts tshetshi uuetishuets, tante kustatshuuts tshetshi animuets nikustanants kakeeshauts mishiue kakeeshauts tshekuanu niuitamankunaets tsheutshimau niuitamakunan tshetshi ushitakantshi mitshuapa kie tshetshi takunits nipinu. Kakitshinauts tshiueshimukunuuts. Stapuetuaiapints eku tshash tshistimaunan amatakun nipin." *Niskueuts Kaitusset*

Katsheniuts niuitamakunants nastesh ama nishishueuts tshetshi atutsheats.

"Napempen amaminuenitamupan uantutanits ute ntenitam nipin uinakimitauts katanuani nimesha tante mitshetipin namesh uta ministukush nta puetuau kie tapueu nastesh ama anuts kataua nimesh napem amatapuetueu Innu Utshimaua tshetshi atukunits eku itiku amatshika tshi peikusin." *Matininish*

"Miste-Pitish kie Shushepish enkutshints esishuets uta Utshimassits, Miste Aush utshimaui pan ataueutshiuapits, eku Miste Kink tau nte eiapits enkue nakatuapatam ataueutshiuapinu ama nastesh takunu tsheanimuats amatakun Innu tshetshi uitamuakanits ama nisenitenan enitinants niui tamakuunan muk tshetaek mitshuapits ntukuunan kie tshikitshinista itutenau nutshimits ntukuunan peik unu ashupite tash mitshuapa ueshitakan tshi 1967 kie peik unuashupite tash minuats tshika ushitakanua

In those days, the priest was always interpreting for us when the government people came. The priest was very strict in those days. People were afraid to speak out against the priest. Many of us today think this was the biggest mistake we ever made.

After Cyr left, there was another priest called Frank Peters. The new priest had a new idea. All government agencies got together with Frank Peters to meet with Chief Joe Rich. Some of Joe Rich's family were there too. The priest was interpreting for us.

"The government officials called a meeting. They told us that very soon the Innu should move to a new location. This place, old Davis, was too rocky, and there was no space for new houses, although there was plenty of water. But to hook up water from one house to another was very difficult. Besides, this place was too small for a new community. The government people told us that they were looking at different places for a new site. The chief and council (also appointed by the priest) were involved in looking for this site. The officials told us if the Innu thought it was a good idea, then they would go meet with the government in St. John's. They also said they were pretty sure the government would support the idea because none of the Innu had the houses yet. They said another meeting would be called for the Innu. The officials told us we needed a new community, and the store would be close by. The store was on the island. We needed a new wharf and school. They said the present school was too small and the population was growing. A few months later, the government agencies visited the community again. This time, it was agreed to move." *Miste-Pinip, elder*

Another time that the government tried to interfere with our lives was when they first tried to settle us, the Mushuau Innu, at Nutak on the coast north of Nain about fifty years ago.

"The government told us to move to Nutak because they were going to shut down the old Davis Inlet Hudson's Bay post. They placed us in some kind of big boat and once we arrived in Nutak the government started to handle the relief. There was a white person there that we called Miste Puntshe. He was the one that gave out the food supplies and relief. There were Inuit at Nutak, a lot of Inuit people and a few white people. We were living on one side and they were on the other. We lived there for one year

until my father decided to go back. The priest told my father that he had to go back and all the Innu decided too. My brother was killed in a drowning accident there in the fall. We left in the spring. I don't know what the government was up to moving us there. I only know the people were making snowshoes." *Meneskuesh, Utshimassiu elder*

When the government was trying to settle us in the sixties, some elders tell us it was Ross King, one of the government representatives, with the store manager Ramsey House, the priest and Chief Joe Rich, who came to see this place and picked it for the new community. They say it was mostly the government people who chose the island for the new Davis Inlet. Maybe the government didn't have enough money for a better place, and that's why we didn't move to the mainland in the first place. They said the land was good for building houses. The water was deep enough for the boats to come in.

They dug a well to make sure there was water. They told us the water was there and it should be enough for the whole community. We were also told once we got a new house there would be water and sewer facilities for every house, and furnaces for heating. They said there was too much wind in old Davis Inlet. Here it was protected on both sides. Later they would find a place for an airstrip.

"We heard the government decided for the Innu to move to Utshimassit. By the time people were settled, they were too afraid to speak out. We were afraid of white people and we did everything white people were telling us. The government told us they would build us houses with running water. They lied. They tricked us. We believed them and now we are very poor with no water." *Family Violence Project*

Other elders tell us they had no say in the decision to move.

"My late husband didn't like the idea about moving here because he thought the water would be polluted and there would be no fish. At that time, there was a lot of fish around this island. Now I know he was right. There are no fish on this island any more. My husband disagreed with the chief about the move, but he was told he could not be alone here." *Matininish, elder*

"Mr. Peters and Joe Rich were the ones who picked

ntukuunah 1968. Kie niuitamakuunan mishiue tshekuan tshika titenau tshitshuats nipin tshika pimpinu eku katshi piseats nastesh amatakun tshekuan nte mitshuapits muk kastapistesi tukuea."
Shankush Katsheniuts Isishueuts

"Shushepis peikusu uetstimaut niuuetishimukunan inua. Kie animuenishni, pase Innuts ama uintutepin tshuute, ute anuts Utshimassits. Eku Shushepish mushinau peikusu utshimaut, eku anuts eshinakuats etshi mitshetits utshimauts uta Utshimassits."
Shapatesh

Pase Innuts nisishueuts ehe kakeeshauts ituteuts tante mitshuapa nete kaushitakantshi nete uipits Utshimassits, kie niminu enitamuanan eshu ushitat Shushepish mitshuapa. Pase Innuts nisishuepants ete tshipa tshimitakanua mitshuapa nete Shanti eku tente tante etukuash shipis kie minuau nipin, eku tante kutakuts amanitutamuts Innuts nenekatenitamuts. Ama shuka umitshumuts eku kutakuts amasenitamuts eshinakunits.

"Tshishue niminuenitenan ueshitakantshi nitshinaia katshi atutsheash eku etuteash ama takun tshekuan kie mitshuapa amaninu ushitakanua." *Miste-Peashue*

"Miste Kink kie Innu Utshimau Shushepis uinuau nakatue-nitamuts uaatukuanits esk eka tshesenitamat tshashine tshi tutakanu nastesh Innu ama senitam enitinanits. Muk nisenitenan niuitamakuunan, uipits Utshimassits tshe pishashu tshetshi ushitakantshi mitshuapa pase inuuts atuseuts, tshe mikauats mistukua mishiue mitshuapa. Utenimanan tsheutshimau minuanueenu etutak natukuaat Innua uta ministukuts. Kie niui tamakuunan ekuta uta menuats. Minisenitenan tshetshi tukuats kamenupuunants eku tsheenitamats, amanukuetu tutenan. Mishiue nisishueuts mishiue tshekuan tshika titenan, tetipuakea kastapistes kapimpint kie nipin eku nastesh ama takun tshekuan." *Shimun kie Manin*

Nistim tsheutshimau ushitapan pushunanu, uta tshetshi akustakan tshi ntapitshitanan uta natamashi tshekuaia nete akuashuutish ekutanta muk ueueshinats pushunanits ekuashunantshi muats muk nekats. Pase ntutusenan tshemikaniseats ueshitakants pushuunan eku pushuunan eku ueshitakants ataueutshiuap kie pise mitshuapa napish tutakanu niuit shaaushinan ueshi takantshi mitshuapa amantapitshitan pepints tshekuan muk mikanipakan kie akitask. Meskeeu

mikanipakanu apitshitau utshimau ueshitat nete uitshuash nipini pempinits.

Nuuitamakuunau kauskatshi mitshuapa tshikatakuats nipin. Tsheutshimau uitamuepan Innua tshika pimpinipan nipin, muk nitshinats nastesh amatakun tshekuan. Muk tukuea kastapistesi mita kapunikantshi mitshuapa minuaua nte ueuetimits, Katshi piseats eku etapinan nispimits niuapaten ueuetimits. Uskats mitshuapa kaushitankatshi tshishue stimashinakuea. Kie niui tamakuunaapan tshika ushitakanua mitshuapa pepushe tante kaushitakantshi ne kutika mitshea. Nistim kaushitakantshi minuau asin tapue eskuake nte tshipatshimitepeni. Eku tapue tshimiskenau tsheuitshinek.

"Muke niseniten, niuitamakunaiapin tshinushinueputshe tshika tipenitenau. Nin maue nits mushinau mitshe tinanu eku minuats mashanikants ushitakanu nits mitshuapa kaushatantshi." *Nian*

Katshi Atutsheats

Katshi atutsheats ute, pase Innuts nitshipinuuts etintutets nutshimits. Pase inuts minuenitamuts uitshuaua eshinakutakanitshi. Tante ntenitenan menuats etutakuunau. Kie ama nisenitenan tshetshi mishats uestumpunikukunak uta stesinats. Katshi puash, pase Innuts kusepents. Pase Innuts atusepints Utshimassits, nimiste ushitanaapin shuneau etuseats neunueapits peik meastakea. Ntenitenan minuau mee en tsheska. Kie tshishue mitshetuuts aueshishits mitshima tshukuts, shishipits, kie nimeshits. Innuts ntuuiuts katits uipits eku eiapits pashueuts nimesha ueuetimits uitshuash.

"Ntatuseapin mushinau nete Utshimassits niuitshi tusemapin akeeshau Pupitents. Natenan ministukuts asninina tshetshi mamumpinitakants uapin eku tshenimista tusen muk ama-neaki tueniten."
Kaniuekutat

Pase Innuts kuspitshuuts nete nutshimits apitshepints atumua tshetshi tats net kie pase ntu uiuts eku nepatataui tshekuanu takushinits ute. Kie amatshi shuka ntu uiunan katinats uipits tshinanu Innuts stitanan ministukuts, tshiustum puninukunan kameskutishi miskumin eku tekuatshishi, nish mak nist pishumua mistishantish eku patush meskuutik-ni tshipatshi ntutenan ete nutshimits muk kustukun. Shakuatshi Innu kustam tshetshi itutet nete miskumits

out the site for Davis Inlet. Ramsey House was the manager of the store then. Also, Ross King was there. He was the head man in the government stores. There was no public meeting then. No Innu were notified. All we were told was there would be work to clear the site. We didn't know what was happening then. We were told we were going to live in houses, and weren't to go to the country again. Fifteen houses were built in 1967 and fifteen more were built in 1968. We were told that we would have everything in the house: running water and sewer. But when we moved in, there was nothing in the house, only a wood stove." *Sango Bay tent meeting with elders*

"Joe Rich was a lone leader. He gave all the advice to the Innu people. There was some discussion; some people didn't want to move up here, where Davis Inlet is now. Late Joe Rich was always alone as a leader; now there are too many leaders in Davis Inlet." *Shapatesh, elder*

Some people say we just said yes to the white people about the move because we saw the houses that were built in old Davis Inlet, and we liked the house that was built for Joe Rich. Some people thought the houses should be built at Sandy Brook where there was a river and fresh water, but others wouldn't listen. People were suffering. They didn't have enough food. Others didn't know what was happening.

"We were happy to hear that each family would get a new house, although we didn't know what the houses were going to be like until we moved. We found out the houses were not properly built." *Miste-Peashue, elder*

"Ross King and Chief Joe Rich were the ones who decided about relocation. As far as we know it just happened. No one really knew what was going on. All I know is we were told old Davis Inlet was too small a space for new houses. Most people were working, cutting the trees down for a new lot for each house. We thought the government was doing a good job moving the community here on this island. We were told this island was a good spot. We didn't know there were going to be all kinds of problems. When we knew this, it was already too late to do anything. Everyone thought we would get everything, like chairs, furnaces and water, but it was just empty houses we got." *Shimunish and Miste-Manian, elders*

First the government built a small wharf for motor boats. We used boats to unload the materials from the freight ships. It was easier to unload materials on the wharf than on the beach. Some of us worked cutting logs for the new wharf. After the wharf, the store was built, and a number of houses were built that first summer. We helped to build our homes and no machines were used, only shovel and axe. All the roads and the manager's well were built by hand and shovel. White people do things the easy way: using tractors, sawmills and so on. They don't use their hands for making things and moving things around.

So the promise of new houses was kept but we had no water. Government people told us we would have running water and sewers, but our homes were like empty boxes. All we had were stoves. The houses looked good from the outside, but when we got inside and looked up to the ceiling, we could see outside. The first houses were poorly built. We were told every year that there would be new housing for those that needed it. More houses were built years after but those houses were worse than the first ones. At least the first ones were built on good soil, because most of them are still there. Now you can't find a good place to build a house.

"The only thing I knew, we were told to take care of the house and in twenty years we would own it. My house is always overcrowded. There was also an extension put on it. My house was built when the houses were first built." *Nian, elder*

After the Move

After we moved here, some families stopped going to the country. Some people were happy with their houses and they thought things were okay. Maybe they thought this was the best thing that ever happened to them. They didn't know we would have all kinds of problems in this community. The first year, most people were fishing. Some of us were working in the community, although we weren't making much money—about $40 a week. We thought it was better than nothing. There were a lot of animals close by, like seals, ducks and fish. People hunted like they did in the past. They also dried fish outside their homes.

"I used to work most of the time here in Davis Inlet with a settler from Hopedale. We used to go away to the islands to pick the stones for mixing cement. It

Child's drawing at school workshop / Auashits kaunishi-natatshet, kaskutimatsheupits kaianumats, 1992

CAMILLE FOUILLARD PHOTO

Miste-Peashue, mukushan at Nutuashish Gathering / Miste-Peashue, mupimepan ete kanatshemaianits Nutuashish, 1992

amatshitutenan ministu kuts eshukum pishuma. Napes peik nipipan pinasitshet esk ama minipinua miskumina eku nastesh ama tshiuitsheanan.

Tapue nimiskenan ntiniun uta ntesinats tshetshi miskuats.

"Ntshisinapin nete nist 1970 pupun ekuninitshinukuts uiuitshiituts. Takun nitshinan muk ama takun katshi tempuntshi kie nipin. Nutaun tshimikaamupin mita nastesh amapitshitau kipimpinua tshekuanu. Muk atuutinam akitaskunu kie utishama. Kie nas pekutshi-shiua nukuteuni. Pase Innuts apitsheepints atumua tshetshi nikutets nete nanikutini ministukuts. Kie nikaun kuapitshepin napinitshi. Kie pepunitshi muk peik ushinu utitshin napitshi tat. Nikaun muk peik ushini utitshin. Kie mushinau akushipin etshi tshisinan, eku eiapits anuts kuetit. Euasiuan mushinau nitshisin, tshishue mitshetuuts mistukuts kie tshishue minuau nipin. Niuitamashun, tshekuanitshe uisheka pimpinits unipimau, kie katshi tempunitshi nete uitshuats, eku miskuts atutshi mistutusepints. Kaskutimatsheutshiuapits, eie mieu utshiuapits, kie ntukutshuapits, kipimpinua nipina. Eku tshekuan tshinan katukunua? Innuts uepinumuts kauepina-shunanitshi uitshuats ueuetimits anuts eia pits. Niskueuts uenape kamashutaui kie etuskataaui uitshuau uepinimuts kauinakamits unipimai mitshima uitshuats. Esk eiapits tutamuts anuts, nastesh mimiskutshipanu. Ama niunipiminan kie ama takun katshite puntshi tshitshinats. Tshekuan mane, tshekuan uishe katuka tshitshinats?" *Shustinis*

Eshipepushi uetishipintshi tshishue tshek tapitu ntitanan. Uta stisinan eiemiutshiuap, kaskutimatsheutshiuap, mitshimitshimaskueuts, ntu kutshiuapits, ataueutshiuapits, kie kamakunueshits. Mishiue misku tinamuts tshekuanu. Pepuashi kauapukuest niui tipenimukunan eniunats. Kiniuapamanapan tsheutshimau etshi mitshi pinitat. Mishiue tshekuanu uiutinum kie stesinanu.

Nimitshetinan etiskuutshits kakeeshauts, muk ama ni-kuetu tinan. Niminueni tenanapin kanishinakushihats uipits. Ama nista tshishika kuunan uipits etuseatshi. Ama nisenitenan eshinakuak atuseun. Amanisenitenan eshinakuatshi mishinanikea anuts tshishue miskuau Innuts apitshi tauts shuneanu tshetshi iniuts Innuts kakeeshau skutimashuun tshishue minuau kaskutimatshe utshiuapits.

Nipin mushinau animeenitakun 1969 nipin mitshipinu. Tsheutshimau, mistuutinumupin shuneanu tshetshi skutimashunanits. Pase mitshuapa takuea mishiunakea kie kauapekaushunants. Minuau kauapekaushunants muk amatakun nipin? Ntenimanan tsheutshimau tshiskueu pinetisha kauapekaushunanitshi. Senitam kaetikunits nipinu stisinash. Kie muk eshinakuats akushun takun mishiuente nispinu stisinats. Nipin muk amatakun. Niminan nipin pase kauinakimak eku pase akushuuts Innuts.

Innuts pase amashuka titamuts nutshimits mitshiminu. Pase mitshuuts ataueutshiuapits mitshiminu. Ntaku-shiskakunan. T.B. akushuun mishiue nispinu stesinats kie tshishue tshinipinu. Inuuts kie auasits akushuuts nimitshetinan pushinukuunats ntukutshiuapits nete Shinantinits.

was hard work but we didn't care." *Kaniuekutat, elder*

Some people continued to go into the country with their dogs to the barrens to make a living. Some would just go hunting and bring their traditional food back to the community. But we couldn't always go to the country to hunt like we used to. We, now people of the island, have a very difficult time during break-up and freeze-up. In the fall, it takes two to three months for the rattle to freeze up. We can't go to the mainland because it is too dangerous. In the spring, people are afraid they will go through the ice. We are stuck on this island for months. A few accidents have happened during the break-up. One boy died from a shooting accident because we couldn't get help for him.

We found out life in the community was very hard.

"I remember way back in the seventies how my parents struggled. We had a house with no heaters or running water. My father used to go out chopping wood on his own without using anything mechanical. He used to take only his axe and snowshoes with him. Sometimes it took him almost a whole day to chop wood. Some people used to go on dog sleds to get wood on or sometimes off this island. My mom used to go out hauling water in winter and in the summer. She would get water by hand. My mom has only one hand. She's been sick on and off since I remember, and today she is still like that. There used to be a lot of trees around this village, and clean water. But I always remember this when I was just a child. I asked myself, why can't we have running water and heaters in the house, so people won't have to work so hard? The school, church and the clinic have running water, but what about us? People began to throw garbage outside their homes like today. Women who did laundry and housework used to throw their dirty water outside their homes. Today, people are still doing that. Nothing changed. We never got water and sewer and heaters in our homes. Why don't we have those kinds of things in our home?" *Shustinis*

As the years went by, more and more people began to spend the whole year in the community. The church, school, Social Services, clinic, store and R.C.M.P. began to really change our lives. We had depended for years on the priests who had taken control of our lives, and then they stopped taking responsibility. But we no longer had the control. We began to depend instead on the government agencies. Our troubles got worse when we saw that the government wanted to rule everything. He wanted to take away our rights and our land.

Many of us got jobs working for white people, but we didn't know what to do. We were better off living our own way. We never got paid for our work in the past. We don't understand the pressures of this kind of work. We don't understand budgets. This is very hard for us because these days people need money to live. White education is very important, and we weren't getting a good education in our school.

Water was always a problem. As early as 1969 the water problems started; the water was contaminated. The government has spent thousands of dollars on studies. Some of the houses even have toilets and bathtubs. What good is a bathtub when there is no water? We thought the government must be crazy to send those bathtubs. They knew there is no water in this community. All different kinds of diseases began to spread in the community. It was the water that was to blame. We were drinking contaminated water and many people were getting sick.

People also didn't have much wild food. Most of them ate store food. We started getting sick. T.B. hit the community and quickly spread. Adults and children were sick. Many of us were sent to the hospital in St. Anthony.

Years ago, when we saw that we would not find water, some of us began to discuss relocation. When the government heard that, they started building the airstrip, a new wharf and a new store. Even after the school burned, they brought in trailers, and built a new school the next summer. After that, people were quiet and we didn't talk about moving. We knew the government wouldn't listen because of all the money they spent on these things.

"Some of the elders say we were always free. We didn't have to worry about anything if a person felt like going out to the country with his family. All he had to do is take a little bit of food and leave. People used to respect the animals in the proper ways. Caribou meat was never wasted. When one person had meat, he used to share with other people. Now when one person kills a caribou and brings it home, the meat is kept in the freezer for a long time. But it doesn't taste very good when it has been in the freezer a long time. In the past,

Pepuashi, tshekuatshe uishekamiskimats nipin pase ninan ntanumuekatenan isheatutsheats eku tshe utshimau petamushipin, eku ueshitakants kapiminashits katueuts, kie pushuunam kie ataueutshiuapits. Katshi niskuatets kashkutimatsheutshiuap eku peta utakanipani kitshinaskunuani mitshuapa, kie ushitakanu katshi nipitsh. Eku Innuuts tshimueuts kie ama nisishueuts tshetshi atutshets. Tante eku tshe utshimau minitutum kie mishiue utinam shuneanu.

"Pase katsheniuts nisishueuts mushinau nikaniun ama nakituenitenan tshekuan Innu tante uintuteu nutshimits. Muk apisis tshipa takunim mitshiminu tshipa atistuteu. Innuts ishpitenimeuts aueshisha tshesthi nipaats. Atikuunash amanista uepinean. Inutipenitam unashinu, eku eshamati ni Innua. Innu tshiuestau unashinu, eku meskuutitati ni neush. Meskuutitakantshi unash neush ama shuka minupukun-ni. Uipits Innu uitshiitupints. Eku tshash ama takun.

"Tshekuan etinak? Utapanisa miskutiskueuts atumua kie katak ushistesi miskutiskamuts inuuta. Tshe utshimau miskum miskutiskatsheu eshiniuau muk tshinan tshiskutimakuunan eshinakuash. Kie pase mitakun tshekuan, kie aueshishits amatauts pise. Mitshen tshekuan ueuskats stesinats. Kipim-pinua tshekuan tshishue tshishimiskakunan. Eku niui itute nan nutshimits kapiminashits kie utapanisa mishiue ushipinu kakeeshau eku amaminu-pinu. Mitshinakutau eshinakushuak. Pase niunitanan tshekuan etshi atutsheats ministukuts. Nimi tshetina-nuatshaattshish kakeeshau. Peikushu muk tshekuan etinats anuts kiminanua. Akaskutimutshits ntuasiminaets tshekuanu Innu kaenitintshi uipits, atutshi papi-nipin." *Innu Tsheutshimau*

Ntisinats nistimaunan amaniutshinukuunan nitshinaia ama ntepishinan tshepiats tshishiue mishau kauepinashunantshi kie mitshimakun mitshuapa uta stesinan. Pase mitshi ushuneaminan tshetshi ui tshinau. Pase ama takun atuseun kie nastesh ama takun tshekuan. Tshenimiste unitanan tshekuan. Eku pepuash, eku utishipinu menash mushinau kie mushinau. Mishiue minuuts. Pase inuts nipanukuts shitaunapunu. Inuts nipuuts nepanushuts, pekistue shinits, kie nte kutakuts tshekuanu etu takuts.

Auasits stimauts eku unitshinikuaua minut inuts pase eshikumutshishi kaua-minuuts kie akushi skakuuts. Amantenitamuts tshetshi iniuts. Mishiue minuuts. Muui-uitshintut kie metshi tapamituts, katshi pupunits eku uetamaututs nutshikatunan etshishipinits utamautuuts eku netshipiniats kanakituenimitshis ntuasiminaets, nitshipinan kashatshatshis Innuts kie nikanishinaents unitshinukuaua nistim uakieuts utu asimuaua kie utuasimuaua metshipinushuntshi. Ninante tapue nashinean eshamiats mistitakun kamenupunts.

"Tshekuan amamunipanipan nete uipits Utshimassits inutshuapish ntitanan, mukuanuts ama nishinakunipan etutamat anuts; kaminatiskuants, niskuteuapun, mitshimitshimaskueuts, utinepints auasa nete uuinitshinukunu katsheniuts nenekatenitamuts. Uiuapameuts auasha tsheshi kau tantshi nushimits. Ama minuau nipin uta utenats. Mushinau tshika ushikanu nipin eshi iniunaku?" *Mani Katini*

"Tshinan Innuts tshipa tshita patenan etaspishunais, eshi stimaunak tshinan muku tshistimaunan uta utenats. Kutukuts utenats Nent (Nain) kie Innu utenats takunu nipinu." *Kaniuekutat*

Pishe stenitenan etaiau uta ministukuts nau kauepinashunants. Inuts muku pipamuteuts, ntuapatamuts tshetits eku metshinits enitits. Tshekuanu tsheutshimau uishi eka uapimitak eshinakushuak tshekuanu tsheutshimau uishi eka tutak tshekuanu? Muku apitshitauts stishinanu eka nastesh tepenitats. Tshishue tsheutshimau tshimiste mishinamakunu.

Mishiue tshisheitenan mishiue eshinakuts Innuts nete uaieu. Mishiue anuts tshiuapatenan. Uatinaui tshekuan uinitam pita tsheutshimau tshiuitamuanan. Pishe tenitenan tshipa skutimakunu tsheutshimau tshetinak kamenupinak. Muku metinu tshipa nutshikenas tshetshi eka ueshimitak tsheutshiman.

Ntuasiminants enkunin uishiniunats nisenitenan niuiaiashinan nitshinats enkun nistim ntanumue-atenanapin tshetshi atukuants nimishetinan mamu tshetshi atuseuts uaatutsheats. Kie niuishapinan niui tamuanan tsheutshimau kie tshetshi minu ininiutshish tshetshi minu punash, nipin kie tshekuan tshetshittimats eku upauitshianants ntuasiminants kie tshenuuts tshetshi minupits mitshuapits. Atutsheatshe minuats tshekuan tshikaishinakun Innuts isishueuts tshetshi tats ministukuts tsheutshimau ushitak kamenupunits.

people used to help each other. Now it is all gone.

"What happened? Skidoos replaced the dogs and outboard motors replaced the canoes. Politics and government funding replaced the traditional way of life. We only follow Canadian law. Part of our culture is missing and the animals are gone too. Those kind of machines can make anyone lazy. Now we want to go to the country in the easy way, by planes and skidoos. This has spoiled our culture. Most of our culture is lost since moving on this island. If we don't keep up with teaching our children our traditional culture, it will never come back in years to come." *Innu Nation*

The promises that were made to us were not kept. In this community we live in very poor conditions. Our houses are not fit for families to live in. There is a lot of garbage and bad smells around each and every house in this community. Most of us do not have enough money to live on. For many, there is no work, nothing to do. We lost so much of our culture. Many of us became helpless and we depend on white people. Too many things were new for us in the community. Over the years, we began drinking more and more.

Many of our people have died because of alcohol, from suicides, drownings and other accidents that have happened. Children suffer when parents are drinking. People drink every day and get addicted. They don't feel like working. All they do is drink. Instead of helping and looking after each other, over the years we began fighting each other. We started blaming and hurting each other. We stopped looking after our children, and they stopped caring for other people and their parents. Parents started blaming their children and our children began getting into trouble. We pushed each other away. Things are declining. We have serious problems.

"Things got worse here than in old Davis Inlet. We lived in tents, but we didn't have the kind of problems we have now: gas sniffing, alcoholism, social services taking the children away from their parents.

The elders are suffering now. They want to see the young people go back to the country. Living conditions are poor. The water is contaminated in the whole community. Do we have to boil the water for the rest of our lives?" *Mani Katinin, elder*

"We Innu can always be recognized because of how we dress, how poor we are. We are the only community on the coast who suffers this much. Other communities like Nain and Schefferville all have running water." *Kaniuekutat, elder*

Some of us feel that living on the island is like living in a dump. People wander around, looking for something to do, and end up doing dirty work. Why can't the government look at us and see what happened? Why can't the government do something? They're just using our land, which doesn't belong to them. The government owes us a lot of things.

Many of us know now that these things have happened to Native peoples across the country. We are realizing more each day. Everything we do now, we have to ask permission of the government. Some of us think the government should teach us and show us what we need to learn so that we can work with the government to solve our problems. But we should be very careful in what we learn from the government.

Our children have no future here. We know we must move our community. We have already started talking about relocation. Many of us know we must work together to make this community better before we move to another location. We must be strong. We must never give up. We must let the government know we want to move for better health, better living conditions, for water and sewage systems, so we can solve our community problems, so we can help our children and our elders live more comfortably, and for better housing. This time when we move again, we will not make the same mistakes. The people who made the decisions to move us onto this island didn't look into the future. We hope the government won't make the same mistakes either.

NIST ETSHITAPATEKEN

TSHEUTSHIMAU

Innuts ama nita uapameuts tsheutshimaua. Ntuuiuts, ntumaniuts kie nakituenimushuts. Eku anush tepenimitak tsheutshimau. Tshishue stipenumukunu tsheutshimau, kaskutimasheutshiuapits, mitshimitshimau, ntukutshiuap, kamakunuest kie ataueutshiuap. Nastesh ama tshiuitamakunan sheshe tshiminikunan. Tsheutshimau tshuuetishumukunu. Tshishue tshiui tutakanu tshetshi mintak kanuna etuuiuak. Nastesh ama shenitamuts eshi iniutshi inua muku tshishue tshuui tipenimukunuts mak stishinanu.

Mitshen tshekuan kakeshau kamenupinitak. Shitaku-napunu kenastinimak. Nishenitenan espinat kie etutatak tsheutshimau. Tshiunitanan eshi niunau ekun eshi eka minupinak, eshinakuats mitshiuapa, shitakunapun, auashits uetatatshet kie kamenupinak. Tshishue tsheutshimau tshimitshipininikunu mishiue asits. Enishits tsheutshimau tshipa atamenimakanuts eshi eka minupinuak.

Tshishue titakish stinitutakunu tsheutshimau. Nastesh ama tshinakutu enimukunu. Nastesh ama tshinitutakunu. Kakeshau muku uatit uitu. Tshishue tshinakitukunu, nau Innuts ama stenimukunu. Aueshish stenimukunu kie nastesh ama tshinakinuenumukunu. Tshishue uuetishimukunu. Tshishue tshitamuts stenimukunu. Tshishue tshimitshenimukunuts.

"Katshi atutshet inuts ekun nastesh ama minupunu, katuuiunats, kantumaniunats, shitakunapun, auashits kamenupinits, ntuun enitinats, nepanushunats kie inuts menakunakanits. Punuts inuts etutets nushimits ekun mitshen tshishue etakushinants. Minuau tapue Innu eutututs kie euka ta kushisteshimit muku tshishue miste atshipinu. Minuenitamuts inuts uskats uenapatats. Eku pakuntak tsheutshimau." *Shuash*

"Tsheutshimau eshipimpit, eku eshi eka minupinuak. Ama tshiminu-pinai. Kakeshau eshinuiut ekun uanishinakushinak. Ekunu Innu eshi eka shakutatkie uestupen. Tshinan tshipa uueshitanan tsheish iniuiak." *Kamamuinats*

Aka nitustuauts kakeshauts etaaui. Eku anush tshinan tshipa aiasti-nushunan. Tsheutshimau kitshiui uuitshinukunaiauau stenimaieu. Tshiminukunu shuneanu. Ekunu enu uatutatak kakeshau eshi iniut. Katshi minukunau mitshiuapa ekun nastesh ama tshitanan nika tapitu stanan. Ekunu tsheutshimau uatutatak. Nau tshimakunikunu stutakunu. Tshiunitanan eshi iniunak. Tshimishetinan etenitamak tshuieshimukunu tsheutshimau. Ekun anush ama tshinitutakunu, nastesh ama tshipetakunu.

"Ama tshikishi etamenimushinai kanispint. Tsheutshimau put tshuui uitshinukunaetshe muku ama minupunu. Tshuui tutakunu tshetshi unitauak eshi niuak." *Etuetish*

Tsheutshimau kuspaeshima mishikanua netutamitshi inua kamenupinitshi. Muku mishinamuts enishiuanits eku tshauepini. Ama uitamueuts utshimamaua etakanits. Muku ushitauts uinuau etenitats eku uenapatinats utshimamaua etenitats.

"Nastesh ama apitenimeu tsheutshimau Innu tshetshi nipintshi. Kustumuts tshetshi mitshetintshi." *Shuash*

"Tshinakituapimukunu tsheutshimau tshetshi iniuakue. Stiniunan kie tshimishimenitenan. Tshuunikuatikunan uta miinistikut." *Kaniuekutat*

"Katshipinishit, tshitshue mitshetuts, nastesh mitshituiunai, mushinau nte tautsh etautshish. Peikuau nuapamauts katshipinishit metshima tipataushu nte atikua etantshi, eku mentshinipanimana, nas nispinu esimitshenimikuau." *Miste-Etuet, (Kanitmuashishet) tshenu*

CHAPTER THREE

THE GOVERNMENT: TSHEUTSHIMAU—THE BIG BOSS

In the past, the Innu never met with the government. We hunted and trapped and looked after our own affairs. Now the government controls our lives. We have become very dependent on governments and their agencies like the school, social services, the clinic, the police and the store. We were given these agencies without consultation with us first. The government makes too many laws. They have implemented a lot of hunting regulations, like permits and licences. They don't know anything about our culture but they want to rule everything, our lives and our land.

Many things that came from the white man have not done us any good. The only thing we gained was alcohol. We know what is happening and what the government is doing to us. We have lost control of our lives and this has created a lot of social problems in our community, for example, family violence, poor housing, alcoholism and solvent abuse. The government has treated Native peoples badly all over the country. Both the provincial and federal governments are to be blamed for the problems we have in this community.

We have been discriminated against by the government. They don't care about us. Our voices are not heard. White people always have their way. We are far behind other communities. Some of us think the government doesn't see us as human beings. They think we are animals and we don't know how to run our lives. They want to control everything in our community. They think we are too lazy. They are racist.

"Since people were moved to the new Davis Inlet, everything seems to be falling apart: hunting, fishing, trapping, alcohol, kids have a lot of problems, sexual assaults, suicides, people going to jail. People have stopped going to the country and there are all different kinds of diseases. It might look good, people using outboard motors on their boats and using ski-doos, but it has been a big change. People were very happy at first to get these things. Now, we begin to see the government is breaking the Innu people." *Shuash*

"The problem with the government agencies are their policies. They are not working for us. We have to follow white man's rules and laws. This is how the Innu have become helpless and why we suffer. It is time we made our own laws. It is the only way we can solve our problems." *Discussion at workshop, Nutuashish Gathering*

As the years went by, we realized that we should never have listened to our white advisors. Now, many of us think we should govern ourselves. The governments try to make us believe that they are helping us in any way they can. They give us funding. But it is because they want us to live like white people do. After we got houses, we felt like we were stuck in this community with nowhere to go. That is where the government wants us, with nowhere to go. It is like the government put us behind bars in putting us here to live. We have lost a lot of our culture. Many feel like we were tricked by government. Now, the government doesn't want to hear about our problems, or hear our voices.

"We cannot blame ourselves for what has happened. It is the government that is to blame. Maybe the government is trying to help but it is not working as planned. He is trying to make us forget our culture." *Etuetish*

Government agents come here and we talk about the problems in our community. These people take all kinds of notes about what we say. Some of us think these people listen to our concerns, take notes, and when they get back to the city, they don't tell their own government

Epa and Manteskueu, People's Inquiry commissioners /
Epa mak Manteskueu, Katepeshenatshets, 1992

Mishetuts Innuts, eshishuetsh etshitatsh mitshimentun katshipinis, tshitshue memishetu aueshish. Enu pitshe atupunitamuts. Kapitshitepitumutshi katshipinist, nta patshitenu umitshimish ueshish. Passe Innuts uapimeuts nipinua ueshisha, auen nepat enua? Minetshimauia, mishetuets Innuts essishuetsh, katshipinitshi enua tutakuts aueshish.

Tshishue piseueshu aueshish eku aiask nastesh muinu. Eiash nespukushu eiapit shishipits mak anesk mushukua tautsh eku. Eiapit Innu peik itatshimu, "nastesh menita uapimauts nissukutshash, etshitaian nte nutshimit niu."

Etuish put ketutakunaiets katshishipinishit esk nte-etu. Kusteuts tshitshue auassit katshipinishinitshi maiash tshitshue kuestimukuau ents Innuts kepapameskautshi Innu uta.

"Nastesh menuenimauts katshipinits, kustikushiuts, tsheuetakushuts kustatshimeuts netuassima. Peikuau nipaiapan, peminatsh ntanish tshitshue aiashikuepan. Nish tatipuneshu. Niui tshipunamuan uitukeia ama nitshisseniten nin nitshipunenashipen nitukia. Enku enu nistam niuapamapatsh katshipinishits. Niuapamau kapepinistashist pemitepitsh nte kapiminashimuash. Tshishikaiu enu, enkun muk kamenuatsh nte nutshimitsh tshekuan." *Kistinis*

Nemishetinan, eshiuiatsh enuia tepenimatsh kashipinitshi, nastesh meneshenakunu tshetshi tshiskuenish. Mushinau tesishueai tshekapiminatsh nte etauitshish. Esk eiapit peminauts.

Tsheutshimau Nenu Manimit Shunianu Nte Utshipanu Ninan Nitassinat!

Tshishue mushinau tsheutshimau eshishueu mushinau niminauts Innuts shuneanu. Shuneau kamitak ekuta ueshipant stishinat kipikunamua kie kitauanu ashini. Ashinin kanutshiakant nete Schefferville ekunu enu Innu utasin. Mushinau shitshikashunai takesses [taxes].

"Meunu tsheutshimau ushuneam. Asits nte utinakanu. Pikunamuts stishinanu. Tshishue inua piuenimeuts mitshiuapa ama nastesh minuaua. Tsheutshimau stutakunu tshetshi petastimipistuak. Stiniminuts stimauts. Tsheutshiman ama apitenimeu. Tshipiuenimukunu." *Innut Utshimauts*

Tsheutshimau Tshimitshipinukunu

Tsheutshimau stipenimukunu muku nastesh ama tshimi-nupininukunu. Tshiminukunu mitshiuapa, mitshiminu stashimukunu mitshiuapa, mitshiminu stashimukunu eku pishe niskumuts. Pishe ntenimeuts sheshe tshiminukunu tshekuanu tshetshi eka stuak. Uskats manikunak mitshiuapa tshika takun nipin stukunai. Muku kakeshau takunu unipim. Innuts enuaa nutshiamupants uishi takunits unipimuau. Mikanipakea ntapitshitaiapin emunatsheash.

Tshishue miskuau tshetshi taiats eka takuats nipin. Niskueuts tshetshi takuats nipin. Niskueuts tshetshi uapikatshet. Ama takun nipin uta. Niskueu uauapikatshetshi tshishue neush ntuapatum nipinu. Emitshetit euen tshishue neush. Nutshikum apitshitauna tshetshi mainaspitat utuasima. Eieskushiu niskueu ekuapitshet. Nipinu uetanipet ama minuanu, aushiskaku mentshi. Mishetuts inuts kie auashits pushakanits ntukutshiuapits nakushitaui. Ntukuastikushu iteu inua ekun uishakushin tante ama minuau nipin. Nipin ekun tshishe Manitu. Nuui atutshenan tshetshi miskimats menuats nipi eminash.

"Nastesh ama takun uskats manikunash mitshiuap, muku katshapistesh, ekun muku. Ama tukuea nipeuna, tetupuakan put kie aspimitshuakeastuka. Innuts kaatuset enuet tshiashuuts ni katshi tshishikuakataui. Nanikutini ama eauts mitshiminu tante uieauts tetipuakea. Auashits ama mitshuuts ni. Tsheutshimau petishaam mitshiminu ama nastesh minuanu. Tshishue uinakun mitshim etauatshi ataueutshiuapits. Tsheutshimau uinipaniskuneu innua. Ama nastesh minushiuts tshitshinapunits

what we are saying. Maybe they just make up their own stories and show these to the government.

"The government doesn't care if we die or not; they're scared of our population growth." *Shuash*

"It's like the government was testing us to see if we could survive. We have survived but we are suffering. We are a forgotten people on this island." *Kaniuekutat, elder*

Low-Level Flying Is Scary

"Low-level flying is a big problem. We just can't live or hunt; they are always in our way. One time, I saw the jets flying over where the caribou were and we couldn't get any caribou. I really hate them." *Miste-Tuet, elder*

Many of us say that today there are fewer animals in nutshimit because they are feeling the effects of low-level flying. The fumes that come out of the military jets stretch for miles and miles and fall into the water and on the land that feeds the animals. Then the animals eat the plants, and of course we eat the animals. We believe the fumes from the planes are ruining the soil and plants which feed the animals. We have even seen a difference in the colour of some trees. A number of us have seen dead animals. Who killed them? We don't know. Many of us believe the jets kill animals. The jets are scaring the animals.

Animals act different and taste different since low-level jets fly over our land. Some say the animals are skinny and don't have a strong taste. Sometimes they are even too skinny for us to eat. Young partridge are getting smaller. There is a different colour and taste in fish and caribou. They are too thin, and they were always fat and healthy before. Ducks and geese are also affected by the low-level flying. One person said that she noticed that there were no squirrels in the country where her camp was this last year.

In the long run, we will start to feel the effects of the low-level jets as well. How? We don't know. It will affect our food supply and our biological system. We will be physically affected, maybe with deformed children or in other ways. The other major problem with the low-level jets is that they frighten our children and disrupt our peace of mind and the peacefulness of the land. We always have to worry about being frightened and harassed by the jets. They are especially dangerous

for people who spend a lot of time on the water in canoes.

"I don't like the low-level flying. It's really scary. It's noisy and they scared my kids. I was asleep one time when I heard the jets flying above us. My daughter was screaming. She is two years old. I tried to cover her ears. I didn't realize that I was covering my ears instead of hers. The children are too afraid. It was the first time I saw the jets so close. I could see the pilots sitting there. This was in the daytime. There are no bad things about the country except the jets." *Kistinis*

Many of us believe that foreign countries should not have the right to destroy our peace. For a long time, we have complained about how the jets fly without warning. The military planes promised us they would avoid our camps, but they always fly over them anyway.

The Funding Is from Our Resources!

We always hear the governments saying they give a lot of things to the Innu. But we know the funding from government comes from the developments of our land and resources. For example, some of us have been to Schefferville and seen the iron ore mine. We ask ourselves, who owns that mine and who has benefited? We know the iron ore belongs to the Innu people. We also pay taxes.

"The money we have is not from government. It is from our own resources. They destroy the land. They treat Natives like dirt. The houses we have are no good. The government is forcing us into land claims. Our people are poor. The government doesn't care. The government is playing with our lives." *Mushuau Innu Band Council*

The Governments Treat Us Bad

We are governed by the government, but many of us believe it is not doing much for us. We get houses and money for food, and some of us are thankful for this. But many of us believe the government gives us money for housing and a few other things to keep us quiet. When we were first given houses, we were promised running water. Only the white people now have running water. We worked for the white people, digging for their water wells and their septic tanks. We dug with shovels by hand.

It is very hard for us to live here with no water,

auashits meuataui. Shitakunapun eapits nepanikuts Innuts. Stemau kie shikeetshits naushiaskakuts Innuts kie ntukuna." *Manteskueu*

Pishe Innuts tapints kutukuts utenats. Niuapatenan eshinakuatshi mitshiuapa. Mishiue tshekuanu takunu, nipinu kie kauapekaushunants, tetipakea, katshepisteshitshi, kauapekatshipitshi. Nanikutini at kake shenitam tsheutshimau eshi stimauautshit. Mishetuts etats eka uitshit. Tshitshinua ama minuaua. Nastesh ama minuau napitshitakatshi eushitakantshi. Kakeshauts ushitauts mitshuapa kie animea. Ama nastesh apitea. Nau kauepinashunatshi, kueshinakuashi.

At Etakuatshi atuseun ekun maiakant ni uaieu kaushipant. Nistimaunan. Tsheutshimau tutam eshinakushuak. Nastesh ama shenitamutshetshi tshimaketeunu. Ninan nishenitenan. Tshiuapamauts inuts etshimakatet. Tsheutshimau tshishue minuanu etat eku tshinan tshetimunak.

"Uskats etaiats ama tshistisheapin shuneau tshashika-shunashi uastepimakeets nete St. John's. Atauetshiuapits $5.00 tshishikashunaiapin, peik pishuma eku anush $300.00 tshishikashunan. Nishenitenan shuneau nte Innuts ushipanu kie usham animin eshi miste tshishikashunats. Nuui apitshitanan mitshim, apitshitauna, utapanisha, pimin kie kamituestish. Ekunu muku tsheutsshimau menuats kakuspinanits etakunits. Uitshinukuts Innuts. Muku tshishue apishashu shuneau kie tshishue animishiu eutinakant kapiminast nete kuspe." *Kaniuekutat*

"Apishashu auash shuneau. Etukuatshi nishuneam $200.00 muku takun. Etaueani ama nitispinni tshetshi tshishikashunan uastepimakeets kie akupa tshetshi eauts ntuashimits. Tshima tshiuapamik kie eiemak tsheutshi-mau. Tshishue pamiste amau." *Utshimassiu Iskueuts*

"Tsheutshimau stukunu tshishue tshimiste mitinau shuneau. Muku shuneau manikunau mishiue stapitshi-tanan nete mistukuts, uastepimakeets kie mitshim nete ataueutshiuapits. Mishiue kau tshiminaieu shuneanu kamitak. Kau tshiminaieu ntenitakun. Kie mitshiminu penetishak ama minuanu, kie shitshikashuna takeses etusheaui." *Kaatushetshit Niskueuts*

Pikunumuts Stishinanu

Katshi mishikat kakeshau utinam asinu kie pikunamueu Innua kanish ntuuiutshi kie utisinu. Tshishue tsheutshimau miste pikunum asinu, nipinu kie uinakutau asinu. Tsheutshimau tshipam shipua kie nishipitau inua utasinu. Tshiuapatenan asin nete Uapush kie Shepepui. Uauitamuts asinu tshetshi paik etitats. Nushimits etaiak tshiuapatenan asin kie nipin uanakutakants, ntate katshipinishits pepaminats nete stishinats. Apitshitauts stisinanu tshetshi metuatshet.

Muku uatshishipants atuseun tshishipanu. Nastesh ama tshhuuitamakunai. Muku ai tshishipinuts. Tsheutshimau ama nistutum. Innuts eshishueuts amau tsheutshimau ueshitat asinu, Tshishe Manitu usitau. Ama minuku Tshishe Manitua tshetshi utinak asinu.

"Tsheutshimau pikunum asinu epipaminat katshipini-shits kie neshipitat asinu. Uiutinumuts Innua kantuuiutshi. Kakeshau tshipaum shipua kie nishipitau asinu. Aka uapimaueu eshi utinak asinu tshika mishiue mestinum eku tsheka nikuatu ntuuiunak. Ekun tshipa kustinanu. Ama tshika muk apinan eku tshitapimanan tsheutshimau enitutatak. Ama tshikatshi uuetishimanu enitutatak. Ama tshikishi uuetishumukunu tsheutshimau. Tshinan tshipa uuetishumushunan." *Auash Kaskutimashut*

"Ama nishenimauts nipa itauts. Tshemitunits ntenimu-shuts. Mushiueu tshekuanu uitipenitamuts asinu, nipinu, utshekitaua, pishuma kie nimenu." *Kamamuinats*

Ama niminuenimau tsheutshimau eshipipinitat asinu. Uipats Utshimassits nimeshits muku nutshiuuaiaets. Eku nastesh ama tau namesh. Tshishue mishetipan aueshish uta mitshima asuk kie shishipits. Meshukua mitshetupuna nte utat nte Kanipiskau-Shipu atik, 10,000, nepaniku nipinu. Kakeshau enu tutam uishinipits atik. Tshishue miste nipu Mushuau-Shipu atik, 20,000, ntakanu ama nishenitamanan uish nipits. Eeshimeuts atauatsheut atikua uta Kanata kie uaieu. Mushinau atik pipapatau itakanu. Ama nastesh tshiminumitshu. Muku pipamuteu. Kutukuts katiuiuts kie kakeshauts nepatau atikua, uepinamuts unashinu eku muk atikua uteskinua meapitsheuts. Kastitikuet shenitam atikua eshi eka punitshi epipamutetshi. Tshipa kutshitanan tshetshi tshipaamau katshipinishits epipaminats nete atikua etatshi.

Uesham Tshiaspitenimunan Nte Tsheuitshimau

Mushinau tshuuitshinushunan eskua tsheutshimau kamantak shuneanu. Etushetshi auen, tshishikuakanu,

especially for the women who do the washing. Water is very hard to find here. A woman has to look for water all over the place in the community. A woman with many children has so many clothes to wash to keep her children dressed clean. A woman can't even clean her house or wash the dishes. Women get very tired hauling water to their homes. Also the water we have here makes people sick. Many adults and babies are sent to hospital because the water we drink is contaminated. When a baby is sick and we take him to the doctor, the doctor always tells us the baby is sick because of the water. Water is God. We have decided to move to another place to find good drinking water.

"There is nothing in the houses the government built for us, only stoves and a range, nothing else. There are no beds, no table and chairs. People who work manage to get those things when they get paid. But their income is low. They sometimes have to go without food in order to get furniture. The kids have to go without food. Food sent in by the government is not fit to eat. The government should eat the garbage they send us to eat. It is like the government is poisoning our people. The milk for babies is often not fit to drink. Alcohol is responsible for a lot of deaths. Tobacco and cigarettes cause cancer to the people, and drugs." *Manteskueu, Innu woman*

Many of us have been to other Innu communities. We have seen the kind of houses they have. They have everything—water and sewers, the kind of chairs they have, stoves, washers. Our houses are no good. They are made out of materials that are no good. White people build these houses and they are very expensive. But they are not worth it.

Sometimes we wonder if the government knows how poor we are in this community. Many people here have no homes for their families. When there is a job in Davis Inlet, it is almost always outsiders who get all the jobs. We are very poor. The government is responsible for the conditions we live in. They will never know anything about starvation. But we know. We have seen it happen before. They don't live in houses without water. They have everything they need, so they don't care about the Innu. We are human beings, not animals. The government lives in luxury while we live in poverty.

"When we first moved here, we didn't have to send money to St. John's for light bills. We used to pay the store about $5 a month. In 1991, one month's hydro bill went up to almost $300. We know the funding comes from the Native Funding Agreement for the hydro generators and building, and it is too much for one family to pay $300. We need other things, like food, clothing, snow machines, gas and telephone. The one good thing the government has funded is the outpost program. It really helps our people. But there is little funding and it is very expensive to charter a plane from Goose Bay." *Kaniuekutat, Innu elder*

"The family allowance is not very much. When I get my U.I.C., I only receive $200. When I buy food with this, I can't even pay my bills or buy clothing for my children. I wish I could talk to government people in person. I have so many things to say to them." *Family Violence Project*

"The government says he gives us a lot of money. But the money we receive, we spend on building material, light bills, for food in the store. We give all the money back when he gives it to us. It is like recycling. And the food he sends us is all bad. Also, we pay back taxes when we work for government." *Women construction worker trainees*

They Destroy Our Land

Once the white man came, he took from the Innu and destroyed a lot of hunting and trapping territory. Governments have destroyed the land and water, polluting the environment. The government has built dams and flooded land that belongs to aboriginal people. We have seen the land destroyed in Wabush and Schefferville. They are talking about building national parks on our land. When we are in the country we are noticing that the land and the water is polluted as well, because of so many low-level jets training over our land. They are using our land as a playground.

Any developments can go ahead without our approval. They don't even bother to discuss them with Innu people. They just go ahead like they own the land. The government is out of control. Some people say the government did not make the land. God did. It does not have permission from God to take over the land.

"The government is destroying our land, like with low-level flying and flooding our land. They are trying to take the land we hunt on away. The white

eku pishish tshashikuakantshi kuet put ni tshimi-
tshipininukunu tsheutshimau emitak shuneanu.
Minakanuts inuts mitshiuapa eka nastesh tshishikats.
Itenitamuts nastesh tshekuan ama tshishikanitshe,
nastesh tshekuan ama tshishikanitshe, nastesh ama
peik shumitshish tshishikamauts nete uitshuash. Eku
anush mishiue tshekuanu uaiats. Usham Innu apit-
sheeu mitshimitshimauau, Innu Utshimaua, emeutshiuapinu kie ntukutshiuapinu. Tsheutshimau ushuneam
kie eshipipit ekun anuts maskutiskak stiniunanu.

Tshimishetinan katsheshenimak eshi pinpant tsheutshimau. Usham tshuui ntishimunan muku enitit ama
minuanu. Eshukum nipin mushinau ntushenitakanu
nipi. Tshekuan uishi ntushenitakau eka takuats nipi.
Pishe mitshuapa takua mishiunakea kie kauapakau-
shunatshi. Tshekua uits takuatshi eka tukuats nipi.
Tsheutshimau amatshi nipuakatshe etitak mishiunakea. Shenitamuts eka takunits nipinu. Ama tshikishi
minuats ushitanan mitshiuapa uta tante tsheska tshika
tshimitanan. Nete tshipa tshimitanan kauiatutsheak.

Tshinan tshipa utshimamitatunan. Innu Utshimauts
tshipa Utshimamituanuts. Eskua ekatat Innu Utshimauts mushinau uitshitunanipan. Eku anush pistuut-
shimauts uuetishueuts. Innuts tshipa uuetishueuts.
Tapin uipats uetshimaut nushimits etaiatshi. Tshipa
kutshitanan tshetshi Innu Utshimauts minupinits.

Tshinan Stipentemunu

"Tsheutshimau meeute nte uish iniut nete nutshimits uta stasinats. Nastesh amasinitam eshinakunits
nutshimits. Tshisenimanu eshinakust. Tshisenitenan
tshinan eshinakuats nutshimits. Nipeten tsheutshimau issishueshipan nituiauts uuashushipin Innuts
asinu. Tshekuanuenu uishinisssssishuet? Tshiseni-
man tshemintun ushitau asinu. Uitamuatau tsheutshimau katinapuet. Tshinispinua nte nutshimits
mamu utuasima kie utiskuema. Putkie esk unte ash-
inuapatumua tshetshi nte ntutet. Kie tshipatshiuit-
shieu a enua utiskuema, utuasima kie put usima?
Tshe utshimau kakeeshau tshintuea enua utiskuema,
kie utuasima nete nutshimits? Stitanan tshinan nutshimits kie tshinika-nushunan kie tshintuuinushu-
nan. Nina nikusits. Kie tshash mamishituuts kie
senitamuts eshi nakunits nutshimits. Tshishue nimit-
shenimau tshe utshimau. Kakeeshauts kitshi uishuka
uitamakunaeutshi tsheenituak. Tshitapamuk.
Nanikutini tshishue nitshuapin tsheutshimau entat-
shi tshekuanu Innu." *Shenum*

Tsheutshimauts nastesh ama nakituenitamueu Innua
utapuentamunu, nisishueu tsheutshimau ntipeeeniten
asin eamiats mistinisishueu. Tshisenitenan tshinan
stipenitenan stasinu. Ama tshikatshi shuka minipunu
Innu tapuetuatshe tsheutshimaua. Tsheutshimau
stipenimukunu tapue katshitutimau. Tsheutshimau
uapatinueu etshiutshimaut ute Kanata. Kakeeshauts
tukushinuuts ute eku itenitam niseniten tshekuan
mishiueniu. Nastesh amasenitam.

Tshinanu ama tshinishinakushinan tsheutshimau.
Tshiuapamukunu tshinau Kanatian (Canadian). Tshinanu stisinu kie tshekuanu. Ama tshisenimukunu.
Uinuau tante nitakake-eshamuts, eku muk tshinan
ama tshinistakakeeshamu-nan. Tsheutshimau tshipani-
tutueu innua. Eskute mishiue tshekuan tshika unitanan, pase Innu tshikasenimushu pase Innu. Pase
tshinan tshika kustatshinan esku nte stuasiminuuts
ama tshikatshisenimushut Inniuits Tshinan tshikutshitanan tshetshiuitshiitunak mamu kamenipunak.
Tshipantuapatenan tsheutshimau tshetshi nistuapamats innua.

Tsheutshimau staikamikunu tshetshi uauitamuak
stassi-nana uta stasinats tshekanita pistenimunak
espish uikastinamak stipentamunu, tshipauiunikapus-
tuanu tshe utshimau. Eka nutshikuak, ama tshika
nitutakunu. Akanutshikuakue tsheutshimau tshikitshinista nitutakunu. Asinu mishiue tshika pikunum.
Kantuuiuts tshikaushitapinuuts mistukuntshuapinu,
eku eieapits nimeshits mitshiuap tshika uapatikanu
shipits. Miskikuntshe tshekuan uta, eku eiapits
tshetuutinas eka minakuts.

Tshipanutshikuanu tsheutshimau stisinanu kuuinut-
shiku-mua. Tshipa naka tuenimanants, katshipinishits
kie kutuk ute stesinan. Kie tshipa anumuekatinan stisinu kie Innuts tshekuanu uaanimue-atas. Innuts uta
Utshimassits ama tapuetamuts tshetshi miskutinikinits
esk eka mishinaushunants. Kitsheniutshi tshishue
uishamakanuuts naanimuanitshi kie unapamakanitshi
tsheutshimaua ashimakanitshi tsheutshimaua
ashimakanishits.

"Tsheutshimau stenimukunu ama tshikanita
pekupinuts, tshipa kutshitanan tshetshi eka minuats
nutekushiak." *Miste-Pinip*

Pase steniman tsheutimau utinamenu Innu
tshekuanu eku nastesh ama tshinutshikuanu. Muk
stashinuapamanu kie tshitapamanu enu epimpint.
Tshekuanu tsheutshimau tshitapimikunaeua eshi-

CAMILLE FOUILLARD PHOTO

Tshenish and Meneshkuesh at school workshop /
Tshenish mak Meneshkuesh nte kaskutimatsheutshi-
uapits, 1993

people build dams and destroy our land. If we don't
see what he is doing to us soon, he will take the land
and we won't have anywhere to hunt. This is what we
have to fight for. We just can't sit back and let the
government do what he wants to with our lives. The
government shouldn't control our lives. We are the
ones who must take control." *Youth Council*

"I don't know what to say about these people in government. They think they are our gods. They think
they rule the land, the sea, the stars and the moon."
Gathering Voices participant

We don't like the way the government is managing
the resources. For example, in old Davis Inlet, the
main economic activity was the fishery. Now there are
hardly any fish here. There used to be a lot of animals
close by, like seals and ducks. A few years ago, ten
thousand caribou drowned in the Caniapiscau River. It
was the manmade dam that caused the caribou to
drown. More caribou have died, twenty thousand of
them from the George River herd. We don't know why.
The LIA (Labrador Inuit Association) is doing a com-

mercial hunt. They sell the meat in Canada and outside
Canada. What other people believe is that the caribou
are always on the run. They never have time to eat.
Wherever they migrate, there are always hunters or
sports hunters. Some sports hunters kill the caribou,
throw away the meat and only keep the antlers as a
trophy. Biologists believe the caribou are migrating
non-stop. We need to stop low-level flying over calving
grounds.

We Depend Too Much on Government

We used to help ourselves before we started to get government funding. Now if a person works, they have to
get paid, and if they get a low salary, they might quit.
Some of us think we are spoiled by the government
with all the money that is given to the people. People
are given houses without spending any money. They
think things don't cost money. They don't have to
spend one cent on their houses when they get them.
Also people now want to buy everything. People
depend too much on Social Services, the Band Council,

nakushuak. Tshekuanuenu tsheutshimau uakanu tshika?

Muk mushinau kie mushinau tshiuitamakunu tanispish kie netutuak tsheutshimau, espish iniuanak? Utishipinu tshetshi miskutinamak tshinan. Tsheutshimau ushitau ueuestat. Pasese tam tsheutimau tshashipint eku kitshikustikunanaua uenikapuustuuak. Tsheutshimau tshisenimukunu etshi uitshinukuak nete kuskunu Kanata kie Akamisis. Kie mamu niuitshitusemanats Sheshatshit, kie nishapinan tshetshi nutshikuutshits tsheutshimau. Tsheutshimau panitutakunan kie papetenan. Niuiuapamanan tsheutshimau. Nipukueniten tshetshi uitamakunats. Tshinan tshipanitutakuunan uaanimuekatimak.

Kauiatukants

"Tshinan tshipa nutshikenan kie tshipa atuskatenan eniunak. Anutsh u eku tshishue nitsheniun kie ntueniten tshetshiapian kiminuau mitshuap, tshetshi taian. Niuitamakun tsheutshimau ama uitshinueu. Mushinau-kake tshika iniunan etshi iniunau anuts. Innu Utshimau kie pituutshimauts tshipa uitshinukunaets keuin. Tshipa te pueuts tshetshi uitshinukuak tante tsheutshimaua tshimi tshinakunikunua. Innu Utshimau kie pituutshimau tshipa kutshitauts tshetshi ushitats mitshuapa tshetshi minuantshi. Kie tshipa takun menuats asin kie nipin. Tshinan mishiue tshipa atusenan. Ue ministuk ama eun uenu Innu uits." *Tuamish*

Sam Napeu (left), land rights meeting / Napeu, assin kaianimutikants, 1990

CAMILLE FOUILLARD PHOTO

the church and the clinic. Politics and government funding have replaced our way of life.

Many of us don't understand how governments work. We depend on them, but their planning is very bad. For example, almost every summer there is a study on the water here. What is the point of doing these studies when we can't find water? Some of the houses have toilets and bathtubs. What good is a bathtub when there is no water? The government must be crazy to send those bathtubs. They know there is no water in this community. Also, we shouldn't build any more houses here because it is a waste of money. The houses will not last long. If we have to build some more houses, it should be at the new site.

We need to work on our own government. The chief and Band Council in Utshimassit was set up by the white government. Before there were chiefs and councillors, people used to help each other out. Now, only the councillors make the decisions. Innu used to decide things for themselves. There was always a leader in Innu camps, someone to lead the hunters. We need to make our council work for us.

We Have Rights

"The government was not born in the country on this land. He knows nothing about life in the bush. We know who we are. We know how to survive in the country. I heard the government saying he loaned the land to the Innu. How could he say that? We all know God made the world. We want the government to prove this to us. Has he ever been in the country with his family? Or will he be going back in the country in the future? Can the government support his family, his children and grandchildren in the country? Do the government people ever hunt to support their families? We have been in the country and we have survived on only country food and nothing else. I had four boys. They are all grown up and they all know everything about life in the country. I hate the government. These people should prove to us that they know about our culture. Look at me. Sometimes I get really mad when I hear what the government is saying to Innu people." *Shenum, elder*

Both governments are still not recognizing Innu rights, and they are still saying the government owns the land. There is too much conflict over this. We know we own our land and ourselves. We have never signed any

treaty. It is not easy for the Innu and governments to agree. The government owes us a lot for what they have done. The government is showing off because they are the big boss of the province or Canada. White people come here and they think they know everything. They don't.

We cannot be like government. They see us as Canadians. We have our own culture, our land. They don't know who we are. They say whatever they want because they speak English. But for us, we have difficulties with English. It is the government's turn to listen to the Innu. In the future, if we lose everything, some Innu will not recognize themselves as Innu. Some of us are scared that our future children won't know they are Innu. We are trying to help ourselves to solve our community problems. We must find a way to make the government recognize us as Innu.

The government has forced us into land claims. We will never give up fighting for our rights. We have to stand up to the government. If we don't fight, governments will never listen to us. More land will be destroyed. Sports hunters will build cabins, and more fish camps will be seen on all the rivers. If minerals are found in our area, developments will go ahead without our approval.

In our fight to get the government to recognize our land rights, we need to get interim protection so that low-level flying and any other developments will stop over Ntesinan. We also need to talk about overlapping claims with other Native peoples and about compensation. The people in our communities will get a chance to see any agreement and to make changes until they are satisfied before we will sign. It is important that our elders be there when there is a meeting with government officials.

"The government thought we would never wake up. From now on, we have to try not to fall asleep again." *Miste-Pinip, elder*

Some of us think the government has been in charge of the Innu and there is nothing we can say or do about that. We just wait and watch for his next move. Why can't the government look at us and see what has happened? Why can't the government do something?

But more and more of us ask how much longer we can wait to help ourselves instead of listening to government and wasting away our lives for him? It is time to change and do things our own way. The govern-

Nastesh amatshisenitean uisheka uitshintak tsheutshimau uaatutsheak. Uaatutsheak tshiustum-puean tshetshinue tshipa uitamakunu. Tshisenitenan ute mitshuapa uishamiats mitshimatshimiteua eku pase amanu kuatu tshimiteua uta. Ama takun nipin. Nastesh esk ama miskutenitakun. Esk peikun kuetenitakuats. Patuapamanan tsheutshimau. Mishiue kitipenitamua tshekuanu kie kiuiutinumua ntesinan. Aue asin ninu Ntesinan.

Uintusenitamuts pita esk eka stutets. Uitushenitamuts pita nipinu espishants uiuapatamuts nete kauiatukuanits. Tshishue nikamiskatenimanats kamiskaaue nipinu. Nisenitenan tsheushitakantshi mitshuapa kie tshenishinakuatshi, tshenispishatshi kie asinu tshetshitipenitak Innu uitshiiuakantshe, kie mitshuapa tshe enishitshimitetshi. Ninan niuipimpinitanan nispish pitetatunuepuna ketan tshenispishetinanikue. Ninan uipimpinitanan tshetshi minupimpints nipin kie tshetshi pimpits nipin mishiue mitshuapints atakuantshe.

Ntaanimueatuaiapints kakeeshauts. Pase Innuts ntenimeuts atutshi ute tauts etautshish atutsheutishe. Kutakuts Innuts tapuetamuts tante pase kakeeshau uitshimeuts Innuuskueua kie tshipauitshuut uta keeuinuau. Kutukuts nisishueuts kakeeshau uta etatshi stisinats nistim pita tshipa uitam.

Mamu tshipa atusean tshetshi minu nakutaak atutshea-ue. Tshinan tshipa pimpinitanan atuseuna stisinats eshiuapataman. Eiapits ntanumuekatenan uipits kaenitinants. Kie ntuenitamuanants ntuasiminaets tshetshi skutimashuts uipits kaenitinants tshinanu muk inuunau muats muk kakeeshauts.

"Tsheutshimau tshipa ueueshakanipan uipits eku tshipa petishinikanu shuneanu kauiatutsheak."
Utshimassiu Innu

"Minuanu enu tsheutshimau uepuupauntshi Innua meska shuneanu. Enkunu enu muk uatshiat innua. Muk nte tapue apishashinu shuneanu eku tshishue mistitshishikuakanu kapiminast nete kuspe. Kaniuekutat katsheniut. Tshishue nistimaunan, tsheutshimau tutam kie ekun tshipa atamenimakanu. Tshipa nitutakunu tsheutshimau anush. Tshipa uitamuanu eshi uinakushuak mamu tshitshinash kie steshinats. Tsheutshimau tshishue tshimistatinukunu. Tshishue miskuau enatimak nipin. Tshenuts tshishue meskuuits euta utenats. Ama ntshinikustashun. Tshishue miskuau. Nastesh ama tshiatusen, nitsheniun mak ntuskeuem eku nastesh ama tshiatuseu. Tsheutshimau tshipa nitutakunu, usham tshinitutuanu. Tshinan tshipa utshimamitatuia. Ekun tshipashi apitshaiu tsheutshimau auitamatan tshekuanu. Innuts tshipa nitutuakanuts. Ekun eku esi apitau. Muku tshenakituapatamau enitutakanu." *Tuamish*

ments have made too many mistakes. Some believe the government is starting to be afraid of us now because we are standing up for ourselves. The government knows we have a lot of supporters across Canada and Europe. If we work more closely with Sheshatshiu, we have the power to fight the government. It is the government's turn to listen to us. We need to be heard. We want self-government. We want relocation. We must never give up on relocation.

Relocation

"Sometimes I remind myself how I used to work hard to survive. Now I am old and I need a good house, a better place to live. I was told the government doesn't support relocation. Will we have to always live like we do now? The Band Council and chief should help us too. They should shout for help because the government people messed up our lives. Chief and council should really try to build better homes at the new location. We need clean land, water. We can all work together on this. This island is no home for the Innu." *Tuamish, elder*

We don't understand why the governments are not supporting relocation. We have had so much trouble asking for relocation. They should let us know soon. We all know that our homes are overcrowded and we have no place to build new houses in this village. We have no water. Nothing is changing. Our living conditions are the same. But we have to go through government. They control everything and want to rule the land. This land is our land.

They want to do a study first before we go ahead. They want study how much water is available and study the soil to see if the place we have chosen is good for a new community. We will be surprised if they don't find water. We have been making our own plans about where to build, how big the houses will be and what they will look like, how far apart to build them, how much land each person should have, what direc-

tion the houses should face. We want to plan for the next fifty years because our population is growing fast. We want to make sure that we have good sewage facilities and that we don't pollute the water around the new community.

We are talking about what to do with white people. Some people think white people should not be allowed to live in the new community. Others believe that if they are married to Innu they should be able to have their houses in the community. Others say white people can live in the community but they must have our permission first.

We must work together to make this community better before moving to the new location. We must run our own programs and community the way we see fit. We are also talking about going back to the old ways. We want our children to learn more about our culture. We should be responsible for our own people, not outsiders. We need to be educated.

"The government should be sued for their actions in the past, and we could use the money for relocation." *Innu leader*

"We Innu are very poor. That's the government's fault and he needs to be blamed for that. The government needs to listen to us now. We have to let him know how ugly he makes us look, and our home and community. Government changed us so much. It's really hard to carry water. It's hard for elders especially and the whole community. I can't even get wood for myself. It's just too hard. I can't do any hard work. I am an old man and my wife is old and can't do any work. Government needs to hear us. We do too much, listen too much. We have to govern ourselves. We don't need government to tell us what to do any more. Innu have to be heard too. We cannot sit back and let this happen any more." *Tuamish*

NEU ETSHITAPATEKEN

EMEUTSHIUAP: INNU EMEUN MAK KAKESHAU EMEUN

WILLIAM DUNCAN STRONG PHOTO

Uitshimakun playing the drum/ Uitshimakun teuenikea nutshikuepan, 1928

Uipats Innuts tapints uta assits. Eskua eka emeun takuats, Innu takunipan utemeun. Aueshisha utipenikuminua nishi tapuetamupants. Mishiue aueshis nishi tapuetamupants. Ume aueshish utipenikuma tshishue uitshepants innua. Mistapeu eku tshishue uitshepan tepenimukut kie eiemepan. Mistapeu eiapits uitshepan kaakushitshi. Tshishue uishanipan eshi shapit. Tan etatupats eku eshi mishikats kauapukueshits? Kauapukueshits mishikauts eku nekatishinats Innu kaeshitapuetamitshi.

"Nitshishinapin euashiuian, tshenuts mak inuts nimipants. Tshash tshishue nuuinimin paset kauapukuest eku uetshipitat teuenikea. Utinameu Innua uteuenikanua. Eskua ama nipunaiapin. Eku kauapukuest nashinimist, ntukunan tshenu kanutshikuat teuenikea ama minuanu etet. Tshishue nikustau kie nistimatshenimau ume tshenu. Ama shuka uapatum. Tshishue nistimenimau ume tshenu. Uenapinits kauapukuest ntuapimukunan. Ntukuna tsheka minuats ituteiek niminatshe. Ama minuau ntukunai. Tshishue nitshuenimukunai. Ama nista unikuatamau katit kauapukuest kautinat teuenikea.

"Kauapukuest ntukunan kie kushapashikan ama minau. Ishishue Innu kueshapatashi eiemieu kamitshitshi. Kakitshinau. Ntenitenan tshishe Manitu minueu Inua tshetshi nutshikuakanitshi teuenikea kie kushapashikan. Nimatiten uipits kaniminats teuenike. Kie kakushapatakants. Tshipishen kushapashakanish. Tshishue niminueniten tshenu nekumitshi teuenikea." *Miste Shishin*

"Kauapuskuet ekun nistamishikapin nete uipats Utshimassits. Muku mupipan tashu ni apishish ama neush tapin. Emeutshiuap takunipan. Nastesh tshekuan pitakamits, ama takuna tetipuakea, Innuts pipitshitukuts apipats eiemaiantshi. Eku nashipats

emeun kie ninan ama shuka minau, miskuts nutshikumats shitakunapun kie meshimenitamats." *Kaniuekutat*

"Emeutshuap itenitamupan kushapashikan ekunu kamitshit utatusheun, eku metinu nekatishinak Mistapeu kushapashikanu. Innuts itenitamuts aka nitustuataue kauapukueshitsi tshika mishiue niputs. Tshishue nimishimeniten etenitats Innuts. Tshiuapamau Kakushapatak eiemiat, shuskueu emeuna nete nushimish, nau anuts kitutikanua emeutshiuapits. Kakushatapak ekunitshe Tshishe Manitu mantak. Tshishe Manitu mineu Mistapeua ushutshiunu tshetshi uitshinuetshi eminuanits, mauats emitshinits. Ekunu muku ama shuka minua Mistapeu nepatshi kutuka Innua. Minuanu Mistapeu etatshi kushapashikanish. Ntukueu Innua nakushitshi. UItshieu Innua tshetshi miskamitshi mitshiminu etuuiutshi. Uitshinueu auenua kie uitamueutan etitshi kutuka Innu enistitshi etuuiutshi." *Shuashim*

Niuitshinukuts kie nimushupinaets mishiue eiemauts, muku pishe eieshimeuau nishi eiemauts tante pishe ushiuts uaskanikanish. Kauapukuest shikanitueu Innua eku manat utishinikashunua. Eskua eka shikanitashuiats, ninan niuinushunan

CHAPTER FOUR

THE CHURCH: INNU SPIRITUALITY AND THE CATHOLIC RELIGION

The Innu have been here for thousands of years. Before we became Catholic, we had our own Innu religion. We believed in the spirits of the animals. Our spiritual beliefs were in all living creatures. These spirits had a great influence on our people. The kamiteut (shaman) was our spiritual leader and he used to speak for us. The kamiteut was also our healer. He had all the power to help our people. How many years has it been since the missionaries came to our land? The missionaries came and tried to get rid of this religion.

"I remember when I was young, the elders and the people were having a *niminanu* [drum dance]. I was just getting up to dance when the priest came into the drum dance and grabbed the drum from the elder. He took the drum away from the people. We were really afraid. My boyfriend and I ran out. We were not married yet. When the priest came in, he told us the old man was doing evil things playing the drum. I felt so afraid and really felt sorry for the old man. He was almost blind. I respected this old man a lot. Next day, the priest came to see us. He told us never to go to the drum dance. He said it's no good. He was really mad at us. I never forget that night the priest came and took away the drum.

"The priest also told us the *kushapashikan* [shaking tent] was evil. He said the people were talking to the devil in the shaking tent. The priest was wrong. I think God gave the people the power of the drum and the shaking tent. I really hate it when the priest took that away from the Innu. I miss the drum dances and the shaking tent. I was in the shaking tent once myself. I respected the elders, and I still do. I love to dance the drum dance. I love to hear elders sing with the traditional drum." *Miste-Shishin, elder*

"Father Whitehead was the first priest to come to old

Davis Inlet. He never came to stay. He was only a visitor and stayed for a few days at a time. The church was on the Hudson's Bay side. It was empty. It had no chairs; people had to sit on the floor. Mass was said every morning at 7:00 A.M. and rosary was said in the evening. We were good Christians. Then the church changed and so did we but not in a good way. We changed into alcoholism and suffering."
Kaniuekutat, elder

"The church thought the shaking tent was part of the devil's work, so they got rid of the shaman and the shaking tent. Maybe people thought if they didn't listen to what the priest said, we would all die. It is sad to think about these things. I have seen a shaman praying with a necklace like a rosary around his neck in the country, just like we do today in the church. The shaman was a gift of God to the Innu. God gave the shaman his power to use in a good way, not a bad way. The only bad thing about a shaman is when he killed someone in spirit. Other than that, the shaman used the shaking tent in a proper way. He cured sick people. He helped hunters find the animals. He helped families know how other people were doing in other hunting grounds." *Shuashim*

Most of our parents and grandparents were Catholic, except for some families who were Moravian because they were from the Chimo territory. The priest baptised the people and gave us our names. Before this, we used to pick our own names. At first, the Catholic religion was very important to us, but we practised our own religion, culture and traditions in the country. We also had lots of holy water to help us get by. We would travel to Uashat (Seven Islands) to meet the priest to be married or to be baptised. Sometimes the priest, like Father Whitehead, would come to Davis Inlet. We

ntishinikashunaia. Uskats tshishipants emeun tshishue mushinau nteiemaian, pishe uipats nishemauts eshemaianits, eshiniuiat, kie enitinau nete nutshimits. Mushina takun tshitshitau nipin tshetshi. Uitshinukunash. Ntutenan nete Uashats tshetshi nipunash kie tsheshi shikuanitashunats. Nanikutini kauapuskuet mishikau Utshimassits. Niminuenitenan uenapimintshishi kauapukuest eku manimist tshipeatuka kauapuskuet eiemitatim pashikea, asinu kie nipinu nete uipats Utshimassits.

Ntititeeaapun uipats etaspishunats. Kauapukuest niminukunan apitshitauna tsheapitshitaiats, ekunu tshashipants napitshitaiats akupa, kishipishunits kie mishina. Kauapukuest ntutakunan tshetshi unikuatumu-tshish uipats kataspishunats. Tapuetuaia eku uenitaiats uipats kaeshi iniuiats. Minuenitakushu tenimanan. Ekun uishiue ntushuminash. Niminukunan mishinaniketshinu tshetshi eiautshish mitshiminu, akupa kie pashikea. Ama nista uistamakuna tshekuan sheshe minikunash kaua-puskuet tshauet ntukunan tshetshi kau minuats ituteiats nete nutshimits.

Tshishue kauapukuest shutshiu. Kauapuskuet meshika-tshi Utshimassits, ataueutshiuap minueu apauanu kie akupa. Tshishue kusteuts kauapuskuetshi. Shenimeuts ama uiuapameu Innua tshetshi stimautshi.

"Niskueuts mushinau ushetshipitanuuts. Kauapuskuet minuatum eushetshepitanitshi Innu uskueua. Innuts tshek kuetenimats minuenitakushu, eku menenimats. Penestimashi tshemishikatshi nuuitamakunan tanta tsheemat. Innuts minuenitamuts aiamieunu. Auashits ama tapuetuakanuts tshetshi pishats aiamieutshiuapits eka uitsheuats ukauaua put kie utauaua. Muku tapuetua-kanipan auash tshetshi piset uashikanituakathsi." *Manteskueu*

"Nimushupe utinuku kauapukueshitshi tshetshi Innu Utshimaut tant ama minu. Kie mishetuuts tsheuish uitshinukut. Minuku nispimitukunu uuits. Nutaun uitshimeuts nimushuma kie ama minu nutaun kie tshetshi nakatuenimat. Mishanu uits eku kutukuts astashutshuap uitshitamuts. Ekunu uishi uakatuts tshenuts. Eshi petaman Innuts kusteuts kauapukueshitshi ekunu teniten kanimituteaiaua." *Kiti*

"Anushishe auasits metueuts. Tshishue shapimikinu eshu metuets. Tshisue minuau ume menetuets.

Niuapatenan eshi kaminupinash. Auashits niuapatinukunaets uipats. Kie tshishue takunikunan. Kauapukuest mishiue utinum tshekuanu Innu utiniunu. Ama nita uitamuaiaets auasits eshi minushits. Eskua uipats auasit nete niskutets. Emeutshiuap utinum enu." *Kiti nete kamamuuinats*

Miste-Kauapukuest (Father Cyr) mishikau katshi kauapuskuet. Ekun nistam kauapukuest epit kie eku tshishue naiastana eshiniutshish. Pikaam emeutshiuapinu eku kuesteshe akamish tshemitat. Ninateu inua tshetshi natshematshi. Estukuats emeutshiuap nete uipits Utshimassits, eku tapitu estats Innuts. Ekun eshi tshishipats matshinash ataueutshiuap mitshim.

Miste-Kauapukuest titam tashiputakanu. Ekunu eshi ushitat uits. Miste-Kauapukuest nau itenitakushu kamakunuest. Tutueu Innua tshetshi eka animishitshi. Iteu inua tshetshi eka pastatutamitshi kie ntuun tshetshi eka tutamitshi. Tshishue kustukushiu. Mushina kitsheshimeu Innua ekunu eshi minuenimukuts. Mushina iteu Innua tan tsheshi nushimits itutetshi kie tan tsheshi kau tukushinitshi. Iteu Innua tshetshi eka minitshi kie tshetshi minu nakatuenimatshi utuasiminua. Estatshi ama shuka minanu. Muku Inuts menitshi nete nika etatuaui.

Miste-Kauapukuest eiapits kaskutimatsheuipan. Niskutamakunan eieme mishinanikanu kie tshetshi eiemi-tautshish. Iteu inua tshetshi eka stutaiatshi utuasiminua tshetshi skutimashutshi nushimits etataui. Nitakunan akaui skutimashutaue auasits tshika utinakanuts tshetshi skutimashuts neka. Kie ntukunan mauats tshika ashumakuna. Auash katsheskutimashutshi, ntuapameu nete uitshinish. Tshishikuakanu eskutimatshet. Emeun eku tshishue tsheskutimakunash. Pishe inuts tshishuts kautamakuts kie kamuskuanikuts.

"Miste-Kauapukuest ekun nikaskutimatshem. Tshishue kustukushiu, tshishue miskushiu. Mishiue niushikunikunan." *Napeutik kie Anishish*

Katshi Miste-Kauapukuest tshiuepit, kutuk mishikau kauapukuest (Frank Peters). Ekunu tshishu eiash eshiniunats, ntukuastikushu, kanutapiteu, kaskutimatsheu, kamakunueshiu, tsheutshimaua atiskueu, mistukunapeu, eiapiuapatsheu kauapukueshi kie Inikieu auashisha. Tshishue nakituenitam kauepinashuma, auasits uanatutshetaui, tshishue asiuateu eku auasits tshastishimats. Tshitshue kustikushiu. Mishiue tshekuanu pipinitau muku ama tshipieieu Innu nut-

liked to see the priest and to get statues of Jesus. Father Whitehead would bless all the guns, the land and the sea around old Davis Inlet.

We had our own traditional clothing. The priest gave us clothes to wear, and we started wearing skirts, pants and shoes. The priest wanted us to forget our way of life. We followed his advice and started to leave our traditional way of life. We thought he was a kind man. That is how we were settled here. We used to get social assistance from the priest. Many of us thought the priest would help us in any way he could. We began to depend on him. He would give us vouchers for everything, like food, clothing and guns. We don't know if it was government money. No one ever told us how we got free food from the store. Before Father Whitehead left, he would always tell us to go back in the country.

The priest had a lot of power. Once when Father Whitehead came to Davis Inlet, the Hudson's Bay Company gave all of the people new tent canvas and clothing. They were afraid of Father Whitehead. They knew he would not want to see the Innu living in such poor conditions.

"The women used to braid their hair and tie it up. Father Whitehead really admired the women with braids in their hair. The people began to realize he was a good priest and they respected him very much. Whenever we heard he was coming to the village, we would gather and give him a welcoming party, and receive him with respect. Then he would announce the time when mass would be held. Innu men and women had great respect for their religion and spirituality. The children were not allowed to come into church without their parents. The only time a child was allowed to come in was when he needed to be baptised." *Manteskueu*

"My grandfather was chosen by the priest to become the chief because he was a non-drinker. Also he had a big family who he could influence. He was supplied with a two-storey house. My parents stayed with my grandparents because my father was a non-drinker and could take care of them. He had the big house while the other Innu were living in shacks. I think that would create friction between the other elders in the community. But as far as I know, people were afraid to speak out against the priest, and that is the greatest sin we ever committed." *Kiti*

"Last weekend, the children did a play at school. It was very strong and powerful. This play was very important. It shows what our problems are. The children showed us our past. This play hurt a lot. It was so real. The priest took everything away from us. We never tell our children how good they are. We have to tell them so they will know that they are good. If we still had our traditional ways, we never would have lost our children in the fire. This wouldn't have happened. The church took this away from us." *Kiti at the Gathering workshop*

Father Joseph Cyr came after Father Whitehead. He was the first permanent priest, and he began to take even more control of our lives. He tore down the church and built the mission building in old Davis Inlet. He would go from tent to tent to get people to go to church. When the church was built in old Davis, the people began to stay in one place. This is when we started to eat store food.

Father Cyr had his own sawmill. That is how he built his house. Father Cyr was like the police. He tried to make people behave themselves. He told us people shouldn't sin or do bad things. He was very strict. He used to preach to us and many of us respected him. He used to tell us when to go to the country and when to return to the community. He used to tell us not to drink and to look after our children. When he was around, people didn't used to drink that much. The only time people used to drink was when they were outside the community.

Father Cyr was also a schoolteacher. He taught us the Bible and how to read. He told the people the children should stay behind to go to school while the parents went in the country. He told us if we didn't send our children to school, they would be taken away and placed where they could attend school. He also told us our social assistance would be cut off. When the children didn't go to school, he would go look for them in the tents. He was getting paid to teach the children. Religion was the main course in school. Some people remember he used to beat the children and make them cry a lot.

"Father Cyr was our teacher. He was very dangerous, very hard on us. He hurt us a lot." *Tent meeting with Sango Bay elders*

After Father Cyr left, another priest came. Life changed even more for us. This priest was Frank

shimits etatshi. Katshi taiats ministukuts, minupunu-shu pishish. Katshi neush taiats, eku tshishue inuts mushunau etats utenats.

Frank Peters aiasteneu Innua. Kauapukuest nistam nateu kakaminitshi ekupatush kaminitshi. Kie iteu Innuts kamiste pastaitutats nika aiakanuts, tante tshika shakuenimuts. Ekuts kamitutash nistam nete aiakanuts. Mushinau nutshikueu kaminitshi innua. Muku atiskueu kakaminitshi eku ama nakituenimeu kaminitshi. Eku tshishue uenakatutshi Inua tante kauapukuest muku nakituenimeu kakamiitshi. Ekuta tshashipants kamenupinash. Kauapukuest minueu apitshitauna. Menenimat enua niskueuts ni. Kauapukuest utineu niskueua tshetshi atusetshi emeutshiuapits. Eiastishitshi kauapukuest. Ntuun utineuni niskueua, eku tsheshuenimituts ni niskuets. Ekunu uishuui uakatunants uta utenats.

"Nikustau kie niman kie nishetshin. Kauapukuest uepestameu nutauna kie utamaueu. Muku Innuts tshitapameuts kauapukuest nutshikuat nutauna, kat-shinutshikuat eku nukumish tsha uetat nutauna. Nastesh ama uitshakanu nutaun. Innuts tshishue kusteuts kauapukueshintsi tante nutaun minipin kie ama tshuapu. Nimiskatenimau kauapuest tshetshi skutimuunimit tshemintuna uta tuseunu. Mauats

The old shaman is crucified (The Boneman, *high school drama*) / *Tshistaskuatakanu kameteut, 1992*

tshetshi utamauat innua. Kutukuts tapints uetama nkuts. Ekun nteniten uish mushinau takuats tshuapun nete Innuts. Innuts uapameuts kauapukueshintshi nutshikashuntshi. Mishenu kamenuats tepatshimakant ume kauapukuest." *Epa*

Meuts muku kamatenitats nutshikakuts kauapukue-sitshi. Takunu kutakanu kamenuats estists. Nisheni-manan mistukunapeuts kie kauapukueshits ntuun eni-tutuats napesha kie niskuesha uta utenats. Tshishue miskuau tshetshi uauita-mats.

"Tshishin mistukunapeuts tsheskutimatshet. Tutaku-naets tshekuanu nete mishiutshiuapits. Etaiashi kaskutimasheutshi-uapits, niuapekakunaets nete nishukinash. Mishiue ntuskueshiuaia. Tshishue nikustaiaiets ume mistu-kunapeuts." *Kamamuinats*

"Tshenut peikushinikupan muk tshekuanu eka mentutak, eukunu usham miste uieshimukushipan kauapukueshin kie kastekupeskueu katshi mishikan ute. Tshipa minuanipan enu eka puntakue kaishit-shissenitak tshekuanu. Mieu ninan etutamats uet-eka-ssentamatsh, ne kaishiniunanuts, tshitshue nipukuenimaut ntshen uentshi kimiste eimiautshi tshetshi tshissenitak nenu mesti-mishan, mantuk tshementu eukunu shatshitunu. Kauapukueshit kie kastekupeskueut, apu kunenitak nenu shatshitunu. Mitshetut kauapukueshit uieueshakanit emitshitu-tuat auassa. Miam ne-kamiste akushit ueshish, iten-itakushut, meu-ents katshitshituauentakushit uentshi. Piuenimeut Innu auassa ute nutem espishan Kanata. Kie tat-nte-uen iakunikut umenu essishueuk, menui-ust-tutuau, tapue ume nas tapuanu." *Mushuau-iskueu*

Niuuenitenan

"Emeutshuap ama minuenitam kanishiniunash. kakeshau eshi pipant ekun ninan eshi pipinash." *Kaskutimashut auash*

Emeutshuap ama minu-pinitau uipats. Mishiue eshishuanu. Emeutshiuap pikunum inua kanishiniut-shi. Innu unitau uipats kanishpimatishit, ekunu emeutship naiastinat inua. Usham nitustuanan kaua-pukuest. Katshi tapitu taiats, uakatuts nikanishinaets mak kaiamaats. Nistam titanan eskua sheshus kaeniu-tuta asits. Nikanishinaets takunipan utemeunuau uipats. Eke anuts ueuenitamats, niustuuinukunan

CAMILLE FOUILLARD PHOTO

Peters. He was more like a leader. He was a mechanic, doctor, dentist, midwife, teacher, government agent, police and carpenter as well as a priest. He even controlled the dump, and if any child wanted to go through his garbage, he would let out this big roar and the children would be gone in a flash. He was very strict. What he said went. He was in charge of the whole community, but one thing he couldn't control was when people decided to go into the country. After we moved onto the island, things got better for a while. It was years later that people started staying in the community.

Frank Peters had his set of people. The priest made sure to visit the non-drinkers first and then the drinkers. He also preached that the people who sinned the most usually sat in the back, because they should be ashamed, and those who were good sat up front. The priest would fight with a lot of people who were drinking. He only worked for the people who were not drinking, and he wouldn't help the drinkers. People were jealous of one another because the priest was good to non-drinkers. That is where the problem started. The priest used to give clothing to the women. The women he liked would go in and get first pick of the clothing. Then women started fighting. The priest would also pick women to work with him in the church. When different priests came, there was always jealousy between the women to see who they would pick to work with them. Many of us think this is where the divisions between people started in this community.

"I was very afraid and I remember crying and being very frightened. The priest kicked my father and hit him with his fist. The people were only watching the priest beating up my dad, and when he finished with my father, my uncle took my father home. Nobody helped my father. The people were afraid of the priest then. My dad was drinking but he didn't cause any trouble. I couldn't believe the priest could beat up people. I thought they only were supposed to talk about God, not beat up people. There were others he beat up. I think this is why there's so much family violence too. People saw the priest fight. There are too many bad stories about this priest." *Epa*

It is not only men who were drunk who were abused by the church. There was other abuse that is very serious. Some of us know that brothers and priests sexually abused boys and girls in this community. This is very hard for us to speak of.

"The brothers that came here teaching did things to us in the bathroom. When we were in school, they used to give us showers and wash our bottoms. We were all girls. They gave teenage girls showers. I was really afraid of these brothers." *Gathering Voices participant*

"The greatest sin that our elders committed was they got brainwashed by the priest and the nuns who came. They should have stuck with their own Innu spirituality. It's not our fault that we don't know much about our Innu spirituality. I really wish that these people who are religious today would know that the greatest gift of all that the Creator gave us is LOVE. The priest and nuns don't have that love. A lot of priests have been charged with sexual abuse. They are sick, sick animals. They are not saints or holy people. They abused Native children all across Canada, and if this is hurting, what I'm saying, I'm very sorry but it's very true." *Utshimassiu woman*

We Are Confused

"The church was against the ways of our traditions. White society, their way of living is our way of dying." *High school student*

The Church made a lot of mistakes in the past. Everyone here says that. The Church damaged our culture. Instead of helping us, the priests made us lose our traditions and spirituality by taking control and running our lives. We listened to the priests too much. Since we were settled here, there has been a lot of conflict between the ways of our ancestors and the ways of the missionaries. We were here before Jesus came on earth. Our ancestors had their own religion and spirituality long ago. Now we are so confused, caught in the middle between the Catholic Church and our spirituality. We have our own legends, like the story of Kuekuatsheu who made the land. The priest told us about Noah's ark. Our parents tell us a legend about the time there was a lot of rain, and this man was asked to put a male and a female of each animal into his canoe so that he could save the animals. Was this a coincidence? We don't think so. What about the legend of Tshakapesh? He was the first one to reach the moon, because he

emeun mak ninan ntemeunan. Takuts ninan atinuei-ets, etipatshimakat Kuekuatsheu kaushitat asinu kie tshekat eshi tipatshimunat. Tshinitshinukunuts tipat-shimuts atinukea kamiste tshimunikea ekun napeu kie niskueu kapushakanits aueshishits nete Innu utish ekunu tshetshi inikaat aueshisha. Tshimiskatenitenau ua? Ama teniten. Eku Tshakapesh katipatshimakant? Ekun nistam etat pishumush epimutshet ukuskua. Uipats tshishue tapin atinue. Mamiskatenitamuts inuts penetats katshi tipiskan pishum auen etat? Tante tsheshi shenitamau?

Ama tshishiuuakanu enukumut teuenikea. Kauapukuest tshishikuakanu eketsheshimat innua. Peikushu muku Tshishe Manitu, muku niueniten tante nishets nishi skutimakun.

"Nutapeu nuuitamakupan tshetshi nakatuenimik aueshish kie ntuun enishinakuats mitshim. Niskuti-makupan tan tshetutuk aueshish. Eshinistutuk nutape, tsheminu nakatuenimit aueshish put tshika tshuauts tepenimukut aueshish. Mauats tshika asamuk. Nuuitamuk tshetshi shatshakau aueshishits mak inuts." *Innu Tsheutshiman*

"Nitshishin uskats kupeshiunan. Ntukuun tshetshi uitamuuk kauapukuest eshi pastatutaman. Nten-imukun tshetshi pastatutamun nishuashutash atatupuneshinan. Etuun etenimik auen, eiapits ten-itinakanu pastaitun. Nika uitamuau kauapukuest eku tshekashamuut eku tsheemaian nutaunan kie Manistatamiskatin Pashenimau mestipastatuta auen tante neush tau katshi kupeshiutshi eiematshi. Kauapukuest niminukunan emeumishi-nanikea, kie niskutimakunan tshetshi nikuminash. Uaieu uuenua nikamuna muku nishats nikamunan. Ama nita peten Innu nikamuna. Muku nikaun penetuuk nepeastuat-shi nishima. Tshishin tshashipitshinash eku emeu mishinanikan tenakunamash kauapukuest kamin-imist." *Kamamuinats*

"Niminueniten nin anush temeun tante ama kitshi kau tshinisheman uipats Innuts kanishemaats." *Shuash*

"Euashiuian tshisue mushinau nuui kanipanueshiun tante kauapukuest tuk tshika atuskuau Tshishe Manitu. Kauapukuest unishinatam mithiuapinu eku Sheshus pitakamits tau. Nuuitamakun enu tshekuan uenishinata eku katsheshinantamitshi eku pamina nitukanu tante ama nishenitamau." *Kamamuinats*

"Nukum nishashutash tatushap tatupunesh nepit kie tshipeatuka shiskueu muku. Kauapukueshitshi minuku. Eshi tapueta ekunu tau utshipeatukumits nukunits. Mishiue utapuetumun ekunu tshepeatuka tamish etukunits." *Kiti*

Nimishetinan katsheshenitimats kakeshau utemeun. Ama nishenitenan eshinakuats kauapukuest shakanit-tuatshi auashisha, apitshitau nipinu kie piminu. Ntukunan kauapukuest nishuashutash tatin eshi-nakuat emeun. Innuts takunipan eshi emaats uipats, etutuats kanipitinu, eshi nipuut inu. Mishiue uepinikanua. Uipats auashish eniutshi nutshimish, kauapukuest eshishueu tshetshi tshetshinue shikanitua-akant, eku auash nipitshe aka shikanituakatshe tshika atamaskamukuts ituteu. Eku anush nistam pita skuti-mashunanu uashikanituakatshe auash. Tshishue meush skutimashunanu eku patush shakanituakant auash. Ekun a eshishuanu eskua eka kakeshau emeun takuats Inuts uipats kanipits kakashikuanituakanits ituteuts a atamaskamukuts?

"Enitautshinan mishen tshekuan tuten tshetshi minu emaaian. Aneaneu etatupuneshinan ekun uskat kuminunan tshetshi tshishiakuun epastatunaman. Tante tshipastatuten kie tshikupeshiun tshuuitamuau kauapukuest eku tsheminisk tshekuanu kaua-pants kauauneats nemeshetshi. Mauats tshika minukun ume eka kupeshiun." *Kiti*

Uipats, Innuts takunipan kie uinuau eshinakitueni-mats kanipitshi kie tshenipuat uitshinua. Mishiue uni-takanu. Eskua takun mukushan. Ekunu neskumut atik katipenimukut eshimisk. Innuts ashasheuts nepatataui mitshiminu. Eku aka minuene, tshika tshuenimuk. Put kie tshika mitshipinan mitshima euianishinak. Eku anush tshuushuneaminan estaiak kamiskutatshepinish tshimitshiminu tante ama tshuuiashashea. Tshenuts stukunuts tshuapuuts aueshish katipenimukut tante ama nastesh tshuui ashashea tshekuan put kie tshipi-uenimanu aueshish kanipiak.

"Innuts nakatuenimepats kanipitshi kie ushitaueuts unikuaskanu. Kauapukuest nikatishinum ne eiapits. Ntshishin nutaun nepit, ushitakanu tshipa minuashi-inu nutaun unukuaskan. Mauats ntau. Nikuaskaia kaminuatshi usham animea, tatshinispan. Napem tshek keushitat nikuaskanu. Eku ueuetaspitak . Eiapits kauapukuest nuuaau. Nishatshauts kanipits kie ama niminueniten kauapukuest tshetshi

kept throwing his arrow farther and eventually it landed on the moon. This legend has been through a lot of generations. Were the Innu surprised when there was actually a man on the moon about thirty years ago? How can we explain that?

The elder was never paid for singing for his people with his drum. The priest is paid for preaching to us. There is only one God, but we are very confused. We were taught both ways.

"My late father taught me how to respect the animals and any kind of wild food. He taught me how to handle them in a proper way. The way I understand my late father, he told me to respect the animals or the animal spirits would get angry with me and would not give me any animals to kill. He was telling me to respect the animals and all my own people." *Innu Nation interview*

"I remember the first time I had confession. I was told that I had to tell the priest what I had sinned. I was even expected to commit sins at seven years old. Even if I just had bad thoughts about other people, I had to tell the priest and he would forgive me by saying so many Our Fathers or Hail Marys. I would know who had sinned the most because he or she would stay in the church long to say prayers. The priest used to give out books and teach us how to sing. These songs were foreign to us but we sang them anyway. I never used to hear any Innu sing any of our songs. But I used to hear my mother sing lullabies to my brothers and sisters. I remember my family going into the country and my parents took the prayer book the priest supplied." *Gathering Voices participant*

"I respect my religion as a Catholic because I know I can never go back to my traditional religion." *Shuash*

"When I was young, I always wanted to be an altar boy because a priest told me I would be working for God. Once a priest drew a small house and picture of Jesus on one side. He told us what it was, but we didn't know what he was saying. The priest twisted our ears because we didn't know." *Gathering Voices participant*

"My grandmother was in her seventies when she died and she had a big cross around her neck all the time. This was supplied by the priest. None of her beliefs were visible except for this big cross. It seemed like

Father Whitehead and Joe Rich / Kauapukuest Kauspuskuet mak Shushepis, 1930

all her beliefs were buried by this cross." *Kiti*

Many of us don't understand the Catholic religion. We don't understand about the sacraments, like when the priest baptises a child, he has to use oil and water. The priest tells us there are seven sacraments. In the old days, when babies were born in the country, the priest would tell the parents to get the child baptised, or if the child died without baptism, he would go to hell. Now, we have to take a baptism course before the priest will baptise our babies. Sometimes it takes a long time before the baby is baptised. Also, does this mean that all the Innu who lived before contact with the Catholic Church went to hell?

"As I grew older, there were many things I had to do to become a good Christian. At the age of eight, I think, there is the communion stage you had to go through for a reward if you had sinned. Just because you sinned and confessed your sins to the priest, he would give you a round-shaped white thing during mass. You cannot receive this unless you confessed your sins." *Kiti*

But in our culture, the Innu must have had their own rituals in the past, our own ways of taking care of the dead, our own ways of marrying people. These practices were abolished. We still have a special ceremony called *mukushan*. This ceremony is to give thanks to

Joe Rich shows how the ceremonial robe is used to attract the caribou / Shushepis uapatnueu etapatshakantshi mistikueia, 1963

RAY WEBBER PHOTO

uuetishuet. Nishenimau ekunu nutapeu eshi ntuenitak. Nishe nimau ama ntuenitan nash tshetshi minuashits unikuaskau kie utukupa. Ushitapan kie uin nikuaskaia. Tshishue nistimenimau ekun tante eniat." *Kamamuinats*

Emeutshiuap anuts miste ashipanu. Pishe tenitenan usham tshipinu eashipants. Innuts tshishue shastsheepants kauapukueshitshi kie emeutshiuapinu. Eku anush nastesh ama mishetinanu eiemaatshi. Pishe inuts eshishueuts eshi unitat kauapukuest eatinat Innu, eku ama shuka uitauts. Ntukunan mishetuts kauapukueshits nekastetsh. Tshenuts mitatumuts uipats kanishemaanits. Itenitamuts usham ama nakituenitakanu emeutshiuap. Muku Innu skueuts kanipuut emauts kie kuminueniueuts. Emeutshiuap apitshitakanu tshetshi aianumats, ueueshitunats, etaueutshiuaputs, eshstshimakanits kie kutuk enistinats eka takuat emeun.

"Ama takunipan ataueutshiuap nete emeutshuahpits. Nishi skutimakunaapin Sheshus nikatishaueu uenapimat etauetshi emeutshiuapits." *Innut Utshimauts Kuspaeshimaua*

"Etuteatshi emeutshiuapits, kauapukuest nikitsheshimikunan kie ntutakun tshetshi shenitamutshish aiamieu mishinanikanu. Ama anush uipeten. Peikun penetiman etuteani emeutshiuapits. Kauapukuest uauitam emeumishinanikanu. Tshishue ntakunikun. Kuestutuats eapits auasha nete kaskutimasheutshiuapits. Ntuasiminaets eiapits mitshenitamamuts. Patshi kake shuka mituten at tatshi kauapukuest." *Utshimassit iskueuts*

"Uipats Utshimassits, Kauapuskuet uitshepan Innua mushinau. Eku anu ueshits kauapukueshits nastesh ama nakituenimeuts Inua." *Matininish*

Mishen tshekuan etenitamats emeutshiuap. Pishe isishueuts tan menuats emeun ninan put kie kakeshau emeun. Mishetuts eskua tshenuts menuenitats emeutshiuapinu kie ama minuenitamuts tshetshi astinikinits. Pishe minuenitamuts etukunits emeutshiuapinu, muku ama tshikishi pipinukunan. Innu auashits tshiuapuuts ashi pikuna stiniunaianu. Kie kutukuts ama stuuts. Kutukuts ama nastesh nakituenitamuts. Eskua Innuts itenitamuts eskua tshipipinikunu.

"Nishikanitashun kie ntapueten emeutshiuap, kie eskua peikun ntapueten uipats inuts kanashi tapuetats. Ntuenitamuauts auashits tshetshishitats iniunu. Eskua nishatshitan emeutshiuap, muku tshipa kutshitanan tshetshi ntuapatimak uipats kanishemaiae. Auashits tshipa skutimuakanuts anuts aiameunu kie uipats inuts kanishemaats." *Kaniuekutat*

"Aka nutshiataaue emeutshiuap, etu put tshipa minupunaiapin tshinitshinukunuts menits kie ama nakituenimeuts utuasimaua. Emeutshiuap tutam. Nau kakeshau kueshiniunak. Ekun uishi unikuatimau kanishi nakituenimauts auashits, etutusheau, kie eshiniunak. Katshi taiau uta ministukuts. Mishen eshi kaminupinak. Stanuenimikunank." *Kamamuitunauts*

"Emeutshiuap ama shuka atushemikun uta utenats." *Mitshimitshimau Kaatushen*

Minuau emeutshiuap an tshe kuuui eiemauutshi." *Samish*

Tshash ama takun uipats kaishi iniunak, ama takun kushapashikan. Mauats minuats tshika uapatenan. Ama tshiskutimashunan teuenikea, kie kutukuts aueshishits tepenimukuts. Anush auashits ama nakituenitamuts, unuespimitamuts piminu kie uskea. Tshenuts eskua nakituenitamuts. Tshasha tshishue tshinikitukunuts tshenuts. Auen tsheskutimatauk uipats tshekuanu. Tshenuts isishueuts mauats auasits tshikishi metuatsheut teuenikea. Muku tshenuts. Auen tshenutshikuat teuenikea?

the Caribou God for having provided for you and your family. The Innu share whatever they kill. If we do not, we anger the gods, who will then not provide us with food. Or something bad may happen to us or someone close to us. Now that we have money to buy freezers, we can't lose our sense of sharing. We have been told by our elders that the gods are angry with us because we failed to share and we failed to respect the animals that we kill.

"The Innu used to take care of the dead and make the caskets. The priest took that away too from the Innu. I remember when my dad died, I had someone make the casket for him. The priest argued with me. He said that my dad should have a fancy casket. I said no to him. Fancy caskets are too expensive. We couldn't afford to get a fancy casket. I wanted a homemade casket for my father. My husband later made one. And I had clothing for him to wear. The priest also argued with me for the clothing. I respect the dead and I didn't want the priest to be in my way. I know this is what my father wanted too. I know he didn't need fancy clothing or a fancy casket. He used to make caskets for the dead. I respect him. He was the man that raised me." *Gathering Voices participant*

The Church has changed a lot today. Some of us think it has changed too much. People used to respect the priest and the Church. Now, there are hardly any people attending mass any more. Some people believe that, since we have stopped going to church, there is more drinking and parents don't care about their children. The priests are not here often, and when they come, they don't stay long. It seems that as the priests have lost their power, there is no longer a full-time priest available. We are told it is because the priests are leaving the priesthood. Some elders miss the way mass used to be served. They feel the church is not being looked after the way it used to be. Now Innu women who are married do the church service and communion. The church is used as a meeting place for government people, as a courthouse, as a place to sell clothing, to show movies and for other non-religious activities.

"There wasn't a store in the church before. The church teaches us that Jesus drove people out of the temple when they were using the temple for selling items." *Band Council employees*

"When we go to church, the priest preaches to us and wants us to learn the Bible. I don't want to hear about it any more. It is always the same thing I hear in the church. The priest talks about the Bible over and over again. I'm sick of it. They do that to our children in the school too. Our children are sick of it now too. We can't be too religious even if the priest wants us to." *Family Violence Project*

"In old Davis Inlet, Father Whitehead used to help the Innu a lot. Now the new priests come and they don't take responsibility for the Innu any more." *Matininish*

We have many different feelings about the Church today. We have different opinions about which religion is good, our religion or the R.C. religion. Many of our elders still respect the Church, but they don't like to see it change. Some people think the Church is good to have, but we cannot let it run our lives. Many young people are angry with the Church for having damaged our culture. Some of us have no complaints about the Church. Some of us just don't care about it. Some people feel the Church is still controlling our lives.

"I was baptised and I believe in the Church, but I also believe in our own religion, our own spiritual beliefs. I want the children to learn our way of life. This is very important. I respect the Church very much, but we have to go back to our old ways too. The children are learning the Catholic religion, but they must learn our traditional way of life as well." *Kaniuekutat*

"The Church is not working in our community." *Social Services workers*

"The Church is okay for those who want to pray." *Samish*

Some of our old spiritual ways like the *kushapashikan* (shaking tent), *misinau, memekueshu* (fish spirits) and *pishum* (sun) are gone now. We might never get them back. We don't practise the drum dance any more, and some of us don't care for the animal spirits, like *tipenimukushi* (caribou spirit). Some young people don't care, and throw out the *pimin* and the bones. The elders still look after these things. But now a lot of our elders are gone. Who will be our spiritual advisors? Elders used to say that young people should not play with the drums. Only the elders are allowed to. Who will continue to play the drum?

PETETAT ESHITAPATEKEN

KASKUTIMATSHEUTSHIUAP

Tshishue mitshen Tshekuan eshi kaminupant kaskuti-matsheutshiuap miste pikunam stiniunanu mak Tshet-uasiminua. Kaskutimatsheutshiuap apu eshi tusemikan en tshipa eshitusemekenipan. En tshitshue eka minu-pants. Tshituasiminuts eka skutimuakants enu uit-shiniuaua eshi niuntshi. Enu kakeshaua utiniunu sku-timaukanuts. Kaskutimatsheutshiuap apu minitak tshetshi shenitamuak uipats Innua kaish iniuntshi. Mitshetuts auasits eka tshistutas enu keskutamashu-nanua.

Uipats

"Takunipan nantim auassit tsheishitusset. Nitshisku-tamakutan tshetshi ashamitsheian kie utapaiaskut-sheiat, miste mitshenupan tshekuan etutaman pets—euassiuian. Peikuau niuitamakun—eka tshissenitamen tshekuan tshetshi tutamen miam ashamit, kie tshetshi mantsheian, ama tshika tshi ntatan nutshimit kie apu ut-tshikut-tshi pekassi-nushun eukun nitikupitsh nikanishit. Eku anutshish nitshisseniten shash nimiste tshitshipin etshissenita-man tshekuan, kie tsheishi pakassinushunan. Nin nitshisseniten eka tshissenitamen Innu pakassiun, apu tshikut nita-tshi-apastain assi. Nin mitshen tshekuan eitutaman nutshimit, nutaun kaishitshisku-tamut kie esk nikuneniten anutshish." *Kaniuekutat*

"Miste eitussenanuipan tapue mak tshitshue minu-entakunupan. Nte uipats mitikuninipan, eshiuat tshekuan, miam shiutisha, kie kutak tshekuan. Muk nutshimiu mitshim, unash mak mina nimitshitan, nikaun mak nukum nte nitshiskutamashunapan, ekussikuashuian, kie missina eushitaian mak mitasha. Niminikunan ne tshekuan tshe apastaiat tshetshi skutamashuatsheiat. Kie nitshiskutamashu-napan eiapit eshiuinitikuanut kie eshi neikuan atikuian." *Epa*

Utshen tshenut esk nete euassiuits, nastesh nte menita pitsheut pitetamit kaskutimatsheutshiuapit. Nastesh menita tshiskutamashut kie menita skuta-mashuts mishineikanu. Muk nutshimit tshetshi tat-skutamashuts. Tshenut mak kie utamuaut, eukun tshiskutamuepan utuassimuau eshiniuts kie eshi-pekassinushuts nte nutshimit. Eukun enitinanipan nte uipats. Nantim pimpini pan ne-tsheskutamashunanut tshekuan, memitshetuit ne-eishitshiskutamashu-nanuipan tshekuan eishitutakan. Napessit mushinau nitutuepan utauau kie uinuau-iskuessit nitutuepan ukauau. Tshenu etenitak tshekuanu anu ispiteni-takunu. Ustinitshut nantim nitutuepan tshenu eukunu uet-mitshenit tshekuanu nestutak.

Napessit tshiskutamuakanipan tsheitistat utassiku-manuau, kie tsheishi ushitat Innu-utinu. Iskuessit tshiskutamuakanipan tshetshi kussikuashut kie tan tsheishi neikuat kie tsheishi tshishinat nitamuk ueshishuian kie tshetshi piminuet kie tshetshi assimet-ashama, kie tshetshi missinitshet, kie miste uauitshiku-pan ukauau - napessit kie iskuessit tshiskutamashut muk etshitapamat uikanishuau mak tshenu etutamen tshekuanu kie kuet-ketshessinuapamat, eitin kie eis-sishuen. Eukunu uetshissenitak tshekuanu, euapatshet eitinanun.

"Pishakessina ni-ushitakanipan kie tan eshinakuian-its ashamits. Auas, tsheskutamuakan tshekuanu tshetshi tutak, miste-uipatsh niskutimashutan eiapit eakanut kie tshetshi—ispitenimat assit tshekuan etakuak. Kie nitispitenimatan nipit aueshish, miam namesh. Kie nitispitenimatan kassinu aueshishet. Ninitutetan eiua-nitshiskutamakunan. Shash mate kassinu tshimamishitinau, shash tshipa nitutenau tshinuau. Nas-uin-tshitshissenimitinau, tshitshue tshipa minuatenau nutshimit." *Menushkuesh mak Tshenish, Tshenut eianimuet kaskutimatsheutshiuapits*

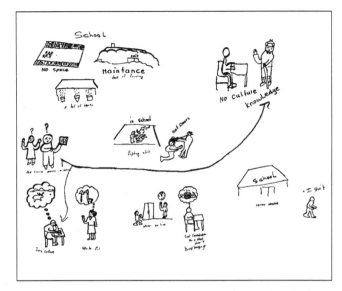

Teacher's drawing at school workshop / Innu katshisku-tamatet mamu unishinateitsheut, 1992

CHAPTER FIVE

THE SCHOOL: KASKUTIMATSHEUTSHIUAP

There are many problems with the school. The school has done a lot of damage to our culture and our children. It has really changed our lives. The school is not working as it is supposed to. The biggest problem is that our children are not learning their culture in school. They are learning the white culture. This is a foreign culture. The school has prevented us from learning our own history. Too many of our children are dropping out.

In the Old Days

"There was always work to do for children. We were taught to make snowshoes, toboggans. There were a lot of things that we had to do when I was a child. I was told once that if I didn't make something, like snowshoes or how to set up a tent, I would never be in nutshimit and would not know how to survive. That's what my parents told me. Now I know I gained a lot of experience about how to survive in nutshimit. I know if you don't have skills, you will never use the land. I did many things in nutshimit that my father taught me. I still have those skills."
Kaniuekutat, elder

"It was really a lot of work, but it was really nice at the same time. In those days, there was no junk food like candy and stuff. All we ate was wild meats and berries. I would learn stuff from my mother and grandmother: sewing and making moccasins, making socks. They would give us stuff to practise. Also we learned how to cut up the caribou and clean the skins." *Epa*

When our elders were children, they were never inside a school. They never went to school or learned from the books. They only learned to be in the country. Elders and parents were always the teachers, showing children their way of life and how to survive in nu-

tshimit. That's what used to happen before. There was a lot of teaching that went on, different stages of learning how to do things. The boys used to listen to their fathers. The girls used to listen to their mothers. Older opinions were more respected. Young people listened to their elders, and that is how they understood many things better.

The boys were taught how to trap and hunt in the country, how to build canoes. The girls were taught how to sew, how to clean and tan the animal skins, how to cook, how to fill snowshoes and make moccasins. Mothers used to help their daughters a lot. Boys and girls learned by observing parents and elders doing these things. Then they would copy them, what they did or said. Then they learned by doing things themselves and seeing what happened.

"There was moccasin-making, and how to make snowshoes. When a child was taught how to make things, they usually picked it up easily when she or he listened. We used to learn how to prepare for the mukushan and how to respect nature. In nutshimit, we respected the water habitat, the fish. We always respected the animals. We would listen and learn. You are all grown up now and you should be listening by now. I am sure you would like it in nutshimit."
Meneshkuesh and Tshenish, elders at school workshop

Our lives as kids before we were settled was not all

RAY WEBBER PHOTO

Mushuau children / Mushuau Innish, 1963

Euassiuiat, meu muk tshetshi atusseiats, nitshiskuta-mashutan kie eiapit pakassiun kie takunipan ne-tshishuk mietuiats.

"Mishiuen niteishi-metuetan, euassiunats. Nipi-pamiskatan, kie niueuepishunan mak eshunaskua-teimat, peputshi etu-minuenitakunipan, tante nishuakuetan mak nishunakuateitan. Emak-miste minuashu assi. Kie miste minuapan mitshim matshi-nat eku napatshi, nimushunan-ni." *Tshenish mak Menushkuesh*

"Nutaun ushitauni tshekuanu tshe metuatsheuk miam mate atshapina tshe apatshinimiki netui-neueutshi. Kie ushieu eiapit nutapaiaskunan tshet-shi shuakueutshit. Mitshetinanipan sheuakuanuts nas patush uetakussitshi punatsh. Tshitshue minuen-itakunuipan. Nantim takunipan tshekuan tsheishimetueiats, ushitau eiapit nutaun nishunaskua-teissina. Eku nte meskumit shunaskuateimat, nanikutini nituanan. Eukun ume itiats uet-ekatshi muestatamat, mak-at-muk tshetshi apinat. Nantim nimisketan—tshekuan tshetutamats." *Kaniuekutat*

Tshenuts Tshiuitamakunu Uipats Innu Kaish Tshiskuta-mashuntshi

"Ete uipats mitukunipan kaskutimatsheutshiuap. Apu tshiskutimashunash nteniunan nte kaskutimat-sheutshi-uapits ninan niskutimashun tsheish inniuiash mak kaish Inniuts uipats Innuts. Kaua-pukuest eapits skutimuepan auasa enku uisisenitam-ash tshetshi mishinantsheash mak tshetshi eami-taeish mishinanikan. Apisish muk nin niskuti-mashun. Apu tshisenitaman etistets nimishi-nanikan." *Tuamish*

"Pishe ninan niskutamashunaepan et Nutak. Apu tukuak kaskutimatsheutshiuap. Ueuetimish nte niskutimashunan. Miste-Kauapukuest nikaskutimat-sheminan. Tikunipan kaskuti matsheutshiuap nete kauish atukants uipats Utshimassits. Kaskutimatshet tshishue uini-tutakushiu." *Kaskutimatshet tshishue kustatenitakushu tshishue ntakunikunan mushinau*

"Apu nita tshiskutimashunan tshashikatshi tante ntatuskuaut nutaun mak nikaun. Tepiskatshi niskuti-mashun. Tshishue animenitakun. Apu minushi nas nikaskutimatsheminan. Tshishue mushinau niutamank. Pese Innuts minuenitakushu, teuts. Tshishue mushinau nimuskuanikunan. Innu Mishinanikan mak emieun niskutimakunan." *Nian mak Anishenish*

"Kamenupuniak enkun etutakunau kaskutshi, mat-sheutshiuap mak tshinan tshiskutimashunaeapan. Eku ta nta uisishipants eka minupuniak. Nte etauae kaskutimatsheutshiuapish Apunita skutimakunak kaish iniuts uipats Innuts. Enkun uesh unikuatimak kaish Inniuts tshutauinuts. Kaskutimatsheutshiuap nte ianimenitenan anuts etits ntuasiminants." *Etuetish mak Akatis.*

"Tsheskutimashunan, kaskutimatshet apu minitutu-nimish niutamanikunan tipaskunikan put kie mis-tukunu. Tshishue nimiste akunikunan. Tshishue papu niuausinakunan etaspishunats. Katshesenita-mutshishi tshesku-timunimish niutamankunan. Nashikuneu nikesapeshunea eku uetamikitshe-unimish mauats niuiuapimauts tshetshi tutuakanits ntuasiminaeets." *Niskuets Kaitusets*

Esi tukuash kaskuti-matsheutshiuap. Mitshetuts Innuts metshimushinits uta Utshimassits. Apu tshinikatats Innuts utuasimuaua ete uatatuaui nut-shimish. Tauts pise auasit uauitshimats utauaua mak akauiuaua ete kaskutimatsheutshi uapits. Mishikatu-aue ute Utshimassits apu unikeketankushits enua kutaka auasa.

Essi mishetu pupush pese tshinan apunit skutimat-tuiak tshikuspinai ete nutshimish etu eminuats tshekun tshiskutimakunaets tshikanishinuts. Mak apu animak esi skutimakuiau. Kaskutimatsheutshiuap atuseun tshi shue miskuau. Kaskutimatshets miste mitshetuau tshiuei tamakunuts tshekuanu. Tshikanish-inuts etu tshiminuskutimakunaepit tshiskutimakunuts esiniuntshi Inua. Kaskutimatshets niutamanku-

work and learning survival. There was also a lot of play time in the old days.

"We used to play all kinds of games when we were children. We used to go canoeing, swinging and skating. In the wintertime, it's more fun than in the summer because you can go sliding and skating. The land was beautiful. We ate healthy food. In the summertime, we picked berries." *Tshenish and Meneshkuesh, elders at school workshop*

"My father would make a toy for us to play with, a bow and arrow for hunting and to get some partridges. We also had a toboggan that our father made for us to slide down hills. Everybody was there sliding until evening. It was pretty fun. We always had something to play with, like my father would build skates for us. We skated on the ice. We used to play ball. These things would keep us going without getting bored or just sitting around. We always had something to do." *Kaniuekutat, Utshimassiu elder*

The First Schools

"In the old days, there was no such thing as school. We didn't learn our culture in school. We learned from our people. We educated ourselves in our culture and traditions. The priest used to teach the children as well. This is how some of us learned to read and write. I learned a little, but not much. I don't even know what grade 1 is." *Tuamish, elder*

"Some of us kids went to school in Nutak. There was no school there; we had school outdoors. Father Cyr was our teacher. We had school over in old Davis. Also, the teacher was very strict. He was very dangerous, very hard on us. He hurt us a lot." *Tent meeting with Sango Bay elders*

"I never went to school in the daytime because I worked for my father and mother. I used to go to school in the night. It was very hard. The teacher was not very good. He used to beat me up a lot. Some people say he was good. He used to make us cry a lot. Innu mishinanikan, what we learned was about the Bible." *Nian and Anishenish, elders*

"Most problems are because of the school. Like us, we went to school. That's when our problems started. When we were in school, just like today, we never learned anything about our own culture. That is why we don't live like our forefathers lived. We really blame the school for what has happened to our children." *Etuetish and Akatis*

"When I was in school, the teacher used to abuse us. He would take a ruler or stick and start beating us. We were in a lot of pain. He used to laugh and make fun at the way we dressed. When we didn't know our work, the teachers used to beat us up. A teacher used to pull down our pants and spank us on our bottoms. I don't want to see this happening to our children." *Family Violence Project*

Now, since the new school was built, more people are stuck in the community. Families can't go to the country without their children. There are kids who like to go in the country with their parents, but they are afraid they will have to repeat their grade again. They want to stay caught up with the other children. Some teachers won't let the kids go to the country with their parents.

Over the years, some of us never wanted to go to school. We wanted to go to the country, because we felt we learned better things from our parents and it was easy to learn. School work was too hard. Teachers would explain things over and over again. But our parents were better teachers. They taught us our culture. Teachers used to beat us when we didn't know what they were trying to teach. Our parents were patient. It was easy to understand the things they taught us.

"In the Mushuau Innu School before it burned down, Sister Martha used to teach us the Innu language. I think an Innu teacher should teach our language. When my late father told us about legends, this is how I learned about life in the bush. When he told us a legend, I could almost picture it in my mind. When I was young I thought legends were bedtime stories. When a person talks about life in the country or animals, then you get an idea of how the people used to live in the country." *Tumas*

"White people tell us we don't have any education. We have more education than they do, because we learn a lot of things. An elder is like a minister. He has a lot of experience in how to take care of his people. Women have a lot of education too, because they know how to do a lot of traditional things, like how to treat the caribou skin, how to sew and so on." *Band Council interview*

There are some of us in the community who have no complaints about the school, some who feel that the

naepints ketshenitamutshishi enu tsheshutiminimish nikanishinants uinuau niminitutakunant mak tshetshiue nesenitamuanan enu tshiskutimunimis.

"Ete Mushuau Innu Kaskutimatsheutshiuapish esk ekaniskuatets siste mata skutimatshepan Innu mishinanikanu. Ntenimau nin Innu kaskutimatshet tshipa skutimatsheu Innu munu. Nutapun natinusetshi, ekun uisisenitaman nte etenitakuash nutshimish. Natininushetshi ni mamitinenitamuan nte nistukuanish miam euapatamuts kuetenitamuts. Atinukuants ntenitenapan tshetshi muk nipemakants auasits. Innu unauitatshi nte nutshimish mak auesisha enuesit tshiseneten kaish itet Innu nete nutshimish." *Tumas*

"Kauapishits tshi uitamakunuts eka nastesh miste skutimashuau. Tshimiste skuti mashunan tante mitshet tshekuan tshisenetenan. Tshenuts ekun nas mestesenitas miste utshimau tshipa itenitakushuts. Tshisenitam tshetshi naka tuenimat utinima. Niskueuts eapits miste senitamuts tante senitamuts kaenitintshi uipats Innu, mak esh minukuakanitshi attik mistekuea. Mak tshetshi kusikuashuts. Mitshet kutak tshekuanu. Tshitutamuts." *Innut Utshimauts*

Passe Innuts uta Utshimassits mui nisishueuts tshikuanu etukakanits nte kaskutimatsheutshiuapits. Passe ntenitamuts nuitshinukunan kaskutumatsheutshuiap. Passe Innuts ntenitamuts tshuitshinikunan kaskutima-tsheutshuap tshetshi minusentamau kakeshau eni-shinuit. Tshetshi miste nistutuau kakeshau unauitakants assin mak ka uiatukuants. Passe Innuts ntenitamu kaskutimatsheutshiuap nanikutini tshuitshinikunan eskutimashunaui.

"Mue kaskutimatsheutshuiap nuitshinukun tshetshi minusenitaman asin espin mak eshinakuats. Tshuitshinukuna tshetshi minu senitamak eskutimashunau." *Kaskutimatshet*

"Ueskats tshashipinants eskutamashunants kauapukuest skutamuepan auasa. Tshash une tshishipaanishipan kaskutimatsheutshiuapinu kanakatuepatas uatshiats kapukueshintshi. Nte kaskutimatsheutshiuap ueshitakants nte natukuants. Ne usikaskutimatsheutshiuap ishinikatepan Mushuau Innu Kaskutimatsheutshiuap. Minau eshinikatets kaskutimatsheutshuap, tshinan tante Mushuau Innuts kie tshinan mue stesinan. Eukun mue uish nishinikatets kaskutimatshet. Minuenitakun mamu

eatuseats. Niminueniten uatshitusemukuau kutakuts Innuts uta Utshimassits. Kuet niskuatet kaskutimatsheutshuap. Minita senitenan uetsh niskuatet." *Manteskueu*

Skutimatshetau Ushinan Stiniunu Nte Kaskutimatsheutshi Uapits

"Uipatsh nte, tshiskutamakunanapan ete uaiu tshekuan nastesh minita peten tshekuan eshinakuats muk eshinikatets, enauitamakunan nte kaskutimatsheutshuapits. Kaskutematshetsh skutamueuts auasa enishinakunits espitaskamakants assinu, mak kanitupunanits, mak nitamuk aueshisha ete uaiu enishinakushintshi. Tan tshipa nishiuitshinikunan enua tshekuaia ete eatisits tsheskutimakunau?" *Innu Nation Kaianumet*

"Ntemauts auasits tshishue ama nistutakuts. Aneminu-kuts ninu eshaianimueuts. Nipetuauts auasits kake-shaunikatamuts tshikuanu uauitakaui. Nuiuapamauts tshikuanu uauitakaui. Nuiuapamauts auasits tshetshi senitats uipats kaishiniunanits, tshishue tshipa minuanu tshi senitats. Unitauaue uipatsh kaishiniunau mak esha-ianimueau nesk tshika unitanan tshikatshitau auen tsheskutamatau. Auasit kapishisutshi nipetustakuts mishinanikanu nte kaskutimatsheutshuapits manakanits tshishue minuenitamuts pinetataui misenitamuts nenu kaskutimatsheutshiuapinu tsheunikuenikuts. Tsheunitats uipat kaishiniunanits. Nenu kaskutamuakanutshi nte kaskutimatsheutshuapits kakeshaua nu utiniunu. Eskunte tshika senitamuts auasits tshekuanu tshesenitats mak tshekuan uenitat nte kaskutimatsheutshuapits. Tshika senitamuts nenu esiunitats utiniunuau." *Kanieukutat*

Metukuea mishinanikea Innuts uipatsh kanishiniuts Innu. Kaskutimatshets uinuau tutamuts mishinanikea. Mishinanikea petishanikanua nte Sheshatshiu mak nete Unamenshipish, utishanikanua muk mishuk nistunimuts mak mishuka nistutamuts. Atinamuts enua etistentshi kanestutas. Astauts nte muk kie esk petipetishanikanua.

"Minisenimauts esi minakanits Innu. Kaskutimatshets tshetshi skutimatshets Innu-aimunu. Pashish put minakanitshentshi. Eukun ntutakunapan esk tsheskutamatshean. Apishish tshishue niminukun tshetshi skutamatshean Innu-aimun, mintispishin

school has helped them. Some people think the education we get from the school is very important because we need it to keep up with white society. For example, we need education for land claims negotiations and for relocation. Some of us think there have been times when the school has worked better than at other times.

"This school has taught us about the world around us, both pros and cons. It has helped us to get a better look on life with a proper education." *Innu teacher*

"When school was first started, the priest was the one who used to teach the children. This is when I found out that the school board was helping the priest. That is when the school was built at the new site of Davis Inlet. The new school was named Mushuau Innu School. This was a good name for our school because we are Mushuau Innu and this is our land. That is how the school got its name. I started working at the new school. The principal asked me to come and work. It was good when we worked. Then another person came and a third principal was hired. We liked working together. It was great working with other people from the village. Then the school burned down. We never knew how the fire started." *Manteskueu*

Teaching Our Own Culture in School

"In the past, we were like foreigners in the school. The school taught us everything that we never saw or heard of before. The teachers teach our children about the universe, wars and animals from other countries. What is the good of these things for us?" *Innu Nation interview*

"I talk to young people, but they don't seem to understand. The language I use is hard for them. I often hear the children name things in English. I want the children to learn our way of life. This is very important. If our culture and our language is lost, there is nowhere in the world where it can be found. My younger children sometimes bring a kind of paper to me from school. They are really proud. I guess they don't really know the school can make them lose their own culture. Whatever they learn in school is white man's ways. I guess one day the children will find out what they have gained and what they have lost from the school. They will learn that they have lost more than gained." *Kaniuekutat*

Father Frank Peters was also the teacher / Miste-Peters eiapits kaskutimatshueu, 1963

There are no books on Innu culture. Innu teachers have to do it themselves. They get books from Sheshatshiu or La Romaine, but it is really hard for them to understand. They have to change the words they can't understand. Many times Innu teachers just put the books away and don't even bother to use them at all. But the books keep coming anyway.

"I don't know how much time the teachers' aides are given to teach Innu-aimun. They probably are given only a few minutes. That is what I went through when I taught school. I was always given so little time to teach Innu-aimun, I didn't have enough time to teach what I wanted to. When I taught at the school, the students behaved very well and they listened too. But since I have not been teaching at the school, the students don't seem to listen to their teachers any more. Maybe the teachers aren't teaching the students very well by not explaining to them about the subjects they are learning." *Manteskueu*

"The school is only teaching English to the older students. I am learning how to write English and I am getting better every day. The saddest thing is that I can't even write in my own language." *High school student*

Our Innu teachers should make more of our own books in Innu-aimun. They need the help of the elders to start these Innu books. They need supplies to make these books for our school. Someone came to the school once and said we could make our own books.

RAY WEBBER PHOTO

uanishiskutamatshean. Tsheskutamatsheani, tshishue nitutamuts tsheskutamukuaui. Esi punan nte kaskutimatsheutshuapits, tshishue minututueuts kaskutimatshemuaua. Put uinuau kaskutimatshets mitshi minu uauitamuetshentshi auasa nenu tshekuan uaskutamuats." *Manteskueu*

"Kaskutimatsheutshuapits auasit kamamishitits muk kakeshamunu skutamuakanuts. Niskutamakun tshetshi kakeshaustaian tshishue tshash nikashiun ekakeshaustaian. Ume muk uestuenitaman mintshi innustai ne eshaianimuiean." *Kaskutimashut Auash*

Innu kaskutamatshets shipaushitauts mishinanikea tshipa innustauts. Tshipa uitshinukuts katsheniunuani Innua ushitats mishinanikea. Tshipa ntuenitakanua mishinanikea tshe apatshitats. Peik auen petutepan nte kaskutamatsheutshuapits eku ntukunan tshipa ushitanau tshimishinanikanuaua. Peik Innu ute Utshimassits mak nte Sheshatshit tshipa utinakanu tshetshi uitshatusemats Innu kaskutamatshentshi tshetshi ushitats Mishinanikea tshetshi Innu stentshi nenu Mushua eimunu. Innu Utshimauts tshipa ui ntuenitamuts shuneanu nenu tshetshi uitshiakanitshi Innu kaskutamatshentshi.

Kaskutimatshetshiup skutimueu auasa akineshau metuan. Minuenitamuts auasits tsheskutamuakantaui uipatsh kanishimetuanits anutshish nastesh masenitamuts auasit uipatsh kanishimetuanits. Eskuenua tukuea uipatsh kanish imetueintsh, muk mitau uen tshipa skutamatsheu.

"Stuasiminuts kakeshaua eshiniuntshi. Uenishinatantsheau atik tshimanituneniman, kaskutamatshets mamitunenimeu katshinuakuentshi "GIRAFFE." Skutamuakanuts auasits aueshisha nte AFRICA kaishinikatenua nte kamisits. Matukunu tshenishinikatauts ntshe aueshishats nte kamisits. Auasits unikuateuts kanishinikatakanitshe aueshisha nte nutshimits." *Innu Kaskutimatshets Nete Kaskutimasheutshiuapits*

Ninan nituassiminantsh tshipa-ui-tshiskutamashut kaishiniutshit, kie kaishi-tshissentamutshit, kie eatinutshanun, entuiunanun, kie enutimeshanun kie eshi-tshissinuastat Innu tshekuanu, kie eshi-mititakan aueshish, kie nenu ueshish tepenimukut kie eshi-pakunan aueshish, kie epashiken maniun kie tan eshi-nakatuentakantau uskea. Kie nituassiminan

tshipa-ui-tshissentamut nenu ntu-iu-assi nte nimushumpinantsh kapimutet kie tshekuan apastakanipan napitshi, pemutanut kie atamutsh eapatshiakanit pepunetshe. Kie tshipa tshiskutamashut Innu uta tshetshi ushitat, ashama, pishakiessia, kie kutakanu Innu atusseunu. Kie tshipa-ui-tshissentamut nenu Innu kaishi metuen. Kie nitenimanan nituassiminan tshetshi tshissentak tshetshi ispitenimat tshenu, kie eshiniutshit kie kassinu aueshisha. Tshitshue ume miste itenitakun, tshetshi tshissentak auassit! Tshenut umenu tshipa tshiskutamueut auassa uipats kaishiniunanun. Metauts nte tshenut tshetshi tshiskutamatshet nte katshiskutamatsheutshiuapit. Tshitshue miste ispitenitakushut tshenuts.

Nishinakun Tshetshi Minu Skutamashunau

"Tshikustenan tshetshi ka senitamauk an eshi skutamakunak enkun aiash ues nispininukunak." *Innu Kaskutamatshet*

Tshuiuapamanut stuasiminuts tshetshi nistutats kakeshamunu mak tshetshi minu sentats uipats kaishiniunanuts. Mitshetuts auasit puniskutamashuts tshe anamenitamuts ninu kakeshamunu. Nishua eshaianimueau INNU-AIMUN mak KAKESHAMUN, animenitamuts meni Innu uasits. Kaskutamatshets misenimeuts auasa esi animenitamin tshi nenu kakeshaua mushinanikanu, mitshetuts kaskutimatshets tsheuenimiats auasa katshesesenitamintaui mak kanestutakutaui. Auasits kusteuts kaskutamatshemuaua. Auasits tshipa skutamuakanuts tshetshi minututuats uitshiniuaua tshipa uitshaiuts stiasiminuts tshetshi eka puniskutamashuts. Auasit kamamishitutshi mishuka senitamuts mak mashuka minuskutamuakanuts. Tshishuskutamashuts muk esk eapits senitamuts nenu tshikuanu kaskutamakuts kauapishintshi kaskutimatshentshi.

"Kaskutamuakantaue auasits uipatsh kaishiniunanuts, tshi nishunu put kie nistunu pupunitshe, stuasiminuts muk kakeshamunu tshika nishaianimuents nte katutshi Innuts ute Kanata. Passe tshash auasits misenitamuts tshetshi inustats utishinikashunuaua mak kutak tshekuan, mitshetuts Innuts tshashitats eskutamashuts, muk esk neaneu put peiukusteu etipitaui ntenitakushuts. Tshishue etitash tshitutamuts mishinanikanu ieamishinantshetaui. Nuiuapaten tshetshi etu skutamuakanits auasits nenu uipats kaishiniunanuts. Skuta-

Someone from Utshimassit should be hired to work in Sheshatshiu with other Innu teachers to make our own books and translate the ones they do into Mushuau aianimuan. The Band Council should look for more funding for the Innu teachers.

The school teaches the children white man's games. We could make our children happy by teaching them our traditional games. Right now, the children don't know about our traditional games. Those games are still with us, but nobody is teaching them.

"Our children are taught about other cultures. In our drawing, the child is thinking about the caribou; the teacher is thinking about the giraffe. We teach about animals in Africa. There are no Innu names for these animals. The children are forgetting the Innu names for animals in nutshimit." *Innu teachers at Nukum Mani Shan School*

Our children need to learn about our traditions and spirituality, about legends, hunting, fishing, about how to read the signs and track down the animals, about animal spirits, how to clean the animals, dry the furs, and about how to take care of the bones. Our children should learn about our hunting grounds, where our grandparents used to walk, and how we used to travel in the summer and by dog teams in the winter. They should learn to make canoes, snowshoes, moccasins and other crafts. They should learn our own traditional games. We want our children to learn how to respect OUR ELDERS, OUR CULTURE AND THE ANIMALS. THIS IS VERY IMPORTANT! Our children need to learn from our elders about the old ways. We don't have elders teaching in the school. Our elders are so important.

We Need a Good Education

"We are afraid to fail, and that has changed us." *Innu teacher*

We want our children to learn English as well as our own culture. But many of our students quit school because the English books are very difficult to understand or even learn. English is our second language. This is hard for Innu students. Some teachers don't seem to understand how hard it is for the children to learn the white books. Too many teachers get angry

when our children don't understand. The students are afraid of the teachers. Children need to be taught things like respect in school. We have to help our children stay in school. Our high school students are not learning very much. They graduate and they still don't know the things that they are supposed to learn from the white teachers.

"If the school doesn't teach our children our culture, in twenty to thirty years' time, our children will speak only English like in other places in Canada. Some of our children cannot even write their own names in their own language. Another thing, some people finish high school, but it is like they are in grade 8 or 9. They can hardly write a letter. I would like to see more teaching of the Innu way of life. This is like an education and it is better. If a child knows about life in the country, that is like she or he finished university." *Shuash*

"In school, we don't get a good education." *High school student*

"I have only seen a few students finish high school. What do they get? Nothing. There are no jobs, just drinking. The school has very big problems." *Shushepmak and Mani Katini*

"Children don't want to go to school. I think it is too hard for the children because it's mostly English. I think it must be hard for the children to understand. My son doesn't want to go to school. I keep sending him. He told me he doesn't understand the books and the work he is asked to do. He says the teacher will get mad at him if he doesn't know what to do." *Miste-Shishin, elder*

The school is too small; we need more classrooms. The children need to learn music and art. We need a classroom for art. The children only learn from books. They are bored with the books and need other things. Students need to learn how to ask about things. They need to learn life skills, things like sewing and knitting. We need a homemaker to teach the children how to cook. Half of the kitchen now is used as a classroom.

Our Children Need Help

Many children cannot listen and learn anything because they have too many problems. It is not good for the teachers either, because if the children are not listening, they are not learning anything. Children have their

mashuts nenu itenitakunu kie etu minuanu. Auas eskutamuakant nte nutshimit tshekuanu, miam tshash tshashiskutamashutshi nte ka miste skutamakunanits itenitakushu." *Shuash*

"Kaskutamatsheutshuapits nte mitshi miniskut." *Kaskutimashut Auash*

"Passe muk nuapamauts auasits tshashitats eskutamashuts. Tshekuanu kanastinats? Tsheska. Matukunua atuseuna, muk minanu shitakunapun tshishue mishau tshekuan metshipininukunau nte kaskutamatsheutshuapits." *Shushepmak kie Mani Katini*

"Auasit mui skutamashuts. Anamenitamuts nenu kakeshamunu. Nikus nui skutamashuts mushinau ntishauau kaskutamatsheutshuapits. Miniseniten ne mishinanikan mak eshiskutamakunan ntuk Nikatshuenemuk kauapishits kaskutamatshet ka senitamutshe enu etishumit." *Miste-Shishin*

Apishashu kaskutamatsheutshuap. Auasit tshipa skutamuakanuts tshetshi nikamuts mak tshetshi unishinatantshets. Tshipa ushitakanu nte auasits tsheunishinatantshets. Muk mishinanikea, kutakunu nte tshekuanu tshipa uitutamuts. Tshipa uitamuts auasit tshikuanu uapitshitataui mak uatutakaui. Nishinakunu tshetshi skutamashuts uipats kaishiniunanuts, nenu kakuskuashunanut mak kasimatanikanua. Tshipatau auen tshetshi skutamuat auasa tsheniishipiminuentshi. Kapiminieutshuap nte kaskutamatsheutshuapits pusk kaskutamashunants ntapatshitakanu.

Stuasiminuts Uiuitshinikushiuts

Mitshetut auasits eka natutakuau kie eka tshisentakuau tshekuanu mak mishenu tshekuanu kamenupanikutsh apu minuantsh kie kaskutimatshetsh mak auasitsh nastesh eka natutas natesh misenitamutsh tshekuanu. Auasitsh tshekuanu kamenupaniktsh etu mishanu nte tamits. Ama tshi ueuetishinamuts kuet mista tshuapits nte atamits. Ama tshinakatamutsh tshekuanu kamenupanikuts nete uitshuats kie apu tshipetustat nete kaskutimatsheutshiuapit. Uinauau ama senimeutsh uinauau ama seninitamuts tshentutets. Kaskutimatshets ama uitsheuts nastesh muk tshuenimeuts, nanikutini auas kastinakanu nete ut ukauia put utauia kie nte kaskutimatshentshi akunu umenu auasits uish punitats kaskutimatsheutshiuapinu ama tanua uenua tsheuitshinukuts.

Ninan nu uintuapmanan uen mestisenitak tshetshi uitshiat nete kaskutimatsheutshiuapitsh. Tshetshi uitshiat auasa nenua kamenupanitshi nete uitshuat put kie nte kaskutimatsheutshiuapits. Ntshe auasits ntuapmeuts uenua tshenatutakuts. Mak tshetshi tantshi kaskutimatsheutshiuapit put kie tshetshi emiat nenu tshekuanu kamenupanit ama nisenitamuanan mishiue tshekuanu kamenupanits auasits etatash uinuau, nu uiuitimakushiuanan. Kaskutimatshets tshetshi emiakanits kie uinuau. Tshuenimeutsh auasa.

Nastesh memenupanu usham mitshetuts auasits puniskutamashuts. Ama minispanu nenu uaishiskutamashut nete kaskutimatsheutshiuapit pase unitauts nenu tshekuanu kaskutimatsheutshiuapits, kie kaskutimatshets natesh muuitsheuts kie pase auasits tshishitauts kaskutimashuts kie pase misenitamuts tshe ntutets.

Mitsheau auasits miste ueshamiputsh put kie uinitshi-nikuaua menatshi kie ama mitshuts tshietshepapanitshi. Pase tshitshue uinipauts kie shiuenutsh. Mak mitshi minuskutimashut tshatsh mitshunanu ntshe uasits kaiapishishishits nte espish neu kaitapits. Nu uintueni-tenan mishiue auasits tshetshi mitshuts.

Mieu muk shitakunapun tshetshi atamenitakants, pase Innuts mitshetinua auasa ekunu neush piminueu tshetshepaninitshi. Ekunu uet Ueshamipits. Muk tapitshitan mita kapunikantshi katshapistesh. Kie matakun nipi kie takaua mitshuapa ekun kamenupant. Kie tshishue neush apu tshitshi tetshi mitshuapa aispishits tshetshi mitshuts tshetshepapanitshi. Kie apu uiueshamitshits. Put kie tshitentsh mitshuapinu kie takunits nipinu nte uitshuats. Auasits mushinau tshikatauts nta nau skuetimashunantshi. Auasits tshika tshi uapekaushutsh nete kaskutimatsheutshiuapits kie itshikaminakanuts kashikueuna nete ut kaskutimatsheu-tshiuapits.

Nu Uiuapamanta Kamiste Skutimashuts Kie Kamiste Senitatsh Kaskutimatshetsh

Nte kamiste senitats kaskutimatshet ute kaskutimatsheutshiuapits mishetuts ute kaskutimatshets natshi skutamashuts kie pase misenitamuts eshapepanits kaskutimatsheutshiuapinu pase skutimatsheuts ute kaskuti matsheutshiuapits kie pase miam auasa kuetenitakushits, skutimatsheuts kuet pushitsh.

Innu kaskutimatshets minita natshiskutamashuts utshimau kaskutimatshet neteu kie kukuetshimat

CAMILLE FOUILLARD PHOTO

Shanutish, 1993

problems bottled up inside; they can't get them out. They have too much anger inside of them; they can't leave their problems at home and they can't bring them to school. They don't know who they can go to. Teachers don't help them. They only get angry at them. Sometimes the child is caught in the middle between the parents and the teachers. This is why some kids quit school. They don't have anyone to go to.

We need an experienced guidance counsellor in the school to help the children with their problems at home or at school. The children need someone to listen to them. They need counselling, someone to keep them in school and talk with them about their problems. We don't know all the problems children have. We need for them to tell us. The teachers need counselling too because they get mad at the students.

Another problem is that many of our students are dropping out. They are not directed in what they want to learn in school. They lose interest in school, and the teachers are not helping them. Some students finish high school, but they don't know where to go from there.

Many times children are late for school because the parents are drinking, and they come with no breakfast. They are too sleepy and hungry. They can't concentrate. There is breakfast for kindergarten to grade 4. We need breakfast for all the children.

We can't blame it all on alcohol. Some people have a big family. It takes a while to cook the breakfast. That's why they are late. We only have wood stoves. Having no water and cold houses is a problem. It takes a long time to heat our homes in the morning. Our children don't have time to eat their breakfasts. They don't want to be late. If the houses could stay warm at night, and if there was water in the houses, the children would be on time at school. The children should also be able to take showers in the school, and the school should provide towels.

We Need Trained and Experienced Teachers

We should have qualified teachers in our school. Many of our teachers are just out of university and they have no experience in how our school works. They start teaching in our school and some of them seem just like kids too. They train here and then they leave.

Innu teachers never went to university. The principal comes to them and offers them a teacher's aide job. They don't know what to do when they enter the classroom. They are not ready.

> "When I started the job, the principal told me to make breakfast. Then I was taken into the classroom and handed some books. After school, I had to wash the floor like a janitor. My pay was very low. I never had any training. I have asked about taking university courses, but no one listens. This will be my final year for teaching." *Innu teacher*

Some people wonder if the teachers' aides know about the kinds of things they are teaching the students. They think the only good thing they can do is to help the teachers. But many of us think our teachers' aides have more experience and are more qualified to teach our children than the teachers. They do the work because the children don't speak English and don't understand what they are being taught. But the white teachers get paid more.

Innu teachers have been in these teaching jobs long enough. The school board was asked a long time ago for university courses. We were told there would be courses here in Davis Inlet. The teachers' aides don't know why they have never gotten any training, or why they have not had more action on this from the principal. Recently, the principal did ask for teacher's aide

tshetshi uauitshiantshi kaskutimatshentshi natesh misenitamuts tshetutats tshekuanu ueskats pase-taui nete kaskutimatshe utshiuapit esk eka senitakau shuka.

> "Ueskatsh tshashipanan etusean utshimau kaskutimatshet nu uitamak tshetshi piminueuts tshetshepapinits kuet ntu staian nete kaskutimashuts utinuash kie niminuei mishinanikea. Katshi shiskutimashunants, nistspautai pipitshitikuts mian ne kaminastashut. Kie ama nita natshi skutamashun. Nu uiten uaskutimashunan kie nastesh ama nitutakun. Anush kapunua ekun masten tshe skutamatshean." *Innu Kaskutimatshet*

Pase Innuts ntenitamuts nenu Innu-kaskutimatshets etu senitamuts mishiue eshinakunits skutimueuts auasa. Ntenitamuts anu minuau tshekuan tshetutamats tshetshi uitshitshits kaskutimatshets. Kie nimitshetinan etenitamats, Innu kaskutimatshets etu senitamuts kie miste skutamashuiats tshetshi skutamutshit auasitskie mak akaneshau kaskutimatshets muk tutamuts utatuseunuau mak auasits ama tshiakaneshamatsh kie minis-tutamuts akeneshamunu eitakantaui. Muk akaneshau kaskutimatshet etu uinuau miste tshishishiuakanutsh.

Innu kaskutimatshets tshash uipatsh skutimatsheuts. Kanakatuapatats kaskutimasheutshiuapinu uipatsh uitamuakanipants tshetshi takunits kaskutimashunants, ute Utshimassits Innu kaskutimatshets misenitamuts uetsh katakunits kaskutimashunanitsh kie tshekuanu eutsh katutakanitsh tshetshi miste skutimashuts.

Innu kaskutimatshets skutimashupants tshetshi ushitats mishinanikeia enu tshetshi nustentshi. Nish Innu kaskutimatshets espinipants nete Uenameushipu ninaneu tatupunitshe shash esi skutamashuts emeunu, tshishue minuapan mak tshishue miste senitamupants esk enua tatamuts mishinanikeaia mak mushinau apatshitauts, ekunu ne muk nika esipushits.

Innu kaskutimatshets ntenitamuts nastesh mana kateunitakanu tshekuan etinashit nanikutini minuanu etenitats mak tshakaishipipinu kasku timatsheutshiuapinu muk apu tat auen tshenatutuat. Put ents pepinitats kaskutimatsheutshiuapinu ministuapameuts enua Innu kaskutimatshetshi kaishuitamatsheshits ishitapakanuts. Innu kaskutimatsheshits ntenitamuts muk kakeshau kaskutimatshets uaitinashi tshekuanu

ente kaskutima-tsheutshiuapish mushinau tapuetuakanu peikuau kake-shau uiskutamakushipan Innu aimunu nastesh ama anushituakanu. Peik Innu kaskutimatshet skutamuepan.

Kaskutimatshets Nutshikuepant Ntuasiminaia

Mishetitpants Innuts tsheshuapits, tante pishe kaskutimatshets kie pitutshimau kaskutimatshet utamauepants auasa kaskutimashutshi. Nastesh minuats manauiuapateia tshetshi timikash. Auasits tshaka tshi senitamuts utamautuaue kaskutimatshetshi, auasits pase punu skutimashupants tante mushinau utamakuts kaskutama-tshetshi, ekun eku tshika punipanu auasits etutuakanits.

> "Nistu pupunitshe en kaskutimatshet ueta mauat nishima, astatukupieu nta uapinekash kuet puskustikua-ishimeu mak nishim ututshiu peikush e utamaut kaskuti-mashushintshi, mishetuts auasits puniskutimashuts tante ekue muk estuat." *Utshimassiu Iskueu*

> "Tshisiten kaskutimatshet nutamakupant nte kaskutimutsheutshiuapish nishunu ashu neu tatu puneshin. Kutshi tapan enu uanishiskutimut kuet utamaut tante manasenitamuau ua nishiskutimut. Nutmakunaiapants kaskutimatshets esk ente kue puniskutimashunan tante nikustaishinapan manaseni teispan kakeshau mishinanikan." *Niskueuts Kaitusets Utshimassin iskueu*

Niskuesits mak napesits ntun nitutakupants uipats kaskutimatshetshi mak usteshimuauts, tsha ka tshinista tshiuni kuatikanu, katakanu ne pase tenitamuts Innuts. Mishetupuna nui animuekatamupants katshi petamash ne Mount Cashel Inquiry.

Kaskutimatshets muk uaetats auasa eteuts maiatshimeuts kie mak uaushinuueuts, kustineuts tshetshi ntutetshi nte mishiutshiuapits.

> "Kaskutimatshets peikuau kustineshipan nte tshetshi tutetshi mishiutshiuapish ntanish pumukuuipan tshash. Kauinakuta Mishiunakan Teshipan." *Utshimassiu iskueu*

Pase kuamuauts mak utamauts mak nukumiats mak nimushumiats ueuetepants auasa nte kaskutimatsheutshiuapish tante estuakanitshi enua auasa, pase uitamuepants utshimau kaskutimatshet tshetshi uitshinikuts mak pase mishinamuepants enua pepinitantshi kaskutimatsheutshiuapinu. Utshimau kaskuti-

courses from the university. We were told there is no funding.

Innu teachers also need workshops to help them make books in Innu-aimun. Two teachers' aides went to La Romaine eight years ago to learn about religion. It was very good, and they learned so much. They still have those books and use them all the time. That was the only time they ever went anywhere.

Innu teachers feel like nobody cares about what they do. Sometimes they have good ideas about how the school should be run, but no one listens. Maybe the school board doesn't even recognize the teachers' aides. People just see them as interpreters. Innu teachers feel when white teachers want something new in the school, the answer is always yes. Once the white teachers wanted to learn the Innu language. There was no problem. One of the teachers' aides was chosen to teach them.

Teachers Abuse Our Kids

Many people are angry because some teachers, including the vice-principal, beat up on students. We don't want to see this happening any more. Children won't learn if teachers beat them. Students quit because of beatings from teachers. This has got to be stopped.

"I remember three years ago a teacher beat up on my brother. He pushed him against a brick wall and bumped his head. My brother had a bruise. This same teacher beat up on other students. Many students quit school because of him." *Gathering Voices participant*

"I also remember a teacher beat me up in school. I am twenty-four years old. He was trying to show me how to do my school work. He started to beat me because I didn't know what he was trying to teach me. The teachers were beating us up. Later, I quit school because I was too afraid. I couldn't understand the white schoolbooks." *Family Violence Project*

Girls and boys have been sexually abused by former teachers and brothers. These things can never be forgotten. Some people think these abuses have been covered up. For many years, people didn't want to talk about these things, until we heard about the Mount Cashel inquiry.

Teachers also call the students names, using bad language and swearing at them. They say whatever they like to the children. Some teachers won't let the children go to the washroom when they need to. Some teachers make fun of the students and laugh at them.

"The teacher once told my daughter not to go to the washroom. My daughter started her period. He told her not to use the toilet and that she would make it too dirty." *Family Violence Project*

Some parents and grandparents have taken their children out of school because of these abuses. Some people have asked principals to help and others have written to the school board. Principals and the superintendent don't do anything. The teachers are never removed. They should not be in the school.

Too Much Fighting in the School

There is a lot of fighting both inside and outside the school. Children fight with each other, teachers fight with the children and the janitor and vice-principal fight with people too. Sometimes there is too much gossip spread amongst the staff.

The children are fighting because they have too many problems. Something is bothering them, and that is why they are fighting like that. The children learn from adults as well. They see adults fighting and they start doing the same thing. If we had a guidance counsellor, the children could go to her and talk about what is really bothering them. Sometimes the teachers don't say anything to the kids when they fight. When Innu children and white children are fighting, teachers seem to always blame the Innu kids. This is not helping our children.

"The school is not working right because many of our children are against each other. I don't want any of my grandchildren hurt by other children. This is why I take my grandchildren away from school. In the country, my grandchildren are happy and free. They work as much as we do. They cut wood, pick boughs for the tent floor. They do everything for us. At the same time, they are learning their culture. Sometimes I have to tell them how we used to live in the country. They learn other things. That is exactly how I want to see them be." *Shenum, elder*

matshe mak kapipinita kaskutimatsheutshiuapinu minista utamupants tshekuanu kena minista nikatishinakanuts na kaskutimatshets. Matsha katshitetauts kaskutimatsheutshiuapish.

Miste Nutshikatunanu Nte Kaskutimasheutshiuapish

Tshishue nutshikatunanu nte pitikimish mak ueuetimish nte kaskutimatsheutshiuapish. Auasits nutshikatuts, kaskutimashets, pitutshimau kaskutimatshet, kaministashuts nutshiueuts auasa innua. Mushinau miste pupukumakanuts kaituseshits.

Auasits nutshikatuts tante apu minupunits takun tshekuanu manamitinenitimuskakuts ekun enu uishinutshikatuts stauapatsheuts auasits nutshikatunanitshi kuet ekunu enu etits, tat kauitshat auasa auasits tshakanateuts tshika uitamueuts enu tshekuanu manamatanenitamuskakuts nanikutini kaskutimatshet mastuteuts auasa nutshikatutshi Innu auasa mak puskustikushut nutshikashutuaui. Kaskutimatshet enua shukuaui atam Euni muets Innu auasa nastesh enu muuitshi nikuts ntuasiminants.

> "Kaskutimatsheutshiuap nastesh minuau eshipipint tante mishetuts stuasiminuts unakashanatuts nin apu uiuapamakua nusimits tshetshi akuaits auasa, ekun enu uishuini katishinikuau nte kaskutimatshe utshiuapish, ete nutshimits nusimits tshishue minuenitamuts mak nastesh mutinminikuts tshekuanu, kuesi atusets esi atuseeutshi, ni kuteuts maiatshiteuts, mishiue tinitutakunaiats. Peik nush enu kaskutimashuts eshi niutshits nete nutshimits kutakunu tshekuanu tshiskutimashuts ekun enu nas uanishuapamakau utetas." *Shenum*

Kaskutimatshets Mesenitamuts

"Frank Peters uapatinepen auasa kashetshimakan tshi enua kaupaisha mak kautatshapintshi. Nuapatinikunaipan enua kautatshapintshi kamenu shintshi mak kakananiutshi, kaupuaishits mushinau kaniuipants." *Innut Utshimauts*

Nimishetinan ninan ute Utshimassits. Me skue nitamash tante kakeshau kaskutimatshet ama nistutueu tante kakeshau kaskutimatshet ama nistutueu Innua mak pisenimeu eshi niuntshi, takunikunaiats ushamikats mishau ua kashinatun mak auasits eapits ke kake shau kaskutimatshets.

En tenitakun kakeshau kaskutimatshets nastesh mapitenitamuts kaskutimatsheutshiua pinu espinits, nanikutini tsheska stuteuts auasa nish muk tshekuanu mineuts tshetshi nue nisishuet auasa ehe kaetutatshi tshekuanu.

Kutak tshekuan kamenupants en kaskutimatshets put kie utshimau kaskutimatshet etakunitshi auasa kemenupunitshi mineuts mishinanikanu tshetshi minatshi unitshinikuaua mishinamuepants enu auasa unitshinikuaua, nanikutini pikupitam auasa mishinanikanu esk eka takushint uitshiuats tenimeu utshimau kaskutimatshet uin tshika mineu enua auasa unitshinikuaua, put ke kaskutimatshet tshipanatuapameu enua unitshinikuaua.

"Pase kaskutimatshets uakashinuets auasa eta spishuntshi. Peik kaskutimatshet uashatusemek uakashamameu auasa tante apu minuaspishuntshi nimitshenitamuan katshi nisishuet. Takunikuaua enu esishuet tante nintsh nitshinuts mak nin tuasimits uauats matshi uapekaue enua auasa ntauni enua Innua kaskutimatshetshi tishumeuts, etenimeuts kaskutimatshets enua auasa uinakushuts tenimeuts, tshika uisenitamuts kaskutimatshets enu katekunits nipinu mak katekuntshi mishiunakeia nte Innu uitshinit nte peikua kaskutimatsheutshiuapish napeu kaskutimatshet Ntekupen tan kasi taspishunaua etaspishut kaskutimatsheshiskueut. Nishakuenimunuk katshi eshit tante tikupa uinakueia mak nastesh ama minuaua, tshika uiakueia mak nastesh ama minuaua, tshika uinakueia mak nastesh ama minuaua, tshika nakatuenitamuts kaskutimatshets esishutui." *Innu Kaskutimatshi*

Kaskutimatshets Miste Minuts

"Utshimau kaskutimatshet peikuaun takupan. Unauitamuat enua kaskutimatshentshi. Innua eshi niuntshi mak eshi pipinitshi mineshipan enu shuminapunu utitipatshimustuat." *Utshimassiu napeu*

Pase kaskutimatshets uta etats tshishue miste minuts, auasits animekateuts kaskutimatshetshi menitshi. Kaskutimatshets matshikauatishiuts nuapameiats kaskutimatshets ueutinas thenisishuets takushinai esishuets ni uestamashiutuaui, tshi uapamamaiats kaskutimatshets menits, kuet matenitats nanikutin maskutimatsheuts tante matenitamupants ni te utakushits, nastesh manakuatutinan uta Utshimassits niuts.

CAMILLE FOUILLARD PHOTO

Manteskueu with children at school workshop / Manteskueu mak auasish nte kaskutimatesheutshiuapits, 1992

Teachers Don't Understand

"Frank Peters used to show the kids movies about cowboys and Indians. He showed us that Indians are bad and losers. The cowboys were the winners." *Band Council interview*

Many of us in the community find it very hard because the white teachers don't understand the Innu and our culture. They hurt us. They don't know how we live. There is too much racism and harassment between the Innu teachers and children and the white staff.

It feels like some white teachers don't really care about what goes on in our school. Sometimes they push too much with the children when they are not causing trouble. They give them two choices. They keep asking them if they did something wrong. The children break under the pressure and they will say yes, that they did cause trouble, even though they didn't do anything wrong.

Another problem is when the teachers or the principal are having problems with a child and they give a letter for the child to bring home to his parents. Children sometimes tear it up on their way home. I think the principal should give the letter to the parents herself, or the teacher should go and talk to the parents himself.

"Some teachers complain about how the children

dress. Once a teacher I worked with complained about the smell, that the children smelled, they had no clean clothing. I really hated it when she said this. It hurts me too because they are my people, my children. The white teachers can't even wash the children. They let the Innu teachers do this. We feel that these teachers think the children are too dirty. The teachers should understand that there is no water and sewage facilities in Innu homes. When I was in school, a male teacher once asked me why I didn't dress up nicely like one of the female teachers. I was very embarrassed when he said that to me because my clothes was dirty and in bad shape. Teachers should watch what they say." *Innu teacher*

Teachers Drink Too Much

"A principal once said he wanted an orientation for the teachers. He did that orientation for the new teachers over a bottle of wine." *Gathering Voices participant*

Some of the teachers who come here drink too much. Children complain when they see the teachers drinking. The teachers do foolish things. We have seen teachers make excuses that they were sick. They were sick from hangovers. We have seen teachers drinking. They get drunk. Sometimes they don't come in to teach; it is because they were drunk the night before. They say they have nothing to do in the community.

School Name

The name we have for our school now has caused divisions in the community. It is not good for families to fight. Some of us feel that the name we have now, Nukum Mani Shan School, has given too much power to one family in the community. Many of us would like to see our old school name back. People wonder why the name of the school was changed. The Mushuau Innu School is a good name, because we are the people of the barrens. We should change the name when we build a new school when we relocate. It would help to stop the fighting if we switched the name.

We Need a Safe School

There are problems with maintenance in the school. The exit doors are important. After a storm, the doors get jammed from too much snow. Sometimes only the

Kaskutimatsheutshiuap Eshinikatets

Eshinikatets kaskutimatsheutshiuap tatipan titinikunau, apu minuats tshetshi nutshikatuts Innuts tatipant etats, pase ninan teniteniten eshinikatets kaskutimatsheutshiuap ushamikats miste minakanu shutshiunu peik Innuts. Uta Utshimassits mishetuts uauapatats? Kaskutimatsheutshiuapinu kau tshetshi eshini katets uipats kaishi ni katets, mamitunenitamupants Innuts tshekuan ushiuiatinikants kaskutimatsheutshiuap kaishinikatets Mushuau Innu kaskutimatsheutshiuap minuapan eshi nikatets tante tshinaiau Mushuau Innuts. Tshika atineia kau kaishini katets en uipats kaskutimatsheutshiuap uskatsh atukuatshe, ekun tshika nitshipinu enutshikatu nants tshi atinimak eshinikatets.

Niuitetenan Tshetshi Kakustuats Kaskutimatsheutshiuap

Takun kamenupunt nte kaskutimatsheutshiuapish nte ueuetimish stukues tshishue apitishut, katshimatshishikatshi nash tshipuakuneau kaskutimatsheutshiuap nanikutini peikusu stukue napatashit, tan tshetimikash niskuatetshe? Mishue put tshika tshipukushunai! Nui apitshaia nash Mushinau tshetshi tat auen tshetshi nakatuapatak ka skutimatsheutshiuapinu tshetshi utinakant auen Mushinau meiauat kuna. Peik Innu kaskutimatshet tutamupan enu tshetshi meiauat kuna takunu enu utatuseun mestatuskanits enu tsheskuti-matshetshi auen esk ente tauts auasits tsheshauentshi nte tsheskutimashuts nete timakash kakeshauts ukaskuti-matsheutshiuapuash shash uinuau utuasimauau atu-tshi tshikutimashunua. Nastesh apu minuats tshetshi tutuaka-nits auasits, etu shuneau tshika mistatuenitakanu tshetshi minu nakatuenitakants kaskutimatsheutshiuap.

Innu Uin Tshapimpinitau Kaskutimatsheutshiuapinu

Nui uapamanants tshetshi minu skutimashuts nituasiminaits, apu minu puninukunash kaskutimatsheutshiuap ninai nui pipinitaia kaskutimatsheutshiuap, mak peik uapamaia utshimau kaskutimatshet tshetshi uitshinimish mauats tshitutamuts nastesh tshemuanu peikuau nima-shanamuaia kapipinitat kaskutimatsheutshiuapinu peikun kuetenitakust. Nastesh apu nitutuuat Innua uatamakutshi tshekuanu nastesh mapitenitam.

Eshinakun tshetshi tusenitamash mak tshetshi uapatamash kamenupuntshi kaskutimatsheutshiuap tshinaen tshika skutimatsheutshiuapinu, mieunu ene kakeshau kaskutimatsheutshiuapinu, mak tshinau

tshipa senimanan kaskutimatshet tshipa atuse nte kaskutimatsheutshiuapish, mak tshipa nitu tuuaiats stuasiminuts tshipa ntusenitamuana tshekuan kamenuenitats nte kaskutimatsheutshiuapits pase teni tamuts tshipa tshipanikanu kaskutimatsheutshiuap katshi tutamaue uatutamak.

Mishetuts kanestutats eshipimpinits kaskutimatsheutshiuap nu mat apu senitamash enu pase kaskutimatshets uish pikupiakanits enuituseniteia esi apatshitakants shuneau nta kaskutimatsheutshiuapish, uipats nete nuitshaia-pants nituasimiats, eku anush etu mistapatshitakanu shuneau nta tshikaskutimatsheutshiuapinash ute Utshimassits.

Nui apatshaiats tshenuts tshetshi skutimatshets nte kaskutimatsheutshiuapish, nui tshishimaits auasits en tshetshi skutimashuts enu kaskutimatsheun pase ninai nuiua pamaia Innu tshetshi utshimakaskutimatsheut tshetshi nue, tshipa uitumiskuaia auenua tsheuitshitusemukut kutakuts tenitamuts tshetshi kanumintshi enua Innu kaskutimatshetshi tshetshi pipinitantshi kasku timatsheutshiuapinu, nui uapamaiats Innuts tshetshi etu uauitshaushits nte kaskutimatsheutshiuapish tshash pase tauts Innuts unauitshinuets nte kaskutimatsheu-tshiuapish, mak auasits tshishue min-uenimeuts.

Tshika uiseniteia tshekuan tshekatshi kustamuk uatutamuak.

"Shash nitsheniun mak nimitshimushin ute ka taianua, ents mak nusimits, enu eshiskutimashuts kakeshaua eshipipinitshi, mauats enu ni aia eshipipinutshits, nimishimenitamunikun eshipipinutshits, nimishimenitamunikun eshipi-pinak metinu katukunuau, auen enu tshipa atamenimakanu. Nete kauishatuants auasits shatshiepants tshenuau mishinau tapants nete unitshinikuau, katshi atukuants uta auasits tshishue aiats tenitakushuts nastesh apu apitenimats unitshinikuaua, nitamenitenan kaskutimatsheutshiuap enu eshi skutimuats auasa eshikupuna aiask muk mamanupu-nu eniun uta Utshimassits. Pase ustinishuts tshishue nita utuiuts muk minishipipinuts enu eshipipinutshi nastesh apu speuatats aueshi-sha, nau kakeshaua kutenitakushits, uin ete eshi niunan, eshi unashit aueshisha tshishue apitinipant, ustikuatshekan naniuekuta kanipan nta mistukush ekun tutua kanipant aueshisha kapasishuau." *Tshenish*

main door can be used. What would happen if there was a fire? We could all get trapped inside. We need to have a full-time maintenance man. There is funding for someone to shovel those doors. One of the teachers' aides has to do the work of a maintenance man too. Teaching is a full-time job. Children are still in their classroom when there are leaks. If this happened in a white school, they would not go ahead and have regular school. This is no good for the children. We need more funding for the maintenance of the school.

Innu Control of School

Our children want a better education, and we want it for them too. The school is not working for us. We would like to take over control of our own school. Now we have no say in how the school is run. Over the years, we have gone to principals for help and they don't do anything. It is like we don't have the right to complain about the school. We write letters to the superintendent. He is the same. They don't seem to listen when people tell them things. They don't care.

We have every right to go and see what is wrong with the school. It is our school, not the white teachers' school. We should speak up about the school. We should make our own decisions about how to run our school. We should decide which teachers will work at the school. We should listen to our children. We need to ask them why they are unhappy with the school. Some of us think the school should be closed if we can't have our way.

Many of us don't understand how the school is run. We don't know why some teachers are fired. We won-

der how much money is spent on the school. In the past, we helped our children. We were never paid for teaching the children in our culture. But now we need more funding for our school in Utshimassit.

We need elders to teach in the school. We need to encourage our students to go to university for teacher training. Some of us would like to see an Innu principal soon. We could find someone to work with him/her. Others feel we need to have certified Innu teachers to take control of the school. We would all like to see more Innu people involved with the school. We have volunteers coming into the school now and the children really enjoy them.

We need to learn not to be scared to do things our own way.

"Now I'm old and I'm stuck in this community. As for my grandchildren, they are learning the white man's ways, not our own ways. I'm sad that our culture is fading away. Who is to blame for that? In old Davis Inlet, the children used to respect their elders and they were always ready to help their parents. After moving here, the children changed. They don't care about their parents. I really blame the school for the way they are teaching our children. Life in Davis Inlet is getting worse every year. Some of the young people are very good hunters but they don't follow our ways. They don't respect the animals. They are like white people. In my day, every part of the animal was important. The skull had to be hung on the tree. It was the same for small animals." *Tshenish, elder*

ASHUTAT ETSHITAPATEKEN

MITSHIMUTSHIMAU

"Uskats ntishamukunapin utshimau. Ama nista uapatean auasis shuneas. Niminikuunan mishinanikeetshin eku eteueats ataueutshiuapits. Ama niseniten esi ashimukuunan muku tshishue nimiste atauen. Ntean mitshim, pasikin, akupa, kie nipakea peik pishum eku patush miskuts kauapukuest eshumuet. Niminukunan mitshiminu mak akupa. Peikuau kamakunuest ntishank tshetshi natamitshi Innua tshetshi takushinitshi Innua tshetshi ashamakanits. Ntuten Shankush (Sango). Kie kau tshiuen Shankush eku mitshimutshimau. Ama nastesh ntshi shikak ntuk tshetshi. Nteshauk muku ama ntapuetuau. Ntukunan ama tshika ashimukuunau. Ama nisenimau tshekuanu eshit nete ataueutshiuapits kamakuatak nent tetauts Utshimassits mak nent. Ntuku shipin tshika ashimukuun uintutene nutshimits." *Tshenish*

"Mitshimitshimau tshinatikuna eku eshimitak, mantak atuseunu kie uetinat stuasiminua." *Innut Utshimauts*

Anuts tshishue ama tshisenimau etenimak mitshimutshimau. Pise itenitamuts mitshimutshimau tshuuitshinukunu eka atuseuak. Nanikutini tshuuitshinukunu tshetshi atuseak tshetshi pipints tshuneaminu. Ama tshuaatanu muku pise uapatamuts kamenipunitshi mitshimutshimaua uta Utshimassits. Ama pise minuenitamuts eshi pimimt mitshimutshimau. Kaeshau mitshimutshimau ama tshisenimukunu kie eshiniuak. Stenimanu mitshimutshimau tshipim-pininikunu. Ushamiats tshiuitipenimukunu. Ushamiats tshimeste eminukunu uauitshinukushiuak. Mitshimutshimau nau eshinakust tsheutshimau ukupaeshima. Tshiuitipenimuku kie tshiuitamakunu tshetuau.

"Mitshimitshimau ntenimau tshimi ntutakunu. Uitsheu Innua kaakushintshi kakatshiatusentshi. Mit-

shimitshimau tshipanakatuapameu kaakushintshi." *Matininesh*

"Mitshimitshimau tshimitshipinukunu etshi iniak. Kie etakumituak. Pise mitshimitshimaskueuts apu nastesh nakatuenimats innua." *Tshan*

"Niskumauts mitshiminu manits kakatshi atuseuts. Uipits tshash ntashimukuun etshi nipit napem." *Innu Tsheniskueu*

"Ntatuskuauts mitshimitshimau tshetshi pipinits nishuneam. Enkunu enu muk muenuenimikuau." *Samish*

"Innuts apitshitauts eashimakanits. Aka asha makant innu tshipa tshimakateu." *Manik*

Utineuts Auashau

Utshimassits uta mitshimitshimau utineu auasa. Ama nisenitamuan tshekuanu uishinikatishinat. Innu mushinau tapitu tapints ama niminueniten a auas eutinakant. Mitshipinitau nete Inua mitshetuuts auasits nika etats. Tshishue ueshiu. Mitshimitshimau uetinatshi auasa. Nastesh ama nitutueu unitshinukunua kie nastesh ama uitsheeu kamenipunitshi ueti natshi utuasiminua. Mentshi ukaumau mak utuamau meeunimuk auas nau emakunukuunan kuetenitak. Tapue tapuanu ama pise nakatuenimakanuuts auasits. Auasits pikunimuts tshekuaia mukuntenimau mitshimitshimau tshipauitsheu unitshinukunua. Mauats tshetshi utinat.

"Peik uskau anuts etutak mitshimmitshimau uetinat auasa eka nastesh minu uitamuat uuitshinikunua tshekuanu uishiutinat." *Miste-Peashue*

"Tshishue misti pistinikanu shuneau auasits nakatuenimakanits kie kaatuseshits tshashiuakanits. Mitshimitshimau tshipauiuitsheu utamuaua kie ukau-

CHAPTER SIX

SOCIAL SERVICES: MITSHIMUTSHIMAU—THE FOOD BOSS

"In the old days, we used to get relief from the store manager. We never saw a family allowance check. We had a piece of paper which we would give to the clerk in the store. We would go to the counter and take the things we needed. I don't know how much the relief was, but we could buy a lot of things. You could buy a lot of food, guns, clothing and blankets with one month's relief. Later, it was the priest that gave us social assistance. He handed out food and clothing. Once a police officer sent me to tell other people that they should come to old Davis Inlet for relief. I went, and when I returned to Sango, he was there as the relief worker. He never paid me anything. He told us we should work for him, but we didn't want to. He told us none of us would get relief. I didn't know he left a message for me at the store in Zoar, halfway between Davis Inlet and Nain. The message was that I would get relief only when I was ready to go to the country." *Tshenish, elder*

"Social Services used to come by and give us welfare, then they gave us jobs, and now they take our children away from their homes." *Band Council*

Nowadays, we have many different feelings about Social Services in our community. Some of us think Social Services help people by giving those who have no jobs some assistance. They sometimes help families out with their personal problems, and they give people work to get their U.I. stamps. Some of us have no complaints. But most of us see very serious problems with Social Services here in Utshimassit. We don't like the way Social Services is run. White social workers don't understand us and our culture. We think Social Services is making a lot of decisions about our lives. We feel like social workers control the lives of our families. They ask too many questions when people ask for their

help. Social Services is like all government agencies. They are trying to control us and tell us what we should do.

"I think Social Services is doing a good job for us. They help many people, especially those who are sick and not fit to work. Social Services is supposed to look after people who are sick." *Matininish, woman elder*

"Social Services is messing up our lives, our culture and our relationships with each other. Some social workers don't care about the Innu." *Tshan*

"I thanked them for food supplies that I got when I couldn't work. I've been living on social assistance ever since my husband died." *Innu elder*

"I worked for Social Services just to qualify for U.I.C. That is the only thing I like about them." *Samish, elder*

"People now depend on Social Services. Without Social Services, people would starve." *Manik, elder*

They Are Taking Our Children

A very big issue for us here in Davis Inlet is the social workers taking children from their homes. Many of us don't like how Social Services is separating families. Innu families used to stay together. This is damaging our families. Too many of our children are away, outside the community. It seems very easy for Social Services to take the children away. They don't listen to the parents and don't give any help to the parents with their problems when they take the children away. If the parents are drinking, the answer is not to take their children away. When a child is taken away from parents, some of us feel it is like being sent to jail. It is true that some parents don't look after their children.

uasits nekatakantaui
①

Ntukuntshuapits Teakanu
mistakushu Iskueu.
④

② Nutshikatunantshi

Iskueu utamauakanu

Nipu mitatakanu

uasits Unishina tanikanuaua
estatsheT Shitakunapun.

*Child's drawing at school workshop / Auasits kaunishi-
natatshet, kaskutimatsheupits kaianumats,* 1992

maua. Utineu auasa tshetshianuenimat uuit-
shinukunua. Ama minuau. Auasits kanakatuenimakanits tshika tshiueuts. Peikun tshenishinakust."
Innut Utshimauts

"Uetinakantau auasits eku tshishue menitshi unitshinukuaua. Mukueatapa auas tau mitshuapish
uetinakantshi auas etu ama minupuniuts unit-
shinuka. Auas uetinakantshi kie kau tshauetshi ama
nitutueu unitshinukua. Unitshinukua auas tshipa
uitshakanua eskua eka mishikat auas tshetshi
minupinits. Mitshimitshimau tshipa uitusemeu
kamenupunits mamu auas kie unitshinukua tapitu
uitshiituuts." *Kaastipets*

"Ama niseniten mitshimitshimau uishuutinat auasa.
Uipits Innu nakatuenimepan utuasima nanikutini

auas piuenimakanipan ama minu nakatuenimakanu.
Tshisin peik iskueu pauenimat ukusa. Mashikuapiteu-
ni kie pepunitshi ueuetimits nikiteu eku meskutshi
ntshi uskatinu. Tshishue nimishimenimau auas.
Nastesh ama nekuatu tutuakanu unapema tshishue
kustiku. Niskueu tshishue mitshenimeu ukusa.
Kauapukuest ntuk tshishe manitu tshika uitsheeu
auasa kie tshika ituteu uaskuts nipitshe. Ama nistutuau. Ama niseniten tshekauanu. Nu uishe kuauistu-
tat nenua iskueua. Tshishue nimitatau kanipit auas.
kauapukuest nitshuanuk katapuetuuk kanishit
tshekuanu. Ekush ume auas nipitshe. Uishamiats
piuenimakanu auas. Eshamiats. Nimistinitutuau
kauapukuest. Ama niminueniten uetinakantaui auasits. Innuts tshipautinamauts mitshimitshimaua."
Miste-Shishin

"Anuts ama ntapuetakuunan tshetshi utamautshis

The kids are getting into trouble. But we think Social Services should try to work with the families, not just take the children away.

"One thing that is very new to me is that Social Services takes the children away, without even explaining to the parents why they take children away." *Miste-Peashue, elder*

"A lot of money is spent on group homes and their employees. Social workers should help parents too. They take the children away to punish the parents. This is very wrong. The children that are in the group home now will come back. Nothing will change." *Band Council*

"When they remove the children, it's like babysitting for the parents so they can drink as much as they want. They just move the child to a different home. When they remove a child, they do more damage to the parents and children. When kids are removed and then returned, they don't listen to their parents. Families need help so that when the children return they can feel free and comfortable. Social Services should work with parents on problems and with children too. Parents, children and social services should work together." *Alcohol Program workers*

"I don't understand why social workers take children away from their families. I remember in the old days, the Innu used to take care of their children themselves. Sometimes a child is abused or not looked after. I remember a woman was really mean to her little boy. She used to tie him up, and in the winter she left him outside and his feet got badly frostbitten. I was very worried about the child. Nobody could do anything about this. The husband was afraid to say anything to his wife. The mother said she hated the boy. The priest said God is with the boy, and when he dies the boy will be with God in heaven. I don't understand this. I don't know why he didn't say anything to the woman. I really missed the child when he died. The priest made me really mad when I believed him when he said it was okay for this child to die because he was so badly treated. I don't know why Innu people let this happen to the child. We listen to the priest too much. I hate to see children taken away

from their homes. The Innu should take over Social Services." *Miste-Shishin, elder*

"Nowadays, we are not allowed to hit our kids. But in the past, our parents used to hit us when we got into trouble." *Manteskueu*

Most of the kids who are taken away are not getting the assistance they need from the social worker. It is wrong for the social worker to separate kids from their families. Families being broken up puts a big pressure on the kids. They have mixed feelings about what is happening to them. The social worker is only doing more damage to the kids. That is why the kids do the things they do. When the social worker takes the kids when they are small, it isn't such a big problem. But the social worker is making more problems in many families.

"They send the kids to group homes, and when the kids are brought back to their community, they are messed up. They don't listen to their parents. They want to make their own decisions." *Tshuash, clinic worker*

We don't understand how Social Services makes these decisions. It seems to be very easy for them to take the children away. There always seems to be money for transportation. Sometimes, when a child is placed in a group home, social workers don't even bother to talk to the parents. It is like they own the children. Social Services should explain to the parents why they have taken the child away.

"Social Services took my family away from us. We don't understand Social Services. Why do they take my friends and family away?" *High school student*

"Parents drink, but they still love their children." *Epa*

Some of us see the group homes as part of the problem in these family crises. Some parents go to Social Services to take their kids because they are sniffing gas and they don't know what to do. As well, the kids are getting into trouble because they want to be sent to the group home in Sheshatshiu. Some of them are sniffing gas so they will be sent away. We know the reason children like to be in the group homes is because they get good clothing, they don't have to do any work with their parents, and they have running water. The social workers are telling the kids if they are abused they should come to Social Services for help. Some of us

auasits. Uipits. Mushinan nuutamankuunaiapin kaestutamatshi." *Manteskueu*

Auasits uetinakantaui ama ashimukuuts mitshimitshimaua. Ama minuanu mitshimitshimau tshe tshi nikatishinat auasa. Auas nekatishinakanantshi tshishue ustapinu nete unitshinukush ama senitamuts espinits. Mitshimitshimau ama senitamuts espinits. Mitshimitshimau ama minupeeu auasa. Enkunu auasits uatits. Mitshimitshimau uetinat episisintshi. Ama shuka matenitakun. Muku mitshimitshimau mitshipintau unitshinukunits.

"Auasits etishakantaui nete kanakatueni-makantaui tshishue ama nistutamuts. Nastesh ama nitutueuts utauaua kie ukuauaua. Tshishue uitipenimushuuts." *Tshuash*

Ama nisenitamuanan mitshimitshimau etutak. Tshishue ueshiu auasa uetinat. Mushinau titim shuneanu tshetshi pushat nanikutini auas teakanu kakeeuenimakant nastesh ama uitamuakanua unitshinukua nas etipenimats itenitakushu.

"Mitshimitshimau ama uitamueu uishu utinat auasa. Mitshimitshimau utineu nitshinuka. Ama nisenimau tshekuanu uishuutinat nitshinukua kie ni uitsheuakea." *Kaskutimashust*

"At minua auas ukuauna kie utauna peikun eapits shatshinuku." *Epa*

Akashuka minupinua kuetenitaman auasits kina katuenimakanuutshi. Pise nantuapameuts mitshimutshimaua tshetshi utinantshi utuasimuaua. Menatisskuentaui kie ekasenimataui tshetutuats. Kutukuts auasits uiust anituuts tshetshi itishinakanits auasa pase minatiskueuts tshetshi tshistishauakanits tshishue tante uskanua utapitshitaunuaua nastesh ama atuseshuuts kie nipinu pimpinu mitshimitshimau iteu auasa piuenimukuunekue tshepetuteek. Enkunu auasits uishunutshikuats pimina auasits uiutinkushiuts. Mitshimitshimau nitu tue auasa eku nastesh ama nitutueu ukuamuaua kie utamuaua.

Nanikutini ama ntispinan shuneau tshetshi nakatuenimitshist ntuasiminaets. Tshishue tshekuan meminuantshi auasits uieauts. Enkunu auasits uishekaui nakatuenitas uipits kaishiniunanuts tshika uintauts eshipimpinitshi nanikutini auas uetinakantshi ntuun mishukua minuanu enitsts kie ama shukaminuna-katuenimakanuuts. Auas na katuenimukutshi Innua ama nispinu shunianu. Nanikutini Innu tipan

apitshitau tshetshi minu nakatuenimat nanikutini uetinatshi mitshimi tshimaskueu auasa utinamueu essi eshimakanitshi nau etshemutimat inua ntenitakushu kie tshauetshi uitshiuats tshishue neush ama takunu ushuneam.

"Utinepan mitshimitshimaskueu ntuasima nete teepin Sheshatshits. Ntukunaiapin tshika mishikau mushinau nipameunu kie apakanu katshi utinat ntuasima nishuau mishikashu Utshimassits. Nepit nikaun tshika mishikau ntenimau muku ama mishikau." *Mani Katini*

"Mitshimitshimaskueu uetinatshi iskuesa nete Sheshatshit itishaueu teakanuts nete menanits ama minu nakatuenimakanuts muku-peikuau eakanua utapitshitaunuaua. Kanakatuenimaukuts menitshi unuetishankuuts nete katats pipamuteuts meskeats tepiskantshi. Piuenimakanuts auasits. Ama minuenitamuts. Peikuau niskueu mituetau Sheshatshit iteu ukauna tshishue nishiuen." *Kaatuset iskueu*

Ntenitean uetinatshi mitshimitshimaskueu auasa ekutanta tshipateakanuts utenats tshetshi-nakatuenimakanits. Tshipanaka tuenimukuuts uikanishiuaua put make tshipa utshutikanu kanakatue, nimakanits auasits. Pise auasits ituenitamuts umenu. Tshipauitshaauts auasits uauitshinukushitaui. Tshi pakustinae mitshimitshimaskueu auasa. Niminu nakatuenimaaets ntuasiminaents.

Niskueuts Kapiuenimakanits

Mitshimitshimaskueu itishaueu iskueua nete kanakatuenimakantshi, unapemuaua. Niskueuts tshitishimuts unapemuaua minatenitamititshi tante uitinikushiuts nete kanakituenimakantshi iskueua. Nanikutini niskueu tau ntukutshiuapits nutshikakutshi unapema. Napeu pise ama minupunitau kie kutukuts niskueuts tshishipinitauts tshuapuunu. Pise itenitamuts uinuau niskueu etukunits enakatuenimakanits kie kutukuts itenitamuts etu ama minupinu mitshimitshimaskueu kie kanakatuenimakanits niskueu mitshiuap ama uinutshikamuts tshekuanu niskueu kamenupunits tshastishauakantshi.

"Mitshimitshimaskueu uiuitsheeu kapiuenimakanitshi iskueua. Ntukuastikushu kie uapameu niskueua nete ntukutshiuapits. Kusteuts niskueua tshetshi ushikuakanitshi ntenimaaets mitshimitshimaskueu kie ntuastukushu enkun tshishue uauitshaats

believe this is the reason why there is so much solvent abuse and gas sniffing going on here. The kids want to be taken away. The social workers listen to the children and they don't listen to the parents.

Sometimes we don't have enough money to look after our children. Sometimes they are bought luxuries. Some of us worry that this causes them to lose their culture and way of life. They also lose their language. They get brainwashed by this white society stuff. Sometimes when children are removed they are put in one home, and then moved to another. Sometimes these homes are not better than the ones they left, and they are not cared for properly. Foster homes are not given enough money to look after these children. They have to feed these kids using their own money. Also, when a worker takes a child away from his home, they also take the welfare money. It is like the worker is stealing from the people. Then when the child is ready to come home, it takes a long time for the parents to receive the family allowance checks.

"A few years ago, a social worker took my child away and put him in the group home in Sheshatshiu. The social workers promised us that our child would come home every holiday, like Christmas and Easter. Since they took our child away, we have only seen him twice here in Davis Inlet. When my mother died, we thought he would be sent home for his grandmother's funeral, but he wasn't." *Mani Katinin*

"The social worker took girls from here and sent them to Sheshatshiu. They were placed in drinking homes. They are not looked after properly down in Sheshatshiu. They were only bought clothes once. When their guardians were drunk, they were kicked out of the homes where they were staying. They stayed out all night on the roads. These kids are being abused a lot. They are not happy out there. One woman got a call from her daughter in Sheshatshiu. She told her mother she was hungry."
Women construction worker trainees

Some of us believe that if social workers have to take children away from their parents, they should place them in the community with families here. They should place them with their relatives. Or we should have our own group home built in the community. Some of our children are asking for this. We should help our troubled children if they need help. We should stop Social Services from taking our children away. We care about our children.

Help for Battered Women?
Social Services also sends our women away to Libra House, in Goose Bay, when they are beaten by their husbands. Most women run away from their husbands when they are drunk because they want to be placed in Libra House. A lot of women end up in hospital when they are beaten up by their husbands. This is an issue we don't agree on. Some of us think the man is the problem. Others think the woman starts the trouble. Some believe Libra House is good for the protection of the women, and others think this only creates more problems. Many of us feel Social Services and Libra House are not dealing with the real problem when they send the women away.

"The social worker is trying to help abused and battered women. Even the doctors are involved when women end up in hospital. They are afraid for the women, that they might be seriously hurt. Some of us believe the social workers and the doctors are the only ones who are trying to do something for battered women, for the sake of the women's lives. We are not doing anything for battered women."
Manteskueu

"I have seen many women depend on Social Services, not for food but for other problems. When a man and his wife get into a fight when they are drunk, the woman can go to the social worker and tell her she has been beaten badly by her husband. The social worker calls Libra House in Goose Bay, and on the same day or the next day, the woman is sent out to stay at Libra House. The man is left behind and charged with assault. The woman takes her problems to Libra House. While she is there, Libra House piles on more problems, and she is sent home. Sometimes the woman starts the trouble first, and it is the man who pays for it. When a husband goes to court, he has to go to jail or pay a fine. The money he spends on the fine could be spent on food for his children. I think the community should solve these problems, not anyone from Social Services, the nurse or Libra House." *Shuashim*

Some of us know this is not a new problem. We must try to remember what was happening before. Women

Mani Anishe and baby; she took her life later that year. /
Mani Anishe mak auasish, 1992.

CAMILLE FOUILLARD PHOTO

niskkueua kapiuenimakanitshi. Ama shuka tshuuit-
shainets niskueuts kapiuenimakanits." *Manteskueu*

"Niuapamanan niskueu uauitshinukushitshi nenu
kamenipunt. Niskueu kie napeu nutshikatutaui
minatenitataui. Niskueu ntuapameu mitshimitshimaskueua uitamuau uetamakutshi unapema. Mitshimitshimaskueu mituestau nete kuspe niskueua
kanakatuenimantshi eku niskueu pushakanu nete ni.
Napeu nikitauakanu eku ueueshakant. Niskueu
ntishimu nete kanakatuenimakant eshi tat nete
niskueu mitshiuapits. Tshek tshishue mitshenua
kamenipunt. Tsha-uepintshi niskueu tshishipi-nitau
nanikuti. Eku napeu etamenimakan eku unapema
ueueshakantshi nanikutini makunakanua put
tshishika-shunua tshashikashut menu-napeu ueueshakantshi tshipa eakanu umitshiminu utuasi-ma.
Nteniten inuts tshipa minupunitauts
kamenupunits." *Shuashim*

Meunush kamenipunau uipits nete tshipa mamiti-
neniten kanishinakuat. Niskueuts pauenimakantau
uipits ama nikuatu ituteuts uipits Utshimassits.
Niskueu nutshi-kakutshi unapema kauapu-kueshintshi
ntishumni. Niskueuts esk piuenima-kanuuts. Nastesh
ama tshiuitshaeuts.

"Uipits naau kueshinakushinau niskueuts kapiuenimakanits. Tsheniskueuts ama eshipiuenimakantshi
niskueua. Muk tshinanu sitapimaiaets pauenimakan-
its iskuets. Enkun peikun stishinakushinaiapan
neskueunak kie muku stintenimaiauts. Ama
tshikamiskatenitenan enkun muk ishinakunipan."
Manteskueu

Shitakunapun tutatsheu uishekaminupunak napeuts
kie iskueuts Tshipa uitshinukushiuts eminits pise stenitenan minuanu enu napeu ueueshakantshi nutshiku-
atshi utiskuema. Kamakunueshits ama nutshikamuts
nutshikashuntshi. Tshikisituteau nutshikatunants minuats. Niskueuts nutshikatunants enkunu uishinikitats
unapemuaua. Napeu ama nishinakushu utiskuema,
tshipaueshakanu. Minuanu nenu niskueu kapiueni-
makant etuapamatshi ntukuniskueua nut-
shikuakantshi.

Napeu unashu kie uiuitshinukushiu mitshimi-tshi-
maskueu. Nastesh ama uiuitsheu kapiue-nisentshi.
Niskueuts mak auasits nakateuts. Tshishue muesta-
timuts kie uitshiueuts. Tsha-uepintaui peikun kueshi-
nakushits napeu peikun kueshinakust. Ntenitenan
napeu tshipa pusha-kanu tshetshi uitshinukushit.

Ntenitenan napeu kie niskueu tshetshi atu-skuatas
kamenupunits mamu. Nanikutini mi-tshimitshi-
maskueu tshistishaueu tshetshinue kie nistim pita
niskueu tshipa uitshinukushiu. Tshipa kukuetshi-
makanu pita. Peikun napeu tshipatutuakanu. Tshekamakunuest kuskunu tusintishaueu auenua. Niskueu
tshipauitshaakanu uta utenats. Mitshimitshimaskueu
mapi-tenimeu kanipuuntshi. Enkunu nanikutini nti-
tamenimanan nekituntshi. Tshipaminuau tu-kuats uta
niskueuts kanakatuenimakanits.

Ama Nispanu Shuneau

Mishetuts inuts kamenenitats eshi ashamakanits. Mitshimitshimau usham miskushiu. Tshishue pishish
tashimikunan. Ama niminupinuanan. Mishetuts
tuasiminuts eku ama ntispina eshi ashamakunats.
Mashetitshi utuasima eku tshishue meshimentak.
Auashits mushinau, shiuenuuts. Auashits ntuenita-
must ueskatsh. Akupa, kie kutukunu ni eauts
tshekuanu. Ama nu uitshinukunan mitshimitshimau
shinuapastamashi nishuneaminanu. Ama ntushen-
imikunan tshetshi ispanansh mitshim. Tshishue
eanushitamuts etuenitamatshi shuneanu. Mitshimitshimaskueu, put kie mitshimitshimau tshipa uitsheuts
inua uaashimikushitshi.

used to go through beatings with no one to turn to. In old Davis Inlet, when women were beaten up by their husbands, they would go to the priest for help and support. Women are still being battered. We are not helping these women.

"In the past, we were like these battered women. We don't talk about ourselves when we were like these battered women. We only look at other women who are battered. We used to be like these women. We say whatever we like about these women. We seem to be surprised about what is happening. We shouldn't be, because these things used to happen in the past." *Manteskueu*

The problem in these family crises is alcohol. Both women and men need big help with their drinking. Some of us think it is the right thing to do to charge men when they assault their wives. Sometimes the R.C.M.P. doesn't do anything about these assaults. We can't let these beatings go on. Women are beaten up and that is why they leave their husbands. Men have no right to beat their women. It is a crime. Abused women make the right decision by going to the nurses when they are beaten.

But men are human too and they also need help. Social Services don't do anything with the abuser. The women and children have to leave the community. They get very lonely and miss home. When they come back, they go to the same situation. The man hasn't changed. Some people think this should be the other way around. Men should be sent out to get help.

Many of us think men and women should try to work out their problems together. Sometimes the social workers decide too quickly to send the women to Libra House. Some of us wish the women would get counselling first. More questions need to be asked. It is the same for the men. The judge shouldn't send anyone directly to jail. Women can get help in our community. Social Services doesn't seem to care what happens to married couples. Some of us think they are to blame if married couples are separated. It would be better if we had a shelter for women here in the community.

Not Enough Money to Live On

Many people are disappointed with the very small amount they get for social assistance. Social Services is hard on us. They only give us a little welfare money. We have very big problems. We don't have enough food to support our families. The people with the large families are the ones who suffer the most. The children are often hungry. Children also need clothing, and parents need other things, not just food. Sometimes we have to wait a week for our next cheque when we don't have any more food. The social workers don't even help us when we are waiting for our U.I.C. They don't try to find out if people have enough food for their families. They always make some kind of excuses when people ask for money. Social workers are responsible to give assistance to people who need relief.

"Now we have a family allowance cheque. We can spend it any way we want, but things in the store are very expensive. We hardly get enough money to buy food for our families. We can't pay the light bills and we can't buy clothing for our children. People on social assistance now suffer the most." *Kaniuekutat*

"The Social Services gives out $86 every month for individuals, which is not nearly enough." *High school student*

"I remember I didn't have enough money to buy food. Social Services wouldn't give me money to buy food for my children. I took my son to the clinic. I was told I was starving my child." *Family Violence Project*

"Before I got my old age pension, the worker took one hundred dollars of my relief, and another hundred dollars from my assistance. I asked him why he did that, and he told me I should work. He knew I could not work because I was sick. He didn't even tell me what he was doing with my welfare money." *Tshenish*

"Sometimes people don't have food to send their children to school and they go to the social worker for emergency assistance. The social worker knows this is true and still won't give assistance. Once I asked her to come to my house to see. She said no. She only gave me fifty-six dollars." *Gathering Voices participant*

The social assistance that comes to us is payment from the development of our own resources. Maybe the government thinks we don't know that. But we know. Other people think we get help from the government, but the money comes from our resources. This money from all over Canada comes from Native peoples' land.

"Eku anush etukuats auash shuneau. Muku uantapitshitaiats ntapitshitanan, kie muku tshishue animin tshekuan nete ataueutshiuapits. Ama ntispinan tshetshi eiaiats mitshim. Ama nanikutini tshitshishiuaiaets uastepimakeets, kie ama tshiaian utukupuaua ntuasiminats. Innuts kaashimakanits ekun tshishue nakunikuts." *Kaniuekutat*

"Mitshimitshimaskueu $86 peik pishuma ashameu inua eku ama nispinuuts." *Kaskutimashust*

"Ama peikuau ntispin eshimikunan tshetshi eiaian mitshim. Mitshimitshimaskueu ama niminuk shuneanu tshetshi eauts mitshiminu ntuashima. Ntusteau nikush nete ntukutshiuapits, eku ntukuun tshekat tshimakateu stuashim." *Utshimassiu Iskueuts*

"Eskua eka takuats nitsheniushuneam, mitshimitshimau utinum peik mitashimitunueapish nete uish ashimikuuts. Tshekuan uish utinamesh ntau, eku ntuk tshipa atusen. Ama tshi atuseuaia tante ntakushuai. Ama nuuitamuk tshekuanu uish utinak nete kauish ashimikuuts." *Tshenish*

"Nanikutini ama nispanu Innu mitshiminu tshetshi itishauat kaskutimasheutshiuapits eku etuapamats mitshimitshimaskueue. Kie shenitam mitshimitshimaskueu eku muui ashameu. Peikuau nuuishamau tshetishi petutet nitshish tshetshi uapata. Mauats tuk. Muku $56.00 niminukush." *Kamamuinats*

Eshimikunau ekuta nta ueshipat stishinash eshi pikunikats. Tsheutshimau ama shenitamuts stenimukunaetshe. Tshisheniterten. Kutukuts itenitamuta tshishue tshiminu uitshinukunu tsheutshimau. Ume shuneau ushipanu uta stishinash kie kutukuts Innuts utasiuats.

Usham Tshimiste Ntenimanu Mitshimitshimau
Ushamiats tshimiste uitshinukunu mishimitshimau. Usham miste nukushu uta kamenupinak. Tante muku tshinatanu uaashimikushinak eku nastesh ama statusesinan. Pishe nastesh ama uituuiuts tshetshi ashamat utuasimaua kie ama uiatusheuts. Muku mitshimitshimaua eku etushumuts. Tshipa skutimashunan tshetshi shenitamak tshekuan eku tshetshi minu atuseak. Nankutini nastesh mapitishu Innu, muku ement.

"Tshipa uitshinushuuts Innuts, anuts tshetshi Iniuts. Mitshimitshimaskueu ashimeu Innua eku tshishue Innuts menuenitats. Eka shimakanits Innuts tan tshipatuuts tshika nikanushut-tsha." *Akatis*

"Uipits Innuts kashimakanits ama shapenitamuts mushinau. Ama mishimenitamuts tante natimuts uaapitshitataui. Kutukuts Innuts muuiatuseuts kie ama uiituteuts nutshimits tante minuenitamuts eshamakanits. Kaashimakanits Innuts nastesh ama mishimenitamuts. Muku minuuts kie ama atuseuts." *Shimun kie Mani*

Tante Eshi Ushitats Ueuetishuets
Tante esitutats mitshimitshimaskueu uetinataui auasa. Ama aianimueuts nete shintshanishish. Nastesh ama ustumpinuuts uapushatau. Eku Innu uanatshishimukushitshi. Mui uitshaakanu. Innu entutisetshi mitshimitshimaskueua tshetshi pimpinitat ushuneam ama takun shuneau etakani. Nanikutini mitshimitshimaskueu aianimueu nete shintshanishish eku patush katshiutinat natutisentshi. Etikuatshi shuneau etutiskantshi minakanuutsha tshetshi utinats Innua tshetshinue? Put make nistim pita tshika aianimueuta shintshanishish?

Tsheutshimau Atuseuna
Amaminupinu mitshimitshimaskueu eshipipinitat atuseuna. Mitshimitshimaskueu atuskeu Innua tshetshi pipinits ushuneaminu. Innuts tshishue apisis tshishikuakanuuts. Ama nispinuuts shuneanu tshetshi pempinitshi ishineamua ama uiashimeuni mitshimi tshimaskueua. Napeu atuset nete Innu Utshimaua eku niskueu etuapatatshi atuseunu mitshimutshimaskeu muuiatuskeeuni tante unapema atusenua. Peik etusetshi ama nispinu shuneanu tshe tshi eat mitshiminu eku auasits shauenits. Eku mitshimutshimaskueu ntukunan shiuenuuts stuasimits kie kuesteshe tshika teakanuuts. kutukuts ntenitamuts uikanishuaua Innu mitshimitshimaskueuts eku nistam maiakanits atuseuna.

"Nipeten peikuau Shintshanishish etusetshi Innu uta tshishue paisis tshishikuakanu eku etu mistitshishikuakanuuts nete Newfoundland." *Shimunish*

Kaatushets Kamenupinits
Nishuuts Innuts etusets ete mishinanikatshuapits anuts. Innuts nakatuapatamuts shuneanu. Amatau mitshimitshimaskueu. Mishikauts nanikutini nastesh neush ama tauts. Amaminuau. Tshipatauts neush utani kie tshipa uitsheeuts Innua kamenipunitshi. Mitshimitshimaskueuts tshishue auasiuts kie nastesh ama seni-

We Depend Too Much on Social Services

Some of us in the community feel that we have become too dependent on Social Services these days. We think Social Services has played a major role in the social deterioration in Utshimassit because people can go over to Social Services and get their relief without having to work for it. We don't hunt to feed our children, and some people are not interested in working. They just go to Social Services for support. We should get training and learn something to get future jobs. Now these people have nothing to do, so they drink more.

"Without Social Services, people could help themselves; people would survive. Social Services give people social assistance and people depend on that. If the people didn't get social assistance, what would happen to them? Would they survive or not?" *Akatis*

"People who have long-term assistance have no worries because help is always there when they need it. Some people are not interested in working or going into the country because they have become addicted to social assistance. People who are on social assistance have no worries. All they do is drink and not work." *Mani and Shimun*

How Decisions Get Made

We wonder how social workers make decisions about things, like when they take children away. They don't have to call St. John's. They have no problems paying for the transportation. But when people are desperate for food, they can't get emergency assistance. Or when people look for work at Social Services to get their U.I. stamps, they are told there is no money. Sometimes a Social Services worker has to call St. John's before they can hire a worker. If there is money for jobs, do they have the authority to hire someone right away? Do they always have to call St. John's first?

Social Services Jobs

We have a number of other problems with Social Services jobs. Social Services gives work to people so they can qualify for U.I.C. People are paid very low wages. They don't have enough income to support their families. Then, when they are on U.I.C., Social Services can't give out anything for people who are out of food and gas. They can't get emergency supplies. The other problem is when a man or woman is working and the other one goes to Social Services for a job, they don't get hired. For example, if the man works at the Band Council and his wife wants to get a job too, Social Services won't hire her because the man is working. When only one parent works, there is not enough money to buy food for the family. Then, when the kids go hungry, the social worker tells us we are not feeding our children and they want to put them in another home. Also, some of us feel that relatives of Innu social workers are the ones who get the jobs first.

"I heard one thing in St. John's that concerns me. I was told that when Social Services employs people for short-term work, people in Labrador are making less money with these job opportunities than they make in Newfoundland." *Shimunish*

Staff Problems

There are only two Innu workers in the Social Services office at the moment. The Innu workers look after the financial assistance. There is no social worker. Social workers come in here and stay for such a short time. This is not good enough. They should stay here permanently and help out the people who are having problems. Sometimes the social workers that come here are very young and they have no experience. They don't want to listen to us about our culture. They don't understand the Innu. They say they can make the decisions because they are the social worker. Some social workers don't care about the people in the community and they don't know what they are doing. They make decisions about our lives and do damage to our families. Then they leave.

There is never any training for Innu Social Services workers. They are told there is no funding. Our workers don't have training but they are expected to do the work of the social workers.

"Last year, Social Services sent a young social worker. She came out of university. I had a real hard time with her. And she didn't know anything about being a social worker. She was supposed to train me, but I did all the training for her. I complained about her to the regional office, and they also ignored me. They didn't care and didn't want to hear our problems. They just wanted me to sit back and be an angel. We are no angels when we see problems. Let's not sit back and let it go. We have to fight for our rights.

"I'd been asking them for a raise, too, but then again they said no. I worked with these people for

tamuts. Nastesh ama nitutakunaets kaeshiniuak. Nastesh amasenimeuts innua. Ishishueuts ninan nika uuestanan tante nimitshimaskueunam. Pise mitshimitshimaskueuts ama apitenimeuts Innua kie ama uintusenimeuts. Pikunimuts kie aia tinamuts Innua eshiniuntshi. Kuet tshiuepinits.

Amanita skutumuakanipants Innu mitshimitshimaskueuts. Ntakanuuts amatakun shuneau. Tante uetinats shuneanu auasa kipusheutshi. Nisenitenan misteapitshitauts shuneanu uetinataui auasa. Kaatusets amaskutimuakanuuts muku itenimakanuts tshetshi ntitusets mitshimitshimaskueua.

"Pupunush mitshimitshimaskueu petishauakanu. Anushishe tshiskutimashu. Tshishue nimuskuinuk. Nastesh ama senitam tshekuanu emitshimakueunanits. Mpaskutimakupin muku nin niskutimuau. Ntaianimuen mishinanikantshuapits nuauinau eku nastesh ama nitutakuun. Ama tshinaka tuenimukuunan kie ama tshuinitutakuunan kamenipunak muk tsheapinek kie tsheanisheuniek ama eutshinan anisheniuts una patiman kamenupunan akaapitau nutshikashutau tshetshiminu pinak. Nteemapints etunuuimistitshiakushiuan eku mauats ntukuts. Mishetipuna ntatuskuauts. Tshek nastesh ama nishapenimauts. Amastapitenimukunuuts nastees. Utshimau mitshimitshimau mishikapin eku eshitni taetatishits eku menits Innuts kie eskua minuuts Innuts. Nastesh mapitenimeu ukupaeshima." *Epa*

Nanikutini kakeeshau mitshimitshimaskueu itishumeu Innu mitshimitshimaskueua tshetshi nikatishinatshin ete auasa nte uts uikanishinu.

"Kakeeshau mitshimitshimaskueu itishumeu Innu mitshimitshimaskueue tshetshinikatishinakanits auasits. Ama eunu Innu utatuseun tshetshi nikatishinat auasa. Mauats ama tshetutuauts Innuts meeunin mitshimitshimaskueu. Kakeeshau mitshimitshi-

maskueu enkunu utatuseun." *Innu mitshimitshimaskueu*

"Tshishue etatusean mishinanikantshuapits tshiskueni-takun. Nimishimenimauts Innuts uta utenats. Nimishi-meniten minamitine-Nita-mani mitshimitshimaskueu katutuat innua." *Epa*

Peikuau ntukupin mitshimitshimaskueu tshetshi nikatishinimitshi. Meu nin ntatuseun tshishue nuuauiutshimuk. Amanistutuauts Innuts ntuk eku tshin tshika tuten ntuk. Amantapuetuau eku tsheuitsheun ntuk kie tsheutuniuun ntuk mitshipinitauts kuet tshiuets tshipauitshakanuuts uauitshinukushitaui. Mitshimitshimaskueu tshipautineu Innua tshetshi atusentshi. Itenimakanu ama nakatuenimats nastesh Innuts uetinakanits ama nitutueuts. Tat mitshimitshimaskueu tshipanitutueuts put. Kaatusesits petakaui etusetaui ama nikuatu tutueuts. Kutuuts Innuts isishueuts uikanishiuaua. Kutukuts isishueuts kaatusesits nutshikatuuts kie eianikantuuts pinetataui tshekuanu etakanuuts. Atu tshitapuetueuts. Kutukuts kaatusesits etusetaui minuuts.

Innuts Tshipa Utinamuts Mitshimitshimaskea Utatuseunu

Innu mitshimitshimaskueuts tshipanitutueuts Innua etukutaui. Tshipauitamueuts tsheutshimauts kamenipunits tshekuanu. Tshipakutshitauts mitshimitshimaskueuts tshetshinituts tants tshentapitshitakanits shuneanu. Innuts kashimakanits tshipaskutimuakanuuts tshetshi mistukunapeuts tshetshi minuatusets nete. Tshe utshimau tshipaistau kishimeua Innua tshetshi skutimuakantshi. Mitshimitshimau tshipani tutakunan kie tshipateu Innu mitshimitshimaskueua. Tshishue tshipauitsheeu innua. Tshipautinean mitshimitshimau utatuseun kie tshipaatinean kie tshipampitinitanam. Enkun muk tshe tshi minupunts.

many years. I finally got really fed up with them. They don't care about the people in the community. I remember when the regional director came in the community. He asked only, 'How many people are drinking alcohol?' And he always asked if the people are still drinking. He doesn't care about his staff." *Epa*

Sometimes the non-Innu social workers make Innu workers remove children from their homes.

"The non-Innu social workers are making Innu workers remove children from their homes. This is not Innu work, to remove a child from his home. I will not do this to the people. I am not a social worker. That is the white social worker's responsibility." *Social Services worker*

"The work I had to do for Social Services is crazy. I am sorry for the people in the community. I feel really bad when I think about the things that the white social workers made me do to the people. I remember once I was told by a white social worker to remove a child from her home. That wasn't my job. She kept pushing me to go to the home. She said that she didn't speak our language and I'd have to go myself. I refused to do it. Then she said she would do it herself, and I had to go with her for interpreting." *Epa*

Innu Social Services workers also have to hire the people for the work projects. They are expected to supervise them. They find that the people they hire don't listen to them. If there was a social worker, they might listen to her more. They find it just too hard when workers miss work. They don't know what to do. Some people complain that the Innu workers only find jobs for their relatives or their husband's relatives. Others complain that the Innu worker fights with her workers when she hires people. They think something should be said to her. This should not be allowed. Some people think that this worker's drinking interferes with her job.

Innu Control of Social Services
Innu social workers should listen to Innu concerns. They should try to explain to the government the problems we have. We want Social Services to find the best possible way, with input from the community, to spend their funds wisely. For example, people who are on social assistance should take training for carpentry, crafts and skills for future jobs. The government should spend social assistance funds on training. Social Services should take direction from us for now, but it would be really good if we could have an Innu social worker. She could really help our people. Then we would have control over Social Services and make our own policies soon. That is the only way to make it work. We could find our own ways to help the troubled children if they need help.

NISHU-ASHUTAT ETSHITAPATEKEN

NTUKUTSHUAP

Innuts uinuau tutamupant ntukuna mak uinuau ntukunushupants tshishue shutshimakanu ntukuna. Mak uinuau Innuskueuts tapants uautuassimintshi niskueua. Eku anutshish tshenutsh tshuitamakunuts tshi mistinitu-tuauits Ntukuastukushuts. Tshiunitanan uipatsh ka nishintukunushunau tshinan.

"Uipatsh nte nutshimits etaiantshi uinuau Innuts ntukunushupants. Ama nita uapamakanipan ntukunstikushu mak ntukuniskues. Mishue eshash eshunitanan uipats kaishintukunushut Innu. Uin muk ntukuatukushu uiapatshitau ntukuna. Nin nteniten tshishue minuaua Innuts etutats ntukuna. Innuts enkushitaui kuet nantuapamats ntukuniskuesa. Tshipa minuanu Innuts eapatshitats uipatsh kaishintukunushuts eku eakushintaui tshitshitaunikunan." *Miste-Shishin*

"Uapamik. Nin nutshimits nte ntiniun apu tat nte ntukuastukushu mak ntukuniskues, uinuau Innuts tutamuts tsheapatshitats ntukuna eku anuts manuitan nte Utshimassits. Naka nte ntitan tshishiue niminuenimun apu tat auen kaueuetishimuk. Nin nuiuetishimushun. Nusimits tshishiue takunits tshekuanu tshipamitshipinikuts." *Shenum*

"Uipatsh nte esimeu kauapukuest Mr. Hettach ishinikashupan netukuat Innua. Misteuauitshiepan Innua eakushintaui. Innuts etataui nte nutshimits, eakushitaui uinuau ushitauts ntukuna tshe apatshitats. Mitishantshuap apatshitakanipan tshitshue minuau eakushitshi auen. Kakeshashau katshi ushitat ntukuntshuapinu, Innuts kuet punitats uipatsh uinuau katutats ntukuna nte assits kautinikantshi tshishue minuapan eushitakantshi ntukuna nte assit uetinikantshi." *Tshenish mak Meneshkuesh*

Katshenuits tshiuitaniakunuts uipats nte tshishue shutshipants Innuts mak minita akushipants esk nte etats nutshimits. Eku anuts mishue tshekuan miminupinu miste akushuts Mushinau Innuts. Nastish apu minupan tshekuan mak miste niputs Innuts. Matukun nipin ute Utshimassits. Mak ne nipin miminuau tshetshi minantsh, miste uinakun eku eakushiskakunau. Mak Innuts mitshetuts T.B. etakushits kuet. Matishuat ni-ntukuastikushu.

"Nte nutshimits etaiantshi miste minuashu asin ama nas apu takuatsh tshekuan tshipa akushiskakunan. Miste minuau nipin menantsh, apu nishinakuats ume nipin ute Utshimassits kuinakuma eukun eakushiskakunak." *Kaskutimatsheuapits kaanumants*

Stakushiskakunan shitakunapun kie pimin eminaman. Kie mitshim nte ataueutshiuapits eapits stakushiskakunan. Nutshimits uetinikantsh mitshim minuapan kie ama shuka nita akushuts Innuts. Kauapukuest shashish tshiuitamakunanapan miste minuau nutshimits mitshum eapits stakushinan kauepinashunantshi nitamuk uepinashunantshi nitamuk uepinikanua eku matshits ni nitamuk aueshishats. Kuet nispant ne uanakuats nte uetanipants.

"Kakeshau mak tsheutshimau eskua tshishue ustinitshiuts eku tshinan ustinitshuuts tshishue tsheniuts. Mishiue ntuun etatupuneshits." *Manteskueu*

Ueskuts uaiatukuants nuitamakunaipan tsheutshimau tshetshi ushitakants ntukuntshuap, tshika mishau ntukunan. Miste petaunakanuts mistukuts. Apishashu ntukuntshuap ueshitakants pase mistukuts apatshiakanut ueshitakants emeutshiuap, kauapukuest tapan etuskuat Innua apu tat ntukuniskues. Nitamuk uapameu kauapukuest eakushintshi innua, kie uin peikueu etukunuet.

Eku anuts ntukuntshuap miste apishashu ute Utshimassits mak mishuka minuau Innuts muk peiuk tepiskaua tshitauts nte ntukuniskuesits tshetshi

CHAPTER SEVEN

THE CLINIC AND HEALTH SERVICES

Tshatsh and daughter / Tshatsh mak ninta, 1992

CAMILLE FOUILLARD PHOTO

We used to have our own medicines and heal ourselves. We had strong medicines. We had our own midwives. Now, some of our elders tell us we listen too much to the white doctors. We are losing our medicines.

"We used to heal ourselves when we were in the country. We hardly went to doctors and nurses. These days, they have taken over everything and Innu medicines are slowly disappearing. It is too bad this is happening. I think Innu medicines were better for the Innu. These days we take pills, and when we get sick, we run to the nurses. I would like to see Innu medicines used again because they were better for us. Now, we have to go outside the community when we are sick." *Miste-Shishin, elder*

"Look at me. I was born in the country. Where I was born, there was no doctor or nurse, only our medicine. Now I stay away from the community. I feel free and healthy. My grandchildren are happy and live in peace." *Shenum*

"In the old days, the Moravian minister Mr. Hettasch was a travelling doctor. He would come on his dog team from Hopedale. He would do everything he could to help those who were sick. In the country when someone is sick, we always use Innu medicine. The sweat lodge is really good medicine. After the government built a nursing station, people stopped using their own medicine. Sometimes Innu medicine is better than modern medicine. In the old days, there wasn't any sickness. People were healthy back then. And when people travelled to Davis Inlet to pick up supplies, they usually brought back sickness with them." *Meneshkuesh and Tshenish, elders*

The elders tell us we used to be strong and healthy. This was because of our way of life in those days. Now many things have changed, and we are often sick. We suffer because of poor living conditions. Some of our people are dying from these conditions. People are sick because of the stress. There is no water in Davis Inlet. It is very hard for us to be healthy when we have no water to clean ourselves. We drink the water; it is contaminated and it makes us sick. People used to get T.B., and the doctor had to operate on them.

"In the country, we live on the most beautiful land, the air is fresh, the water we drink is so tasty, not like the water we drink in Davis Inlet. The water here makes us sick." *School workshop*

We are sick from alcohol and gas sniffing. The foods we eat now from the store also make us sick. When we were in the country, we were always healthy because we were eating wild foods. The priest told us once the wild foods were like medicine. As well, we are sick because there is dirty, smelly garbage everywhere, around each and every house. People throw their honey buckets in the community. The ground gets dirty and it goes down under and the water gets dirty.

"The white man and their government are still looking young while our young adults are looking old. This applies to all our people, men and women of all ages." *Manteskueu*

When we first moved here, we were promised a big clinic for our community by the government. There were a lot of materials for a clinic, but they went into building the mission. There wasn't a nurse when we moved here. Only the priest worked as doctor and

ntukuntauts. Kie pase Innuts itenitamuts minuanu ntukuniskuesits etats ute Utshimassits. Mak peiuk Innu nisishueu aiask minupanu ntukuntshuap.

"Mashuka niseniten espants ntukuntshuap, muk nteniten ntukuntshuapi ekute mestuitshiakanits kaiakushits Innuts." *Manik*

"Ntukuntshuap tshuitshinikunan matshui eatapa nispini-kunai." *Kashetan*

"Minuau ntukuntshuap ntukuastikushuts mak ntukuniskuesits miste uitshieuts kaikushintshi ute Utshimassits." *Shimunish mak Miste-Manian*

"Tshiunitanan uipatsh kaishintuunushunau. Auas eakushitshi kuamuauts kuet ntutats nte ntukuntshuapits. Tshi miste ntenitenan Ntukuntshuap tshetshi Uitshi-ikunau." *Innut Utshi-mauts*

Pase Innuts minuenitamuts espanits ntukuntshua-pinu. Uipatamuts tshetshi atinikanits eshipimpini-takanits. Mushinau uapatamuts kamenipunits ntukuntshuapinu ute Utshimassits. Muk minita nisishueuts tshekuanu.

"Mashuka takun tshekuan eshapitshitakan nte ntukuntshuapits. Mashuka tutsh katusets, mak eishapitshitakants tshekuan kie ntukuna." *Kamamuinats naianumants*

Amanispanuts ntukuniskuesits. Meshikatshi ntukuastukushu pishish muk tau ni minipishiu tshet-shi minu ntusenimat auenua muk ntukuna mineu. Mitshetuts Innuts uauapamats uesham apashish tau. Kutakuts Innuts isishueuts tshekuanu kauitaua uta ntukuastukushu tsheska eanimpinu. Miste mishau akushun ute Utshimassits.

"Ete Kuspe miste mishau ntukuntshuap eukun tshekat espishat Utshimassits. Ekuta Utshimassits apishashu ntukuntshuap mak nishuts muk ntuku-niskuesits, nish tepiskantshi tshipa atuseuts mak nish tshashikantshi?" *Miste-Tuma*

"Auasits eskushiueuts ntukuniskuesa. Mak mentu-aui Innuts. Ntuapameuts ni ntukuniskuesa katshi tshipanikanitshi mak eakuatepiskantshi. Eakunu nenu uishekauitantshi shuka ntukuniskuesa, kus-teuts nenua Innua ntukuniskuesits." *Patinik*

Passe ntukuniskuesits mak ntukuatukushuts meshikataui minuenitakushuts mak passe mitsheni-takushuts. Miapitenimeuts innua, muk nenu shuneanu put uishipapinitshentshi. Nanikutini misteapaten-imukunuts. ntukuniskuesits mak ntukuastikushuts. Passe tshinan mitshiminuenitenan tshetshi uapamatau kaskutimashut ntukuastukushu. Mitshisenimanu meshikatshi eshi ntukuastukushuit. Nas put ntukuas-tukushu put mak kaskutimashut ntukuastukushu muk uiapatshitau stiniunanu tshetshi skutimashut uan-tukastukushuit. Mak passe Innuts ntenimeuts ntuku-niskuesa, muk ntusenitamueut Innua mikunu, kie tshetshi tshishuntshi kuet minats ntukuna kue tshi-uetishauats. Passe ntukuniskuesits mitshenitakushuts emeutshni nakushintaui innua, tshipa nitutueuts Innua uatamakutaui nakushintshi. Mak passe Innuts ntenimeuts ntukuniskuesa kakeshauts muk tshinistipa uapamakanuts nakushitsui eku Innuts uauapamatui ntukuniskuesa. Neush ashuapatamuts tshetshi uapa-makanits.

"Ete Kuspe pushkantaui Innuts kaiakushits ama shuka minu ntusenimakanuts miam kaneapiteni-mataui Innua kuetutuats ntukuastukushuts. Miam nte nitamuk aueshisha katutueutshi." *Shimun mak Mani*

"Kutakuts ntukuniskuesits uenapamataui katshen-uintshi muiuapameuts uinenimeuts." *Mitshimitshi-mau Kaatusets*

"Innuts isishueuts ntukuniskuesits mapitenimeuts Innua eakuatui. Passe ntukuniskuesits mainustushi-uutshimeuts Innu." *Mamunitau Staianimuanu, Innu iskueu*

Mitakun shuka tshekuan tshipa apatshitakanu nte ntukuntshuapits eakushitshi auen. Tshipa tshi uitshi-akanuts Innuts takunits nenu eshapitshitakanits nte ntukuntshuapits. Mishetuts Innuts pushakanits uaku-nakantaui mak uantusenitakantaui mikuaua. Tshi-pushinikunan uantusenimukunaui mak nastesh mat-shuitamakunan etakushinak. Neush tshishue stishinu-apatenan tshetshi uitamakunak etakushinak kuet tshi-ueunikunau esk mitshisenitenan etaushinak. Mak peiuk Innu tshamatshi utuasima miste ustuinuku.

Mitshetuts Innuts etenitats usham neush. Ntuku-niskues ashinuapameu ua pushatshi auenua eakush-intshi. Mushitauts Innuts nakushitaui muk nastesh akushiunakushuts. Ntukuniskues uitamueu nua mis-takushin iteu. Ntukuniskues manatshi Innua ntukuna kauatshinukuntshi nua tshipa pusheu tshetshi uapa-mantshi ntukuastukushua nte Kuspe. Ntukuniskuesits

nurse. This priest would see any patient, day or night, even though he was alone.

Now we do have a clinic in our community. This building is very old and very small. It needs repairs. People can only stay there for one night. We depend a lot on nurses and doctors these days. Some of us think we depend on them too much. But most of us think it is a good thing that we have this clinic. Some people have no complaints with the clinic. One participant said that medical services have improved in Davis Inlet.

"I don't know much about the clinic, but I think the clinic is here to help the sick, so I have no problem with the clinic." *Manik, elder*

"The clinic has not changed our lives. The clinic is here to save lives, not to change them." *Kashetan*

"The clinic is no problem, because doctors and nurses are doing a great job helping the sick in Davis Inlet." *Shimunish and Miste-Manian*

"We are forgetting our own Innu medicines. When a child gets sick, the mother takes the child right away to the clinic. We depend on the clinic too much." *Band Council*

But many of us have had problems with the services of the clinic, and the health care we get. We would like to see some changes. We see these problems many times in Davis Inlet, but no one complains.

"There is a lack of medical services in our community—a lack of staff, equipment, supplies and treatment." *Discussion at Nutuashish Gathering workshop*

There is a shortage of nurses here at all times. When the doctor comes to the community, he only stays a couple of days. He does not have time to do proper examinations, and just prescribes pills. There are many people that are wanting to see him. The short stay is not good. Some of us ask why we can't have a doctor here instead of a travelling doctor. This community is not like other communities. We have big health problems.

"In Goose Bay, there is a hospital the size of a community. Here there is a clinic with two nurses. Why can't we have four nurses, two in the night and two in the day?" *Miste-Tuma, elder*

"Children give the nurses a hard time. That is the reason why we don't have nurses. Also, when people

drink, they go see the nurses and give them a very hard time. They go after hours and late in the night. That is the reason why the nurses don't stay here properly. The nurses are afraid of people here." *Patinik*

Some of the nurses and doctors who come here are really good; others are not. Some nurses come here and don't really care about the people. Maybe they come here only for the money. Sometimes we don't get good care from nurses and doctors. Some of us don't like to be seen by a student doctor. We don't know when the travelling doctor comes if he is a qualified doctor or a student doctor practising his medicine on our bodies. Some of us think that when the nurses treat patients, all they do is take your temperature, take your blood pressure, give you pills, and send you home. Some of the nurses give us a hard time. They argue with people when they are sick. They should just listen to what the patients are saying. Some of us think the white people get better service, that the nurses will see white patients right away, but they don't rush to see Innu patients.

"Here or in Goose Bay, people are not treated properly because some doctors don't care much about Innu people. They see them as animals." *Shimun and Mani*

"Some nurses, when they see the old people, they hate to check them, because old people smell." *Social Services workers*

"People complain that the nurse doesn't care if she hurts people when she is treating them. Some nurses don't think we feel pain." *Gathering Voices participant*

The clinic here doesn't have much medical equipment. Lives could have been saved if the clinic had proper equipment. Too many people have to be sent out. People are sent out now for X-rays and blood tests. We have to go out to get checked for any diseases. Sometimes we go out for tests and return after a couple of days with no report on what is wrong with us. Sometimes it takes a long time to find out what is really wrong with someone when they are sick. Sometimes we come back, we don't know what is wrong and we are still sick. Also, it is hard when only one parent can escort a child when he or she has to go to the hospital.

Many people feel that sometimes the nurses wait too

mui ntukueuts uenua patush miste akunukuts. Katsheniuts ama miminuenitamuts unapamats usumuaua eshinakushintshi. Tshipa uiuitshaiuts Stuasiminuts esk eka unitats mishue uipats Kaishiniunanuts. Nishinakunu tshetshi natutuauts stuasiminuts. Uitshatusemauts mak emiauts, kie Uitshinushunak punitaiak eminak, tshipa nitutakunuts. Tshishatshianuts stuasiminuts mak uinuau tshi shatshinukunuts. Tshishue stuasiminuts tshika miste espitentakushuts eskunte tshi shinitautshitaue.

Innuts pushitaui Kuspe ama pitikianuuts nete ntukutshuapits. Tamek nete mitshiuap kataiats itakanuts ant nash mistakushitaui. Eku uatshiuepitaui nanikutini nikitauakanuts. Nanikutini ama nistutam kakeshamunu. Mitshetuts uatshiuepinits muku ama tshitshi uepinuts. Tshenuts uinipuuts nete utasiuats. Ntukuastikushuts tutueuts nte ntukutshiuapits tshetshi nipintshiu. Ama minuau. Innu tshipa shenitam tshetshi nipit nete utasits, ntukuastukushu tshipa tshiuetishaueu.

Innu uskueu pushakanu uautuashimitshi nete ntuku-tshiuapits. Tapints nutshikuats nuskeuts uetuasimitshi kie shenitamuts tshetutuats. Eku anush eatapa tutakanu. Nanikutini niskueu peik put nish pishuma ashinuapatum tshetshi minushit.

"Peik pishuma ntishinuapaten tshetshi minushinan tshitshue nimuestaten. Ama nishenimau auen nete kuspe. Nimitatau ntanish kie napem. Katshi mishikaian ama nishenimuk ntanish. Tshishue miskuau niskueu tshetshi nika tat. Tauts niskueuts tshipa tutamuts auasha uaniutshi. Mishetuts auashits eniuts nete nushimits, euitshinukuts Innu uskeua. Eapits nikatishinikanu." *Epa*

Ntukuna eapits ama minuaua. Nanikutini Innu ntukuun minakanu ntukuna. Ama takuea nakushinaui ntukuna. Ama tshiminu uitamakunan eshinakuatshi ntukunan. Kutukuts eshishueuts tshetshi mishinanikanitshi ntukuna maiakataui. Ama tshikishi uinushunan mishinanikanish muku tshetshi ntuapatamak ntukunau. Usham tshimiste apitshitanan ntukunan. Ama tshishenitenan eshinakuatshi ntukuna. Ama shuka uitshinueua ntukuna. Ntukuna ama minuau.

"Anutsh ntuapamapin ntukuniskueu eku uatimuut etakushiuts. Minuats natau eku tuk ama tshinistutatin kauitamuun. Eku tshekuanu uish mint ntukuna." *Utshimassiu Innu*

Anuts uauapamakantshi ntukuniskues nistam mishinanikan tutakanu eku patush katshiuapamat ntukuniskues Innua. Mitshetuts Innuts etenitats ama tshika situtakanu mishinanikan uauapamakantshi ntukuniskues miam miste mishatshi ntukunshuap kuitutakanua mauats tshikatshiuapamuk ntukuniskues eka miste akushim. Pase katsheniutshi Innuts misenimeuts pishumukaia eku puminuats eka senimats tshenuts pishumukaia Innuts kakanistutuatsh kakeshaua eukuntsh miste animenitats. Kaetantaui auenua tsheutunikakuts. Kie matatamuts kamituetishintshi pase Innuts. Pepushi mak napishi mitshetuts Innuts etats nte nutshimits. Pase muk tatamuts takapishenikea, miminuanu tshetshi pita mishinauakanits uauapamataui ntukuniskuesa eakushitaui. Ntukuniskuesa eakushitaui. Kie Innuts etutetaui nte ntukuntshuapi tshishue neush ashuapatamuts tshetshi uapamakanits. Kuet nanikutini tshiuets mitshi uapameuts ntukuniskuesa kuet miste akushits. Uapamatakue ntukuniskues nenua Innua tshi-pa tshi uitshiepan tshetshi eka miste akushintshi. Uneshamipinaui nta kauitamakuiak tshetakushinau, tshitshue nitshue-nimuk-ni ntukuniskues. Mak ntukuniskues tutam mishinanikan tsheuapamantshi ntukuastukushua uamishikantshi. Ka uanakantshinta Innu. Mitshiuapameu nenua ntukuastukushua. Uipats nte muk eshinakust auen uauapamatshi ntukuastukushua uapamepan. Meshikantshi.

Nanikutini mitauts ntukuniskuesits etuapamakantaui nte ntukuntshuapits. Miste apatshitakanu shuneau tshetshi mushinau tats ntukuniskuesits nte ntukuntshuapits mestiakushitshi auen matshikastinakanuts ntukuniskuesits. Innuts kaetitats kamituetishintshi mitshimituestauts, eku pemutets etuapamats ntukuniskuesa. Nanikutini muinutemuakanuts put kie mitanua ntukuniskuesa nte uitshuaunits. Nakushitshi auen nte neka atashi pineshuakantshi mitshi ntukuniskuesa uitshinits. Mak kaetatshi ntukuniskues nte uitshits miste animenitakunu kameskuakantshi.

Tshuaputs pishe inuts tante ama uitaapimukuts uitshuat inuts kamiste akushits kie katsheniuts. Ama uinateuts inua nakushitshi tshetshi ntutetshi ntukutshuapits. Pishe ntukuniskueuts tshuaputs uashamakataui. Itenitamutshe-tshi Innua uitshuaua uinakunua. Muku ashinuapameu mushinau tshetshi etu akushitshi.

CAMILLE FOUILLARD PHOTO

Shuash, Akat and Katinin at Nutuashish Gathering workshop / Shuash, Akat mak Katinin nte Nutuashish kamamuitunatsh, 1992

long to send people out when they are sick. A person can feel where the pain is but might not look sick. The nurse tells people there is nothing wrong with them. When the nurse prescribes pills and they don't help, the nurse should send the people to see the doctor in Goose Bay. It seems like the nurse won't do anything until the person is really sick, then they send the person to Goose Bay. When the doctor finds the problem, it is too late. We have seen this happen often. But sometimes we also see the mission plane coming in the night for emergencies.

People go out to Goose Bay and they are not admitted right away. They are told to go to the Friendship Centre, even when they are very sick. When it is time to go home on the mission plane, sometimes the patient is left behind. Sometimes this person can't speak English. Sometimes people want to come home and they can't. Many elders want to die in the community. Doctors let them die in hospitals. This is not right. If a person decides to die in their own community, doctors should let them go back.

Pregnant women now have to go out of the community to the hospital for a long time. There used to be midwives and they knew what they were doing. Now it is all changed. Some women wait one or two months for their delivery.

"I waited for a month when I was pregnant and I was really homesick. I didn't know anybody in Goose

Camille Fouillard Photo

Ketshastipeneu and Akatis at community workshop /
Ketshastipeneu mak Akatis nte kaianimuanits, 1992

"Peikuau napem mistakushu. Nuuishamanan ntuku-niskueu eku ama takushinu. Eku minuats uashamit-shish, ekunu tekushint tshash tshishue ama tshi atshinua napema." *Shanutish*

"Peikuau takushin nipit eku etuapamik ntuku-niskueu. Ntuk tshepetuten uapashe. Ama nista nipan tepiskats kie ama tshi nipan. Tshishue ntakushin." *Kamamuinants aianumeun*

Nanikutini Inuts ituteuts ntukutshiuapits eku ama tanua kautuniatsheshitshi. Mishetuts inuts kanestutats kie kakatshi uitamuats etakushits kie auasha etitshi. Tshenuts ama tshi uitamueuts etakushits tante ama kashiuts kakeshamunu. Tshipa tau Innu kenashiut ekake-shamut. Tshishue miskuinuku Innu tshetshi uauitak eshinikatetshi akushuna. Ekunitshe nanikutini ntukuastukushu kie ntukuniskueu uish eatapa minuets ntukuna. Stiniminuts tshipa tauts nete ntukuniskuets ama tapuetam tshetshi tshimakanitshi. Ama minuau tshetshi pushakant Innu epekushit eka nistutak kake-shamunu. Kustatshuuts penekushitaui.

Nanikutini nakushitshi auenia etuapamatshi ntuku-niskuesa, eku atat ni shitakunapun staushiskakunau.

Eku stenimanatsh ntukuniskuesits nastesh mapiten-imeuts nakushitaui mak nas kaitenimeutshi tshetshi nipintshi. Muipusheutsni tshenistipa, patush nas kakatshiuitshia-kanitshi emiste akushintshi kuet pushatsh. Mak ntshe kastipetsh tshuitamakunuts etu kaui minusenitamutshi ntukuniskuesits mak ntukuas-tukushuts etenitakunits shitakunapunu, mak tshipa skutimashuts tshenish-uitshiats kakushiskakuntshi shi-takunapunu.

"Ntukuniskuesits mineuts Innua ntukuna. Minuts matshitaui Innuts ntukuna, senimeu nenua etintshi ntukuniskues, muk inishatsh mineu. Innuts kamin-utshi shitakunapunu minakanuts ntukuna, "Lib-rium" nishinikatenua. Librium miam ntenitakun shi-takunapun, miam uatshatshi etu tshetshi minitshi Innua katutueua ntukuniskues." *Kastipetsh*

"Peiukuau nuitamuau ntukuniskues tshetshi pushat peiuk Innua nte ntukuntshuapits. Nistam tshipa uintukakanu, eku ntuk ne Innu tshekuan nte uistu-tamen, esk ne Innu minu shitakunapunu." *Shuash*

Katusets nte ntukuntshuapits uapatamueuts nenua Innua umishintinikanu entakushinitshi mak uetuniku-

Bay. I missed my little girl and my husband. When I came home, my little girl didn't want to come to me. She didn't know me. It is really hard for women to be away from their families too long. We have midwives in the community. They can look after the deliveries. Many Innu children were born in the country with Innu midwives. That's all been taken from us too." *Epa*

Pills are a problem. Sometimes people are given the wrong pills. We can't get pills for pain. Other times, we don't get enough information about how much medication to take. Some people think it is not good to give the children the same medicine over and over. Others complain that you have to have it written on paper in order to get a prescription. We don't like to have to make an appointment just to get a bottle refilled when the nurse gives us the same medication. Some people say we depend on pills too much. We don't know what we are taking when we take prescription pills. A lot of pills don't work, even antibiotics. Pills are not good for us.

"Not too long ago, I went to the nurse and explained to her about my problem. The second time I went to see her, she told me she didn't understand what I was saying. Why then did she give me pills?" *Gathering Voices participant*

Today we have to make appointments to see the nurse. Many of us think, this is a small clinic and we shouldn't have to make appointments like in a big hospital. The nurse won't see you right away unless you are very sick. Some of the old people can't tell time. This is no good for them. The people who can't speak English are the hardest hit when there is no one to help them. No more than ten homes have phones. During the winter or summer, many people are away from the community. Some camps have bush radios, but it is crazy to have to make appointments from a camp to see the nurse or doctor. If someone is sick in a camp, does he or she have to come to Davis Inlet to make an appointment? Then when people go to the clinic, they always have to wait. Sometimes they have to go home without being seen because they had to wait too long. They go home and sometimes they get seriously ill, and the nurses have an emergency on their hands. These emergency situations could be avoided if the nurse had seen the patient. Sometimes, when we are late for our appointments, the nurse gets mad at us. Also, the nurse

makes a list of people for the doctor to see when he comes. If a person is not on the list, sometimes he or she can't see the doctor. In the past, anyone could see the doctor whenever he came.

Sometimes, the nurse is just not available. After hours, the clinic is empty. We are told it is too expensive for nurses to stay at the clinic at night. We don't know what Grenfell means by that. [Grenfell Regional Health Services, a provincial government appointed body, administers health care to communities in the Northern Peninsula and Labrador portions of Newfoundland]. In the night, when a person is sick, it is hard to get the nurse. For the people who have no phone, they have to walk to the nurses' residence. We go to the nurses' residence and they don't open the door. Or they are not there. If we bring a patient from the camp at night and it is an emergency, we take the patient to the nurses' residence. If the nurse is not at the nurses' residence, you waste your time trying to find her.

People are upset because it seems that most of the nurses won't do home visits to people who are bedridden or the elderly. They don't like to go even when the person is too sick to go to the clinic. Some nurses get mad when they are asked to come. Maybe they think Innu homes are too dirty. It is like wait and wait, until the person is very sick.

"Once my husband was very sick. We called the nurse but she wouldn't come. We called a second time and the nurse came this time, but my husband was already unconscious." *Shanutish*

"One time, I had a really bad toothache and I went to the nurse. She told me to come back tomorrow. I was up all night and couldn't sleep. I had too much pain." *Gathering Voices participant*

Sometimes people go to the clinic and there is no interpreter. A lot of people here don't speak English and we can't tell the nurse about our problem or our child's problem. The old people can't tell what is wrong with them because they don't speak English. A good interpreter is very hard to find. Sometimes an interpreter cannot find the name of the kind of disease the person might have. Maybe that is why the doctor or nurse makes mistakes and prescribes the wrong pills to the patients. We need our own people in the clinic. Sometimes when someone is sick, the nurse won't allow

ataui. Eku unauitamuats nenu Innu utakushunu muk eshin akushintshi auenua uitamueuts. Apu minuants nenu etutats. Minishinakunu tshetshi uauitakanits Innuts etakushits. Akueuts nenua etutuats Innua unauitamuat etakushintshi. Kutakuts Innuts etutetaui nte ntukun-tshuapits kustatshuts tshetshi uauitas nenu nas etakushits. Kie mitshetuts Innuts etenimats ntukuni-skuesa tshetshi emiats ni nenua katusenuani nte ntukuntshuap. Mui atuseuts ni eakushim-puetaui.

Ama minuanu ntukuniskuesits katshipamutshi kauapekaushunanits ni nte ntukuntshuapits. Nishinakunu tshetshi uapekauakuts stuasi-minuts. Mushinau uapekauakanipantsni auasits nte ntukuntshuapits. Passe ntukuniskuesits uaka-kanuts uanakushintaui auasa. Mitshetuts stuasiminuts uetikumits. Katusets nte ntukuntshuapits stapauepants ni auasa ustikuanua uetikamintshi tshash ne minita tutakanu. Mak auasits uminisimuts, mipimpi-nua nipina nte tshitshinats eku mitshiuapekaushunan. Nuiuapatenan tshetshi uapekaushuts Innuts minuats nte ntukuntshuapits, takun nte nipin pempintsh. Kie Innuts mitshikuapitsheuts nte ntukuntshuapits, senitakaue Innuts kuapikanitshe nte, mishue auen tshikau, kuapi-tsha ntakanuts. Kakeshauts muk tapuetuakanuts tshe-tshi kuapitshets nte ntukuntshuapits.

"Nitshuenimuk ntukuniskues mitshimukuauts stuasimits ntuk. Ntshiuetishank tsheuapekautau stuasimits ntuk nteskushin mushinau esikuapitshean. Tshipa senitam ntukuniskues kapempinits nipinu nte mitshuapits." *Mitshimitshimau kaatusets*

"Ntukuniskues eapits uitamueu Innua tshenitshintau mak pepeskupintaui stikumuauts stutakuauts iteu. Matshi senitau ntukuniskues kapempinits nipinu nte mitshuapits. Misiuapekaushunan eshikum tshishikaua nenu kakeshau katua. Eshikum tshishikaua put tshipatshi uapekaushunan pimpints nipin nte tshitshinats." *Mani Katini*

Matshuishuka tapuetuanuts ntukuniskuesits mak ntukuastukushuts eshimukunaui ntukuna.

"Tshash tshi matishikun mitshetuau, mashuka nuiu-

atapuetuauts ntukuastikushuts, ntukuastukushuts ntenimauts nipeuts innua." *Miste-Nishapet*

"Mitshetuts Innuts eanimenitats ntukuntshuapinu etukuakantaui. Passe tshitaunakanuts nte kuspe. Ntukuntshuapits mak passe minita petaunakanuts, niputs nte kuspe ntukuntshuapits put ete kuestetshe assits. Eku mishuka tshuitapuetuanuts ntukuniskuesits ute Utshimassits. Mue nin mushinau ntakushin muk manuiuapamau ntukuniskues mashuka nuitapuetuau tshekuan esishuetshi." *Matininish*

Passe tshinan stanamenitenan neu ntukuniskuesits uaiapatshitats nutshimits nte assits uetenikanitshi ntukunu. Matshisenitamutshe tshenishapitshitat. Muk put uintusenitamutshe etenitakunitshi nutshimit assit ntukuna.

Innuts Uinuau Tshetshi Pimpintats Akushiu-Atuseun

Matshiminuenitenan passe eshi pimpinitakants ume eakushinaui. Misenitamuts eshi niuak. Ntukuastukushuts mak ntukuniskuesits tshipa nitutueuts Innua uatamakutaui tshekuanu.

"Ntukuastukushu uimatisheu nutauna katshi nipintshi. Minui tapuetuau muats ntau. Matishakantshe enkunu enu tshe uishisenimakant uets nipit ntuk. Maniuiuapamau uiu nepit. Kuet matishuats ne nastesh matshekuan tshinisishuen, mantshishukustishen uamatishakanits nutaun uiu katshi nipit." *Utshimassiu Innu*

Nui uapamanants ntukuniskuesit mak ntukuastukushuts tshetshi mushinau apits ute Utshimassits ntukuntshuapits. Nuiuapamanan Innuskueu tshetshi ntukuniskueut, eakun ne Innu ntukuniskueuts auen tshipatshi nistutaku Innua uantukunukushintshi innuaianimuet. Mak tshipa minuananu tat tsheuitshat nusheskueua uaminushintaui niskueua. Atukuantshe, nuiuapatenan tshetshi mishatsh mitshetits katusets. Antshe paushitakanu ntukuntshuap tshetshi tats kaiakushits tshetshi eka pushakanits mak tshetshi tukuatshi mishue tshekuan etapatshitakant nte ntukuntshuapits.

an escort to go with them. It is stupid to let a person go to the hospital by himself or herself when they don't speak English. They are afraid to go alone.

Sometimes when a person goes to see the nurse, she says people are sick from alcohol. Some of us feel that the nurses don't care about Innu people when they are sick from drinking. They don't care if they die or not. They don't send them out, only when it is too late. Also, our workers at the alcohol program tell us that the nurses and doctors need to know more about alcohol problems and how to treat them.

"The nurse gives the people pills. People take these pills when they are drinking. The nurse should be able to tell that the people are drinking, yet she still gives them pills. People who are drinking are given pills called Librium. Librium is like alcohol, and people can get addicted to them. It's like you are helping the person to drink more." *Alcohol Program workers*

"Once I asked the nurse to send a person to the hospital to dry up. He needed medical help first. The person told me that was a crazy thing to do. This person is still drinking." *Shuash*

The staff at the clinic see the patients' records or they know things about people when they interpret. Sometimes they talk about the patients' illnesses to the public. This is no good, and it should not be allowed to happen. The patients' medical records should be kept confidential. The patient's personal life is being violated when the nurses' aides talk about their illness to someone who is not employed at the clinic. Then, when people go to the clinic, they are sometimes afraid to let the nurses know what their real problems are. Some of us think the nurses should also talk to the clinic aides about their drinking. They don't come to work because they are hungover.

It is a problem that the nurses cut the showers at the clinic. We need to bathe our children and babies. We used to be able to do this. Some nurses even complain when our children are dirty. Many of our kids have head lice. The workers at the clinic used to clean the children's heads for lice. They don't do that any more. Children also get boils. We don't have running water in our homes. We would like to see people taking baths at the clinic because this is a place with water. Also, Innu people can't get water at the clinic. They are told that if people see or learn about it, everyone would come to get water. But white people can get water at the clinic.

"The nurse was mad at me and said that I don't clean my children. She sent me home and told me to wash my baby at home. I am really tired of carrying water. The nurse should know by now that we don't have running water." *Social Services worker*

"The nurse once told people the rashes, itching or red spots on the skin was caused by lice. If only the nurse knew there is no water in our houses. We can't have baths every day like white people. We probably would if we had water in our homes." *Mani Katinin*

Some of us just don't trust the medicine of nurses and doctors.

"I have had operations, and I don't trust doctors. I think doctors are killing people." *Miste-Nishapet*

"My other concern is that clinics are hard to trust any more, because many people are treated in the clinic. Some are sent to Goose Bay hospital, and some never come back. They died in the hospital, in Goose Bay, or elsewhere. Now it is very hard for us to trust clinics in Davis Inlet. Like myself, I'm sick but I don't want to see the nurse because I can't trust her any more." *Matininish*

Some of us worry about the nurses who try to use Innu medicines in the clinic. We don't know if they know how to use it. They might just be testing it.

Innu Control of Health Services

Some of us don't agree with the way Grenfell is running our health services. They don't understand the way we live. We think doctors and nurses should listen more to what people want to do. We need services for when people are in camps in the country. There might be emergencies. Camps need C.B. radio contact with the community all the time.

"The doctor wanted to do the autopsy on my father's body. I kept saying no to her. She said that was the only way they would know what really happened to him. I didn't want my dad's body cut open. They did it anyway. I couldn't stop the doctor from making this decision." *Gathering Voices participant*

We would like to see permanent nurses and a doctor at the clinic. We need a Native registered nurse, someone who could talk to her patients in her own language. We would like to have a midwife. When we relocate, we need a bigger clinic with more staff. It should be a place where people can stay if they are sick instead of going out, and it should have emergency equipment.

NIANEU ETSHITAPATEKEN

KAMAKUNUEST

"R.C.M.P. nishitshitapatikinu Royal Canadian Mounted Police eku nin ai eshanimiash apu takuash. Mishiue nishinikateuts R.C.M.P. kie put mountie, eukein eshini-katetits enu kakeshnmunu apu senimitshis tshe ni shinikatitshitsh enu eshian-imueutshish. Ninai muk eshitshitapimitshish enu ataspeshut, enu ntishinakataets-kamakunuest, nishinikateu, 'the man who locks up people.'" *Shustinis*

Tshe peshashu nte etaiash. Aiask muk ueueshakanuts innuts nte kuestetshe epishasi assina mesteueshintunanu eapits, uipats ete minita pikuneaiapin tshekuan. Etu ish minanu, ete Innuts pikunumuts tshekuanu kamakunue-shits nemetshipininukunqiits ntenimaiaits. Uesets kamakunueshits etat ute, mushuka mishetuts Innuts pa-kunats tshekuanu, eku tshash mishituts minakunakanits, pise apetenimeuts mak pise mapitenimeuts. Tshishue mishiueu tshekuan eta pakunamash. Ntakutunai mak nimimamishimitunai eku minamiti-

Mani, Miste-Nishapet and Epa at worskshop on recommendations / Mani, Miste-Nishapet mak Epa nte kautshimuanimanits, 1992

nenitamash. Eku pise usham nimistispitennimanan kamakunueshitsh. Pise kamakunueshitsh ntenimaiaitsh pikunumutsh enua Innua 'law' ute etatuai ntisinash. Nisenimaiaitsh pakunashi Innua Eshipimpantshi, tsheutshimau misenitum eshipantshi Innua, eku kaueshintunantsh mak kamakuneshitsh minustueu Innua, mak ninai minustuaiaits.

"Kamakunueshitsh mak tshe utshimau nastesh meatishiutsh nui entishumukunaits tshe, nishimpipi nutshish enu kakeshaua." *Utshimassiu Innu*

"Ete uipats tshishue nikustaiaits kamakunueshit pise Innuts mushinau tshishipitshuts mak pise tauts pitakamish eku muk uitshatshuapishuts eta shipuastenitakanish enu tshe tshi kanatukuts." *Kashetan*

Pise Innuts minuenitamuts entantshi kamakuneshitshi nte ntisinash Innuts ne intenimeuts nakatiuapimikunaits kamakunueshits, enu uistats kamakunueshit tshekatimikinitsh tshekuanu ntukunu nanikutini tshekuanu tshe tshi uitshinimist. Innuts eushikuataui uenua tshika tshi utinakanuts. Pise ntishueai nastesh mitutakanu tshekuan etataui, kamakunueshits. Kamakunueshits aiantineutsh kaminishintsh. Eku kamakunueshits ntenitakushut kanani kamatsheshits muk nanikutini apu minupinash, pise kamakunueshits tshishue uiuitsheuts innua, eku pise kutikuts iash ntenitakushuts mapitenitimuts tshekuana etutshishi tshekuanu pise uakashanueuts innua. Nanukutini kamakunueshits minuteseuts mak nanukutinu miste iatapa enituuts.

"Nastesh matukun tshe kuan tshenisishueian mak nastesh matukun tshe anamuekataman." *Shenum*

"Tastesh uma minuau tshe tshi tats kamakunueshits uta, miam nte tepenitats ntassinanu." *Auash Kaskutimashut*

CAMILLE FOUILLARD PHOTO

CHAPTER EIGHT

THE POLICE AND THE JUSTICE SYSTEM: KAMAKUNUEST—"THE MAN WHO LOCKS PEOPLE UP"

"The R.C.M.P. stands for the Royal Canadian Mounted Police, but in our language we don't have those words. Many of us say R.C.M.P., or police, or Mountie. We say these words in English but we don't know what we should call them in our own language. We just see R.C.M.P. on their uniform. The word we use in our language, *kamakunuest*, means "the man who locks up people." *Shushtinis, Native court worker*

We live in a small community. The number of crimes here is increasing. The number of problems in the community is increasing too. In the past, we didn't break any laws. Since there has been more alcohol, a lot of people break the law. We blame the police for some of these problems. Before the police came here, not that many people broke the law. Now, many of our people end up in jail. Some of us care and some of us don't care. We have a lot of problems with the law. We hurt each other and bring each other to court. Then we feel sorry for that. Some of us think we depend too much on the police. Some of us think the R.C.M.P. break Innu laws when they are in our communities. But we know even if they break our laws, the governments would never recognize our laws. The police and the court don't understand the Innu, and we don't understand their laws.

"The police are not different from other government agencies. They want all of us to follow the white man's way." *Gathering Voices participant*

"In the past, we were really scared of the police. Some Innu always stayed away from the community when they were in town. Other people would stay at home peeking out of their windows to make sure that the police did not come to their homes." *Kashetan*

Some people think it is good to have the police in our community. They think the police are here to keep an eye on the people and to protect us. The police are here to prevent crimes and tragedies from happening. There are times when we need their help. People who hurt other people or damage other people's property should be arrested. Some of us say that the community seems quieter when the R.C.M.P. are stationed here. The police can deal with drunks. So the R.C.M.P. are like peace officers for some people, but others say the police do not give us security and sometimes just cause more problems. Some police who come here really try to help the Innu. But others are different and they don't care what happens to us. Some of them are racist. Sometimes the R.C.M.P. do a good job and other times they make big mistakes.

"I have no comments and no complaints. I don't need them and I have no problems with them." *Shenum, elder*

"It is not a good thing for the police to be stationed here all the time because they act like they own our community." *Youth Council member*

"I like the police being stationed here, but they should always try to be there when people need their help. It is their job to prevent tragedies from happening in the community. Police should prevent crimes from happening and respond to people who need their help." *Manteskueu*

"Back in the old days, there were no laws about fishing and hunting. There was no such thing as trespassing. We walked without any fear on our land and hunted wherever we wanted. But today, we can't do anything without getting a licence. Everything has to be registered. Back in the good old days, we were free. It is still our land." *Tshan*

"Once when I was coming back from hunting, the

"Menuau kamakunueshits tshe tshi tats muk tapue mushimau tshakatshi tauts etimikinitshi tshe kuanu uta ntsinash. Kamakunieshits tshakatshi nanakaimits tshe tshi kashuka tshiskuanits mak tshetshi uitshats enua uashamukutaui." *Manteskueu*

"Uipats ete nastesh metakun 'Law' nutemeshantshi mak etuuiunantshi. Minita pete tshetshi pastueten tshekuan. Nipimutenan nastesh minikustatshinan ute ntisinash muk uautuiunash kue ituteash. Eku anush mantshituteiai tshekuan patish kannu kapit-shaia mishue tshekuan tshika mishinianikinu, uipats ete minuapin, nastesh minutshikakunai, etu esku ninai ntisinai." *Tshan*

"Peikua katshi tukushinan etuiunan kamakunuest nteshi-napimukushipantsh eta nashipetimish, uiuap-atum niutinu, metakuna tshekuanu nta eka tapuetuk muats etik petute ntuk ete kamakunueshits tshi-uapits. Natutshea niutinu muk nastesh mimeskum tshekuanu." *Kaniuekutat*

Piekushu muk tshekuan eka minuenitamash kamakune-shits uakustinimist ntuiunanu. Ntenitakushuts kakustisheshits aueshisha. Innuts ntuiuts eku muk kusteuts kamakunueshintshi. Nanukutini Ueshakanuts etuatau utuassimaua. Ueshishits Innu mitshum. Ntuiun eshiniuats, minuiunitaiai ninai nanikutini nuituapateia tshemitshinash nte naka. Nisentenan menuatsh. Niminiunai mak nishut-shiuskuakunai, kamakunueshits ntukunaits tshetshi kashuka mistenapeik atiuk. Matapuetakunaits tshetshi ntuintshish shakunitshi enua shisipa mak niska. Nuikanumikuakunaits enu nutuuiunu mak nutemeshantshi mak kutekena tshekuanu. Aiask mitsheua enua 'Law' katuiunantsh kanaui kustinikunaiatsi ntuiunn kuetenimikua me un eshiniunash. Nastesh minashanakunu tshetshitutunimist. Kamakunueshits nana skakunaits ute ntiniunash.

Tshishue misheua tshikuaia ekaminupinash minustu-tumuts kamakunueshits enu eshipi-pinutshish mak Innuts mishetuts eka nistutatan en kakeshaua 'Law'. Mineseniteiai nastesh eshipimpinantsh enu kakeshau kinishimpimpinua minuinispiniunai auen pakunashi tshekuanu. Mineseniteia kanispiniunai. Mishuka-tauts kautunikatsheshits enu Innuts uashamukutaui kamakunueshintshi. Minustuteai enua tshetshi nishin-

uakuats nta teshe kakeshau 'Law'. Kamakunuest uati-maski nishinakun tshetshit kastun. Innuts minestuta-muts nanukutini kamakunueshits minatutemuts enu 'Law'. Nanukutini kamakuneshits Innua attuteeuts tshetshi eminukuts esk aka emats kauitshinueshintshi. Eku uauitshinukushinashi nimaetestuaia peta tshishue animentakun. Nimishetinai tshetshi itikuau tshekuanu kamakunueshits enu ekamunupinuts.

"Tshashu tshimakunikun kamakunest autimut pak-inumuts 'Law' minestutuau. Minesenite tshekuan pakunuman ntuapimau kautunikatshest, muishuapeikepu kamakunuest nanikutini utinakunu uen eka tutatshi tshekuana. Eatapa utinakanu. Ekaninistutuatshi auen kakeshamunu nastesh matakunu tshenanikani kut kuet muk uitshat kamakunueshintshi. Kamakunuest mineu mis-hanikanu emitaueu kuet muk uinushuntshi mak pat tshipeatukustau eukun kamakunuest etutuat Innua ute eku tiapuemakinitshi." *Shushepmak kie Mani Katinin*

"Nanukutini Innuts muimineuts mishinanikinu kamakunueshintshi. Eku muk meskamut tshekuna tshetshi kustatshimat Innua mak tshetshi shetshiat. Eukunu enu uishtapuemikunash nte kaueshitu-nantshi, tshe kamakunuest uitamueu tsheitutuak-intshi. Eukan tshekuan mushinau etimikash tsheka-makunuest etiski matshuinisihue tshekuan itisk etu tshash nante tshiminuen tshenishuen nte kaueshitu-nunants. Tante eku tshikatshi nisisheu tshekuanu eka nastutak kakeshamun. Kamakunueshit mishinamuet esishuentshi uinua uitamueuts enitutats etu nte ueshitunatsh pisk metakuaua enu kauitumuats." *Shimun kie Manin*

"Piekau ntutanikun nte kamakunueshiutshuapits eka utunikakunan mishuka nustutuan kakeshau nituapineuts tshe utunikuntshi kuet ueueshinakunan muk. Mushinau tshika-nantuapamau auassa uauapi-matshi mak Innua ntuasim pisishipan ntutakanu ntukuntshiuapits." *Kaianumet*

"Peikua nuapimau kamakunuest nte taueutshi-uapits, nuitamak ma tshinista minauuts auassits ntuk eku ntau muats ntapueuan enu etek eku ntek tshetshi shikashun nishuneapis ashu petetash eku tshashikashunan eku minista ueshinakunn kat-shishikashunake kamakunu-kunapen." *Tshenish*

"Nusim uishamakanu kamakunuetshiuapits. Uiutin-

R.C.M.P. was waiting for us on the beach. He asked to see my hunting bag, but I didn't have anything. When I said no, he asked me to come to the police quarters. They checked my bag but found nothing."
Kaniuekutat

One thing we don't like is when the police interfere with our hunting. R.C.M.P. are like wildlife officers. People go out hunting and they are afraid of the police. Sometimes people get charged for hunting for food for their families. The wildlife is Innu food. We need to eat this country food to survive. Hunting is our tradition and culture. We don't want to lose it. We sometimes want to get fresh meat from nature. We know it is good for us. It makes us healthy and strong. The police tell us they don't want the Innu to kill too many caribou. They don't want us to hunt out of season, like ducks and geese. We have to get licences for hunting, fishing and so on. There are more and more laws on hunting. It seems like they are trying to put a stop to our hunting. This is not our way of life. They have no right to do that to us. The R.C.M.P. are interfering in our lives.

A lot of our problems happen because the police don't understand our culture, and because many Innu people don't understand the white man's laws. We know nothing about the legal system. We don't like to get involved when someone breaks the law. We don't know how to react to it. There is a lack of interpreters when Innu have to deal with the police. We don't understand our rights under the white laws. If a police officer asks you a question, you have the right to remain silent. People don't know what is meant by that. Sometimes the police don't seem to respect their own laws. The police have misled some Innu and forced them to make statements without a lawyer. When we want help from a lawyer, we have to call one outside the community. This makes it very difficult. Many of us have stories of times when we had problems with the police.

"I have been to jail myself. When the police told me I had broken the law, I didn't know what he meant. I didn't know what I broke. I asked for an interpreter. This officer was not in his uniform. Some people get arrested when they haven't done anything

wrong. They are arrested by mistake. If this person does not speak English, he has no choice but to co-operate with the police. The police writes a statement for him, reads it to him, and they ask him to sign. It doesn't matter if it is just an X or his signature. This is what the police do to people here, and then they are found guilty in court." *Shushepmak and Mani Katinin*

"Sometimes people don't want to make a statement to the police. But the police always find a way to scare you or say other things to make you nervous. This is the way police force us to make statements. If we make a statement to the police, it means we are already found guilty. The second guilty verdict is at the judge's hands. These things happen over and over again here. When a judge asks you to say anything before he sentences you, you have nothing to say because your statement was read out in court. When a person is arrested and he speaks very little English, the police have to force him to make a statement. But how can a person make a statement when he speaks only a little bit of English? The police make up the statement for him. They make up their own story, and in the court some of the things the person said are not in his statement." *Mani and Shimun*

"One time, they took me to the cabin without a translator. I didn't understand English very well. They didn't look for someone to translate for me and they took me to court. They should always get an interpreter when they see children or adults. My baby was little at the time. She was taken to the clinic." *Gathering Voices participant*

"Once I met the police officer in the store. He asked me if I had been giving drinks to young boys. I told him I wasn't and that I was telling the truth. He told me I would have to pay a $25 fine. I paid the fine in the store although I never went to court. If I hadn't paid the fine, I guess I would have gone to jail." *Tshenish, elder*

"My grandson was asked to go to the R.C.M.P trailer. The police wanted to take a report. My grandson told him that he never did the things the police were asking him about. But the police kept saying he did. They didn't believe him. They pushed my grandson to say he did the things he didn't do. My grandchild is not a troublemaker. I watched a show one time about

CAMILLE FOUILLARD PHOTO

Peashueshish, Nutuashish Gathering mukushan /
Peashueshish, mupimepan ete kanatshemaianits
Nutuashish, 1992

imeuts esishuentshi nusim minitatute tshekuanu kanuuitamakutshi kamakunueshits. Metutam tshekuanu. Mita puetueuts kamakunueshits tutueuts tshetshi nisishuentshi ntuten enu ekatutamantshi meue nusim kaka pikunak tshekuanu. Peikuan nishatshiman innu ueshiakanu nepatatshet minepeu uenua e kakeshaunipeu, nikuste tshetshi tutuakanits Innuts." *Utshimassiu Innu*

"Nastesh mintapuetuauts kamakunueshits enu katshi pisets nitshinash eka tutamats tshekuanu, nuitamakun kamakunueshits ntuapatamuts shitakunapanu nte mitshuapits. Tateshekamuan mukuanumuts tshetshi pisets. Nau nuistuten nuinatapen. Nipaseken, nta ntestan espimitshuakentikush eku tetueshetatshetsh, munuitute-muauts kuet taskuats stukea, kuet pisets nipu nta peik kamakunuest kuetipiskum mishiue nipinu pipitshitikush nuikashinen nipasikan eku uetamauts kamakunuest nisishikeuth katshi tshekat piek meastakanits ntakushipan nui pasuk nikakatshinamuk. Nastesh minista pasau auen etshi niunan eku nisishuetshe eatapa ntitan enu uetamauk eka tuta tshekuanu. Minita ueshinikun, ueshinikunaiakue mishiue kaui-tamuapan tshekaunu tshekamakunaest. Niminunish nisishuk esk minita minuau." *Tshenish*

Kamakunueshits tshaka minuuitamueuts enu 'Law' tante minastutuuaiits. At eapits etatshi kashuitamatshest, eapits mushuka minustutum. At kutshi tauts muk mushuka minuitimuts tante mushuka tukueua enu 'Legal' tshekuau ninai Innuts minasentenan etshianimashi eshuitikintshi. Nukutshitanan tshetshi kaianimash esishueash muk mashuka tshinistuteai eku 'Crown Prosecuter' kie put tshekamakunuest memenuuita makutshitse enun ue ueshakantshi muk tshishue animenu ekun tshishue animen ninai inu. Kuekuetshimikunank tshe neush minimiskeai kanishiuitumu aiai. Eku uinuau nastesh manimenitamuts ank uinua kakeshamuts mukuanisikuets tshekuanu tante kakeshamuts.

"Uishakaminupunash tante kakeshamun ntinustanan man Innu nakakeshaustaia nui uniuemukunan kuet mitshi pinua uatumuataui kamakunuenshintshi. Naniku-tini nte kaueueshitunant, Innuts misenitanuts eku kuet pistenimuts, mapitenitanuts tante animenitunuts usham nin tanimeniten, muk nukutshitan enistutanan esishuan-tshi eshukun puna. 'Law' miskutshipinu, nashikupini-nukunai tante minustuten, etuish muk animea." *Shustinis*

Kamakunuetshiuap Ama Uitshinueu

Kamakuneshits mushinau makuneuts Innua ntenimaiets muk-et-utineuts kuet kapetenamats. Nastesh mapetenineuts katshimakunakantaiu, muitsheuts innua. Innuts uiuitshinikushiuts enu aushiskakuatshi shitakuaapunu meuts entsh 'criminals'. Muitshia kanuts katshi makunakantaui nte kastipeutshiuapits uipiseuts muats nte kamakuneshintshiuapits.

"Nastesh mukusteats Innuts kamakunueshintshi. Innu uaueshakentshi enu nutshikashutshi mak put pakuatshi mitshuapits makunakanu ete Kuspe eush ueuetishinakanu kuet petepeik nuskuteuapunu." *Etuetis*

"Kamakunueshits nanukutini mestetutueuts innua. Kaminist utinakanu, ueshiakanu kuet makunakant. Katshi ueuetishinakantshi nastesh muskutamuakanu tshekaunu mak nastesh makustem tshetshi makunakant. Nte minakunakant, muk mitshu, atuseu mak metueu. Nastesh Innua mamupistaku, mak nastesh muitamuakanu euu metshipant mentshi." *Kaianumants*

an Indian guy who was charged with murder. He never killed the guy. The white guy was the one who murdered the person. I'm afraid that this will happen to the Innu too." *Gathering Voices participant*

"I would never trust any police officer myself because once they broke into my house for no reason. I was told the police were searching the houses looking for home brew. I locked the door. They were doing this without a search warrant. I was just about to leave to check my fishing nets and I was going to take my gun with me. I put it on the table when they knocked on the door. I didn't open it for them so they kicked in the door and broke in. I was standing there. One of the officers spilled the water bucket all over the floor. I was going to clean the gun when one of the officers hit me in my right eye. A few days later, he was saying he thought I was going to shoot him, which is not true. I never shot anyone in my life. I guess he was just saying that because he knew he made a mistake of hitting me for no reason. The police never laid any charges. If I had been charged I would have explained everything to the judge. My right eye has been bad ever since." *Tshenish, elder*

The police should explain to the Innu about the laws, because nobody really understands them. Even when there is an interpreter there, he or she has a difficult time with the two different languages. They try to translate, but they can't understand how some of the words translate. We don't have any words for a lot of legal things. We as Innu don't know how to say these difficult words in English. We try to say it in an easy way that we can understand. When a crown prosecutor or a judge asks a question to the accused, wanting him or her to explain it better, sometimes the accused doesn't know how to. These things are hard for us as Innu. These questions take a long time to find the answer. But it is easy for them, because they have it all in English. They can say whatever they want because they speak English.

"The problem is both translating English into our language and our language into English. It gets confusing and often turns into a mess when people give a statement to the police. Sometimes in court, people don't know how to say it in English and they give up. They don't care because it is too hard to explain it in English. This is all new to me, and I find it difficult. But I do my best as long as I can understand what

they mean. Every year, the laws change. It seems that it is getting us down because most of us don't understand. It is getting more and more difficult." *Shustinis, Native court worker*

Jail Doesn't Help

The R.C.M.P. are always taking our people to jail. Many of us think the police only send the people to jail and then forget about them. They don't care about the Innu in jail. They are not helping the people. People need help for their alcohol sickness. They are not criminals. They are not treated for the sickness while they are put in cells. People need to go to a treatment centre, not to jail.

"People are not afraid of the police. When a person is charged with something like assault or break and enter, he is sent to jail in Goose Bay. On the same day he is released, he comes home with a load of booze." *Etuetis*

"The police sometimes do a lot of damage to the Innu. A drunk person is arrested, charged and sent to jail. Once he is released, he has not learned anything and he is not afraid to go back to jail. While he is in jail, he just eats, works and plays. No Innu people visit him. He gets no counselling for his drinking problems." *Gathering Voices workshop discussion*

Treated Badly in Jail

The conditions people are put in when they are locked up are very bad. Some of us say we do not like it when our people are put in cages. It is really dirty in the lock-up. The cells smell bad because of the buckets that are used as shit buckets. Many times, the prisoners ask the police to take away the stinky buckets, but they don't listen to them. Some people have been arrested and just left on a cement floor. We think the trailers and the lock-up should be cleaned up.

"Before they had trailers, the R.C.M.P. used to arrest a lot of drunks, tie them up in the basement of the manager's house and just give them a bucket; people were treated like dogs. It is not a crime to drink; it's only a crime if you do something wrong. I don't know who fed them." *Shuash*

"My son was in jail once. He told me he was locked in a room where there were no lights, just dark. I don't want to see other young people treated this way." *Gathering Voices participant*

*Child's drawing at school workshop / Auasits kaunishi-
natatshet, kaskutimatsheupits kaianumats, 1992*

Essi Eka Mintutakunats Miakunikunatshi

Ama nimitutakunan nete kamakunuetshiuapits. Eshinakuats nte kamakuntunants nastesh meminua tshitshue uinakun nte kamakuntanants tshishue uishekan
matshapusikua, mushinau. Nteut tshetshi ueue
stakantshi kamakunueshintshi muk minatutakuts
pise Innuts utinakanuts kuet muk nikatakanits nta
uapenekash. Ntenitenan tshika kashinikunua kamaku-
tunan tshi.

"Esk ekatukashi kamakuntunantshi, kamakunueshit
makuneuts kamatenitishintshi, makuputeuts nette
tamatuaush nte utshimaua uitshinish. Nau kuestu-
uakanits atumam Innuts. Meun tshetshi utinakant
auen ment eka tutaman tshekuan." *Shuash*

"Nikus makunakunu piekua, nuitamauk
atishekanikanu nte eka uastentsh muk tipiskanu,
munuiuapinau kutak auass tshetshi tutuakant."
Utshimassiu Innu

Nastesh eiapits ntuassiminaits muitshikanuts pakunashi 'Law'. Utinakanua utuassimuaua Innuts. Eku
katshi mishikataui, auassits kuet uitamuats keteka
auassa, nastesh mukusteuts auasits kamakunueshintshi.
Muk uiutunikushiut natesh muitshakinuts. Peikua
kamakunuest utineu auasa eka uitamuat ukumauan
mak utamuaua. Patush tsheseninats ete tan nua Kuspe.

"Nastesh miniminuenitemauia estuakanits ntuassiminaits eiash uapatamuts tshekuanu nistam ket-
shestinuapimeuts tshe nish pikunats 'Law'. Kutuk,

katshimishikataui kuet uitats enu eshipikunikintshi
'Law' kuet-kustamuats, ekun eshi pampintsh
anush." *Shustinish*

Nanikutini utinakanuts Innuts enu nastesh eka
shuka espitenitakunitsh. Nanukutini kamakunueshit
enua utineats menenitakushintshi Innua kuet maku-
natakue metshenitakust. Nanukutini kiketshinameuts
uitshiniuaua ekue uetinat kante tshishue animenitum
enu kekatshanamakant. Nastesh meapitenimeu
kamakunuest uaui tshinushintshi muk enu apitshitau
kamakunuest uatimakat uenua. Nastesh misenimeu
kamakunuest tshika tapuetueu mushuka ntusenita-
muts, enua muk uatimakeut ekun ienua muk napitshi-
tauats eku kuet makunats eku katutamiatshi utetese-
unuau nishinakuna.

"Niseniman auen piek, tshe mushinau utamaueu
utiskuema, nastesh kamakunueshits mistuteuts eku
napeu mapitenimakanu." *Niskueuts Kaianumets*

Kutukuts mamishimituts. Kamakunest nteu tshetshi
mamishimantshi minuats tutaske nteu. Kuetenimikuau
kamakunueshits kui shunuapemeutshi tshetshi etu
tutamantshi tshekuanu.

Metauts kamakuneshits uapitshaken taui, metauts
nte ntisinash, tshishue neush metauts uashamakantaui
ute. Pise ntenimeuts tshetshi tantshi mushinau
kamakunueshintshi tshi tshue miskuau nutshikatunantshi eka tat kamakunuest muk nta ueshitunatshi
etats. Mineseniteia eshutinakanits kamakunueshits

There is also no help for our children who are breaking the law. Children are taken away from their parents. When they come back, they tell other children about the group home. Children are not afraid of the police. They want to be taken away so they break the law. This is not helping our children. One time, the R.C.M.P. arrested a young boy and never even told the parents. When they found out, he was already in Goose Bay.

"We do not like when our children are taken away from our community, because when they go away they see a lot of things that are very different from here. First, they learn from people outside how to break the law. Second, they come back and tell stories about what they did outside the community, and they show other people how to do it. This is how we pass these problems on to each other these days." *Shustinis*

Some people are arrested without a good reason or for nothing serious. Sometimes it seems like the police take the good people and put them in jail, and the bad ones get away with things. Sometimes people lie about other people. Then the accused person has a hard time dealing with the law and the lies that were told to the police. The police don't care about what the accused is trying to say to defend himself or herself. The police only use what the informant tells them. The police don't know who is telling the truth. They don't investigate enough. They use the informant's story to send the accused to jail. Maybe this makes them look like they are doing their job.

"I know this one guy. He always beats up his wife. The cops don't do anything about that situation. They let the man get away with it." *Family Violence Project*

Sometimes people want to press charges on another person. The police tell them to press charges if the person causes trouble again. It is as if the police are waiting for something serious to happen before pressing charges on people who are causing trouble.

The police are often not here when they are needed. When they are not in the community, it takes a long time for them to get here when something bad happens in the village. Some of us think we should have police stationed here all the time. It is really hard when there is fighting and the police are not around. Most of the time, we don't have R.C.M.P. to look after the people,

only when the court comes in. We don't understand how the decision is made to have police here or not. Why were there two full-time officers in Davis Inlet for a while after the fire in February? They should have been here before that even happened. Was it because of the drinking or because of the children breaking the law? Why have they left again? Is it because they have no housing? Many of us think they should be stationed here full-time and permanently.

Even when the police are in the community, they are not available when we need them. You call them and sometimes they never bother to check it out. Other times, they don't bother to stop fights when they start. At night, it seems like their phone is off the hook. We can never reach them. They should be in their trailer at night when people are looking for them everywhere. We don't ever see them much in the community. They don't help our young people when they are doing activities. But when there is something going on in the school, they will go. They only hang around with the white people. They don't seem to care what happens to us. They should try to get along with the people, both adults and children.

"I once called the police for their help, but I couldn't reach them. I called everywhere I could think of, but I couldn't get in touch with them. So finally I had to go out and try to find them myself. I found them at the school. I asked one of the officers for his help at my place. He asked me why I was looking for him and what kind of trouble was I having at my home. They told me to go and they would be by shortly. But I had to wait a long time for them to arrive. I thought the police weren't doing their jobs. It is as if they were waiting for something serious to happen. It's not that I want them to go away. It's just they should respond to people who need their help." *Manteskueu*

"One time, a kid broke a window of the school. We called the police and they told us that we should take the matter into our own hands. They were too busy and didn't want to be bothered. So we went to get the kid and took him to the police station. But the police weren't busy at all. There was nobody there, just him and a female teacher." *Clinic worker*

"I have seen police officers drinking when they were on call. I find some officers racist. I have heard them calling Innu bad names." *Gathering Voices participant*

tshetshi tats nta tshekuanu uistats nta Utshimassits katshi niskuatents nta epishinimiskeua. Uipats uta tshika ta pants esk eka timikinits enua put menanu kie put auassit pekunumuts 'Law'. Tshekuanu minuats katautshi? Enua pat muitshuta uta tshika tauts uta mushinau.

At eapits etataui, eku metauts uashamakantaui. Tshikamituastuauts eku tshikitshi tikushunuts. Nanikutini muinanikamatsheut nutshikatunantshi, tepiskantshi nanisipitimuts kamutuetishimau kuetenimitshit. Nastesh mantshi kastinaiats nte tshika tapents utshuiash, mishue ete etuapimakeantaui. Minesta shuka uapimanants nastesh minista uitsheut ntuasuimunaia menetuentshe eku muk etinantshi nte kaskutimatsheutshiuapits, kuet itutets mishue nua uitsheuts kakeshaua. Nastesh kanta petenimukunau nitshi keuteni-mikuau tshipa kutshitauts tshetshi uitsheuat Innua mak auasa.

"Nimituestimuauts peikuau kamakunueshits eku amatatikits uauitshinukushinan. Ama tshika kastinants mishiue nte. Eku tshek etuapamukuau. Kaskutimatshe utshiuapits nimiskuauts. Eku uatamuuk kamakunuest tshetshi petuet nitshinats. Tshekuan uishiuintuapaminats kie taetinants. Nte tshitshuats. Eku tshiue mentukuts amanika ne ustan. Tshitshue neush ntashinuapamauts tshe tshitukushinits. Ntenimautshe katutimutshi utatuseunuau. Kishinuapatamutshi tshetshi nutshika tunanits. Ama eunuenu uanikatishaukau. Tshipatituteuts uauitshinukushunanitshi." *Manteskueu*

"Peikuau auas pikuam kaskutimatsheutshiuapits. Nimituestimuanan kamakunuest tshinuau nte natik. Tshishue nimiste atusenan ekun etshi nutshikuunam ntukunaiatik. Eku natitish auas eku etutatshish kamakunueshintshi. Ama atuseuts kamakunueshits. Amataianunte mukuin kie kaskutimatshesheskueua." *Kamamuitunants*

"Ntshiuapamauts kamakunueshits menits etusets. Pase kamakunueshits mitshenitakushuuts. Ntshipetuauts entataui inua." *Epa*

Nanikutini ustumpuninikuuts niskueuts. Kamakunueshintshi niskueu minukunakantshi uininutshikueutsh. Uitutueuts ni menakunataui. Peikunu nteshipin niskueu tshika ueueshintin uintuun nitutuune. Eku uneuetishinikuke kamakuntunanits.

"Peikuau kamakunuest niutshipituk pikupitum nip-

itshueanishinu. Pusk nimusheskitepituk." *Niskueuts ishishueuts*

Kakeshauts eash tutuakanuts. Etutashi Kakeeshau kamenuantshi ama nutshikuakanuuts. Ntuun enitutuataui auasa ama apitenimakanuuts ni tante kakeeshauts. Kuetenimitshits kamakunueshits kuuikatautshi. Kakeeshau metuestimuatshi kamakunueshinintshi tshetshe tshinue tikushinuuts uatipamuats kakeeshaua.

Nimishetinan kamenueanataui pinasataui atumua kamakunueshits. Mitshimanta paseuts mitshuapits kie uitshuats kustukunu enu. Amaminua uas tshetshi uapamat penuasua ntshi atumua. Kamakunueshits neka nte tshipa pasueuts atumua. Nanikuti ama apitenimeuts kie meekateuts. Nepakanits atamuts akushiskakuuts enua Innuts. Peikuau ntakanuts tshetshi pasuats uiakashentshi. Amanists takushinuuts. Katshi nishumuastukeants minuats atum makameu Innua eku patush pinasuats atumua.

"Nimishetinan kamenenitamas kamakunuest eshi pashut atuma, peikuau tshekat nipashuk penashuat atuma." *Shankush Tshenu*

Tenimaaets kamakunueshits tshipa makuneuts kamaste-nitamintshi tepiskatshi eskua eka ushikunishutshi. Pishe ntenitenan tshipa kuetipunum shitakunapuna uipats katutash. Mushina tshipa tapuetakunan tshetshi ntuuiunak enakituenimikunak. Eku anush stukunan muku tshetshi taiak uta utenats.

Nuui uapamauts Innu kamakunueshits uta utenats. Kie tshinan tshipa uuetishumushunan. Kamakunueshits tshipa uuitshinueuts uta nete kastipanits kie auasha emetueakanitshi.

"Tshipa nakituenimaaets stiniminuts mauats uaiieu ueshipanits. Tshipa skutimakunan enispish uueshitun. Eku patush tshipa naketuapamauts stiniminuts. Tshishue mishen eshinakuats uta eshi tats kamakunueshits. Tan tshenishinakuats mushinau tataue kie mishetitaueu inuts kie aka nikuatu tuteaue kie aka ashapitshe utenats. Mukua tshika apinan, tsheminak kie tsheuapatinauts stuashiminuts euishipeak. Put make mushinau tshika uueshinikunan eshukum pishima kie pupun. Tan tsheshi ashinuapatimak tsheshi uitshinu-shunak muku tshenitutuau tsheutshimau eku tshishue tsheka minupinak tsheutshimau tshimakunikunan nastesh ama nikuatu stute-nan." *Shustinis*

Sometimes women have their own problems with the police. When they put women in jail, they go after them. They try to do things to them while they are locked up. One time a woman told the police she would charge him if he tried to do things to her. He released her from the lock-up.

"One time, a police grabbed me and pulled my coat and shirt off. I was half-naked." *Family Violence Project discussion*

White people get treated different. It seems like white people break the law and they get away with it. Our children have been sexually abused and people get away with it because they are white. Some of us think the police are covering it up. When a white person calls the police, they are there right away to protect white people.

Many of us don't like the way the police are shooting the dogs. They shoot them in front of the houses or near their trailer. This is very dangerous. It is bad for the children to see them shooting the dogs. The police should take the dogs far away when they shoot them. Sometimes they just leave them around and don't bury them. These dead dogs can make people sick. One time, they were asked to shoot a dog who had bitten someone. But they never came. After two weeks, the same dog bit another person. That is when they finally shot this dog.

"The people in Davis Inlet are not against the police, but the police almost shot me when they were shooting dogs." *Sango Bay camp elder*

Some of us think that police should arrest drunks for an overnight stay in the lock-up before they hurt each other. Others think the police should dump the home brew buckets like they used to do before. We should be allowed to go hunting when we are on probation. Now we are told we have to stay in the community.

We would like to see Innu police in this community. We now have two people from here in British Columbia training to become First Nations police officers. It is also time that we made our own laws in this community. The police need to get more involved with other programs in the community, like the Alcohol Program and the recreation activities of the Youth Council.

Child's drawing at school workshop / Auashits kaunishi-natatshet, kaskutimatsheupits kaianumats, 1992

"We should be responsible for our people, not outsiders. We should get educated about the law. Then we could look after our people. A lot of things are happening in our community ever since the R.C.M.P. was brought onto our land. What will happen if there are more and more people, and they have nowhere to go, and if nothing changes in our community? Are we just going to sit around, keep drinking and show our children we are alcoholics? Or are we going to put ourselves in court every month, every year? How long more can we wait to help ourselves instead of listening to the government, and wasting away our lives for him? The government put us behind bars in putting us here to live with nowhere to go." *Shustinis*

PEIKUSTEU ETSHITAPATEKEN

ATAUEUTSHIUAP

Mushuau, 1963

Uipits

"Uipits Innuts ama nista titamupants atauetshiuap-inu. Ama nista eakanupan nastesh tshekuan tshetshi inika-nushunants. Muku ntuuiunanipin mak tapitu-inanipin." *Kaskutimashust*

"Uipits Utshimassits uipits Innuts tshishue apisis eapints mitshiminu peik pupuna. Ntuuiuts kie nime-sha mueuts. Kauapuskuet etat tsheutshimau minepan shuneanu ataueutshiuapits mak kaua-pukueshintshi. Innuts ekute eapints mitshiminu eku etutets nete nutshimits. Nanikutini pise nikatamuts shuneanu tante ama tauts Innuts. Innuts uuenu minakanuuts shuneanu. Innu etutauaui tshetshi umaniunu utshimau minueu mishinanikeetshinu tshetshi eiakanits mitshiminu. Mestinipatashi Innu umaniunu eku iau upasikan eku miskuts manuet umaniun." *Kaniuekutat*

Uipits ataueutshiuap, nanikutini tshishue mishen tshekuan eiakantshi ataueutshiuapits mitshim kie apits-shitauna. Katshi tsheutshimau ataueutshiuapinu uti-nak tshipatshi esk ntutaua tsheapin maniuna. Eku anuts ama takun. Innuts apitshitauts tshekuanu nete ataueutshiuapits. Nete uipits Utshimassits mitshim uepinikanipan minesipints. Anuts kuuskaua ataueut-shiup. Ama shuka minuau put uipits Utshimassits. Pase tshinan stenitean nete Newfoundland tshe utshi-mau ushitau tshetshi tipenitak ataueutshiuapa.

Katshi atutsheats nete ministukuts, eku ataueutshi-uap nistim ushitakanipan. Innuts amauats eauts tshekuanu nete usteshe uaiu. Ninan nteanan tshekuan uaiaitshi ute ataueutshiuapits.

Anutshish etshishikats minuau tapue ataueutshiuap etukuats uta stesinats. Kie muk niuiuapatenan tshetshi minkunakuats ataueutshiuap. Muk peikushu tsheut-shimau ataueutshiuap ute kie Innuts tshetshi atauets uaiats tshekuanu uaapitshitats.

Nititautshiuapinan Tshitshue Stimashinakun

"Tshinan stataueutshiuapinu mitshinakun Utshimas-sits ata-ueutshiuap eamiats miskuau. Amanista nista uapaten ataueutshiuap eshinakuats etshi aniunan kie eshinakuak uipits Utshimassits ataueutshiuap. Kutak nte ataueutshiuapa utenats tsheminuaua ataueutshi-uapa. Utshimassits ataueutshiuap tshishue mitshi-nakun." *Samish Mistinapeu*

Kutaka ataueutshiuapa tshishue mishiue tukuea tshekuaia. Ekuuta Utshimassits ama shuka takun tshekuan ataueutshiuapits. Stitaueutshiuapinu. Nanikutini tsheska mesteueua. Eshukum pupuna, ataueutshiuap mushinau nutepinu mitshim kie kutak tshekuan. Shakuashi ataueutshiuap nutepinu ashinina uantuiunan tshi. Kie shakuatshi ama tshianan uas-tenipimakeaskua uta ataueutshiuapits. Tshinan kie stenitean tshinan tshiuepinean. Kauepinashunantshi kie eskupintshi niskustuana. Tshinan tshiuauitenan ataueutshiuap meishinaitsheak mishinanikea. Muk

RAY WEBBER PHOTO

CHAPTER NINE

THE STORE: ATAUETSHIUAP

In the Old Days

"In the old days the Innu never had a store. We didn't have to buy anything for our survival. We only got it for free from hunting and gathering." *School workshop*

"In old Davis Inlet, people would buy very little food from the store or things they needed to supply their families for the winter. We would hunt and fish to get food. When Father Whitehead was the priest here, the government used to allocate money to the store and the Mission. People bought supplies for the year and went to live in the country. There must be something left of that money because the people weren't here all year to pick it up. This money was supposed to be for the Innu. When people sold their furs, the store manager used to give vouchers for supplies. If there were a lot of furs, where did that money go? People say we had to pile up furs as high as a gun if we wanted to buy a gun." *Kaniuekutat*

The store in old Davis Inlet was a Hudson's Bay Company store. Sometimes there would be a lot of different things we could buy in this store, from food to women's clothing. After the government store took over, we still sold our furs there for a while, but not any more. People used to be able to charge things to the store. Now they only accept cash before you can buy any food. In old Davis Inlet, food was thrown away if it was expired. The new government store is worse than the one in old Davis. Some of us think the Newfoundland government must have made the decision to take over the store.

When we moved on the island, the store was the first building to go up. People didn't have to order things from outside at that time. We could buy the things we needed at the store.

Nowadays, it is good to have a store in the community, but most of us would really like to see some changes with this store. There is only one government store here and that is where people have to buy the things they need.

Our Store Is the Worst

"In Davis Inlet, there is hardly a store. I've never seen a store in my life like the one in Davis Inlet. Other coastal communities have better stores. Davis Inlet's store is the worst." *Samish*

In other stores, they have everything. Here in Davis Inlet, there is hardly anything in our store. Sometimes the shelves are empty. Every winter, the store runs out of food and other things. In the spring, the store runs out of ammunition for hunting. This spring we can't even buy candles at the store. Many of us think we are sent the garbage and leftovers. We have already complained about the store by writing letters. But the government still must not know that we don't have that much money to order everything from the outside.

The manager says they overspend in one fiscal year. They probably overspend because they bring in things that are not needed. Or they fly in things in the winter by plane, which is very expensive. But many of us don't understand why the store overspends. Whatever the store has, whether it is food or clothing, we don't get it free. We pay a lot for it, and the money goes back to the government. We think the government is to blame for how bad our store is run.

"What kind of a government do we have? Every time there is an election, government people come to Utshimassit for support. How can the Innu give support to the government when our store has nothing? In Happy Valley, all the stores have everything. What

tsheutshimau ama senitam nenu tshinan tan nispish shuneau uantuentimak tshekuan nete uaiu.

Utshimau nisishueu peikupuna. Ntuun tshekuanu eauts eataui kie eka apitinits. Muk ninan ntuenitean tshekuan pepushi kapiminast apitshiakanu enkue tapue tshishiue nanimishit eku ninan amanisenitenan tshekuan ataueutshiuapapitish. Tshekuan ataueutshiuap etukuats mitshima put akupa, nastesh shetshen tshetshi utinamak. Tshishue tshimiste tshishikean. Eku shuneau espint tetshe tsheutshimau. Stenitean tsheutshimau uinenu mitshinakutau ataueutshiuapinu eshinakunits.

"Taeshinakusts tsheutshimau eteak? Mushinau kituku-nua etakanikants kie tsheutshimauts petuteuts ute Utshimassits uauishinikushit. Tshekuanu ne Innu uauitshiat tsheutshimaua nenu katukunua ataueutshiuapits tshe-kuanu. Netema apipani mishiue ataueutshiuapa tukun tshekuan. Tshekuan eshinakuats kamitsit utitaueutshiuap nete Newfoundland? Ataueutshiuap nastesh ama minunakun. Nastesh tshekat ama takun tshekuan." *Shenum*

Amatakun Shuka Mitshim

Tshishiue ama shuka takun mitshim ataueutshiuapits. Peikun muk matshi matshinash kuestukuesteshe muk, eku etakushinash ni. Tapue ama shuka takun mitshim ataueutshiuapits auasisis umitshimishuau kie tshitshinapunits.

"Eshikumupina, mitshim mushinau ama shuka takun. Nanikutini kapiminast petautau mitshiminu. Kie nanikutini tsheutshimau kauimistipetishamua mitshiminu napinitshiuta tekushipintshi. Nas tshipa mistipetautakanu nispishteik pupuna." *Miste-Peashue*

Ama shuka takun mitshim kaminuats nete ataueutshiuapits. Niuauitenanapin uipits tshash, kie niuitamakunaiapin tshetshi mitshim petautakants. Kapetautakants mitshim mishuka tshimitshinan, mitshim ume eshinakuats kukushunash kie uishekea. Kaminuats mitshim kapetautakants kapiminashit tshishue uinakuea, kanutimaskuatshi kie uapaminits. Kie pinakamatshi tshishatinuaia uinakuea pise nete tamits. Kamiskuututshi mitshima minuats kau miskutitauts kauishekinitshi. Mushinau, nete kamiskutshitapinish pikupinu kie eku nta uishimitshash. Kie tshishue neush tshetshi ushitakants.

Mishau mitshim tshetshi eaiats kie tshetshi minupikuats. Muk ninan kutuk nteanan eku eiaiats. Pase

Innuts eauts tante amasenitamuts eshinakunits. Kutuk tshekuan mitshim tshash tshikamesipanu. Eishikumpuna tshika nikatishinikanuants kaistakantshi. Esk tapue mitshim takun a taueutshiuapits tshe meshipints kie Innuts esk eiapits eiauts. Katsheniuts put kie Innuts ama senitamuts tshetshi tshitapatats kakeshamunu etuku nits kie etshineush astents neta kaasta kanits.

"Tsheutshimau tshipasenitam mitshiminuessi neush astents ataueutshiuapits kie etshineush astents. Nanikutini tsheutshimau stenimukunu tante Innuts stenimukunu, kie nastesh minakatuenitam mitshiminu etamitak." *Tshenish*

Tshishikatenan ue mitshim tapue kauinakuats. Amatshimitshinan. Kie tshiuepinenan kamiskutak unash put kie tshikashinuaia uinakuea. Mitshim stakushiskakunan. Stuasiminuuts akushiskakuuts eapits. Kie tshishikenan mitshim eiapits kuetuuepinimak. Ama tshiminukuunan tshuneaminu kie tshiunitanan tshimisteunitanan etshishikamak kauinuak mitshim.

"Nipake tshishatinuan peikuau uinakun. Tshishue ntakushin kie amaniutuasiminapin. Nusheskueu tshipa minuanunas umitshim." *Mitshimitshimau Kaatusets*

Nanikutini mitshim uinakun esk ataueutshiuapits. Ataueutshiuapits utshimau amuepinum enu mitshiminu esk eiapits ntutauatsheu.

"Pase mitshim ataueutshipits ama nisenitean. Muats Innuts ute utenats ama nistuunimutsh tshepiminuets. Tante Innu amasenitam tshetshi eemitat kakeshamunu. Pase mitshim katakuak kie ama neakituenitamuts tshetshi eiats tante amasenitamuts tshenuuts tshetutats. Enkun shuka ataueutshiuapits shuka kimistitikunua tshekuan. Tshishue tshipaminuau ataueutshiuap ntuenitakantshi tshekuan Innuts uaapitshitats." *Miste-Pinip*

"Ataueutshiuap takun miskuts mitshim eshinakunikunau kie peseueau. Eku matshinau tshikatinuaia nete ataueutshiuapits eku nakushiau." *Tshan*

"Kakeeshau kustisheu shiustimakea uta ataueutshiuapits. Atutshintutamakanu Innu. Eku muk Innu tshipa mueu Innu paueshikea. Ekumuk kakeeshau tshipa mueu kake shampuaueshikea." *Innu Tsheutshimau*

kind of devil government is in Newfoundland? The store is no good at all. It almost has nothing."
Shenum, elder

Food Problems

There is hardly any food in the store. We are eating the same thing over and over, and we get sick of it. There is often a shortage of foods we really need, like milk and baby foods.

"Every year, the food almost runs out. Sometimes the government charters the plane to bring food. I sometimes wonder why the government doesn't bring all the food in the summer, while the CN boats still run. They should bring enough food to last through the winter." *Miste-Peashue, elder*

We don't have much fresh food in our store. When we complained in the past, we were told we will get fresh food. But a lot of the food that is brought in is not fit to eat. Food like pork chops and chicken, turkey, is spoiled or rotten. Fresh food that is brought in on government charters is often rotten, like bananas and apples. We open cans, they are rusty or it is mouldy inside. Frozen foods are thawed and frozen again. A lot of times, the freezers and coolers break down, and everything goes bad. It takes a long time to get them fixed.

A lot of the food we buy is not that good and it tastes bad. But we have no other choice. We have to buy it. Some people buy it because they can't tell the difference. Another thing is the food that has expired or is out of date. It has only been a few years that they have to take these off the shelf. It still happens that food in the store is expired and people still buy it. The elders or the people who don't read English really have problems because they can't tell how long it has been sitting on the shelf.

"The government should know that a lot of food at the store is beyond its expiry date. Maybe the government thinks that because we are Innu, it doesn't matter what kind of food they sell to us." *Tshenish, elder*

We pay for this food that has gone rotten. We can't eat it. We have to throw it away, like when the frozen meat or tin cans are spoiled. The food makes us sick. Our children get sick too. We are paying for food that we have to throw away. We don't get a refund for it

Ketshastipeneu cleans a porcupine while children watch / Ketshastipeneu patakuepan nakatuapamaku auasa, 1992

when it is spoiled. We are losing a lot of money paying for food that has gone bad.

"I opened a tin of stew once, it was garbage. It really made me sick and I was pregnant at the time. Pregnant women need real food." *Social Services worker*

Sometimes food that is spoiled is kept in the store. The store manager doesn't throw out the bad food, but puts it on sale.

"Some of the food in the store is not known to us. No Innu person in the community knows how to use it when cooking, because most Innu don't know how to read English. Some of these foods are on the shelf and no one bothers to buy it because they don't know what it is for. That is why the store looks so full. It would be nice if the store could order other things that people need." *Miste-Pinip, elder*

CAMILLE FOUILLARD PHOTO

RAY WEBBER PHOTO

Utshimaskueu making bread / Utshimaskueu paueshikanishepan, 1963

"Innuts tshishikamuts mitshiminu eku amatshimit-shuuts. Tshitapamaeu tsheutshimau ueshitat shuneanu nenu etishamatak uanakunits mitshimit-shinu kie uanakunits." *Manteskueu*

Tshishue Animin

Misiue ataueutshiuapits tshekuan animin. Tsheutshi-mau tshipasenitam ama shuka uenutishiuts Innuts. Kie tetauts tshipauetitishitakanua. Atusenman, tshi mistit-shishikakuun tshipaiauan tshituasimits mitshiminu tshashikakuuni. Tshin kutuk ama pimpinu tshuneam. Eku ama tshiatauen utakupuaua stuasimits. Eku Innu ute apishashua etukuatshi tshuneam put kie mitukun nastesh. Put kie stashimukunan eku uinuau ama tshi tshishikueuts uastenipimakea pisis ueshuneamitaui.

Eku mitshim neush etistetshi. Ataueutshiuapits esk eiapits animin peikutau tuteu. Eku eiapits utshimau ataueutshiuapits ama uepinam kakaminants mit-shiminu enuts eapits ntutauatsheu. Mak eiapits akupa kie pakupinukuaui eiapits ntutauatsheu. Utshimau ama minueu kie ntutauatsheu.

Menui-Mishinamakunan

Amauats mishinantsheu ustumpunu ataueutshiuap eka mishinimatunants. Kie ama ntshianan mitshim eka takunamats ntishinants shuneau. Eka ushuneamin nimeshamuakan eku nastesh atutshi umitshimin.

Nanikutini uapushinani kapiminast amatueu masten-tuskanu uapushikanitshi eku tshinan shiuenan.

Etu Tshipa Takun Tshekuan

Etu tshipapetishanikanu tshekuaia. Kie ama tshiseni-tenan. Espishats ataueutshiuap kimishaua. Tshitshue tshipamitshen tshekuan ataueutshiuapits mpaiaan muk amatakun nastesh tshekuan tshetshi eaiats. Enkun muk meshash ataueutshiuap etitimak. Tshishue tshipamistitikun tshekuan. Anuts muk takun tshekuan takun tshetshi ntuenitamak. Mushinau tshipatakun tshekuan ataueutshiuapits. Tshipatakun tshekuan uan-tutakan tshi. Muk etuseau tshekuan eku uantuenita-mak-ni.

Pase tshinan utshimau ataueutshiuapits amanaka-tuenitam etuenitashi tshekuanu. Uantuenitamuaui tshekuanu eku ama takun ni uatamuaui, stenimanu ataueutshiuapits utshimau ntuenitamuenu eku muk amatutum. Kutukuts ntenitamuts ataueutshiuapits utshimauts ntuenitam tshekuaia Innua etuenitamintshi uaepitshitantshi, muk uin minista ntuenitamuts. Tshekuan ama nista petishanikanu. Nanikutini ninan nipushinan nete kuspe tshekuan uaiaitshi. Pase tshi-nan tshekuan etishamakunak ete Utshimassits tshishue uinakun. Eku uanakuashi pinetishanikantshi ute kue-steshe nete kauiitishamutshi.

"Ataueutshiuapits utshimau kutshitau mitshiminu nete Shintshanishish. Eku ama petishanikanu. Put kie mitshim petautakantshi kapimishinantshi, kie mitshin mitshin, ataueutshiuapits." *Kaatusets*

"Tshishue miskuau tshekuan tshetshi takuats ataueutshiuapits. Tshekuan tshinan uishuui apitshi-taiak ataueutshiuap etukuatshi uapukuna." *Kaatusets*

"Ataueutshiuap amashukatakun Innuts tshetshi eiats, ue niskueuts uantuenitataui—uskatshikua, shestikuapints, mitishits, pitshueana, tukukumana. Eku napeuts, shinukuanikea Innu ut pitshuean, Innu ut tshistaskuanisha, kastapistes tshistaskuaia kie kutuka kimisheuani tshekuaia. Auasits kie uin-uau uieauts tshekuanu eku mitukunu ni uaiataui ataueutshiuapits. Amashuka mitshea apatshitauna nete ataueutshiuapits, muk pitshueana eku tshipau-tikupiashuuts takunitshi. Tshinanu Innu ama tshi staspishunan kakeeshau etaspishut. Tsheutshimau tshipasenitam etshi apitshitak shuneau etuenitamak tshekuan nete uaiu." *Tshenish*

"The store has changed our food, diet and health. Now that we eat canned foods from the store, this has made us weak." *Tshan*

"The white man cut the yeast from the store. It is not to be sold to the Innu. So the Innu eat only bannock, and the whites eat bread that is mixed with yeast." *Innu Nation board*

"People pay for this food and we can't eat it. It seems like the government is making money by sending us spoiled and rotten food." *Manteskueu*

High Cost

Everything in the store is expensive. The government should know we are not wealthy people. The costs should be cut 50 per cent. If you work, you have just enough money to buy food for your children with one week's pay. You don't have any other income. You can't buy clothes for your children. Most people here have low incomes or no income at all. They are on social assistance. They can't pay the bills with the little money they receive.

Even when the food has been on the shelf too long, the price stays the same. Or the store manager doesn't throw out the bad food. He puts it on sale. This happens too with merchandise or products that are torn or broken. The manager doesn't give it away. He tries to sell it.

No Credit

Another problem we have with the store now is that we can't get credit. We can't buy food unless we have cash in hand. If you don't have money on Friday, that means you don't have food for the weekend. Sometimes the mail plane doesn't come in for a week and the whole family suffers.

We Need More Stock

We don't know why they built the store so big. There are many things the store could sell that they don't have and that we would like to buy. It is the only big store we have. It should carry everything. Now we can only get some things with special orders. These things should be in the store at all times instead of special orders. We should have some say in what is sold in the store. The only way for it to work is if we are involved in ordering the stock.

Some of us think store managers don't care about

what they order in. When we want something they don't have, and we ask for it, we wonder if the store managers order it when they say they will. Others think the store manager probably orders the things that people need, but he never gets them. The stuff never arrives. Sometimes we have to travel to Goose Bay to get the things that we need. Some of us think the stuff that is sent here is junk. It is stuff they can't sell anywhere else.

"The store manager tries to get food from St. John's. They don't send it. Or the food comes in on the plane, and a lot of it has gone bad." *Store workers*

"There is hardly anything in the store. What we don't need in the store is stock like flowers." *Male construction worker trainees*

"The store doesn't sell a lot of things people need, like for women—needles, beads, thread, cotton print material, scissors. Men need files, canoe canvas, canoe tacks, stove tacks and so many other things. Children too need so many things that we can't buy at the store. There are a few clothes in the store, but the clothes are for children and young people. There are old women who still wear skirts and they need cotton material to make their own clothes. We Innu can never dress the way white people dress. The government should know we don't have that much money to order everything from the outside." *Tshenish*

We need more healthy foods, fresh foods, meats, vegetables and fruit. The store should carry all kinds of merchandise—outboard motors, hardware, canoes, skidoos, chainsaws, lumber and rope. We want the store to carry things we need when we go in the country, like tent canvas, candles and stovepipes. We would like to see furniture, like chesterfields and beds for babies, and washers in the store. We would like to see clothing for men, women, children and babies, including shoes and boots. We need enough clothing for everyone. The merchandise should be in good condition, not torn or broken.

Staff Problems

Some people have problems with store clerks who argue with customers who come to buy groceries. They don't like to see this happening with elders. People don't need this when they go shopping. People go to the store to be served by the store clerk, not for an

From a wall hanging by Ketshastipeneu / Astemitet kakutaken, Ketshastipeneu kaushitat

Tshinanu tshipantuenitenan tshekuan kaminuats mitshim, kaminuskakunak mitshim, unash, kie kashiuatshi. Kie ataueutshiuapits tshipantuenitamuts eshinakunits kaapitshitakantshi. Kataushistesi, apanikeets inuuta, utapana, katshimputatshepintshi kie apisha. Ntuenitenan ataueutshiuapits tshekuan tshetshi eaiats eku uaapitshitaiatshi nete nutshimits. Ue ntinuutshiuapinan uastepimakeaskua kie nikastapiste shiminan kie kutiskueua. Kie niuiuapetenan tshetshi tukuatshi tetipuakea katshinuaskuatshi kie nipeunisa auasisits, kie kauapekantshepintshi ataueutshiuapits. Kie niuiuapatenan apitshitauna napeuts, niskueuts, auasits, kie auasisits, kie misina tshetshi tukuatshi. Kie nas tshipanishpinanua akupa mishiue Innuts. Kie tshipa minuaua atutshi pikupinua etutauakantshi.

Kaatusesits Mitshenitakushuts

Kaatusets ustumpunuts. Pase Innuts ustumpuninukuuts ataueunisha etauetaui mitshiminu. Kie Innuts amauiuapatamuts tshetshi ustumpunitshi katsheniuntshi, Innuts mauats amauiapatshitauts enu etauetaui. Innuts etutetaui tshe tshi minuitshinukuts ataueunisha etauanikutaui, muats tsetshi nutshikatuts. Pase Innuts matenimeuts kutshemutimakantaui etauetaui. Kaitusentshi ataueunisha. Ataueunishits ama niminuenitamuanan unapatimatshi atutshi sheshe mineuts

etauentaui uikanishuaua. Kutukuts ntenitamuts ataueunishits nasteesku-shitaui kie neush etusetaui uipits.

Usham Tshimiste Apitshitanau Ataueutshiuap

Uishamiats mishiue tshekuan tshuutinean ataueutshiuapits. Innuts mishiue utinamuts ataueutshiuapits mitshiminu. Eku pase ama ntuuiuts. Auasits ama shuka uimitshuts nutshimits mitshiminu muku nte ntenteshe tshikatinuaia put kie kishiuanua. Tapue tshishue mistimitshuuts kishiuanua. Nastesh ama minuanu.

"Ataueutshiuap esk nishinakun kie mitshin mishinanikantshuap. Innuts kustimuts pase tshetshi, ntuuiuts nete nutshimits tante ataueutshiuap enkunuenu nakatuenitats. Uipits nete nastesh amau nakatuenitenan ata-ueutshiuap. Mushinau nistutenan. Kie ama shuka nakatuenitenan ataueutshiuapits mitshim kie eka kaetukuatshi. Kie pase nte Innuts utinamuts nete kakeeshaua umitshiminu eku eapits pase Innuts naushishkakuts mitshiminu." *Shimun kie Manin*

Innu Tshipa Tipenitam Ataueutshi-Uapinu

Innu tshipa tipenitamuts ataueutshiuapinu. Tshinaiu mamu tshipaitusenan nete ataueutshiuapits.
Innuts nete kiituseutshi ute ataueutshiuapits eku tshipantuenitamuts mitshiminu nenu inua uaiantshi ataueutshiuapits. Nistim tshipauitamueu Innua uaiaau tshekuanu tshipa minuau tshinan ntuenitamak. Kie tshipauitshintunaik mamu.

Tshimishetinan tinapuetamak kie tshetshi pimpinitaiau stitaueutshiuapinu. Tsheutshimau atutshi pimpinitau atuseun unta uta stasinats. Kakeeshau pempinitat stitaueutshiuapinanu eku nastesh ama minupuntau. Tshishue tapue shapiu uatutatshi tshekuanu. Ama niuiuapitshianan kakeeshau tshetshi tshekuanu nutshiak. Innuts tshipa ueuetishitamuts tshetshi minupinitats tshetshi—minuants mitshiminu eku tshipa minumiskuutitats napintshi, ataueutshiuap tshipa nutenikanu masteutiskan.

Ataueutshiuap tshipa tipenitakanu, atutshi ntuun miminakanu kakeeshau. Tshinanu tshepaushitanan stitaueutshiuapinu. Innu Utshimauts tshipa utinamuts ataueutshiuapinu, eku shuneau tshipa nataikunan. Anuts tshipa eaan tshekuan eku shuneau ute pise ushipanu Innuuts. Niuitamankuunan shuneau nitikuunan, muk shuneau ushipinu nte kanata kie ute Inuuts utasiuau.

argument or a fight. Some people feel they are cheated sometimes when they pay for their stuff. They don't like to see clerks giving things to their family without paying for them. Others think the store clerks need a break when they have been working there for a long time.

We Depend Too Much on the Store

People depend too much on store food. They don't do enough hunting. The children especially don't eat wild foods and they depend on canned food or junk food. They eat too many sweets. This is bad too.

> "The store is about the same as Social Services. People are afraid to go to the country because the store is all they care about. In the past, we didn't care much about the store. We were always on the move. We didn't care whether the store had a lot of food or no food. Now people have gotten addicted to white man's food, and some people get sick from this food." *Shimun and Mani*

Innu Control of the Store

We should all work together and complain about the store. We should have Innu workers in the store to order the food and materials people want to buy in the store. At least, the store manager now should ask the people what stuff he should order for the store. He should consult with the people about what we want. It would be good if we could do the ordering. It would help the community.

Many of us believe we should run the store. Governments should not be running our businesses in town. The reason why the store is poor is because white people are running it for us. We have the power to do anything. We don't need white people to do things for us. Some of us think the store should be changed to a co-op with members having a say in how they want the store to operate. We could fill it up with fresh food. People would be able to use the freezers in the summer. The store could stay open on Saturday.

If the store is not a co-op, it should be transferred to private hands. We could build our own store. If, for example, the Band Council took over the store, the money would come back to us. Now we buy things and the money goes back to the government. Part of this money is Native funding. We are told this is tax dollars, but it is money from all over Canada which comes from Native peoples' land.

Meneshkuesh stretches the caribou skin to be painted and made into a ceremonial robe / Menshkuesh nuthsikuepan mistikuea, 1963

Ray Webber Photo

PEIKUNU ETSHITAPATEKEN

UTINITAU STINIUNU

Tsheutinamau

"Uipats mushinau, tshinipaapin. Kakeshau mishiue tutam tshekuanu. Stenimanu kakeshau mishiue senitam muku ama stapuenan. Kanti shumitauts am minupinu." *Shushepmak kie Mani Katinin*
Tshipa unikapunan tshetshi uuetishumitunak tapitu tshika atusenan kie shenimushunan. Tshipa uuetishumushunan tshenispish iniuiak. Ama tshikishi ntamenimitunan. Tshinan tshipa tutenan tshetinak ama tshikishi muk apinan kie tshetshitapamak kakeshau tshetshi tutamatak. Tshitutamaue peik kamenupinau tshika shenitenan tshekuan kenastinimak.

Tshinan tshipa utshimamitashunan kie tshipa pipininushunan. Tshinan tshipa tutenan kamenupinak, meieu kakeshau. Tsheutshimamitatunak. Tshipa utinean tsheutshimau kapipinistats, kaskutimatsheutshuap mitshimitshimau, ntukutshuap, kamakunuest, atauetshuap kie mishiue. Tshipa kutshaauts Innu kaskutimatshets, Innu mitshimitshimauts, ntukunis-kueuts,kamakunueshits kie mishiue. Anuts ama stiteauts metinenitats inuts tshetshi utinats. Tshipa tutuauts auashits tshetshi minu skutimashuts nete uaieu.

"Tshetshi kau utinamak stiniunu, tshipa unikapunan tshekuan etuenitimak tshekuanu tshenuts etuenitats. Tshinan tshetshi pisteinushunau meu tsheutshimau tshepistintak." *Kaskutimashutshuap*
Innuts kaatuset ntukutshiuapits, kaskutamatsheutshiuapits, kauueshitunats, mitshimitshimaskueu, kie ataueutshiuapits niskutimashunan tshetshi atuseats. Uin atuseuts uin tshipa ukanumu. Kanum etusetshi pepushi atuseun. Inu ma-uaatusetshi uimistiskutimashu Innu, eku tshashikuakanti ni. Innu atuseu uetunikatshet nete ntukutshuapits put kauueshituan-

nits, kaatuset kaskutimashut. Tshishue nakatuenitakanu atuseun kautunikatshets etusets. Mushinau tshipa utunikatsheuts etataui uta stisinats.

Innuts tshipa ntuenitamuts tshetshi skutimashuts, kie ntuueniten tshetshi tutaman tsheininiuian mishinanikea. Ntuuenitenan Utshimassits tshekuan kie shuneau tsheapitshitaiats. Mishinanikea niuitshinukunan. Ntapuenan tshetshi isishueats tshekuan tshe kushkunu tutamats. Ue ntapitshitanan mishininanikea tsheskunu tutamats. Tshipa tshishipinan tipenitamash mishinanikea.

Tshipa nisishuenan auen tsheatuset ntisinats. Tshinan tshipa utinanants mitshimitshimauts, kaskutimatshets, ntuniskuesits, utshimau kaskutimatshet kie kutakuts. Uets penetutepints unuuitamish tshipa skutimashuts ute stasinats. Nas tshipauinispinan kaitusesii nishunu-a-shu neu tshipaituseuts nitukuntshuapits. Kie kutak kaituset nete mitshimitshimaskueua nas peik tshishikaua tshipatuseu. Kamakunueshits ute tshipa tauts eiapits mushinau.

Muk kinisishue, mitshimitshimau ntatuskakunan tshetshi uitshaat kapiuenimakanitshi auenua, kie uetinakanitshi auasa uitshuash, put etishauat niskueua kakeuenimanitshi. Ntuetenan tsheanumue atimat niskueuts kie auasits. Menants muk uestumpunuets uetamauakanits auasits, eku unitshinukuaua auasits tshipa uitshinukuuts tsheekaminits, kie tsheeka minatiskuets. Niuintumuskenan auasits kakeuenimakanits ute stesinats. Kakeuenimakanits auasits, nipukuenitenan tshetakuats ute. Innuts tshipantusenitamuts tshetshi uasa eka utina kanitshi. Kie nika ntumiskenan niskueuts tshetats utamauakantaue uta Utshimassits. Pase Innuts ntenitamuts napeu tshipa nikatishinakanu tshipa uitshiakanu etit.

Mitshimitshimau tshipa skutimueu inua kaashamat, tshetshiskutimashut mistikunapeunu, kakusikuashu-

CHAPTER TEN

REGAINING CONTROL OF OUR LIVES: RECOMMENDATIONS

We Need to Take Over

"In the past, we were like we were asleep. White people were doing everything for us. We thought white people knew everything, but we were wrong. The advice they gave us never worked." *Shushepmak and Mani Katinin*

We need to stand up, have confidence in ourselves, make our own decisions. We can really work together and be proud of ourselves and who we are. We have to set standards for ourselves and goals for our lives. We can't always blame others. We have to take responsibility ourselves. We should do things ourselves instead of sitting and waiting for white people to make decisions or do things for us. If we can solve one problem, then we will know we are gaining.

We must govern and run our own affairs. We need to solve our own problems, and not have the white agencies do it. We need self-government. We have to take over all the government institutions: the school, Social Services, the clinic, policing, the store and so on. We should have Innu teachers, social workers, nurses, police and so on. At the moment, we don't have many educated Innu to take over these institutions. We must encourage our students to attend colleges, universities and other training institutions.

"To regain control of our lives, we need to stand up for what we want, what our elders want. Our freedom is ours, not the government's." *Teachers' workshop*

Our people who are presently working for the clinic, the school, the courts, Social Services and the store need on-the-job training. Where qualified, they should be certified based on their years of work experience and expertise. If people are expected to do the work of university-trained people, they should be recognized and paid accordingly. People working as interpreters, for example at the clinic or with the courts, need training to do this work. It is very important to have skilled interpreters in these jobs. As well, there should always be an interpreter available to provide services in this community.

While our people are getting training, we need to have more and real input into the decisions made about our lives by these agencies. We need to be consulted on what we feel our community needs and how program funds could best be used. These agencies are here to help us. We have a right to say what we want them to do. These agencies need to take their direction from us now. We should begin developing our own policies for these institutions.

We want a say in who will work in our community. We should play a role in hiring social workers, the principal, teachers, nurses and so on. These people coming from the outside need to learn about our community and culture. We need to provide an orientation for them. We should have enough staff to work in these agencies. For example, we need a full-time social worker, and we need more staff to provide twenty-four-hour service at the clinic. Police should be stationed here permanently as well.

For example, Social Services should work with us to develop the best ways and means to deal with family crises, rather than just removing children from their homes, or sending women to Libra House. We want family counselling for the man, the woman and the children. Alcohol is usually the problem in these crises, and parents and children should be helped to deal with their drinking and sniffing. We want to provide foster

nants, kie nas tshetapuetikants atuseun.

Kaskutimatsheutshiuap, nipukuenimanants ntuasiminats tshetshi kashiuts kakeeshamunu kie inumunu. Nas tshipa minu skutimashuuts kaskutimatshet atusets tshetshi mistiskutimashuts Innu kaskutimatshentshi. Kaskutimatshets uaiu ushiuts meshikataui, kakeeshauts kie kutakunu eshaianimuets. Innu kaskutimaskueuts tshipa ukanumuts pepunitshi etusetaui. Pauitshinukunan kaskutimatsheutshiuapits tsheuitshakanits auasits kamenupunits nete kaskutimatsheutshiuapits. Nikaskutimatsheuapinan niuitshinukunan ntuuasiminaets eka utamauakanits. Kutukuts Innuts uiuitshutumuts kaskutimatsheutshuapinu eshini katents. Utshimassits tshipa senitamuts. Ntuuenitenan etu shuneau. Apishashu kaskutimatsheutshuap tshash nimitshetinan nuuspinan. Niuintuenitenan ka pisiseatshi kie niuiuapatenan kaunishitanikants kanikuminants kie kapiminuats.

Innu kaskutimatsheshiskueuts tshipa animueuts kie inumunu tshipa skutimatsheuts. Ama niuiuitshinu enan eshishuats Sheshatshit, ekute nte uetishanikantshi tshekuaia kie ekutente uetishanikantshi Quebec, nipukuenitenan ka-tsheniuts nete kaskutimashunants. Auasits tshipa skutimashuuts eshiskutimashunau kaskutimashunau. Niuiskutamuanants auasits tshetshi eiemitats kie tshetshi mishinaitshets eshaianimuets kie mistuskutimashutaue. Kie ntuasiminaets tshetshi ntutets nutshimits.

Ntitenitenan aiamieutshiuap, nimitshetinan uaapitshatshish kauapukuest. Eiemieu tshuapit kauapukuest

Miste-Etuet and grandson / Miste-Etuet mak usima, 1993

tsheinuemit, eku tshetshi minuenimau. Tshetshia-pits Innuts tsheuiskutimashuts. Innuts etu tshipa uitamuakanuts manakintaui ni tukuna. Uatimau metuestaiau tshipa mitshetuuts kaatusesits nitukuntshiuapits natshintukushinaui. Aiamieutshiuapits tapuetikanu Innu Patikakantshi tshetshi eiemituakant. Innuts nas tshipa minuntutueuts.

Etu tshipa takun tshekuan ni ntukuntshiuapits tshetshi uitshinukunan mestakushinak. Kie ntukuniskuesis tshipa tauts neush. Eku etu tshipa senitamuts eshinakunits etauak. Kauitshinuet ntukuniskues niskueua tutshimis-kuts pushiu uetuasimitshi. Kie etu tshipa mistiskuti-mashunan nitukuuna etaiak nutshimits. Kie mushinau tshipa mpinitakanu kanitutakants eshukum tshishika etaiak nutshimits eku tshipa animuenani nitukutshiuapits mestakushitshi Innu.

Tshinan tshipa ushitanan tshenispinak uta utenats, tshenishanuenimak auen pikunashe. Tshipa uitamuanan tsheutshimau eshinakunitshi eshipipinuak.

Kamakunuesh atutshi nutshiakanuuts entuuiuau. Etatauai uta tshipatintuteuts uashamakantaui. Tshipa minuuitamueuts ueueshiakantaui. Tshipa makunakanu Innu mentshi menatenitatshi. Eku eiapits tshipa apishipeu menatenitatshi. Eku eiapits tshipa atishekauakanu. Nas tshipa tshita pimeuts menitshi eshinakunikunits shitaunapunu. Kamakunest tshipamintutueu Innua kie kakeeshaua uta stesinats. Kamakunueshits tshipanikati-shineuts atumua uta Utshimassits esk eka pasuats. Kamakunueshits tshipa ntuusenitamuts kie atutshi katueuts Innua etitaui.

Niuiua patenan ataueutshiuap tshetshi minu takunimats. Put patshitipenitenan ninan. Muk peta mpatshi tapate-nan espints ataueutshiuap, kie auen tsheutinakant ata-ueutshiuapits tsheatuset, tshekuan mitshim kauintueni-takanua.

Pishe inuts kustatshuts kie shakuenimuts tsheutshimaua meshikantshi Utshimassits. Tshipa shapinan naianumeak. Tshipa uitamuanan tsheutshimau eshinakuntak. Kie tshipa mishineian tshekuan eshi tuenitamau eku tshipa minaieu tsheutshimau. Tshipa ntusenimaieu eshi pipint tsheutshimau kie metinu tshipa tutuanan.

> Tsheutshimau nas tshipa tshi tapamakanu. Tshipa senimukunu tshinanu Innu kie stipenitenan stesinu. Nipukuenitenan Ntesinan tshethsi nakatuapatamats kie amaniuiuapamanants katshipinishits, tshetshi pikunas ntesinanu.

PETER SIBBALD PHOTO

homes here in the community. If children must go to a group home, we want that group home to be here. People here should make the decision about whether a child should be removed or not. We want to find our own ways to provide shelter for women who are beaten in this community. Some people think the man should be sent away to get help.

We want Social Services to provide training for people on social assistance—training in carpentry, crafts, and in skills needed for future jobs.

In school, we want our children to be well educated in both Innu and English. We need experienced teachers to work in our school and training for our Innu teachers. Teachers coming from outside should be trained in teaching in English as a second language. Our Innu teachers should be certified based on their years of work experience. We need guidance counsellors in the school to help children with their problems, and to help them stay in school. Our school needs guidelines on disciplining children to put an end to the abuse. Many people want the school name changed. The community should make this decision. We need more funding for the school. This school is already too small and our population growth is very high. We need more classrooms and we would like to see an art room, a music room and a kitchen.

Our Innu teachers should have workshops on teaching Innu language and culture. We want resources now to begin developing our own books and materials about our culture and language. We don't have any say in the curriculum centre in Sheshatshiu, and the materials we get from them or from Quebec are in a different dialect than ours. We want elders teaching about our culture in the school. Children should be learning our traditional games in school. We want more focus on teaching our children to read and write their own language at all levels, including the high school. We want our children to be able to go into the country as part of their formal education.

With regard to the Church, many of us believe we should go back to our own traditional spiritual practices. As for the R.C. Church, some of us want a priest who can speak Innu-aimun, so we can feel comfortable talking to him. Some recommend that Innu be trained to take over as laypeople. Others believe the Church needs to be more present when it is needed, like when

people die. They should be there to help people with their grief and be more active in the healing process.

The clinic needs more up-to-date equipment, especially for emergencies. We need nurses to stay here permanently. They need to get to know the community. People need more information about the pills they take. We need more staff so that we don't have to wait so long to see the nurse or doctor by appointments. We also want a midwife so that women will not have to leave the community to have their babies. We need to learn how to use our own medicines again. We need medical services for our camps. They should have twenty-four-hour radio contact with the clinic in case of medical emergencies.

We need to set up our own community policies, to make our own laws and set up penalties for when they are broken. We must let the government know that we have to have our own laws in our own community.

The police should not interfere with our hunting. In the community they should always be available when called. They should work with interpreters to get statements from people. They need to better explain their laws to us. Police should make arrests or lock people up when they are drinking to protect others. They should clean up the lock-up. They should work more closely with the Alcohol Program and other agencies to address the problem of alcohol. When people are jailed they should get help for their alcohol problems. The police should treat the Innu and whites the same in our community. The police should remove dogs from the community before they shoot them. The police need to investigate cases more, and they should not cover up others.

We would like to see the store changed over to private hands. Or we would like to take it over ourselves as a co-op. In the meantime, we should have input on how this store is run, what foods and supplies need to be stocked, and what staff is hired.

Some people are afraid to talk or too shy when the government comes to Davis Inlet. We must have strong voices for the government to hear us. We should tell the government what he has done to us. We need to make a list of all the things we need, give the list to government and tell them we need to do it on our own. We need to learn how government works, but we should be very careful what we learn from the government.

CAMILLE FOUILLARD PHOTO

Tepi, 1992

Mamu Tshipa Atusean

Ninan uta Utshimassits tshipa tapitu atusenan kie tshipa uitshitunan. Tshipa punan enutshikatunak, kie emitshenimitunak kie epiuinimitunau naianumeau put kie emashitunak. Ama tshikishi utimikatunan. Tshipa shatshitunan. Atuseaue tapitu, tshika nitutakunuts inuts kie tsheutshimau tshika itenimukunu keastishiutshi.

Utshimauts tshipa tapitu atuseuts kie uitshituuts. Mishiue tapitu tshipa atuseuts. Utshimauts itenimakanuts tshetshi uitshaats inua, tshipa uitamueuts tshekuan uatutakaui, asin uenauitakantshi, kie kueui astukanua. Inuts mamu utshimauts tshipa isushueuts tshekuanu uaupatash utasiuats kie eka minuenitats tshipa tshipaamuts utshimauts.

Tshipa kutshitanan tshetshi shapits tshiutshimaminuts. Uipats inuts utinepants utshimamaua. Tenakanikatshi inuts tshuenimituts. Tenakanikatshi tshiustapininikunu. Uatakakushitshi Innu uitamueu inua tshetit takauakatshe. Tshipa miste aianimuanu. Tshipa punan tsheshi apitshitaiak shitakuna-pun tenakanikatshi. Usham mishau mitshenimitun kie

tshuapun kie tshiunitunan euitsheuakenitatunak. Tshipa apishipeuts utshimauts. Eminu utshimaut Innu ekun tshishue tsheapitish.

Tshipa uitutenan tshetshi eka tamenimitunak kamenupint uta Utshimassits. Tshipa atamenimushunau ekun muku tshetshi kau utinimak stiniunu. Ehe, tapue shitakunapun stakunikunan, meieu ene muk kamenupinak. Tauts inuts kamenits, ama nist minupinuts. Nauitamakue meshats kamenupinak. Peikun muku tshetinak tapitu tshika ntushenitenan tshekuan kamenupinak. Ama tshikishi tshinan tshipa tutenan.

Tshinan Tshipa Kutshitanan Tshenishipipinak

Tshipa skutimashunan uipats kanish pipinak, eshiniunak kie eshe emaiak. Tshika nitutuaiats tshenuts kie uitshaiauts. Ekun tshipa utshimaminan kie tshipa uuetishumukunuts. Auashits-tshipa skutimuaiaets uipats kanish iniunak. Innua tshipa ishi iniuts. Tshipa uitamuauts uipats kie tshetshi nitutatauts kie shenitats.

"Etaiak uta utenats mishen tshekuan kamenupints uenapatamak. Etaiak nete nushimits mushinau tshimeskenan tshetinak, kuesheau. Ekun tshipa ishiniunai. Kaetuuiunau tshinutshikenan mista. Ekun iniun." *Kamamuinats*

Eskua ama pitastunuepun tshash tshiunitanan stiniunu. Tshipa kau nishiniunan kanishi iuiunak. Eskua tauts tsheshenitats nete etuteats kie eshi tuuiunats nushimits. Ama eskua ama tshika tauts tshenuts, eku tsheka tat auen tshenishuitamatak nushimits. Pishe Innuts eshishueuts tshinan stutenan iush uenitaiak uipats kaish iniunak. Tshipa uitshitunan tshetshi mushinau ituteak nete nutshimits kie tshe apitshitaiak asin.

Tshipa skutimashunan uipats kanish inuinau. Tshenuts tshipa skutimakunuts tshetutamau uskea, kushapa-shikan, mitshishatshuap kie uipats ntukuun. Tshipa meatsheieuts aueshishits. Ekun tsheshi kau kastinimau stiniunai.

Tshipa etu tuuiunai. Inuts tshipa skutimueuts auasha tshetshi shenitamitshi eushitakanitshi tshekuan. Tshipa ushitanan mishinanikan uipits eshi iniunak kie staianumanu. Tshipa minuenitamuts stuasiminuts skutimua-uts uipats metueuna. Tukun eskua metueuna muku ama skutimashuts uipats metueuna. Tukun eskua metueuna muku ama skutimuanuts auashits. Mushinau tshipa itutenan mushinau tshipa

The government must recognize our rights. They must recognize that we are Innu and that this is our land. We want our land to be protected from the destruction of future developments. We want an end to low-level flying because it is destroying the wildlife we depend on. If we work more closely with Sheshatshiu, we have the power to fight governments. We must gather voices from across Canada and other countries to help us put pressure on governments. The government is afraid of us now because we are standing up for ourselves. They know we have a lot of supporters across Canada and Europe.

We Need to Work Together

We, the people in Utshimassit, need to work together and support each other. We have to stop being against each other, hating and hurting each other either through verbal or physical contact. We don't have time for this. We must respect one another. If we work together, people will listen to us, and the government will see us as a different people.

Leaders should also work together and support each other. All local organizations should get together more often. Leaders are elected to help the people, to explain to us what is going on with such things as new developments, land claims and relocation. The people need to have more say with the leaders about what is going on in the community, and if we disapprove of anything, the leaders must try and stop it from happening.

We need to find ways to make our leadership work for us. In the old days, people used to pick their own leaders. When there is an election now, people get mad at each other. Elections are a problem. If people are running in an election, they should tell everyone what they will do for us when they are leaders. This should happen at public meetings. We must stop using liquor for our elections. It brings too much hate and violence, and makes us lose our friends. We need sober leaders. Good leadership is very important.

We have to make sure we don't blame each other for the community problems. We need to take responsibility ourselves. This is the only way to regain control of our lives. Yes, it is true that alcohol is part of the problem, but it is not the whole problem. There are people who don't drink and they still have problems. It is time

we discussed our major problems. There is only one thing to do. We must get together and try to find ways to deal with these problems. We don't need outside experts to do it for us. We have to keep it in our hands and do it our way.

We Need to Practise Our Ways

We need to learn our way of life and keep our culture, traditions, values and spirituality. We need to listen to and respect our elders. They should be our leaders and advisors. The children need to learn our culture. We want them to live as Innu. We must talk to them about the past more. They will listen and understand.

"When we are in the community, we see a lot of bad things happening. When we are in the country, we always find something to do, like fishing. This is the way we should live. When we are not hunting, we can cut and haul wood. This is the life." *Discussion at school workshop, grades 5 to 8*

It is not even fifty years since we have been losing our culture. We can still go back to our traditional ways. There are a few old people here who remember how we used to travel and hunt in the country. Once the elders are gone, there will be no one left to tell us how we used to live. Some people say it is our fault we are losing our culture. We should encourage each other to keep going into the country and using the land.

We need to do research on our culture. We should let the elders teach us about sacred things, like what to do with the bones, the shaking tent, sweat lodge, and things that we used for medicine. We need to respect the animal spirits. That is how we are going to regain control of our lives and our culture.

We could depend more on hunting for our food. Men and women should work with the children to teach them how to do Innu crafts. We need to produce books on our culture and language for the school. We can make our children happy by teaching them our traditional games. Those games are still with us, but nobody is teaching them.

The Outpost Program is run by the Band Council. It helps people to go to nutshimit to live for up to three months. The program assists with aircraft charters to camps but also sometimes with supplies and fuel for skidoos. We should go into the country more and have the Outpost Program. We want Outpost Program funding available all year round. This will help people

takun kakuspinats peik puna. Ekun tshetshi uitshinukuts inuts tshetshi punitats eminits kie kau
tshetipenimushut. Tenimauts pishe inuts tshetshi tats
nushimits peik pupun. Auashits tshipa uitshimeuts
unitshinukuaua. Tutamae mishiue tshika nikitenan
kashetshimakanits, kanitutakants kie mishiue
tshekuan. Nete nushimits tshipa skutimashuts uta
eushitakanitshi. Tshipa auashits nitutueuts atinuaia
nepataui. Enutshikuakant teuenike tshipa skutimuakanuts. Tshipa tutuakanuts tshetshi mupistuats
utinimaua.

"Tauts inuts tshetshenitats inu uta. Innuts upau-
nakanits nushimits, tshipa kau mishikauts uta Utshimassits. Auashits tshika skutimuaets uipats kaish
iniuau. Eka skutimuakut auashits uta eshiushi-
takantshi ama tshika nista shenitamuts. Auashits
itenitamutshetshi ekuta muk mitshima tshipa ntu-
uiunanu. Tshishue minuau nushimits etuuiunats shishipits. Etu tsheutshimau tshipa minukunu
shuneanu tshetshi uitshimats tshenua. Tshipa kau
tshiueuts nipinits uta tshipa apitshitauts. Tshishue
auashits tshipa uitshinukuts. Auashits tshipa uapatamuts tshetshi skutimashuts. Ntuenitamuauts
auashits tshetshi skutimashuts stiniunanu."
Kaniuekutat

Mitshiuapa tshipa tshimitakanua eshi tuuiunats nete
mushuats. Kie tshipa ushitakanua mitshima tshetshi
apitshitats inuts etuuiutaui.

Tshipa minu nakatuenimaaets tshenuts, entshe katshi uitshinushutshi kie stuasiminuts. Tshipa skutimuakanuts auashits tshetshi tats nushimits. Tshipa
ntuapatenan tshetshi minu iniunan, tshetshi eka kakeshau nutshikatak. Uipats inuts meatsheepants
aueshisha kie asinu eku tshipa kutshitanan tshetshi kie
tshinan ituteak kaitutets.

Tshipa Aianumean

Tshipa aianumean, uishamauts Innuts, tsheapinau, kie
tsheuauitamau kamenupinak kie tshetinak eskua eshi
iniunaue. Tshipa ntuapatenan tshekuan kamenupinak
kie tshetuapatamak tsheish minupinak. Akaui uauita-
maue kamenupinau aka ui tapitu atuskatamaue. Tshetshi anumeatimak tapitu ekun tsheshi tutamak
kamenupinak. Nteshiue Innuts tshipa uishamakanuts
tshetshi aianumets, kie tshetshi nitutuauts. Tshipa
apitshitunan.

Innuts tshipa etuteuts naianumanitshi ekunu tshesh-

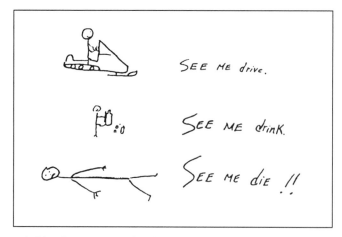

Child's drawing at school workshop / Auasits kaunishi-natatshet, kaskutimatsheupits kaianumats, 1992

enitats enitinanits. Tshenuts tshipa tapituuiuts kie
tshipa uauitamuts tshetinats. Kie auashits tshipa
uishamakanuts eshishuetau tshekuanu. Inuts tshipa
tipatshimuts uitamueuts enishishuanits naianumatshi
nistam tshuiutsheuakanuts kie tshikanishinuts tshipa
uitamuauts. Katshi aianumatshi tshauetaui Innuts
tshipa tipatshimuts enishishuanits.

"Niskueuts tapitu tshipa anumeatimuts
kamenupinanits, kie tshipa uitshinueuts. Niskueuts
shapiuts naianumetaui. Tshipa uitshinueuts uta utenats." *Kaatushets*

Meieu muk enu utshimauts tshetshi mushinau
aianumets. Tshipa tapitunanu tshetshi aianumats. Tenitenan nishuau peik pishuma tshipa aianumanu. Ekun
muku tsheuitshitunak. Tshipa tapituinan tshetshi ntuapatamak kamenupinak uta utenats.

Naianumeaui tshipa mishineai enishishueak eku ama
tshikishi unikuatenan.

Tshipa takun tipatshimun mishinanikan tshetshi
shenitats inuts enishishuanits. Tshipa takun kanitu-
takant tante pishe ama nistuunamuts mishinanikanu.

Shitakunapun Tshipa Tshipenan

Tshipa punan eminak kie stuasiminuts tshetshi punits
eminastuskuets kie nikatishinean shitakunapun kie
tshetshi Innuts kutshitauts tshetshi punits eminits.
Ekun muku tshetshi uitshinushunak Innu tshi-
tapimushutshe emit kie uitshinishutshe. Tetauts
putaue inuts eminits tshipatshi put kutshitauts
kutukuts tshetshi punits eminits.

to stop drinking and regain control of their lives. Some of us believe families should leave the community and go into the country for a year. Our children need to be taken into the country. Some of us think that when we do this, we should leave all the things of the white culture behind, like radios, tape recorders, T.V. and so on. In the country they can learn to make things like canoes with only a hammer, nails and canoe canvas. Children would learn from legends told to them at bedtime. The drum dance should be taught to them. They would also learn to visit their neighbours more.

"People here can still make canoes. If people can be flown into the country, I'm sure they could canoe back after break-up. Some of our children would learn our culture. If we don't teach our children about how to build canoes, how to use canoes, they will never know. Maybe the young people think the coast is the only place to hunt for birds. There are a lot of good places in the country for migrating birds like geese. The government should give us more money for outpost program training for our young people. In this program, young people would get flown into the country with a couple of elders and family. The group would then return to the community by canoe after break-up. This would be very important for our young people. Children have to see it to learn. I want all the children to learn about our culture so it will continue to live on for years to come." *Kaniuekutat, elder*

Cabins could be built along the route to Border Beacon. [Border Beacon is about 180 miles west of Utshimassit, or an eight-hour skidoo ride by day. The government built a weather station and an airstrip there during the last war.] They could also be built around the bays for the future safety of the people who are always going hunting.

We need to take better care of our elders, especially those who cannot help themselves, and of our children. This plan to teach our children and grandchildren how we used to live in the bush is very important. We must find a way to live in peace, not bothered by white people. Our ancestors respected the animals and the land, and we must try to follow in their footsteps.

We Need Meetings

We need to have meetings, invite all the people, sit down and talk about our problems and our future in public. We need to look at the causes of our problems and find ways to solve them. If we don't discuss our problems in public, nothing will change. These problems will not go away just like that, but if we work together and talk, we can begin to solve them. When we get together at a community meeting, people should listen. We need to hear one another.

People have to go to meetings so we can find out what is going on. Elders should gather and discuss what we should do, and men and women as well. The elders should be there. The young people should be asked to participate at meetings as well to include them in our discussions and get their input on future decisions. People who come to meetings should talk to other people about meetings to get them interested in coming. First we can talk to our friends and families and then to other people. Not just leaders should do this, but everybody. People should go to the homes to let everyone know about the meetings.

"If the women got together and talked about the problems, this would help too. Women have strong voices when we all look at the problems. This would help our community." *Women construction worker trainees*

It doesn't have to be the Band Council organizing the meetings all the time. Public workshops can be held at any time. Some of us think we should have regular workshops, twice a month. Maybe that is the only way we will understand each other. We need workshops to help us develop our own plans to solve our community problems.

When we have meetings or workshops, we should write everything down that is being said, so that we don't forget anything important.

We should have a newsletter so people will know what is going on. We also should use the community radio for communication because some people can't read.

The Alcohol Must Stop

We need to stop drinking, and the children need to stop sniffing gas. We must get rid of alcohol and feel like a new people. People are trying to stop drinking now. The only way we can solve our problems is if people are willing to look at their drinking and help themselves with their problems. If 50 per cent of our people are sober, we can do things. More people will want to stop drinking.

"Teniten tshetsh nakituenimushunan punae eminan shitakunapun. Nipun eminan eku tshishue niminueniten kie ama nista akushin. Mushinau ntakushin eskua eminan. Nakituenimauts nushimits anuts. Menani nastesh ama nakitueniten atik mistikuen tshitamin, muku nimin. Eku anush niminuenimun, niminueniten kie nushimits minuenitamuts. Mitshima tauts. Shitakunapun nuieuetishumukun. Nuiu uapaten utenats tshetshi eka minats, eku patush tshipa uitshitunan." *Miste-Shishin*

Tshipa uitshiakanuts inuts tshetshi uitshiakanits eminits kamenupunits. Eminiats mitshipanu. Innuts nipuuts. Tsheutshimau tshipa minukunu shuneanu tshetshi inuts punitats eminits eshi mitshipininukuts menits.

Unitshinukuts kie auashits tshipa uitshakanuts. Tshipa ituteuts kastipetshi naianumentshi. Tshipa uitshinukunuts eminuau. Inuts tshipa shenitamuts etutakuts shitakunapuna, tan eshi akushiskakuts. Tshipa apinan mamu tshenuts kie auashits kie mishiue kamenupinau. Tshipa uitamuaets stuashiminuts eshinakuats uipats. Kie tshetshi eka uinuau nishinakushits. Tshipa nitutuanu katipenimitak. Katipenimitak tshipa uitshinukunu tshetshi punitauak eminuak. Inuts uikanishuaua tshipa kutsheuts tshetshi punitshi eminitshi. Tshipa uitamuaiaets stuasiminuts etutakuts tshianishinuts nepits shitakunapunu etutakuts. Tshipa mamitinenitenan tshekuan uishi minan. Tshipa ntuapatenan kie ama tshika katanan tshekuan kamenupinak uish minak. "Tshipa eiemaaets auashits kaminits nanikutini. Tshipa aianumanu peikuau katshi nishumeastakeatshi. Tshipa kamakunuest uitamuanan tshetshi eiemaat auasha. Auashits uitamueuts kutuka auasha eku uenauinats kutuka kauiuitshinukushitshi. Ama tshikitshi nitutuaets auashits kauauinats kutuka auasha eku put tshipa nitutakanuts. Ama tshikishi uitamuauts tshetits. Muku tshipa uitamuauts etutatshets shitakunapunu." *Kamamuinats*

Etu inuts tshipa pushuts nete kaapishipants mitshiuap. Pishe inuts ama shenitamuts enistinanits nete kastipants tante ama shenitamuts kakeshamunu. Shenitats etu tshipa uitshinukuts. Inuts tshipa etuteuts nete uashats kaapishipats mitshiuap. Tshenuts kie tshipa pushuts kie tshipa uitshakanuts. Tshishue apitishuts kie tshipa nitutuauts. Tshipa pushuts nete kastipants mitshiuap

entshe kaakunikuts shitakunapunu eskua eka tats nete astukantshe. Pishe tshipa uitshakanuts uta utenats katshi pushuitshi. Ntuenititau tshinan tshetshi titimak kaapishipants mitshuap. Nutshimits tshipa takun. Tsheutshimau esk eka nipinak tshipa minukunu shuneanu tshetshi takunits apishipeutshiuapinu.

Tshimishetinan eshishueau tshetshi eka takuats shita-kunapun nete astutsheaue tshipa uitshitunan tshetshi eka petustaiak shitakunapun nete kitshiui astutsheaiaua kie tsheminu iniunak. Inuts tshipa punuts eushitats shitakunapunu. Etu tshika minuenumunan nete tshitshinash.

Ntukuniskuesits kie ntuastikushuuts, Inua natikutaui Utshimassits tshipa skutimueuts shitaunapunu eshini-katents.

Emeutshiuap tshipa uitshinueu Innu ueshukunikutshi shitakunapunu, kaiamituatshet tshipa mishikau peikuau put nishuau put etinatshi uta tshetshi uitshat Innua sheneshintshi. Kastekupeskueuts tshipa uitshinueuts.

Innu Utshimauts tshipa punuts eminits. Utshimauts nete Innu Nation, kastipets kie Innu Utshimauts tshipa tshitapatamuts eminits. Inuts tshita pameuts pushitshi eku eshinuapamats tshetshi mishikantshi tshetshi petautatshi shitakunapunu. Ama uitshakanuts Innuts. Utshimauts tshipa punitauts shitakunapunu epatautats. Innua nakituapimikuts eku kie uin etutamitshi. Ama nitutakuts inua menastenitakaui. Utshimauts petautauts shitakunapunu kie Innu tshika petautau. Patush tapitu uitshitunaue tshishue eskua tshika mishau shitakunapun uta.

Tshinitshinukuts eapits utshimaushuts. Aka uitamuatshe utuasima tshekuanu kamenuats, ama tshika nista shenitaminua. Tshipa uitamuauts stuashiminuts etenitakuats eminau.

"Ama tshishenitenan tshetshi eka petishinimau kamenupinak nete astutsheaue. Tshash tshipa tshishipinan eapishipeak. Muku ama tshishenitenan tshetshi nikatishinimak kamenupinak." *Kistinis*

Auashits Uiuitshinukushiuts

Auashits uuitshinukushits. Pishe ama nastesh nakitueni-tamuts tshekuanu. Uinitshinuka auash tshipa minu nakituenimuku. Tshipa uitamuauts eshi shuenitakushits. Ekuts tsheaiastinash eskute. Tshipa

"I think we can regain control of our lives if we stop drinking alcohol. I quit drinking for a while now. I am very happy and I don't get sick. I was always sick when I was drinking. I look after my grandchildren now. While I was drinking, I didn't do any work like cleaning caribou skins. I was lazy; I only drank. Now I feel good about myself. I clean caribou skins too. I am happy; my grandchildren are happy too. They are very close to me. The alcohol was controlling me. I would like to see the community dry up, so we could help one another." *Miste-Shishin, elder*

Our community needs a lot of help with our alcohol problems. This is a crisis. Our people are dying. The government should be spending more money on services to help people to stop drinking rather than services to deal with the problems that happen because people drink.

Parents and children need professional counselling. We need to go to A.A. meetings regularly. We need workshops for people to learn what alcohol does to them, how it makes them sick, how alcohol affects the whole family. Alcohol is not just a person's own problem. For us, it is a community disease. We need to sit down together, from elders to small children, and discuss all the tragedies that have happened. We have to educate our children about what has happened in the past; we don't want to see this happen again. We need to hear the warnings of the Spirit. Our spirituality will help us to stop drinking. People should talk to their relatives about their drinking. We also need to talk to our kids about how our relatives, our children and our people are dying from alcohol. We need to ask ourselves why we keep drinking. We need to look at the problems we are hiding from when we drink.

"We should try to talk to the young people. We should have regular meetings, once every two weeks for the young people only. We could have the R.C.M.P. officer in to talk to the young people. Some children will talk to the others and say bad things to those people who do the counselling. But if we pay no attention to this, young people will know we are trying to teach them good things, not bad things. We are not going to try to tell them what to do. We just want to remind them about the alcohol problems in our community." *Discussion at community workshop on recommendations*

More people should go out to the treatment centres. Some people don't understand what is happening at treatment centres because they have trouble with English. If they understood, it would help them a lot more. Our people should be able to go to the Innu alcohol treatment centre in Uashat, Quebec. We should send elders too and help them. They are very important and we need to hear them. People who have a drinking problem and have jobs in the community need to be really encouraged to get help to stop drinking. Some people say that those with drinking problems should go to an alcohol treatment centre before we move to the new location. We want a mobile alcohol treatment program for our community so that people won't have to go away to get treatment. We also want our own treatment centre. We want a treatment centre in the country at Border Beacon. The government must provide more funding for alcohol treatment now before more people die.

Many of us are saying we should leave our home brew buckets behind and ban alcohol in the new community. We need laws to stop the alcohol from coming into our community. We should try to help ourselves and work for better living conditions by not bringing alcohol to the new location. People should stop making home brew. We would be much happier in our homes.

Nurses and doctors, as well as other people who come to work in our community, need training on alcoholism.

The Church should get involved in the healing process around alcohol-related deaths. Some of us recommend that the bishop should be asked to come to Utshimassit once or twice a year, or during tragedies, to help when families are in shock from these situations. Sisters should also get more involved.

The leaders should stop drinking. Leaders in the Innu Nation, the Alcohol Program and the Band Council have to look at their drinking problems. People see them go out of town and wait for some of them to come back with booze when they get off the plane. This is not helping the people. The leaders should stop bringing booze into the community. People look at the leaders, and it is booze they are sharing with the people. People don't respect them. They don't want to listen to their leaders when they drink. We will never

Kiti, 1993

PETER SIBBALD PHOTO

apitshiauts auashits tante tshiui apitshinukunuts. Tshipa uapatinaets eshi nakituenimauts kie tshipa minukuaiaets. Innu mentshi unikuatum utuasima etuenitamakut put kie nantuenitamakut. Tshipa minu nakatuenimauts auashits.

Tshipa uitatushemauts tshetshi eka animishits. Tshishue animin auash tshetshi minuenitak kie tshetshi eka animishit. Tshipa uitshinushunan. Tshipa skutimuauts kie euitamuauts stuashimits uipats kaenitinanits. Tshipa ntuapataenan tante tsheshi minupinan tshiastutsheaue. Miuatshe mitshiuap tsheshitetshi, tukuatshe nipin tshika minuenitamuts auashits kie tshika nitutakunuts.

"Nteniten tshetshi auashits uitsheutauts. Tshi pitetash tatunuepashe, auashits tshika pipininukunuts kie stasinanu. Paminueniten aka mitshipinits. Eskute ekun anush auashits tsheutshimauts, tshika uapatamuts mishinanikea kanish pipinitatshi utshimaua. Eku kaminuenitakaue tshekuanu eku tshetshuapits." *Miste-Pinip*

"Tshinishunueputshe, ama nuui uapamauts auashits tshetshi eka nastesh apitishits put tshishauts tshipa ushitanan meskeieu tshetshi shenitats etuteak. Aka skutimuauts auashits eshi nutshikuakants tsheutshimau, peikun tshenishinakushits anuts eshinakushinak. Unikapui kie mashishetau anuts stuashiminuts." Nutuashish.

Auashits pukushenimeuts unitshinikuaua tshetshi punitshi eminitshi. Punaue eminak, tshika nitutakanuts stuasiminuts. Stuasiminuts uiminu skutimashuts tshetshi mushinau tats kaskutimasheutshuapits. Stuasiminuts uimetueuts. Ntuapatamuts tante tshetats katshi puniskutimashutaui. Tshipa takun

kashunaskuatanikants kie kanakituenimakanits. Nitueniten mamu tapitu tshetshi tats.

"Tshipa makituenimaaets stuasiminuts. Tshipa minu iniunan kie nipin tshipa takun. Tshipa minukean stasinu tshipa uitshauts Innuts kie auashits kie tshenuts. Tshipa minuenitamuts Innuts. Mauats nuui nutshikuanan pimin kie shitakunapun. Nuui minuenitenan. Niminuenimauts nitshinukuts. Nimitsheniten shitakunapun." *Shanet kie Tan Mani*

"Nuuimistintuenitenam, mitshim niuinikeenan tshetshi eka nutshikatunants. Niuintuenitamuanants tshetshi eka nutshikatuts. Amaniniuapaten katshishatish shitakunapun. Kie kaushitakants. Niuitshinukunaets tshetshi eka minits. Kie niuiuapamaaets ntuasiminaets tshetshi eka minatuskuets kie tshetshi eka akushits. Nipukuenimanats tshetshi minu skutimashuts. Niuinitutuanants katsheniuts eku te nte tante kinastinimats mitinenetshikan. Etunituenitenan metueuna kanukumunatshi etu kutuka tukuatshi katshiskanikanishits, kaniminants Innu umuetueuna kashuakuants, kaashinaiats, kie kapipamaskuanikants katuaiants nete masteutiskan ke meastakan. Kie auasits atutshi pikuaumuts mitshuapa. Kie patuenitenan kakeeuenimakanits auasits. Kie tshipa ntuenitakanua menuatshi ntukuuna. Kie niuiuapatenan Innuts tshetshi minu inniuts, uitshiituts. Tukuatshi menuatshi mitshuapa kie tukuatshi nipina, eminuats enipaiats. Kie tshipa takun kauepinashunants uenapenashunantshi. Nas etu tshipa minuaua utapaia ne eshinakuats kamishats utapan Super Jag." *Auasits uauitamupants etipitspitetash kie anianeu*

"Tshipa nisishueats tsheka akatukuats niskuteuapun stisinats, uauitamakuunak. Tshipantuenitenan tshetshi minu uitsheutunak. Utshimasiunuts etu tshipa ituteuts nanimuantshi kastipanits. Tshetshiminuniuak, atutshi minan. Tshipa uitshianants stuasiminuts. Mishiue tshekuan tshipa nikitenan, eku mishiue Innuts tshipa minuenitamuts kie tshipa shatshiituts. Kie tshipa atinenan stisinu, muk nte uaatinamauk eku minuats tshipa uskasisipinan. Nistim tshipa tshitapatenan tshenispishats asin nete uaushitakantau mitshuapa. Kutuk nte uaatutsheak, mishiue kamenunipunikunak tshipa uepinean. Muk put niskuteuapun atutshitakun. Put kie tshipa minuau eskutimashunak, tshipa tatshishinan." *Auasits Kamamitits*

change if our leaders don't change. If leaders drink, people will drink too. If leaders bring in booze, people will do it too. Unless we work together and help each other with this, there will always be too much alcohol in the community.

Parents are leaders too. If they don't let their children know good things, they will never know them. We need to tell our children what it is like when we drink.

"We can't make sure that we won't move our problems when we relocate. We have already started a process of recovery and we should continue. But there is no guarantee that those problems will be eliminated." *Kistinis*

The Children Need Our Help

The children need our help. Some of our children don't care about anything. The parents have a responsibility to listen to their children. We need to tell them how good they are. Children are so important. They are our future. We need our children and they need us too. We must show them that we care about them and that we want what is best for them. When people drink, they forget about what their children want or need. We need to take better care of our children.

We should work with them so they won't get into trouble. It is going to be very difficult to make our children happy and free from trouble. We have to help ourselves first. We need to help our children understand our past and present problems. If we move, things might change. But we have to find ways to solve our problems first. When we have good warm houses with running water, this will help the children to be happier and to listen to their parents.

"I'm sure our children will follow our ways too. In the next fifty years, our children will be running their own lives and the community. I hope they don't make the same mistakes we made in the past. In the future, when our children take over as leaders, they will find the old records of how the Band Council used to run the community. If they don't like what they find, they will be angry and frustrated." *Miste-Pinip, elder*

"Twenty years or more from now, we don't want our children to say we were useless and crazy. We have to make a road for them so they will know where they are heading. If we don't teach our children how to

fight governments, then they will be the same as we are now. Let us stand up and fight for our children." *Nutuashish Gathering workshop discussion*

Children want their parents to stop drinking. If we stay sober, our children will listen to us. Our children want a better education and to stay in school. Children want more recreation activities like those organized by the Youth Council. They want a place to hang out in, like a drop-in centre. The community needs an arena and a playground. We want a group home here so our children won't be sent out of the community. We want both parents and their children to stay as one family. We need family counselling so our families won't have to be separated when they are in crisis. We need sex education for our children, to stop the high numbers of teen-age pregnancies.

"The parents should take care of their children. We would like to be healthy, and have water to clean ourselves and our houses. We would like to clean our village up. We would like to help people and children. We would like to help the old people. We want people to be happy. We don't want to sniff gas and drink. We want to be happy. We like our families. We hate alcohol." *Tan Mani and Shanet, school workshop, grades 5 to 8*

"We need more food so we won't be hungry. We want the fighting to stop; we want people to stop beating each other up. We don't want Labatt's Blue or home brew. We want our parents to stop drinking. We want the children to stop making themselves sick from the gas sniffing. We want more education and the kids to be kept in school. We want to listen to our elders about the past so we can get some ideas from them. We want more recreation activities like games, lip sync, more tournaments (like pool-table tournaments), a dance club, snow sculpturing, Native games, sliding, checkers, and floor hockey in the gym on Saturday and Sunday. We want the kids to stop breaking into houses. We want a group home here in Utshimassit. We want better medicines. We would like to see people healthy and helping one another. We want good houses with running water, a good place to stay and to sleep. We need a place to throw our garbage. We want better skidoos like Super Jag." *Children's discussion at school workshop, grades 5 to 8*

"We need to ban alcohol from our community, and

Kauiatukuants

"Tshipa uitamuanu tshe utshimau tshetshi minu ini-
uak, kie tshetshi minupinants nipin kauitakuats, eku
tshipa minupinan, eku tshipa uitshianants katsheniuts tshetshi minuatshi mitshuapa." *Kaniuekutat*

Amanipukuenitenan ntesinan tshetshi mitshash.
Kuestetshe atutsheakue kutak ustumpuninukunau
mauats muk Utshimassits make te nutshimits. Innuts
minupintaue eku tsheminuats. Akamintaue punitataue
tshika minupunuuts. Niuikutshitanan tshetshi uskisi-
shipinash kie tshetshi minuenitamats.

Tshituteatshe uste ministukuts nas tshipaminutaka-
nipi mitshuapa kie nipin tshipa pimpinu kie kapimp-
intshi katshapistesi. Uitshuaua tshipamishitakanua.
Kie tshipa minukukunua mitshuapa. Stisinan tshipa
nas tipenitenan. Atutshinista miskuts mitshipini-
tananapin uta ministikuts, kie tsheutshimau atutshi
mitshipinitau. Kaatukuants peikunen. Enkunu enu
Innu esishuet muats tsheutshimau put emeutshiuap.
Tshinan tshipa pimpinitanan tshitasinu eka uitshintau
tsheutshimau.

Tshitapatetau esh kamenupunak uta esk etanak ministukuts eku tshipa kutshitanan tshetshi nikatamak.
Kie tshipa anumuekatenan eshikaminu punak. Eku
ntuapatamak tshetshi minu punitaiau. Niuiatutshenan
anuts muats neush. Tshipa uitamuakanuuts auasits
tshetshi atukuanits.

Tshipa mamitinenitenan tshekuan stishinats
tshekaminuakue. Eku tshipa ushitakanua ueskatshi
mitshuapa. Tshishue tshikimistiuepinean shuneau
ushitakantshe mitshuapa. Innu Utshimauts tshash
atuskatamuts kauiatukuants. Inuuts tshekeuapata-
muts ueskants tshekuanu. Mishiue tshika animuanu.
Tshishue tshika mishanu Innuts tshetshi tapuetats.
Innu Utshimauts tshikaminu uitamueuts inua.

Innu Utshimauts tshipa kutshitauts tshetshi nas
minuan-tshi mitshuapa atukuantshe. Tshinishitshi tapatenan tsheushitakantshi menamisha tshi mitshuapa,
kie tanis-pish Innu tshetipenitak asinu uitshuats. Kie
atutshi nutshitamuts kuestikunits atukuanitshe. Uit-
shinatshe uikanishuaua mitshima tshipa. Uitshitueuts
patshitukenan tshipetastatu nu utishipints, kie tshipa
mishetinanu tshash. Nipukuenitenan tshetshi takuats
apimpints nipin eku mishiue mitshuapits tshipa takun.

"Tshipa ushitanan mistukutshiuap tshenuaskuatshi
mitshuapa atukuantshe. Kantuuiuts tshipa apitshitauts kie tshipa mupimanu kie tshipa minukikinua

Sheshkun, 1992

uskea. Tshipa skutamashunan aueshishish tepenimitak imuk. Kie tshipa inuniminanu teuenike. Ekutanta tshenuuts paskutimakunaets. Kie pauit-
shinukunaets enitits. Tshipa tshitutenan. Kie
tshipatshi tapatenan nitukuuna. Tshipasku tumua-
iaets stuasiminuts metueuna. Niskueuts tshipa skutimatsheuts apitshitauna akupa eiapi tshitakants
maniun. Eku Innu atutshiminu." *Utshimassits Kaan-
imuats*

"Nas tshipa mistaanimuenan uaatutsheak. Muats
mushinau atutshi mishetinan. Pase tshipaanimuean
uaanimueak." *Shuash*

"Tshishue tshikemiskuak tshenakatamau. Kaus-
tumpuninukunak, muk tshipa tuskuatenan kie
tshipa uauitenan tshitasinan." *Niskueuts Kautintshet*

Innu Utshimauts tsiba takunu umishinikenueau uta
stisinats. Atutshi takun tshekuan kamenupinits auasits

CAMILLE FOUILLARD PHOTO

do what we are told to do. We need to get along with each other so God can help us get to where we want to be. The people in Utshimassit need more counselling and need to go to A.A. meetings regularly. To regain control of our lives, we have to stop drinking. We need to help the children that need our help. We must leave everything behind, so we can live better and everyone can be happy when we move with our families and friends. We could move our community to somewhere else, and we could start all over again. First, look for enough land where we will move to build all our houses on. If we get to move to another community, the problems will pass away. Maybe the alcohol won't be there. Maybe we will have a good education, better ideas for the kids. We have to be cool." *School workshop with high-school students*

Relocation

"We must let the government know that we want to move for better health, better living conditions, for water and sewage, so we can solve our community problems, so we can help our elders live more comfortably, and for better housing." *Kaniuekutat*

We want to relocate before the community gets worse. If we don't move soon to another location, we will have other problems, not only in the community but also in the country. When people have better living conditions, they will change. They will be more comfortable, and this will help people to stop drinking. There will be fewer problems. We want our lives to be more stable at this new location. We want to start new lives for ourselves.

We need to move away from this island so we can start off with proper housing which has water and sewer, basements and furnaces. The houses should be big enough for our families. We should also take good care of our homes. Our village should be on the mainland. We will never again make the same mistakes we made when we were moved on this island. We will not allow the government to make the same mistakes either. Relocation is the number one priority. This time it is an Innu project, not the government's or the Church's. We must make our own decisions and run our community the way we want to, without outside help from the government.

We should look at our problems now, while we are still on this island, and try to leave the things that make

us suffer here. We need to discuss these problems and try to find ways to solve them. We need to plan for relocation now, not later. It is important to plan if we expect to see this relocation take place. We need to talk to our children about relocation.

We should think about what the new community will look like. We should only build new houses at the new site. It is a waste of money to build any new houses here. The Band Council is now working on a design for the new community. People will be able to see this new design soon. Everyone needs to talk about this at meetings. It will take a lot of talking for people to agree. The leaders will have to explain a lot to the people.

The Band Council should really try to build better houses at the new location. The plans so far look at where we should build, how big the houses will be and what they will look like, how far apart to build them, how much land each person should have, whether to build duplexes and houses of relatives close together, whether the new community should face sunrise or sundown. We need to look at the dangers of the rattles [narrow channels with rapids] near the new site. We want to plan for the next fifty years because our population is growing fast. We want to make sure we have good sewage facilities and that we don't pollute the water around the new community.

"We should build a lodge or a longhouse at the new location. This lodge would be for the hunters. It would be a place to hold mukushan and to clean the caribou bones. We would learn about the animal spirits in this lodge. We would hold drum dances. This would be a place for the elders to teach us their ways. This would help us get back our culture. We can do it. Also we could practise our own medicines. We could teach our children our own games. The women could learn to make traditional clothing, like coats with fur. This would help people to stop drinking." *Discussion at community workshop on recommendations*

"We have to do a lot of talking about relocation. It doesn't always have to be in big groups all the time. Just a few of us together can talk about it wherever we can." *Shuash*

"It will be hard to leave our problems behind, but we can work it out if we can talk about a dry community." *Family Violence Project*

utapanisa pempinitats, tshipa nepaats atumua, mena-tuskuets, Innuts menatenitats pepimpinitats. Ntisinan nas tshipa pasteu kie atutshitakun niskuteuapun. Nim-itshetinan esishueats niskuteuapun. Nimitshetinan esishueats niskuteuapun tshetshi takun ekun eatukuants. Petustaaue tshitaunapuminua tshiatukua-ntshe nastesh tshikitshi minuau. Mushinau tshipaan-imuanu tshetshi pastets stesinats.

"Kamenits Innuts nistim tshipa uitshiakanuuts. Nisenitenan pase Innuts tsheakunikuts, eku tshipa sentamuts pase inuts. Eku atutshiuiminuuts. Kamenits Innuts passe mitshenimeuts menitshi Innua, nastesh ama niitshenimitunan. Enkun menu-ats. Tshipa uitshintuuts tshetshi eka minits uiatukuanitshe." *Kaianumeatikantshi tshekuan tshetinants*

"Muk nishinankun tshetshi eka petustaiak kamenupini-nikunak. Innu Utshimauts tshipa itusheuts Innua nitutakuts. Mauats niskuteuapun tshikitshi takun ntesinats. Mauats niskueuts kauti-nakanits. Muats kauapats tshekuan. Muats kauauin-tuts inuts. Ama tshika akuitunanu." *Kaskutimat-sheuts kaanimuets*

"Innu Utshimauts uinuau tshipa tutamuts uta kisti-tananua. Eku mpauishamukunaets papeik Innua tshipaminu uita-mueuts tshekuanu. Enkunu enu-muk tshipatshi tutamuts. Ene tuaue tshipauitamuets kie tshipa uapatineuts uta eshinakunits. Put pase katsheniuts uipetamutshentshi eshinakunits." *Miste-Pinip*

Tan tshipa ntenitamupints auasits katantakueni, kashe tshimakanitshi, kie kakeeshaua umuetuakanua? Put kie uiskutimashutshentshi eshinakunits tshimete-

unu. Ntuenitenan tshetshi minuats nipin kie asin. Atutshi pikunean kaminuats stesinu kie uaatutsheau. Atutshiuepinean kauepinashunantshi uauepinimak ntuun. Nas tshipa minukenan stisinu.

Uantuapatamak tshekuan mishiue tshipa tuuts. Mishiue Innu nantuapatum tshetshi ustukuanimit tshetshi pimpinitat ushuneam. Minuanuenu Innu etuta eatusek. Innu atutshi minu eatuset. Atuseun tshipanispinu shuneau. Innu Utshimauts tutamuts tshetshi atuskaats Innua tshepimpinits ushuneaminu. Innu uetinakant tsheatuset. Atutshi pitaam eku pita, a kanakitu enitak etushumakant tshipa niskuashakanu. Tante minu. Eku Innu tshipa nistutum. Eku uiitutet nete nutshimits uiuitsheuat utuasima, Innu Utshimau tshipa uitshinuku.

Ntapitshitanan ntisinan etaiats. Ntaianimuetuanants kakeeshauts. Inuuts isishueuts kakeeshauts ama tapuetuakanuts tshetshitats uta nistim pita tshika uita-muts. Pase inuts ntenitamuts. Kie pise tapuetamuts tante nipuuts inua kie tshipa ushitauts uitshuaua.

"Tetauts stitanan kake eshauts kie esimeuts. Sti-tanan kie mushinau tshika tanan, tante tsheutshi-mau ninanu inuuts. Tsheutshimau stutakunu muk nastesh amatutenan. Nishuuts tsheutshimauts una-patas tapueu innu uta stesinan. Enkutshinan eniu-nak kie eshiniunak. Eku maku tshipa uninanapin. Ena-miats tshimistinipanan. Tshekuan tshipeku-nikunan. Tshueuepinu katshipinist. Katshiuniak ama euts muk katshipinishits uestumpunitauts. Takun kutak tshekuan kamenupuninukunak. Tshipa kashineanapin eni panak. Tsheutshimau stenimukunu tshetshi eka uniuak. Amanikatshi minuats enipaian." *Miste-Pinip*

The Band Council must have the authority to make laws for our new community. There should be laws about things like young children driving skidoos, about killing dogs, gas sniffing and drunk people driving. If we want to see the community dry, they should make a law banning alcohol. Many of us are saying alcohol should be banned in the new location. If we bring our home brew buckets to the new location, things will not look good. We need to have public meetings to talk about having a dry community.

"If relocation takes place, maybe the Band Council should first build houses for those people who don't drink. I know this will hurt some people, but people who drink might learn a lesson. They might want to stop drinking. Some people will think non-drinkers hate drinkers, but we do not hate each other. This is just an idea. It might help other people to stop drinking when relocation happens." *Discussion at community workshop on recommendations*

"The only way to make sure that we don't bring all of our problems with us is to make a lot of rules. The Band Council should set up by-laws or rules for all the Innu people to follow: No alcohol in the village. No family violence. No anti-white stuff. No harassing other people. When these laws are violated, penalties will follow to the violators of this Innu society. In other words: 'No pain, no gain.'" *Teachers' workshop*

"The Band Council should make community laws. They should invite every person in the community and explain to all of us about these laws for our new community. There is another way they can do it. They can invite a few people and ask them what they would like to see for community rules. Maybe some elders will have some good ideas about what rules are needed." *Miste-Pinip, elder*

How will the children feel if there is no T.V. and no white man's games? They might want to learn our traditional games.

We want a healthy environment. We need clean land and water. We should try not to spoil the beauty of nature where we relocate. We shouldn't dump our garbage wherever we please. We should keep our new village clean.

When we move everybody should try to find something to do. We need more employment for people. It would be really good for the people if everybody had jobs. This way, people wouldn't drink as much. These jobs should pay enough money. The Band Council and other organizations should try to employ most of the people in this new location. Persons who are hired should follow the rules. A warning should be given to them if they do not. If he or she doesn't care about the rules, this person should be fired. This goes for drinking on the job. People would learn a lesson this way. For those who want to go in the country with all their children, the Band Council should help fly them out.

We need to be able to decide who can live in our new community. We are talking about what to do with white people. Some people say white people can live in the community but they must have our permission first. Some people think they should not be allowed to live in the new community. And others believe that if they are married to Innu they should be able to have their houses in the community.

"If we can live as we always did in the past, we can prove to governments we are Innu. Governments will not complain because they will know we are changing. Both governments will see the true Innu of Ntesinan. If we can't do something about our lives and culture now, the next generation will be worse off. It is time to get up now. We have been sleeping all along. Something woke us up, and it is the noise of the jets. When we woke up, we saw that the jets were not the only problem. There were a pile of other problems in our community. It is time to clean up the mess while we were asleep. The government thought we would never wake up. From now on, we have to try not to fall asleep again." *Miste-Pinip, elder*

Mashisheu Tshetshi Minupanits

Nikumu kie mau
Uteuenikea uetamauat umitinenishikinist
ehe, menat.
Eshi uitutak tshekuanu
shenitan tsheustapit
eshi uiuitshat uitshinua eka minupinitshi
shenitam tshika eanikaeu
auenua eka shuka ssenimat.
Tshetshi minupit, tshika matshisheu
tsheutshimau, kakaminupinitat
tsheutshimau utinima petishaueu
ushinueu eku, etuenitamuat asinu
shenitamuts tapue eshi metuets
itenimeuts tshetshi shetshaats
uapatineu nete uaitutet
eku muk tshiam apissish petakushut
tshissentam shash ututshipinu utipeiken
tshetshi ui-unuitishinat utinim.

Kistinis

Struggle for Freedom

He sang and he cried,
the drum beating in his mind.
Yes, he cried...
for the things he had tried.
He knew it was a struggle,
to help his people when they are in trouble.
He knew he had to argue
with the person he hardly knew.
For freedom, he struggled.
With government, it was trouble.
The government men were sent.
He smiled at them and asked them for land.
These people knew how to gamble.
They thought they could make him tremble.
He showed them a new sight,
while they only gave a sigh.
For he knew the time had come
for his people's freedom.

Christine (Kistinis) Poker

INNUT KANTUSSENIMAKANIT ESPANIT

"Katshi tshishitakan neme uskat mishinikan Innut kapet eshitipatshimut espinit nte utat. Eku mitsheti-pan uentshi etu tshessenitak espinit nte utenat (Utshimassit) kie eitutuakanikuen Innuts. Mitshetut uentshi esk tekushinits nte Innu mishineikentshuapit. Tshatapatak kamamunikan aianimuan mishinikan. Uapatamut nene eis-sishuanuikupan kie tshekuan tshipa tutakanipan kie meshuka issi-minanu kaissi minant ute Utshimassit. Kie uinuau Innuts ui-tshissenitamut tan-uaishi-uit-shitishut. Kie Innuts issishueut, ninan nika tshissenite-tenan tsheishiuitshinushunat. Innut uiauitakau ume kaishinakushit, eukunu nenu minuat kau-uiauitak nete kaissishuet katutakanit mishinikan kantussenimakanits Innut kaishiniuits kie kaeitutuakanit. Ui-uapatamut mishinikanu etapuemakanit. Ute Innut issishueut nene kaissishueiat nte katipatshimuiat mishinikan nas nte kassinu tapueun takun. Mitshet-uau shash nitaianimuenan euauitamat ne-uentshi kemistutuanutshi kie kaui-atukan euauitamat. Miste-mitshetuau nta uinuau Innut uapamitut euauita-matut tshekuanu kie ninan. Nantim nintussenitenan. Tshekuan nipatutenan. Passe Innuts uinuau nakat-uenimushut, uinuau pimpinushut. Niteniten tshima ishinakuat tshetshi uitshikunat. Ume netussenitakan tshekuan tshetshi uitshikunat nte ua-ishi-uitshi-nushunat." *Tshatsh, Pitu-Utshimau*

Uapukun-pishum 1993, katshi peikupuna unuipan-takan. Kamamunikan aianimuan mishineikan, Royal Commission Innuts minuat shitshimepan Innu Nation, etu-tshetshi nitussenimakanit Innut espinits nte utenat (Utshimassit) kie nte nutshimit etatau. Innu Nation utshimaut tapuetamupan kie itenitamupan etu tshipa tshitapatakanu, nte utenat eshinakuak kie nte nutshimit eshi-uitshinushut Innut. Ui-tshisse-nitamut tan-tshipa tutamut etu put nte tshipa itishinikenenu

shuniau kie tshetshi etu-atuskatet enitussenitakan nte utenat etu tshetshi minupinits kie mak etu tshipa nitussenitakanu tan tshipa tutakanu etu tshetshi mit-shetit Innuts ua-kuspit nutshimit. Innu Utshimaut issishueut, eukun ume nantim niuauitetan tshetshi ishinakuak. Katshi ne-tutakan mishinikan. Sheshatshit kie uinuau itenitamut tshetshi mamunak uteimunuau eku nte Utshimassit shutshimakats. Nene tshekuan shash pietamak espinikue nte utenat, ne-mishiniken kaunuipantaken.

"Nin-niteniten minuau tshetshi etu nitussenitakan kie nitenimauts tsheutshimauts tshipa kusput nte nutshimit eku tshipa uapameut. Nenu nas Innu eku anutsh ishinakushut tsheutshimauts ama tshinistua pamukunuts. Tshekuanitshe tsheutshimau eka-kue-spit tshipa tau nte nutshimit tshipa uapatam eshi-minupinuak." *Miste-Etuet, Tshenu*

Eukun ume nishuau etutakan mishineke kamamuna-mak staianimuanu kie ekun eiapits tshekat tapiskut eshinakuak. Innu Nation nenu utinepan uenu tshenakatuapatamen umenu atusseunu nete Utshimas-sit tsheminakanit kie uetinakanit tshenakatuapak umenu atusseunu, Tshenish Pastin, Miste-Tuma Rich, Shunin Shantes, Manteskueu Mistinapeu, Patnik Rich, Ipuan Asta, mak Nanishi Tshak. Eku ntshen etuskatat, Shimun Pukue, Tshan Nui mak Camille Fouillard utinakanipan tshetshi uin pempintat umenu atuskanu, Tshatsh mak Penash Rich, Shuash Kenikue mak Kiti Rich eukun tshetshi tatak etisten nenu mishinineke. Eukun ne-tshatapateken uskat mishineikan, tshetshi kutak takuak mishinikan kie eukun tsheitenitakuak kie ekun tsheitistet tshekat. Ntshen nutshikak umenu mishi-neikenu, euku tsheua-pamat uenu kie mak mamu tshika eimieut, ekukuet-shimat tshekuanu mamu napeu kie iskueu, tshenu kie ustinitshu kie iskuesa. Passe eiapit itisheikenipan

EPILOGUE

FOLLOWING UP ON THE PEOPLE'S INQUIRY

Shimun, 1993

"After the People's Inquiry, people were more aware of what was happening in the community, of what had happened to them. People still come into the Innu Nation office, flip through the pages of the *Gathering Voices* report. They see what was said, what was going to be done. There is a decrease in alcoholism in the community now. People are more willing to offer solutions themselves. People often say now that they are the ones who will find the solutions to problems. And when people talk about these issues, they repeat that they have said it in the Inquiry, that it is in the book. People tend to see the Bible as the truth. But here people say what they said in the book, *Gathering Voices,* is the truth. We have had a lot of meetings around sexual abuse, on relocation. There are a lot of consultations going on between Innu people. We have been doing a lot of research. Some people are taking control of their own lives. I hope this study will help us to keep moving towards that direction." *Tshatsh, Innu Nation vice-president*

June 1993. A year after *Gathering Voices* was made public, the Royal Commission on Aboriginal Peoples (RCAP) invited the Innu Nation to carry out a community-based research project. Innu Nation leaders agreed to participate and decided the focus of the study would be on the differences between life for us in the community and life in nutshimit, the country. They wanted to know whether most funding and services should continue to go towards making life in the community better, or whether more efforts should be made to help people go to nutshimit. Leaders felt this was a question we were always talking about. The study was seen as an opportunity for Sheshatshiu to carry out its own gathering of voices and for Utshimassit to build on what we had learned through our People's Inquiry.

"This research project is a good idea. I think the government people should go to nutshimit and see what the Innu people are all about. Still the government is denying we are a people. Why doesn't the government stay in nutshimit and see the big difference?" *Miste-Etuet, elder*

This second gathering of voices was organized in much the same way as the first. A committee was appointed by the Innu Nation to oversee the project. In Utshimassit, the committee included Tshenish Pasteen, Joseph Raymond (Tumas) Rich, Julianna (Shunin) Saunders, Marie Georgette (Manteskueu) Mistenapeu, Patrick (Patinik) Rich, Yvonne (Ipuan) Asta and Nancy (Nansi) Rich. The researchers were Simon (Shimun) Poker and Tshan Nui, and Camille Fouillard was hired to co-ordinate the project. George (Tshuash) Rich, Penash Rich, George (Shuash) Gregoire and Katie (Kiti) Rich served as peer reviewers. The research focussed on gathering voices as opposed to compiling information from books. Our researchers carried out detailed individual or focus group interviews with men and women, elders and youth. Questionnaires were also distributed to all the homes. We held school workshops for all the classes in school, with elders Tshenish and Meneshkuesh as resource people. We talked with people of different clans and with different life experiences and points of view. We included people who have spent a lot of time in the country and those who haven't. In all, we reached 119 people in the community.

This epilogue includes excerpts from the responses of Utshimassit participants in the research project. The

CAMILLE FOUILLARD PHOTO

passe mishineikea nte mitshuapit, uen ua-uitak etenitak, eukunu tsheapastat mishineikenu. Kie nte eiapit
kaskutimatsheu-tshiuapit ntaianimuenan euapamitshit
auassit, mamu tshenut menuskuesh mak tshenish,
uishamakanipan tshetshi uitshiaushit kassinu niteimi-
aten uentshi at-eka uakanishitatut kie ntshen eiat-eshi-
matenitak espinits kie eshu-apatak tsheispinit nte esk
aiskat. Kie eiapits niuapamants ntshen nantim kakus-
pit Innut kie ntshen eka nta kuspit. Eku mamu 119
tashut uentshi uiapamitshit nte utenat (Utshimassit).

Ume mishinikan etutakan tapan nte eiapit Innut
uiaui tshiaushit umenu minuat etuskaten mishinikenu.
Nene mishinikan katutakan *Kamamuetamak Tshen-
tusentamak nte Steniunu Utat Anutsh Kie nte Nikan.*
Kie eimiakanipan passe Utshimaut nte Utshimassit
nene pishimussa 1994 tshetshi uauitak tshekuan tshat-
shipan nte Utshimassit kie takunu nenu eissishuet uta
mishinikan.

"Nitshi pintau-ma-petima, mamitu nenitetau tan
tshipa-tutenan tshetshi-ut-kastinamak nene
kaishiniuiak. Kie tshipa kukuetshi mushunan, shash-
au-stishinakushinan tshetshi uitshiakut kutakut
uentshi tshetshi tshiskutamuakut eshiniuak kie
tshetshi nas Innu itenimuiak?" *Kashetan*

Nene mishinikan katutamak. Tshimitshetitan
essishueiak, etu tshika-ui-tshiskutamashunan nene
kaishiniuiak, tshika-ui-nitumaskenan tshetutamak kie
tshetshi nukutaiak eshiniuiak, kaitapastaiak kie kaishi-
tshissenitamak tshekuan. Esk-au-Innut tshika itenimu-
nan untaiak stiniunu? Passe stissishuenan tshukui-
tanan nte nutshimit patush tshetshi tutamak ume
uatutamak. Tshiui-nitussenitenan minuat etu-tshetshi
minu nistutamak eshi-matenitamak espiniak nte etaiak
utenat (Utshimassit) kie eshiniuiak nte nutshimit etaiak kie tante uet-tshi-untaiak ne-kaishiniunak. Tshiui
minu tshitapatenan ne-tshekuan eka menupinikuiak
kie tan eshi-uitshikuiak kakuspinanut kie tan tshipa
tutenan tsheut-tshi minupintaiak ne-tshekuan eka
menupinikuiak kie tshiui tshissenitenan tshekuanu
metshiminikut Innu uet-eka-tshi kuspit nutshimit
anutshish, tshekuanu tshipa tutuakanut Innut etu-
tshetshi minuatak ekuspit nutshimit? Eku nte masten
tsheui minu tshitapatamak nantim tshetshi takuak
ume eshiniuiak, at-nete tshi-atukantshe?

Uipats nte Innuts, muk tshiam apastapan nenu uinuau eshiniuit. Ama tshitshissenitenan tshetshi apastan
ne-eimun eshiniunanut nete nas uipats. Anutsh tshi-

uauitenan Innu Kaishiniut-muk eminu tshitapatamak,
passe uentshi ishissishuet, muk tshiam tshuauitenan
ama nukan tshekuan. Tshekuan-en-Innu kaishiniut?
Uen Innu mak Innu kaishiniunanut, nishuit itenitakun
kie kassinu eshiniuits uentshi. Miste mitshetuit itenitamut uentshi ute utenat (Utshimassit) tan tsheishiniut
uen tshek ishinakuak tshetshi nantim kunenitamak
steniunu.

"Niteniten nika-tshi-nantim pekassiunan miam
Innuts. Uipats nete shauenants nitiniunan, kie nitshi
pekassiunan tante nitshissenitetan tsheishi-uitshi-
nushunat nitshisse-nitenan tsheishi-ntunushunat.
Tshetshi nukutaiat kaishiniunats, kie kaishi-
tshissenitamat nika-uikutshipintanan tshetshi
tshiskutamashuiat kaishiniuiat." *Manish Tshakapesh*

"Nika inniunan at-untaiat kaishiniuiat kie
kaishikunentashuiat muk-e-miam ne tsheiteni-
takushiat miam uinipaunuts eshinakushit nete
"ghettos" nete Upistuneussit (U.S.) miam ne-kake-
shaut nika itenitakushinan, muk uin-nika inniunan
kie nika-tshi pekassinushunan." *Tshatsh*

Passe uentshi nas tapuetashut tshetshi eka nta
untat, utaianimua, kaishi-pekassinushut kie kaishiniut.
Kutak tshekuan, tshitshue Innu uen etenimut tsheku-
tshiskutamashu nenu kaishitapuetatishut nte nutshimit. Passe uentshi issishueut untaiak kaishi-pakas-
siuiak esk eiapit miam Innu tshika itenitakushinan.
Tshinistunaku-shinan, nte tshishikanat enunakushinak
kie eshinakushinak puntaiak ne-etshiskutama-shunak
stiniunu, miam eka etatau Innut tshika itenitakun.
Miam nepiak tshika itenitakushinan. Kutakut
issishueuts, untaiak staianimuanu, miam eka Innu
tsheitenitakushiak. Anutsh ume esk miam Innu eteni-
takushiak, miam itenitakun esk tshiminukapunan kie
tshishutshenimunan. Peikushu ne-tshekuan uet-iten-
imunak niuntan ne-kaishiniuiat tante tshiuntanan
nene kaishi-shutshenimunak, eukun uet-nantim mit-
shi-uauinukuiak. Passe Innut menu-utinamut nenu
eshi-miskutshipinits nenu eshiniuak, tante issishuet
nitapue-tatishunan nantim Innu tshika itenitakushinan
at-apastaiak ne-tshekuan pempin miam skitu etenitakuak kie at-nte taiak utenat (Utshimassit). Eiapit
miam Innu tshika itenitakushinan, eiapit nte utenat.

"Tshika-tshi tshiskutamashunan eshiniuiak kie nte
nutshimit tshika-tshi eiapit tutenan. Niteniten nin
ama-tshika-tshi nita untanan stiniunu. Tante muk-

report from that research is called *Kamamuetimak Tshentusentimak nte Steniunu Utat, Nitshish, Kie nte Nikan / Gathering Voices: Discovering Our Past, Present and Future*. Interviews with community leaders were also conducted in December 1994 to provide an update on developments in the community. Their comments are included here as well.

"We need to stop now and think of how we can regain our culture. We need to ask ourselves: 'Have I contributed myself to help others preserve our heritage and pride as Innu?'" *Kashetan*

In the People's Inquiry, many of us said we needed to practise our way of life more. We had to find ways to preserve, promote and revive our culture, values and spirituality. Some of us said we needed to spend more time in nutshimit to do this. We wanted to do this research project to better understand the split we experience between life in the community and life in nutshimit, and how our culture is being lost. We wanted to look at the problems and benefits of *Kaupaunantsh* (the Outpost Program) and nutshimit, and at what we can do to solve the problems. We wanted to know what keeps people from going to nutshimit today and what would encourage more people to go. And finally, we wanted to look at how we can make sure that our culture will be alive and well when our community is relocated.

In the old days, people were just living their culture. We don't know if the word "culture" was used in those days. Today we talk about our culture, but when you look at it, some of us say it is all talk and not a reality. What is Innu culture? Being Innu and the Innu culture mean different things to different people. There are many different opinions in our village about what it means to be Innu and about whether our culture can survive.

"I think we will survive as a people. A long time ago, when starvation hit, we survived because we had the knowledge and the skills to survive. We knew how to hunt. To revive our culture and spirituality, we need to practise our Innu way of life." *Manish, elder*

"We can survive if we lose our culture and values, but we will live like black people in ghettos in the United States. We will be living like white people, but we will survive." *Tshatsh*

Some of us don't believe we will ever lose our language, traditions and culture. For some, the key to being Innu is to practise our spiritual beliefs. Some say that even if we lose our traditions, we will still consider ourselves Innu. The colour of our skin makes us Innu. Others say that if we stop practising our culture, it will be like there are no more Innu, like we were dead. For some, once we lose the language, we will no longer be Innu. For some of us being Innu means standing tall and proud. One of the reasons we feel we are losing our culture is because we have lost this pride. The racism we face in this society is responsible for this. Some people accept that changes are a natural part of cultures. They believe that we can still be Innu even if we have accepted things like modern technology or living in communities. We can be Innu and practise our culture in the community as well as in the country.

"I think we will never lose our culture. We are just going around the circle from living in nutshimit and then in the community." *Shimunish*

"I think we can survive because every year we seem to change." *Miste-Manian, elder*

"I don't think we can survive as Innu if we lose our traditions. We can't live like white men. There would be a lot of drinking. Without our culture, we won't survive. Without our grandfathers, their knowledge, our mothers and fathers wouldn't know how to take care of us or provide for us. Without the kamiteut [medicine man] and mitishantshuap [sweat lodges] years ago, we wouldn't have survived. If we wouldn't have had teuenike [drums], we would have starved. Without the knowledge of our ancestors of how to survive in the barrens, we wouldn't be here today. Our culture, I think people will get it back, not all of it, not five generations ago, but some of it. Elders still drum, women still dance, people still have mukushan." *Nupi*

HEALING OURSELVES

To survive as a people and a culture and to regain control of our lives, first we need healing. This is what we said in the People's Inquiry. We have to look after ourselves to make us strong. We need to heal our children, the parents, the grandchildren, the grandparents, uncles and aunts, the whole family, the whole community. There are a lot of people who are on the healing path now and we are proud of this. We have been

utshi-tshi nikuanutenan, nutshimit stanan nanikutini kie nanikutini ute Utshimassit." *Shimunish Nua*

"Niteniten nin tshika, inniunan tante eshikum-pun tshimisku tshi pinan eshiniuiak." *Miste-Manian, Innuskueu*

"Niteniten nin ama tshika itenita kushinan miam Innu, untaiak ne-kaishi-uitshinushunak. Metshikit-shi-tshi-ishiniunan miam kakeshau, usham tshika miste minanu. Ekatakuak ne-kaishiniuiak, apu-kie-tshinan tshikut inniuiak. Eka takunintakue tshimushuminut eshitshissenitak, tshutauinut kie tshikauinuts atut-tshi-tshissentamupan tshipa-ishi-nakatuenimukunut kie tan tshipa ishi-uitshikunuts. Eka tatakue uen tshessentak tshekuan, miam (kakushapatak) kie eka takuakakue mitishan uipats atut-tshi-iniunanapan. Eka-tatakue teueikan, shash tshipa-tshi-tshimakate nanapan. Eka tshissentaka-kuen tshimushumpenuts nte mushuat, atut-tshi-tananapan u-anutshish. Ne-kaishiniuiak, niteniten kau-tshika miskenan, mauat mishiue, passe muk tshika miskenan. Mauat nete uin-petetat tatua espish uikanishi-tatuiak, muk passe tshika miskenan ne-kaishiniuiak. Tshenut esk apatshieut teueikea, kie kukuminashit esk Innu nimut, kie Innut esk mupimeut (Mukushan) atik-piminu." *Nupi*

Ntukunushutau

Tshinan Innuts, uikutshitaiak tshetshi ishiniuiak miam Innu kie tshetshi kunenitamak stiniunu kie tshinan ui-nakatuenimushunak, petima tshika-ui-nitukunushu-nan. Eukun kaissishueiak nte mishineikan katutakan. Tshika-ui-minu nakatuenimushunan tshetshi shut-shiak. Tshika-ui-kutshianut tshetshi uitshiakut stuas-siminut, tshikauinuts, kie tshutauinuts, tshussiminuts, tshukumishinuts kie stussinuts. Kie kassinu mamu tshikanishinut, kie kassinu espishat tshutenaminu, (Utshimassit). Mitshetut shash Innut ua-uitshinushut anutsh, kie tshitshue tshinapeutshenimanut. Tshitshue tshimiste akuikutan tshekuan. Muk anutsh tshi-mashikenan tshetshi-ut-nistunamak stipentamunu. Ishinakuak etu tshetshi mitshetit Innut uapuntat emi-nits, eukunu tshipa nashamut atut-tshi-pistenimut.

Tshika-ui-nikeinan shitakenapun shash nte pet nishupuna utat mitshen shash tshekuan etutamak mamu eatuskatamak tshetshi nikeimak shitakenapun. Kutak tshekuan eka menupinikuiak. Animan ume-

meskinu metimeiak put nta uste 70% tashitshen uentshi ntshen tshesheniutshenitakushit ua-kutshitat tshetshi uitshinushut. Passe utshen Innuts esk menuts kuet puntat-ni-minuat. Ekun tsheishinakuak, kie tshit-shissenitenan Innut esk tshika-ui-uitshinushut.

Katshi nish-eputs, katshi-tshistakan mishineike, Innut umishineikenuau kauauitak essi-eka minupanits, esk eiapit nantim peikun essi-eka minupanits, nte Utshimassit. Nishtut uentshi nepanushut utat nte 1992 etisten atshitashunu. Taut eiapits eka euassiut uanipanushut mitshetuau ume ishinakun. Nene tshep-ishum 1993, ashutats auassit, miskuakanishepan nte mitshuapit enutshikuat pimina kie tshitshue takanu nenu mitshuapinu etauakue. Niui-nipinan issishueutsh itakanut. Eku nitshitishauatan mak nte kutakut peikunueshut-ashu-peik, ntshen tshitshue etutakut pinima-eiapits nitshitishauatan nte (Poundmakers) Alberta apishipeutshiuapit. Kuatu nitutuanan ute, ama takunu tshipa ishi-uitshiakanut ute. Minu-nakatuenima-nishipen nte kie mitshenishepan tshekuanu tshessenitats essi-tat nete, kie eukunu nenu eshitutu-anits kaui-tutakushit tshetshi uapatak essi-shatshi-akanits. Eku minuat kau meshikat, ekun aku-minuat eshinakushit nte uitshuat, peikun tante kueshinakuak nte Utshimassit, nastesh metshekuan atshipinu. Muk neuts ntshen auassit kapushiakanits eka nutshikuat pimina. Uikanishuau eiapit ui-uitshiakanu. Passe-etishiat ninan etuteiat eianimuanut nipetenan kie nit-shisse-nitenan essi-animats eitutakut auas nte-uiat pimina. Passe ukaumaut kie utaumauts ama nenu esk tshissenimeuts etutatshen pimina nenu auassit kutata-ueutshi pimina. Kie shash ute eiapits petautauts auas-sit ntamuk eshinakunits ntukuna.

Passe eiapits tshenut ishinakunu tshetshi uitshi-akanit, muk mui-nanukushut nte uauitshitunanun tante issishueut ama shuka neush shash niketshi-nanukushinan passe ents-shash pistenimuts. Kie ani-minu tshetshi tshissenitak eitinanun. Uauitshiaushit tshenuts tshitshue tshipa minupenu kie etu tshipa tshinipikanu ne-tshekuan uaishi-uitshitunanut.

Passe eiapits Innu esk nenu mui-unui-tishinamut tshekuanu iakunikut kie ui-uitshinushut. Innut tshika-ui-minutshi-tapimushut uinuau nistam. Kassinu uen muk eshinakust, uin tshika tshissenitam ui-punts emi-nits. Ishinakunu tshetshi issishuet ekun, shash ntespin eminianie tshika itenitam nika tshissituauts eku nitu-assimits, nteskuem kie mak ninapem. Passe Innut nas

hurt a lot, but now we need to fight for our rights. If there are more people who are willing to take the risk to quit drinking, GO FOR IT! And don't give up.

The alcohol must stop. Over the last two years, we have taken many actions as individuals and as a community to try to put an end to the alcohol and substance abuse. This is not an easy road. About 70 per cent of the adult population is working on their recovery. Some of these people are drinking and then quitting again. This is to be expected. People still need treatment.

Two years after the People's Inquiry, tragedies continue to plague our community. Three of our young people have committed suicide since 1992. Most of the adults have attempted suicide, many of us recently. In January of 1993, six of our children were found sniffing gas in a cold shack. They said they wanted to die. We had to send them and eleven other chronic sniffers far away to Poundmakers, a treatment centre in Alberta. We had no choice. There was nothing for them here. They were well cared for there and learned a lot. They learned what they want, that they need to be loved. Then they came back to the same problems at home, the same conditions in the village. Only four of them have not gone back to sniffing. Their parents also need treatment. Some of us know from attending conferences how devastating solvent abuse is on young bodies. But some parents still don't know the effects of gas sniffing. And now other drugs are also making their way into our community from the outside.

Some of our elders need healing. They don't want to participate in the healing process because they say they won't be around in the future. Some of them have given up. It's hard for them to know really what is going on. If they got involved, they could help speed up a slow process.

Some people still won't admit there is a problem and don't want to help themselves. People have to really find themselves first; everyone has to decide to quit themselves. They have to say, "That's enough for me. I'm going to think about my kids and my wife or husband." Some have to hit rock bottom before they stop. We are realizing that one of the first steps to healing is to stop the denial and to tell our stories.

Some of us say that our dependency on governments and their money is the reason why people drink. We have lost ourselves and our culture. Others say we

Getting high on gas / Kautatanikants pimin, 1993

drink because our lives are so hard in these villages, the housing conditions and the water conditions are so bad. That is why we have a lot of suicides. Some people say that it is loneliness that makes them drink. People quit and they still think about doing it. They think when you drink, you have a lot of friends. Non-drinkers lose friends when they quit. We don't visit each other any more except if we have alcohol. Also, people pressure each other to drink even when we have quit. When somebody is sick from drinking, they can't stop drinking. It's like their medicine. They drink when they have a bad hangover to feel better. A lot of people have in their homes the white stuff to drink when you have an upset stomach. Sexual abuse is another reason people drink. Disclosures have been made in our communities and there will be more. We don't know how to deal with this, and many of us need healing. It's not only sexual abuse, but physical and mental abuse too. Victims are living with a lot of pain.

Treatment and Education Programs

"In the summer, we organized a women's camp to learn about culture. We had a healing circle and a sweat lodge. We started working together and there was a lot of communicating. We plan to have another one next summer again. The women started getting together Christmas presents for the kids. Every month this year, the women gathered together and had birthday parties, baby showers, just to get

PETER SIBBALD PHOTO

stimankut shitakenapunu eku patush punits eminits. Tshitshissenitenan ui-uitshinushunak nimieu tshetshi kataiak tshekuan, tshika-tshi-tapatenan ne-tshekuan eakunukunak.

Passe stessishuenan, usham tshimiste shutshe nimanu tsheutshimau kie nenu shunianu mantak, eukun uets miniat stissishuenan. Tshinan-u-tshiuninushunan kie tshuntanan kaishiniuiak. Kuteket uentshi issishueut. Usham nitanimiunan ute Utshimassit eukun uet miniats, kie mitshuapa nastesh memenuaua kie metekun nipin, nastesh memenuau nipi-nte uetanpanuts, eukun. Uets mitshetit uentshi nepanushut. Kutaket uentshi, usham nimuestatenan uets miniat issishueuts Innut kutakes puntaut eminits muk eiapit nantim, mamitunenitamut tshetshi tutak tshekuanu, miam eui-nipanushut. Meniat shitakenapun tshitshue mitshetut niuitsheua-keits puntat uen eminits shitakenapunu, unieu passe uitsheuakea. Kie ama mupistuakanu uen patush etitak shitakenapunu. Puntat uen eminits shitakenapunu shuka ni-ai-kam uiminiakau ui-tutuanu tshetshi minuat minits. Uen eiakushiskakut shitakenapunu emints, animentam tshetshi puntat. Miam ne-ntukun ishitshita-patamut nenu shitakenapunu iakushiupetau kuet minuat menits, kuet minuat kau-minuenimut. Mitshetut uentshi kuenenitak nenu kuapakamua ntukunu kemenanua, eku iakushitau nte utauats, eukunu nenu menits, kuapakemenua ntukunu. Kie kutak tshekuan, usham mishau ne-auassit kemistu-tuanutshi eukun kutakut Innut uets minits shitakenapunu. Mitshena nte shash pietakuak, auassit kemistutuanutshi nte Utshimassit, esk mak nte kutaka takunutshen nastesh ama nissenitenan nipa tutenan tante, nistam ninan nikui-uitshinushunan. Nimieu ne-muk auassit kimistutu-anutshi auassit, uen matenitam nte uiat kie nte ustikuan, katshi tutakan tshekuanu. Eku ntshen kamistutukanits tshitshue mishanitshe tshekuanu iakunikut.

Kauitshitunants Kie Kaitshiskutamukan Uen Atusseun

"Napitshi, ninan eskueunats nimamuinan nte ineka ninatshuitshinan, tshetshi etu tshiskutamashuiat, eshiniuiat, nitutenan ne-kuaskapinanua ua-uitshitunanut kie mamu nimitishunan. Uskat-etshitshipiniat nas mamu niuauitshitunan kie mitshen tshekuan uiauitamatunats. Minuat nipitshe eukun eiapits tshetutamats, minuat eiapits niskueut tshika mamuiut peshinakunits kanipaiamianunts, tshetshi atemiskuat tshekuanu auassa eshikum pishuma anutsh peputs nantim iskueut mamuiut kie metueut uenu uetshishikumin, kie kutaka uitsheuanuau neskueu etan utuassiminu. Mamuiut, muk tshetshi minuatak. Napeuts eiapits, kie uinuau mamuitut, tshetshi uauitak utiniunuau kaishiniuts kie uauitamut tan tshipa ishi-minupinu eui-uitshiakanits Innut. Napessit mamu neskuessit, eiapits mamuitut tshetshi nantuatats tan tshipa ishi-metueieut uituassuau. Nanikutini napeut kie neskueut nte tuauts nte kaskutimatsheutshiuapit. Kie nishuau peikupuna, ute Utshimassit Innut mamuitut tshetshi Innu metuet kie eshikum-puna mamu tshitshipitshut Innu tshetshi mamuitut. Nete mamuitut natuaiashit, nte kaui-atukants." *Nupi, Kastipeutshuapit kaitusset*

Takun nte Utshimassit tshipa ishi-uitshianut Innut uauitshinikushit, eka menupinikut shitakenapunu. Taut ntshen kauitshipet, eka menits, mamu-ni-aianimueuts uiauitak eitutakut shitakenapunu A.A. kamamuitut ishinikateu, kie nenu kuaskapinanua eiapits nenu tutamuts. Kutakets ents-uentshi ituteut nte kastipeutshuapit tshetshi uauitamakushit eitutatshen shitakenapunu. Neuitshen nte kaitusset kastipeutshuapit. Tshiuapatamuanan essi nukutat tshekuan ntshen kaui-uitshiat Innu eka menupinits. Nantim tshipa uauitenan ne-tshekuan eka menupinikuaik, tshetshi eka aiatshuka mishat, tshekuan eka minupinikuiak. Tshipa uauitenan ne-tshekuan eiakunukunak, atut-tshi uakashinatut. Kie tshipa-ui-tshitapimanu uen nte atamit uiat, iakunikut tshekuanu, nimiute nte muk ussit tshetshi tshitapamak uen. Ne-uen nantim kenutshikashua takunu tshekuanu iakunikut kie ui-uitshikushiu, kie ntuapatam tshetshi uitshiakan miam kutak uen eshi-uitshiakan. Kie atut-tshi-shakuenimutatunan. Tshiam eiemiakants uen, uitshiniku nenu, nta eka menupanit nte utiskuem kie utuassim, kie tshipa-ui-nitutatunan eimituiak. Peik uen tshessenimat uitshinnu netutakut, kie uin kue-nitutuat, kie kuetshi uitshiat kutaka uenu eka menupinits.

Tshimitshetinanan shash katshi-ituteiak nte apishipeutshuapit, tshetshi uitshinu-shunak ne-eka menupinikuiak shita-kenapun. Shash nte passe uentshi tshi-pushut nete tetshe Nova Scotia kie New Brunswick, kie uepistikuiat, kie Ontario, mak nete uste. Passe uentshi issishueut, niuitshinikunan tshit-

together. Men also had their meetings. They talk about culture and it was a healing circle for them. The kids have a Youth Council that organizes games for youth. There are gym nights for women and men. Sometimes, maybe twice a year, the community gets together to play Innu games. The community has a gathering every year. They camp in the Nutuashish (Sango) area, where people want to move." *Nupi, Alcohol Program worker*

A number of services are available in our communities to help people deal with their drinking problems. We have A.A. meetings and healing circles. Some people go to the Alcohol Program for counselling. It is staffed by six people. Many of us see the value of support groups. We should always talk about the problems that we are having so the problems will not grow. We have to talk about our pain and break the silence. People need to forgive each other. We need to look at the person inside, not the person outside. Sometimes when a person is always causing trouble, it is because he or she is hurting and wants to be loved like everybody else. We also have to not be ashamed of one another. Talking honestly has brought out many marriage problems. We need to listen to each other and trust each other more. When one person knows that the person is listening, they will also listen, and in turn support others who are still not in recovery.

A number of us have been out to treatment to get healing for our alcohol problems. We've gone out to programs in the Atlantic area, in Quebec, Ontario and out west. Some of us say treatment programs have helped us a lot. Many people have attended workshops held for the community. The Youth Council organized workshops like "Flying on Your Own" by Bearwoman and Associates. The Alcohol Program has held workshops on different topics. Some people say we need more community conferences to address some of these issues. We also still need a prevention program for people who may want to kill themselves.

"People have started talking about their thoughts of suicide in support groups. This is a good sign. It is what people should be doing. By talking, they are healing themselves. In the past, people would just go and do it. They would take pills or shoot themselves." *Penute, social programs co-ordinator*

We need to help the whole family. Children need our

Children returning from Poundmakers / Auasits meshikauts, 1993

help. We need to develop programs that will meet the special needs of children. We need workshops on parenting for the adults.

"We should try to be strong to help our children the way the other Natives from Poundmaker have helped our children who have problems. The kids think they can take care of themselves at a young age, but the parents should take care of them." *Shanutis*

"I really believe we have to heal the parents first. What we learn from our parents, that is our role model. What happened in the past to our parents is what happened to us as adults. We were training the child to be the way we were, to be dysfunctional. When we stop the cycle for family violence, that is what our children will learn. They will know how to be well, and that is what their children will learn." *Penute*

The Nechi Institute of Alberta has been training front-line workers, leaders and other people in the community. Seventeen of us in Utshimassit have graduated from the first phase of counselling training. We have begun the second phase in advanced counselling, which we will complete in March 1995. The training has opened our eyes to the way we were looking at drinking and our attitudes towards people. We have not been facing the reality of our problems of alcoholism and codependency. We learned that we are solely responsible for our thoughts, actions and feelings. We are also getting training in how to deal with sexual abuse.

Community caregivers need to work together to educate more people about alcoholism, other substance

PETER SIBBALD PHOTO

shue katshi pitsheiat nte apishipe-utshuapit. Kie mit-shetut uentshi nantim etutet eianimuantshi nte Utshi-massit, mak eiapit tshitshi pintapan, auassit, ustinit-shut tshetshi mamuitut eianimuets, eukun umenu ishinikatenipan eianimuets "Upaui epeikussin" Mask Iskueu mak uitsheuakea pimpintapen umenu. Kastipet mitshetuau nenu mamuitut kie mitshenu nenu tshekuanu uiauitak. Passe uentshi issishueut etu-nan-tim tshipa-ui-mamuitunan ute Utshimassit tshetshi uauitamak ne-tshekuan eka, menupinikuiak. Kie tshipa eiapit tutenan tshetshi takuak tshetshi tshissenimakan, uanipanushut, tshipa-ui-nakatuenimakanu tshetshi eka nipanushut uen.

"Passe Innut shash uauitamut nenu etenitak tshetshi nipanushut, uitamueut nenu kaui-uitshinikut uenu, kie minuanu nenu etutak, eukunu nenu kutakuts uentshi tshipatutamut, tshipa unuitishinamut nenu kuenenitak tshekuanu nte ustikuanuats etipat-shimushut, uitshinushut nenu itenitakushut. Uipats, ishinakushipan uentshi, muk tshiam et-tshituteut kuet tutashut tshekuanu, miam ntukuna mitshut kie mak passushut." *Penute, Uetshimaut nte eianipinits tshekuanu*

Mamu uen utiskuem kie unapem mak-utuassim tshika uitshiakanut, tante eiapit auassit ui-uit-shinikushiut. Tshipa-ui-tshitshipintanan tshekuan tan tshipa ishi-uitshiakanut auassit. Tshipa tshitshipin-tanan tshetshi mamu aianimueiak, tshetshi uitamuakut tshenut tshipa ishi-nakatuenimeut utuassimuau.

"Tshipa-ui-shutshinan tshetshi ishi-uitshiakut stuas-siminut miam nte Poundmakers Innut kaishi-uit-shiat stuassiminu, eka menupinits. Passe auassit itenitamut ninan u-niketshi-nakatuenimushunan essi auassiuiat, itenitamut. Muk ishinakunu uikanishuau tshetshi nakatuenimukut." *Shanutis*

"Nas nin niteniten nistam ukaumauts kie utaumauts tshipa uitshiakanut. Nene kaishuapamakut tshikan-ishinut eukun ne-kau miam tiapiniak. Nekan tshikanishinut. Kaishinakushit nte pet utat, eukun-u-kie tshinan miam eshinakushiak. Miam itenitakun tshitshiskutamakunan tshetshi itenitakushiak miam tshikanishinut kaishinakushit. Tshi-tutamak tshetshi punpen ne-kianimpinutshi kanipuits uentshi, stuas-siminut tshika minutshitapatamut nenu kie tshika tshissenitamut kie uinuau tsheishi uitshinushut. Eukunu tsheut-tshi tshissenitak auassit." *Penute*

Nechi kaskutimashunanut nte ut-Alberta tshiskuta-muepan nenu nikan etan, Innu uetshimaun kie kutaka Innu ute Utshimassit mak Sheshatshit. Nipeikunueshi-nan ashu-nishu-ashutats tshastaiat tsheskutamakuiat eketshessimakan uen. Eku shash minuats nitshi-tshipi-inan tshetshiskutamashuiat eku nta uiniskupishum 1995 minuat tshetshistaiat. Kie ume tsheskutimaku-nats, shepinu nissishukunan, kaishi tshitapamitshit Innu miatenitak kie kaitenimunats meniats. Ninan apu-ut-nistuapatamat ne-eshinakuikuiat kie etutakuiat shitakena-pun kie uet-eka-tshi puntaiat. Eku anutshish nitshissenitenan ninan e-eshipin etutamat, kie etenita-mat kie eshutinamat uet-ekatshi puntaiat eminiats. Kie eiapit niskutama-kunan, tsheishi-uitshiaushiat ntshen auassit kemistutuanutshi.

Nte Utshimassit kauauitshiaushit mamu tshipa-u-atusseut, tshetshi etu minuuitamuat Innu etenitakunit kie etutatshen shitakenapunu. Kie kutakenu tshekuanu miam ne-mate takun en-kutak shitakena-pun eshinikatet tshekuan muk mieu e-tshetshi mnatiken, kustikun tshetshi minateken, eukunu nenu tshipa uitamuakanut Innuts tshetshi minu tshissenitak, kie tshipa uitshiakanut nte eka menupinits nte unipunuats, kie kassinu tshipa uitamuakanut tshekuan tshetshi ut-tshi-uitshinushut kie-uinuau ntshen kaui-uitshiat Innu, esk-ents tshisku-tamuakanut. Kie ntshen katshiminakanit Innut tshetshi pimpintat atusseuna tshipa kutshitaut tshetshi mamu uitshituse-mitut etu-takau tshekuanu. Kaitusset nas tshipa-ui-tutamut tshetshi uitshiat Innu muk eiapit kie uinuau tshekui-naka-tuenimushut kie tshika-ui-minuasteieskusiuts uit-shiatau Innu, tshetshi eka usham miste uesham atus-set. Kassinu ents kaitusset, uinuau tshika-senimushut tshetshi eka shuka numat miste eieskushi-nushut. Nanikutini miste kushikunu tshekuanu nutshikat, miam uiapamatau uenu kie uauitshiatau Innu. Nanikutini tshika-ui asteieskushit tshetshi eka uesham-atusset.

Mitshetuit ne-itenitakanu tshipa ishi-uitshitunanu. Memeshue Innut itenitamut tshetshi uitshikunak ne-tshekuan eshitusseiak, miam ne-mamu keianimuanu, kie ntun tshekuan ketshi-tshipin-takanu. Mitshetuit nenu itenitamut Innut, tan tsheispin ne-kui-ntukuianua Innut, kui-uitshianutshi. Memeshue Innut. Issishueut, tshika minupinu ume tshitshi-pintakanua, kaui-uitshi-akanit Innut. Passe Innut ishi-tshitapatamut miam nenu kau uetinamuak kakeshau kaishi-niut, essi-

PETER SIBBALD PHOTO

Simeon, peacekeeper and chief / Shimu, kananikamat-shesh mak utshimau, 1993

abuse, fetal alcohol syndrome, marriage problems and so on. These caregivers still need more training. The different organizations should give each other support as well. The workers have to be committed to helping their people, but at the same time they need encouragement and support so they won't get burned out. It's up to the individual to look after himself or herself so they don't burn out. Sometimes very heavy stuff can come out for counsellors when they are working with people. They need to take time out to deal with their own issues.

There are different opinions about healing. Not everyone believes that these programs and workshops help us. Some people feel that we are accepting the white man's way again with the Nechi training. Or young people are accepting too many things from a different culture in the training, like sweetgrass, feathers, dream catchers and other things that don't belong to us. Some of us worry that the people trained with Nechi are still not healed enough to help others to heal.

"Why do we need elders from Nechi to help us? At the treatment program in Border Beacon, we had our own elders, Tshenish and Pien and their wives. I feel the Nechi trainees put people down when they tell them they are sick and need to be healed. This makes the person feel very worried and unwanted, or miserable inside. The problem is we don't communicate with each other. We are ashamed and afraid to talk to each other. We can heal our own community in our own hands, if we trust each other. The Nechi training

has made people different, and that makes people not trust them and they don't trust others. That's why I say that first we need trust to heal." *Shuash*

We know there is not one solution to our problems. There are different solutions, and it is up to each individual to get treatment for his or her alcohol problem. People have to pick what is best for them. But most of us believe that some kind of intervention is needed.

Healing in Nutshimit

Some people ask to go to the country to hunt and fish. They say that is their way of healing, when they go out on the barrens. They say that going to nutshimit is better than going out to a treatment program, or that the Outpost Program is like a treatment program. But others say that when people with a drinking problem go to the country, it is like they are running away from all their problems in the community.

"The culture in nutshimit is healing. There is a lot of healing in the old ways. The land, if you pray to the land and the animals, and to your family, that is part of healing. Culture is part of healing. Like if you were in the country for a year, I know you would feel better. There is no alcohol or drugs, or people abusing other people." *Nupi*

"People still have problems even when they are in the country. The country is not enough to help them. Sometimes kids still sniff. One person tried to commit suicide even in the country. People still need treatment. They hold their pain inside; they're not showing it. I have a lot of pain inside me now. If I go to the country I will be happy out there, but the problem will still be inside me. It's like running away from it instead of dealing with it." *Utshimassiu woman*

"When I was in the country, it helped me with a lot of things. But it also brought out some problems. I started remembering how it was before my parents started drinking. I cried for them. There is still a lot of pain, loneliness and grief that I have to deal with. I can't run away from my problems in the country or in the community." *Penute*

When people return to the community, their problems are still there, and they start drinking all over again. Nothing has changed. Going to the country does not fix their problems. These problems hit them again;

tshiskutamashuiak nte (Nechi). Kie mak-shash passe stuassiminut shash nenu utinamut, iatshenu kaishiniun, essi-tshiskutamashut nte Nitshi (Nechi) shash nenu utinamut, meskushua, mikua kie nenu puamunu kautshipitak (dream catcher), kie mitshen nte kutakenu shash uetinak, nte iatshinits tshekuanu tshinan ume eshiniuiak, metshinita nenu passe uapatenan tshekuan, kie nimieu ne-tshinan nte uetshipin tshekuan, uaiu ne-utautakanu tshekuan. Passe Innut itenitamut, utshent, nitshi katshiskutamashut. Meshuka ents kie uinuau minupinut tshetshi uitshiat uitshiniuau.

"Tshekuanu ents-uet-apatshiakan, Nechi tshenut tshetshi-uitshitaushit nete katanut ashuapunits, tapen nte tshitshe niminut, Tshenish mak Pien mak Utiskuemuau? Nin niteniten utshen Nechi katshiskutamashut, usham nas nashuk tineuts Innu, kie iteut stakushinau, tsheui-nitukunushunek? Eku ne-uen etakan, stakushin, tshitshue mishimen-tam kie nastesh memenuenimu, miam eka nas enakatuenimukuian itenitam, nte atamit uiat. Ume tshekuan uestapinikuiak, usham apu ispish eimitunak. Tshishakuenimutatunan kie tshikusti-tunan tshetshi eimituiak. Tshipa-tshi minupintanan ute Utshimassit, tshinan mamu nustaiak, ishinakuak tshetshi minu tapuetatuiak tshekuan essishueiak, anutshish stishinakushinan apu minu utentuiak. Nechi katshiskutamashunanut, tutueuet uenu tshetshi aiat-itenimun kie eukunu uet eka tapuetakut Innu kie kutak Innu kueka nitutuan. Eukun uet issishueian. Nistam tshekui, ntukutanan, kie mak tshekui minu nistutenan ne-eimun-eshinikatet minu utintutau, kie mak tapuetatun." *Shuash*

Tshitshissenitenan metshikitshi peikushu tshekuan tsheapastaiak tshetshi ut-minupunushunak. Mitshea nenua tshekuaia tsheapastaiak kie uinuau ents muk Innut etenitak, ui-uitshi-nikushitau, nenu shitakenapunu eka menupinikut, napeu kie mak iskueu. Innut uinuau tshika utinamut tanenu nenu menuant tshekuanu etenitak tshetshi uitshinikut. Muk passe etishiak, stissishuenan tshui-apastan ne-tshekuan tshipa uitshinikunan.

Tshetshi Etu Minueniuin Nte Nutshimit

Kutakut Innut nituenitamut tshetshi tat nte nutshimit tshetshi ntuiuts mak tshetshi pestauat. Eukun ume ninan nitutetan uauitshinushunat nte etaiat mushuat,

issishuet passe Innut. Anu nte nutshimit minuau tshetshi tat uen mak at-tshetshi itishauakan nete uaiu apishipeu-tshuapit kie mak anu nte nutshimit miam apishipeu-tshuap itentakun. Muk kutaket Innut issishueut Innu kauitshipet ekuspit nutshimit miam itenitakushu miam tshatishimutak nenu unipim.

"Ne-uen kaiapistat nenu kaishiniut nte nutshimit, uitshinusshu nenu iteni-takunu, miam itenitakunu ntukunushu, kie miste mishashipan nte eshi uitshinushut uen nutshimit ueskat. Miam ne-assi epukushenitakmen kie aueshishet, eiapit en-tshiuitshinushun itenitakun kie ne-tshinan eshiniuiak eiapit nta takun tsheut-tshi-ui-tshinushunak. Miam mate-peikupuna tain nutshimit, nitshisseniten tshitshue tshipa minuenimun, atut-tshi-takun tante shitakenapun kie kutak tshekuan, kie atut-tshi tau uen tshetshi piuenimit." *Nupi*

"Innut esk nte eiapits memenupinuts nutshimit etatau, nutshimit meshuka ispish shutshimakan tshetshi ut-uitshinu-shut Innut. Nanikutini nte nutshimit eiapit nte nutshikueut auassit pimina. Peik nte uen ui-nipanushushepen essi tat nte nutshimit, Innut ishinakunu tshetshi uitshiakanit. Innut muk kunenitamut nte atamit nenu tshekuanu iakunikut, mui-mushestaut nenu. Nin anutshish miste mishau tshekuan iakunu-kunan, eku kuspinan nipa minuenten nte nutshimit taian muk ne-tshekuan iakunukunan esk en-nantim nipa kuneniten nte niat. Miam ne-nipa-ite nimushun, nitshitishimuten ne-tshekuan uestuentamikuian, menui-kutshitan tshetshi inekatishiniman." *Mushuau-iskueu*

"Nte nutshimit etaiana, mitshen tapue tshekuan eshi-uitshikunan, muk takun eiapit tshekuan eka menupinikuian. Nimamitunenimauts nikanishit tan ishinakushuakupen esk eka nutshikat shitakenapunu. Nimuskuataut, essi mamitunenimikau, esk mitshen tshekuan eiakunukunan, emuestataman, ekassenita-man ume tsheui-uitshinushunan esk. Mentshi ituten nte nutshimit tshetshi pepamtishimuteman ne-tshekuan uestuetamikuian kie etaian nte Utshimassit, eiapit nte nimateniten." *Penute*

Innut katshi metapetau nte Utshimassit, esk nenu kunenitamut tshekuanu eka menupinikut, kuet minuat kau minits, metshekuanu miskutshipinit, at-katshi kuspitau apu tshekuanu uitshinikut. Nenu tshekuanu eka menupinikut eukun kau niataukut kie muestaten-

they are lonely again. They see people drinking in the community. They see themselves falling down again. They need more than the country to heal. They need help from treatment and counselling.

In the People's Inquiry we said we wanted a treatment centre in nutshimit. We knew that going to nutshimit was not enough to heal, but that nutshimit can help us heal in many ways. It is the best place to get the counselling and treatment we need to heal our spirit. This is where we can practise our way of life, cut wood, feed our families, hunt. The country or barrens is the place to express our feelings freely. This is where we can get our anger out, where we can yell out. We can be a part of nature, walk in the woods, look at the trees, talk to the Creator.

In the fall of 1994, we held our first treatment program in Border Beacon. People have been going out to places all over Canada. Now it costs less for people to get treatment, and we can be near our families. Whole families can get treatment as well. The centre is a camp in the wilderness. One good thing about having our own centre was that the resource people were from here.

"We had thirty-three participants—six families. Only three people dropped out. We ran the program ourselves. A counsellor from Poundmaker just looked on. He told us we did weeks of work in just the first few days. People started breaking down and crying. There was a lot of sharing. Children would start crying when they heard their parents' stories. The men were crying, and the counsellors as well. Then people would hug and hold each other. We also involved the elders. They brought people into the sweat lodge. They shared their knowledge about how to interpret dreams, about why we shouldn't abuse the animals and all other living creatures. We gave the elders a day at the end of each week. People felt the elders should have had two whole weeks at the end of the program to share this knowledge." *Penute*

Healing from Sexual Abuse

When we held the People's Inquiry in 1992, a few of us had started talking about the problem of sexual abuse in our village. Since many of us have quit drinking, more and more disclosures of sexual abuse have been made. We need to get it all out in the open rather than leaving it in the closet. The whole community has been

RAY WEBBER PHOTO

Aneshenish making moccasins / Aneshen mesineshepan, 1963

affected by sexual abuse directly or indirectly. People need help in healing from sexual abuse. We need to understand the enemy within and without. Both the victims and the abusers need help. They are both at high risk for attempting suicide.

Workshops have been organized in the community which have helped people to begin to deal with their history of sexual abuse. People are asking for more workshops. People have been dealing with their problems through circles, mostly women amongst themselves, but some men as well.

Some people say we need to help ourselves and not just look outside for this help. We have held community meetings to try to figure out how to deal with this crisis. At one meeting, people agreed not to get involved with the courts when we are dealing with a sexual abuse case. They felt that some offenders should not go to court. We are supposed to report all cases, but the system does not work to help either the victim or the offender. The court system is not safe for victims,

tamut. Kie uapameut uitshiniuau miatenitamen, kie
uapameut kau piatshinit kie pestenimun. Nutshimit
etenitakuak etu nte emishat tshekuan tshukui-apastan
patush tshetshi minueniuin. Tshika-ui-apastan kauit-
shitunanut kie kaketshessimitunanut.

Nene mishineke katutakan (mamuetetau) stissishue-
tan, tshetshi takuak apishipeu-tshuap nte nutshimit.
Tshitshisssenitenan ekuspiak menispinu tshetshi uitshinushunak. Muk nutshimit takuak apishipeutshuap
tshika mitshen tsheishi uitshikunak. Ekute nte tshitshue menuat ekatshessimakan uen kie eui-uitshiakan,
tshiui-nitukunu-shunan nutem espistiak kie eutat-
shakushiak. Ekute nte muk tsheut-tshi minu tshiskutamashuiak kaishiniuiak, kie eshi-nikutanut, eshi-pekas-
siat uen utuassim kie eshi-nitunushut. Nte nutshimit
kie mak nte mushuat eukun ne-assi tshematenitamen
essi-minu-enimuin. Ekute tshipa-tshi unuitishinen kie
tshipa neketenan. Ekute nte tshipa nanukushinan, uet
ntautshik tshekuan assit. Tshipa pepamutenan nte
minaskuat, tshipa tshitapamanut mistikut, tshipa eimi-
anu katipenimitak.

Tekuatshik nene 1994, eukun ueset tshatshi pinita-
iat apishipeutshuap tshetshi uitshiakanit Innut, nete
nitutenan metshima Border Beacon ashuapunits.
Ueskat kassinu nte niteitishauaten nitiniminan ua-ui-
thinikushit, nete Kanata. Eku anutshish etu apishish
apastakanu shuniau ua-ui tshiakan uen kie etu mitshima nitanan nituassiminan etat. Mamu uen utuassim
itishauakanu uauitshini-kushit, nutshimit nte tutakanu
tshetshi uitshiakanit Innut. Peik tshekuan menuat ne-
etutekan tshetshi uitshiakanit Innut ekuta uta uetinakanit tshenut tshetshi uauitshiaushit.

"Nistunu-ashu-nist nteshetan mamu nete etaiat nutshimit, muk nistipen uentshi pestenimut. Ninan en-
nitshimatan peik tshenu nte ut-uaiu, muk menuit-
shikunan muk ntshitapamukunan. Miam mitshetu
minastakan etusseiak stishinaku-shinau, at-tapue
anutsh shuk tshitshipinau nutkunan, ne-tshenu nte
ut uaiu. Nastesh meneush taut ntshen uentshi uauitshinikushit tshash kuet tipatshimushut kie mauts.
Mitshen ne-tshekuan etuteken eshusteieskatunanut,
miam put nipa issishuen mamu uitshitunanu. Kie
ntshe auassit muskumukut uikanishuau tepat-
shimushun. Napeuts kie ntshe kaitusset eiapits
mauts. Kie akussintut, kie metshikuntut ntshe uauit-
shiakanits Innut, tshenut eiapit ntapatshianan tshetshi uauitshiaushit, uitipimeut nenu tsheskutamuanit,

kie uauitshiakanit uenu nte mitishantshuapit. Nenu
eshitshi-ssenitak kie eshinakunit Innu upuamun,
tshetshi eka piuenimat aueshisha kie nitamuk eshinakust aueshish, nte etat unuitimit. Peiku tshishikau
niminanan tshenut tshetshi uitshitussemimit.
Eshikum katshi peikuminastan. Kutaket Innuts
itenitamut minuat nte nishuminastan tshipa taut
tshenut, tshipunantshi ume etutakan kauitshiakanit
uentshi (apistipeutshuap)." *Penute*

Tshetshi Uitshiakanit Ntshen Uentshi Kemestutuakanutshi

Nene katutamak mishineiken (Kamamuetamak)
kaishinikatet nene 1992. Tshimitshetitan uiauitamak,
ne-eshinakuak essi-mishat ute Utshimassit, ne-kui-mis-
tutuanu tshi auassit kie kutakut uentshi. Eku shash
tshimitshetinan puntaiak e-miniak, kie muk-aiat nantim petakun kie unuipinu tipatshimun, nenu uentshi
kui-mistutuanutshi. Kie nutem ume espishat Utshimassit tshimatenitenan ne-kui-mistutuanutshi auassit,
nasni-mushe tshipetenan nanikutini. Kassinu uen
tshikaui uitshianu nenu eshinakust. Tshiui-minu nistutenan ne-eshinakuak nte uet-tshitshipin kie tan
etenimitut ntshen uinuau, put napeu mak iskueu.
Tapiskut ents enishit tshika-ui-uitshiakanut. Ne-kami-
stutuaken kie ne-katutuat nenu iskueu put kie napeu.
Tante tapiskut ents-enishit tshipa-tshi ishinakunu
tshetshi ui-nipanushut.

Tutakanipan nte-mamu tshetshi aianimuants, kie
uitshinikupen nenu passe uentshi tshetshi nenu shash
tshitshipinit euauitak, kaietutuanikuen nete uipats
euassiut. Kutakuts Innuts issishueut, tshipa-ui-uitshi-
nushunan tshinan, atut-tshintuapatenan nte uaiu
tshetshi uitshinikuiak.

Mitshetuau tshimamuitunan tshetshi uauitamak, kie
tan-tshipa tutenan ume tshekuan eka menupinikuiak.
Nte miamuituiak, mitshetut uentshi essishuet, menui-
ituten nte kaueuestakan, tshetshi uauitamat ume eiani-
mak tshekuan, kemistutuanutshi uentshi. Kie kutakut
itenitamut Innuts atu-tshi ueueshiakanu Innu ne-kat-
shi mistutuat iskueu kie put napeu. Tshipa mamishit-
shemutan ni-pieta-mak uen eshinakushit muk-e-at-kat-
shi makunakan uen kie katshi ueueshiakan Innu,
tapiskut enishit nastesh nenu muitshinikut ne-kamis-
tutak kie ne-kamistuapkan, tapiskut muitshinikut.
Nimiute eshinakuak tshetshi itutakan kaueuestan,
tante muen kaniu nte kaueuestanits. Muuitshiakanut
nte eiapit at-katshi ueueshiatau uitshiniuau. Kie kass-

and they are not winning their cases. They don't get any help even if they do. We also know the abusers are sick; they need to be helped so they can be well again. We don't think offenders should be put in jail. When they go away, they come back and nothing has changed. Some say they should be punished, but not in that sense. They should receive treatment to understand what they have done. Some people are concerned about what we should do now with offenders if we don't use the court system. Some abusers say what they did was long ago. They don't realize what harm and pain they have caused. Some offenders have gone for alcohol treatment, but we don't know if they have disclosed this problem. They may not have had to deal with it in their treatment. We need to find a way where we know they have dealt with it. These discussions have been hard ones. Sometimes there have been tensions between the men and the women.

There is still a lot of sexual abuse going on. There are a lot of unreported cases. A Family Violence Committee was set up in the fall of 1994 to organize an alternative to the court system. We are still waiting to resolve this issue. We have formulated a proposal for a program where the community takes care of the case. We are ready to present this to the provincial Department of Justice. In this program, the offender comes to a group and talks about what he or she has done in front of the victim and their families. The circle is also a safe place for the victim to talk to her abuser. There is healing that happens for everyone in this way.

GOING INTO THE COUNTRY
The Good Life

"When people were first settled in the communities, we missed the old ways of the country, the traditional foods, the way we used to live. We have always been thinking of going back to living in the country. In this community, people are always drinking, but in the country they are sober for three or four months. Ever since settlement, people don't feel at home, they feel like something is wrong. The country is where the people's lives are, where the things we depend on, like the caribou, are." *Akatis and Etuetis*

More and more people are going to the country now, even young people who have never gone before. This is something we said in the People's Inquiry we must do if our culture is to survive. But there are also some of us who never stopped going, families who didn't listen to the warnings of the priests, Social Services or school authorities. They didn't send their children to school. They didn't care if their family allowances were cut off.

"I still practise what my grandmother taught me years ago. I am very happy that I remember all the things she taught me. My children also enjoy themselves and are very happy when they kill the wild food. I always tell my children about our ancestors, about how they used to live, like how they used dog teams and canoes. My children say that it would be nice if we could go back to the old ways and use the dog teams again. But I tell them it can't be done. Everything today is run by machines and they are a lot faster than a dog team." *Shanutis*

"I find it very interesting that many young people like to go to nutshimit today even if they don't have the knowledge of the land or the culture. When I was out in nutshimit last month, it was the first time I had been in a long time. I told stories to Penute and Shuash's families. They asked me questions about life in the old days. That's what I do best being in nutshimit. It's like working. My grandson told me that he really liked it in Davis. I told him that as a child I liked it very much in nutshimit because of the beauty of the land. It was like a home. I had everything I needed, but in the village, I don't know much." *Kaniuekutat, elder*

"I always had the fear before that if our elders like Miste-Pinip, Miste-Etuet, Tshenish, Shushep, if those people fell ill, they wouldn't be able to go to the country and we would never learn the things they know about that life. These are the people who go to the country regularly. Without those skills, we can't go into nutshimit. I never went to the country before this spring, when I went for just one month. When I was there in the fall, that fear was gone. I noticed that young people like Eric Mistenapeu have learned from their parents. They have the skills of nutshimit—children like Theresa (Tenesh) Rich, whose parents often travelled inland in the spring and fall when they were young. When I was there, I had a hard time, but I found it good. It was the first time I ever travelled so far on foot. The boys who were with me were younger. They had more experience and were in better shape. But they were there to help me

inu tshitshissenitenan, ntshen kamistutak akushut itenitakushut, kie tshekuui-uitshianuts ents kau tshetshi minueniuts. Nitenitenan ninan atut-tshi makunakanut ents kamistutuat iskueu put kie napeu. Atmiakunantau, pushiakanut eku minuat kau meshikat, nastesh metshekuanu miskutshipinut kie muitshinikut. Passe Innut issishueet, tshipa anuenimakanut muk mienu tshipa ishi-anuenima-kanut, nte tshetshi makunakanit. Tshipa-ui-uitshia-kanut kie tshipa-ui-minu nistutamunianut, nenu eshinakunit katutak. Kutakut ents Innut ama shuka minuentamut nenu uaishi-uitshianits kamistutamen, eka apastanits kaueuestaken. Passe ents issishueet, kakamentutak, uipats ne-nitutenapan, messinitamut nenu essi miste pikunak tshekuanu kie essi miste ushitat akushunu. Passe ents shash katshi pushiakanits nte kauitshiaushinanunts mitshuapinu (apishipeutshuap), ninan mentshessenimanan tshetshi kassinu tipatshimushut nte katshi pushit. Atut-put-nenu tipatshimushut eshinakushit nete, kanatshu-uitshinikushit nete uaiu. Tshika-ui-nitussenimanut, tan ispinuakupen nete pushit apishipeutshuapit, uitamuakupan kakeie nenu tshekuanu eiakunikut. Ume uiauitamat nanikutini animpinu nte uinuau iskueut mak napeut.

Esk tshitshue nantim unuipanu ne-kemistu-tuanutshi uentshi, esk mitshena eka nta tipatikentau nenu kemistutuanutshi iskueut put kie napeut. Anutsh-u 1994 utinakanipan ntshen tshenakatuapak nenu uentshi eka minupinitutshi nte utiskuem, unapem kie utuassim, kie eukun uts, tsheueuestat tan tshipa tshitutenan tshinan tshetshi nustaiak ne-tshekuan, eiakunikut uen, miam ne-tshipa itenitakun Innu kaueuestakan. Nitutetan ne-mishineikan eshi-pimpintaiats uauitshitshit uentshi, ninan nipa-ishi-tutenan, pimpintaiat. Utshen tshessenitak eka mentutak, nateut nenu, kauauitshiaushin, napeu kie iskueu eimut kie eimieut nenu kaustuentamiat, iskueu put kie napeu kie uikanishinu. Ume kauaskapinanut mukustikun tshetshi eimit uen, kie iskueu put kie napeu, minakanu tshetshi eimiat nenu kaustuentamikut, kie kaiakunikut put iskueu kie mak napeu eku minupinu kie kassinu uen uitshiniku umenu eshi-pimpintaken.

Ekuspit Nutshimit Etu Minuenimu

"Uskat ute nas metshimushiniat ute Utshimassit, tshitshue nimitatetan kaietiat nte nutshimit kie nene nutshimiu mitshim kamitshiat, kie nene kaishi-

pekassinushunat. Nantim nitenitenan tshetshi kau taiat nutshimit. Ute Utshimassit usham miste minanu, kie mitshetut Innut menits, eku nte nutshimit etatau enuet apishipeut, nistupishuma kie neu-pishuma. Katshi ute mitshimushiniat Utshimassit, tshitshue iat-itenimut Innuts, tshissenitamut eka menupinits, nutshimit nte ekute tshitshue tekuak pematishiun, tante tau nte atik, tsheut pikassiua tsheiat." *Akatis mak Etuetis*

Muk-iat-mitshe tut Innut, uiapatak nutshimit, kusput ent-eiapit auassit kaka-nta kuspit. Eukun ume kaissishueiak, tshipa tutenan tsheut-tshi-iniuimekak ne-kaishiniuiak, ekun issishuanuipan nte tshimishinikenu katutamak (mamuetetau). Muk esk eiapit taut Innuts nantim keuspit nutshimit, ntshen kepua kakanitutuat kauapukueshin, mitshimitshimau, kie kaskutimatshen. Menakatuenimepan tshetshi itishauat utuassimuau kaskutimatsheutshiuapit, menakatuentamupan at-nike-ikenets utuasseshuniamuau.

"Esk nitapastauan, uipats nukum kaishi-tshi-skutamut. Tshitshue niminueniten esk tshessitamuk nenu kaishitshiskutamut. Kie nituassimit eiapit tshitshue miste minuatamut kie tshitshue minuenitamut nepatatau nutshimiu mitshiminu. Kie nitipatshimustuaut ni-nituassimit, ishi-pekassiuipan nikanishinan, kie ishinakushipan esk atuma iapatshiat kie esk pemiskat Innu uta iapastat. Nituassimit issishuet tshitshue tshipa minuau, kau nene utinamak kaishiniuiak, kie minuat atimut apatshiakanit. Muk animan tshetshi kau ishiniuiak nene uipats kaishiniuiak, tante anutsh kassinu tshekuan pimpinu eiapastaiak, mate utapanish (skitu) etu-tshipinu mak at-espishipinit atimut. Ntauts nin nituassimit." *Shanutis*

"Tshitshue nimiskatenimaut anutsh ustinitshut shuka kemitshetutshi ua-uapatak nutshimit ema eka shuke tshissenitak nte nutshimit kie eka shuka ssentak kaishiniuak. Kutak na-pishum kakuspiat, eukunu ne-minuat enush neush etaian nutshimit. Nitapatshi-mustuaut ni-Penute kie Shuash mamu utuassimuau nitussenitamut ni-tan itenitakunupan nte uipats etatau Innut nutshimit. Ekute nte tshitshue menutusseian nutshimit, miam ne-uen-etusset ekun etenimuian. Nussim ntuk tshitshue niminuaten Utshimassit. Eku ntau, nin nete euassiuian, tshitshue-nitshi minu-aten nutshimit, essi miste min-

out. They laughed at me when, for example, I missed the duck I was shooting at. But you learn regardless of your age differences. There is always going to be somebody out there to help you out." *Tshatsh*

"When I was young, I really hated going to the country, but I never had a choice. Since then I never really bothered going to nutshimit. I was afraid I'd get homesick and bored. But since my two and a half years of sobriety, I have been really wanting to go with my family to learn about our way of life. I know I made a big mistake to not bother or care about learning our traditions. I feel that it is extremely important for my children to participate in the Outpost Program because I know they will learn and I will too, before I lose it." *Utshimassiu woman*

People like to go to the country for many different reasons. We go mostly in the spring and the fall. For some of us, it is a welcome break from our jobs in the community. We get away from problems like beer and crime, from the white man's world. We get to learn about and practise our culture. In nutshimit, our life still rotates around hard work and hunting for food. We don't have Social Services out there. We go where the caribou is roaming, where it is plentiful. There is always the challenge of finding wildlife, of figuring out where it is, of having to do things like going through rapids. This motivates people to find the food necessary for their families. We hunt for goose, caribou, partridge and so on. We take pride in what the hunters get when they come back from a trek.

"This family was in the country every year all the time with all the children. When they were back in the community, the kids would steal and vandalize their home, sniff gas, and do a lot of that stuff, but not when they spent a lot of time in the country." *Tamene, 1993 Outpost Program co-ordinator*

"Sometimes the work in nutshimit is very hard. Like in the wintertime, we made a hole in the ice using only an ice pick, not the modern technology ones used today. The ice was very thick, and it was only when we could make a hole in the ice that we can have something to eat. In the winter, it is also hard to hunt because you can easily get frostbite. I would go to nutshimit in the springtime, anywhere, because I need to eat caribou meat again. Whenever Innu are in the country, we hunt and eat a lot of traditional

Fishing / Kuskanu, 1963

food. We get to see the land and we are all happy." *Utshimaskueu, elder*

"When I was in the country, I did the things my mother used to do. I would think about my grandmother and my mother. But I had to learn myself without depending on my mother. If my mother was there, I would have let her do all the work and not learned anything. I didn't have time to go for a walk in the mountains. There is always so much work to do around the tent. I like watching the people cleaning the caribou, or drying the meat. I learned while I watch them. I like listening to the old people telling stories. I like to hear them singing in the morning. They always do that, the old people. We built a sweat lodge there. It was hot. We tell stories in there. We talk about things, spiritual things. I like listening to the people talking about themselves there. They talk about how they feel when they are in this community, how they feel different when they are in the country. They feel safe in the country, they feel free. When I am in the country, I like to watch the sunrise in the morning, and sunsets. I took a lot of pictures when I was up there and I did some sketches. I can also hear the loons in the morning." *Kistinis*

"There is a lot of freedom and happiness in nutshimit—the beauty of nature, sharing and communication. I also see how the elders and young children develop a special bond together." *Tshan*

RAY WEBBER PHOTO

uat assi, miam nas nitsh kuetenitaman. Nta nutshimit kassinu tshekuan nimiskan uaitapastaian, eku nte Utshimassit ama nisseniten nipa issishuen." *Kaniuekutat*

"Nantim nimishimenimauts tshenuts, Miste-Pinip, Miste-Etuet, Tshenu, Shushep, ntenimatit akushitau eku tsheka-tshi kuspit nutshimit kie ntshisk nene tsheka-tshi kuspit nutshimit kie ntshisk nene tsheka-tshi-nta tshiskutamuimits, kaishitshissenitak nte nutshimit, ntetenapen. Eku eukushipents uts nantim tsheuapatat nutshimit. Eka ssenitamat nte nutshimit, atut nita ntshi kuspinan. Nastesh menita uapatenapan nutshimit eku anutsh-u-shakuats nikuspin peikupishuma. Nene kuespian peikuau tekuatshik, nas nene metekun kaishikustaman tshekuan, nitshita-pamau essi-euassiut Enik Mistinapeu, essiminu tshiskutamakukue uikanisha. Passe auassit tshitshue minu tshissentamushe pen nutshimit, miam Tenesh Rich, eukun uin uikanisha nantim tanipan nutshimit, shakunit, kie tekuatshinit, esk nete kepua euassiut. Nin nete etaian nutshimit, tshitshue nitani-meniten, muk tshitshue niminuenimun. Tante eukun ne-enutsh tshitshue pemuteian eapastaian niskata. Ntshe napessit uatshimikau etu auassiut espititshiuk. Etu uinuau tshissenitamut kie etu uinuau minuaiatshiut. Muk niuitshimukutit tshetshi uauitshimits. Nushinakut ni-petaumek shishipa tiassumek. Muk eiapits uen tshi-tshiskutamashu nutshimit, meapitinu nenu, etatupuneshit. Nantim nte tshika tau uen tsheuauitshinisk." *Tshatsh*

"Euassiuian, tshitshue nitshi-mitshenten tshetshi kuspinan nutshimit, muk mentshesseni-tenapan nipa ishiutinen. Eku menita nakatuenten tshetshi uapataman nutshimit. Nikustenapan tshetshi muestataman kie tshetshi eka takuak tshekuan tshetutaman, muk essi nishupuna mak pusk essi eka minian, tshitshue nipuku-enten tshetshi uitshimikau nikanishit kuespitau tshetshi, kie nin tshiskutamashuian nutshimiu atusseun. Nitshisseniten mestiuntaian nene ka-ka nakatuentaman kie ka-kaui-tshiskutamashuian ninan kaishiniuiat anutsh niteniten tshitshue miste itenitakun nituassimit tshetshi kuspit nutshimit tante tshika tshiskutamashut Innu atusseunu esk eka untat." *Utshimassit iskueu*

Mitshenu tshekuanu uet-ui-kuspit nutshimit. Shaku-

atshi mak tekuatshik ekuta, mushinau kuespiat nutshimit, ekuta nta tante menuat miam tshetshi nakatamat uenipissish nitatusseunan. Niui-nakatenan uenipissish tshekuan eka menupinikuiat miam shitakenapun kie kutak tshekuan nte uetshipants, kauapishit utassit. Nte nutshimit tshika tshissenitenan kie eiua tshika tshiskutamashunan kaishiniuiak. Nte nutshimit esk ne-tshinukutanan kaispish miste atusseiak kie eshi-nitunushunak. Metau nte mitshimitshimau nutshimit, muk tshintua-pamanu nte etat atik, kie nte matshetit. nantim ishinakun tshetshi miskuakan aueshish nte nutshimit, tshissenimeut nte sheshikan tshipa tanu ueshish netuapamatau miam nte mate nakana katat ueshish, nte mate shipissit metshima, eituteut Innut netu-uiutau. Ne-uen tshitshue kantuiut mishikam mitshiminu tsheut pekassiat utuassim. Netuiuiat mishiue tshekuan ninituatenan, nsk, atik, pineu kie kutak eishinakushit aueshish. Kie niminu utinamuan uen nepatat tshekuanu ka tshi nituiut.

"Ume Innu mamu utuassim nantim kuspu eshikum pupun. Eku-katshi mitapet ute Utshimassit, utuassim nantim tshimutinu kie pikunaminu tshekuanu, pimina nutshikuenu kie mitshenu tshekuanu etutamen. Eku nte etat nutshimit, menita itenitakushinu utuassim." *Tamene, Kakuspinanun etuskatak*

"Nanikutini tshitshue animentakun nte nutshimit, mate nte peputshi, animin eka takuak assun, tshetshi pukueimin nte etshispiketik, eukun muk assun apastakanipan pekuetshanut, metekunupan nte tshetshi pimpin tshekuan, miam mue anutshish eshiuetshit uen ua-pu-kuetshet nte miskumit. Kie peputshi tshitshue tshispiketin. Eukun muk katshi pukuetshit uen katshi mitshun utuassim. Kie peputshi animentakunupan enituiuants tante takau kie tshitshue tshetshe-nue miskutshikueutshu uen nin nikuspin nte shakuatshi. Ntun nte nitan, tante niui mitshin atikunash. Nutshimit etatau Innut mitshut nutshimiu mitshiminu kie uapatamut nte kauapatats uipat kie minuenimut." *Utshimaskueu*

"Nete etaiani nutshimit eukun eishitusseian nikaun kaieshuapamik. Nimamitunenimaut ni-nikaun kie nukum. Muk anutsh nika-ui-tshiskuta-mashun tshekuan nin tshetshi atuskashunan tshetshi eka nantim itishimutuk nikaun. Ueskat nitishinakushinapan etatshi nte nikaun uin nenu muk ntatuskakupan nastesh menui-tshiskutamashunapan. Eku anutsh

"Families are together and close when they are in nutshimit; everyone pitches in and helps out. It is a sober environment. We go to sleep early and wake up early but well rested for the next day." *Tan*

"In nutshimit there is more talk between elders and children. My father and my daughter Hillary were talking on the radio. She asked him about what he had killed. He said he hadn't killed anything, but he had seen two bees!" *Kiti*

"People enjoy the scenery, the view and life in nutshimit. People's health is good because the spring water is so clear and there is no garbage. The environment is clean." *Innu peacekeepers*

In camps, we go often to each other's tents and visit. In the community, we don't see each other as much. That is sad. Before we spend time with people in the country, we might know their names but not their inner thoughts. In the country we find out what each other's fears are, what we want in our lives. We talk about our problems, like drinking. We get to know each other. We open up more to each other about our different emotions. And there is a lot of laughter. People feel safe and feel good about themselves, who they really are as Innu. In the community, everyone is only out for himself or herself.

People say they are healthier when they are in nutshimit. They get a lot of exercise and the exercise keeps them healthy, like when people go walking for hunting. Some people say a lot of Innu traditional medicines are used, not like in the clinic. And people are more healthy because of the wild food we eat out there. They are stronger.

Our children learn from their parents and grandparents in nutshimit. The kids look at their mothers and fathers as their role models. We have our own identity again. Children learn how to carry the canoe, how to build things, how to make things like moccasins and snowshoes, how to hunt, what their parents eat. They can watch their parents carve up ducks and geese. By watching, they learn how to clean the animals and cook them. They learn to survive in the wilderness. You don't see some of the animals in the villages, for example bears. Children are distracted when they are in the community, whereas in the country the children spend a lot of time in the woods discovering and learning.

There are so many things that our children need to learn—Innu games, how to travel with just the basic stuff, how to get the wild foods, hunt the animals, how to get near them, figure out directions, the lay of the land. For instance, when you are going after a beaver and you see the beaver house, you have to know what direction to go in and how the wind is. The caribou as well have a very strong sense of smell. You have to be careful about the wind and the direction that you approach him from. There are a lot of hand signals we can use to not make noise for the animals to hear us. Young people need to learn how to tan the skins, make *komatiks* or canoes like we had when we were still nomadic. We also need to look at what people used to use as medicines, how people were cured if they were sick. Children need to learn how to respect the animals and birds. They need to learn all the names for the many different places out on our territory.

At our school workshop, the children in grades two and three said they like boat rides, fishing, getting caribou, swimming, playing tag and volleyball, walking in the woods, playing outdoors, hunting, going on the plane, long skidoo rides, living in a tent, the jets and the caribou. They also like swinging, berry picking and the trees. A number of the children said they liked everything about the country.

"We played outside. I washed the clothes. I like fighting in the snow, and playing with strings, climbing trees. I like the candles and the plane and to skidoo. I like the toboggan going bumpy. I like playing baseball. I like killing bambies, making fires. I like hunting caribou and partridges. We like to hear stories." *Penute and Kistinis's children*

When we are in nutshimit some of us say we become more aware that we are the caretakers of the land and have to look after the animals. In nutshimit, we don't have to follow the laws of the governments. We just follow the laws of nature. It strengthens our spiritual beliefs. We never waste animal meat in nutshimit. But some of us mess up our campsites and leave our garbage behind. Some of us are beginning to realize that it is important to keep our camps clean. We don't want to make the place dirty like in Utshimassit. We want to hold the land more sacred. We are more environmentally alert. We have to think about what we are doing. We can't let the boys go hunting all the time. We should only kill what we need.

nutshimit etaiani, nastesh menita ispishin tshetshi pepamutenan nte takuts piskutinats usham mishau nte ntatusseun nitshinash. Tshitshue niminu-nuauts uentshi uanitikuetau, kie piassauantshetau, nitshi skutimashun en-itenitakun muk etshitapamikau. Kie ninitutuaut tshenut tepatshimutau nete uipats tipatshimunu, kie tshitshue niminutuaut, nekamutau tshietshepaushin. Nantim nenu tutamut tshenut kenekamutshi ni-tshietshapapintshi nimitishunan ni-kie tshitshue tsheteu kie eitipan-kaishitshissenitak Innu, tshekuanu nte unuitimit tekunit, miam aueshishash, kie nenu uin eshitshissenitak tshenu. Kie tshitshue niminu-tuaut tshenut tepat-shimushutau, tipatimut nenu etenimut nte etatau Utshimassit kie essi-eiat-itenimut nte nutshimit etatau nastesh nte memeshimentamut tshekuanu kie etu minuenimut. Nene kataian nutshimit tshitshue niminunuau pishum piatshimut kie shiakastuet tshi-etshepapinits tshitshue nimiste akuntshenapan nte nutshimit kataian kie nunishinatantshen kie nipet-uau ni-muak iashikuet tshietshepapentshe."
Kistinis

"Nte nutshimit nastesh metikun meshimentamun muk minuentamun takun, essi miste minuashet tshekuan nte uet nitautshit assit, kie miste mishau nte uauitshitun, kie euitamatunanut tshekuan. Kie niuapimaut tshenut mak auassit eshi-mitshimau mamu tat, kie essi ushitat tshetshi etu metshima nis-tuapamitut." *Tshan*

"Ukaumaut mamu utaumaut, nas uitshitussemitut nte nutshimit mamu utuassimuau, kassinu uitshitut eishitussetau, nekutetau mianikashutau, tante metikunu tshekuanu tshetshi apastat tshetshi-mit-shipinikut kie ninan euassiuiat uipits-ni-ninipanan kie uipat nuninan nas miskut niminu asteiekushi-nan, ume tshashikat." *Tan*

"Nte nutshimit tshenut mak auassit nantim ni-eimi-tut. Nutau peikuau mak nitanish Hillary tipat-shimustatut nte takapitshenikinits nitanish kukuet-shimeu tshekuanu nepatan nutauiu, eku itekutik, metshekuan ninipatan muk nishut uiapamikau amut itikutek." *Kiti*

"Nte nutshimit Innut tshitshue minuenimut kie minunemut tshatapatakau, nte unuitimit. Kie tshit-shue minu-eniut Innut tante tshitshue minuanu nip-inu menits nastesh nte metikun tshetshi uinakamit

nipin tante muepinashunanu nte, muinakun nastesh assin." *Innu kamakunueshit*

Nete nutshimit mamu etatau Innuts, mushinau mupis-tatut nte upitshiantshuapuat, eku ute Utshimassit menita shuka uapamituts, ustuentamunakun ume eshi-nakuak esk eka uitshekuspimit Innu nte nutshimit, tshitshissenimanut eshinikashut, muk nastesh met-shessinimanut etenitak nte emamitunenitak ustikuanu-ats, eku nte nutshimit tshitshissentenan ne-tshekuan kakustimak, kie tshekuan en-ua-apastaiak nte stiniu-ats. Kassinu tshekuan tshiuauitenan eka menupinikuiak miam shitakenapun, kie etu tshiminu tshissenimitunan ama tshikustenan tshetshi uauitamak ne-ei-tenimunak kie nantim tshui-unishintunan kie tshipapinan. Nutshimit Innut nastesh metikunu tshekuanu tshetshi mishimentamikut, nantim minuen-imut, kie tshissenimushut uentshi ents tshitshue nas Innuts. Eku nte Utshimassit muk uin tshitapimushu uen iskueu put kie napeu.

Kutakut Innut issishueut, etu niminueniunan nut-shimit etaiatshi. Tante nantim aiatshiut kie essi eka tshiampit uen, muk aiat minueniu, miam mate Innu epimutet netuiutshi. Mitshetut Innuts essishueuts, esk nenua nitapastanan nutshimiu ntukuna, uipats Innut kaishi-nitukunushut, nimiu etenitakuak miam nte ntukuntshuapissit. Kie Innut etu minuaiatshiut. Kie minueniut kie etu shutshiut, tante mushinau nutshim-its mitshiminu mitshut.

Nituassiminan ekute nte uets tshissenitak nutshimit etenitakunits etshiskutamakut uikanishuau kie umushumuau. Auassit tshitapameuts nenu utauau kie ukauau, eukunu nenu tsheui-eshitusset nenu kaishiua-pamatsh uikanishuau. Nte nutshimit kau tshinistua-pumushunan eshiniuiak. Auassit eiapits tshiskuta-mashut tsheishi-peketat, Innu utnu, kie tsheishi ushi-tat tshekuanu, tan tsheishinakutat pishakessia, kie ashama, kie tan tsheishi-ntuiuts, kie tshekumitshiminu matshin uikanishuau. Tshitapameut uikanishuau epeskunan shishipa put kie nska. Muk eketshessen-nuapit, tshissenitamut tsheishi neikuat aueshisha kie tsheishi piminuet. Kie tshissenitamut tsheishi-pakassi-nushut nte nutshimit. Ama mishiue tshiuapamaut aueshishet ute mitshima Utshimassit, miam mate mask, nutshimit nte tau. Auassit naste menakatuen-imushut kie metshekuanu apitenitamut ute etatau Utshimassit, eku nte nutshimit, nantim nte ueuetimits taut, kie nte minaskuat pipamuteut, kie uiapatak nenu

When we are in nutshimit we see many old Innu camps. This keeps us in touch with our past. There is so much to discover. We see the old sticks where people had their tents, but they are rotten now. We might find a shoe and try to imagine if it is maybe fifty years old and who the family was that camped there. We wonder if the camp was built in the summer or fall, if they killed caribou and so on.

Many of us go to nutshimit because of the Kaupaunantsh (Outpost Program). This is the only program we have which is really Innu, helping us become proud to be Innu again. It helps people to go out to the barrens with charter aircraft, skidoos, fuel and sometimes other supplies. Sometimes the Kaupaunantsh co-ordinator works with the clinic for each camp to have a medical box. He makes sure the camps are equipped with a C.B. radio and keeps in contact with them. When there is an emergency, he co-ordinates a response. It could be medical, or people have run out of supplies. Kaupaunantsh really benefits the elders, who otherwise would not be able to go to the barrens and experience the life they know and appreciate. Some say there would be more benefits if more people were out in nutshimit.

"The Outpost Program encourages people to still use the land. We need to see more on the land, and our children need to experience the land to keep their Innu culture. Parents are able to show their children how to hunt and which direction to go in. We eat traditional foods in nutshimit. Children are happy when they are not in school. We can save on a lot of our food supplies when we are eating wild foods." *Youth Development Council*

"There are more families going now. I would like to see even more people going into the country and spending time, maybe four or five months at a time. I would like to see more young people going out by themselves with their families. The program should continue, because eventually as young people spend time there with their families, their children will want to also spend more time in the country. We are following in our ancestors' footsteps. We haven't forgotten. It is part of the life here." *Tamene*

"The Outpost Program is a good idea. In the old days there wasn't anything like that. There weren't any charters. People travelled by foot and together.

If there had been charters with store-bought food, people would have loved it and they would have stayed in nutshimit without moving to Utshimassit." *Meneshkuesh, elder*

Problems in Nutshimit

"There were no problems in nutshimit back then. Today we have many problems and difficulties." *Manish, elder*

"In the old days, everybody was in nutshimit and everything was fine, except for the starvation. The food would run out and that's when the problems started." *Ueniam, elder*

"One of the things you have to remember is that you have to have the skills to be in the country to survive. When you don't have them, you can't survive. You can't survive when you don't know how to make snowshoes, when your wife doesn't know how to make moccasins. You also have to know the area around you. The last time I was in the country with my family was ten years ago. We were just one family, no one else. My father and mother used to have these skills. I would like to learn those things my father used to do. But my mother is not well now. It's too late for me to go back in there. My parents can't go any more." *Tamene*

Life in nutshimit is not without its problems. Many of these happen because some of us have lost our traditions. Or we are not practising them. Many people say that there is too much influence from the white society, not just in the village but also in nutshimit. We have become too assimilated. We use more modern ways. This is something we don't agree about. We used to depend on our own resources. Everything was handmade. We travelled by canoe, dog sleds and toboggans. Today we use planes, helicopters, speed boats and skidoos. Some of us say we want the easy life too much. We just hop on the machines and let the machines do the work for us. We will be weaker if we don't use our physical power. We use other white technology like radios and lanterns. There was less expense involved in the old days. Today, if there was no Outpost Program, some people worry that nobody would go to the country. Some people say the Band Council buys too many supplies for people. But others complain they can't go to the country if they don't have speed boats and

tshekuanu eka nta uapatak, kie eiua-etshiskutamashut.

Miste mitshenu stuassiminut esk tshekuanu tsheui tshiskutamuakut, miam mate Innu metueun, kie tan tshipa ishi-utapeut etshitshipitshit uen, tan tshipa ishi-ntuapatam nutshiu mitshiminu, kie tshipa ishi-ntuiu, tan tshipa ishi-katshimaieu ueshishash enatat, tshetshi peshuapamat kie nte tetshe tshipauts nateu, kie nte tetshe eshiminuat tsheut-tshi peshuapamat. Miam ne-tipeikatshetau amisk. Ntumiskuein, uapatamut uist tshika-ui-tshisseniten tshetshi metinu eitin, kie tshekui-tshissenten nte uetik tetshe. Atik eiapit tshitshue tshika nakatuenimau uapamit, ekua-uin tshika pishuau, namuniskut tshika pishuau. Nas tshika-ui-nakatuenimau tshetshi eka namuniskut. Mitshen nte eiapit eishiuasteitshet uen utitshina eapastat, tshetshi eka petakut aueshisha. Innu auassit tshika-ui tshiskutamashut tshetshi tshishintshet, tshetshi ushiat uta-panaskua, uta miam nene kaishiniuiak esk pepampitshiak. Kie eiapit tshika-ui-tshissenitenan tan, ishi-apastanikupen Innu ntukuna, kie tan etakushit nenu uen apastakupen, kie tan eshi-uitshinikut. Auassit eiapit tshika-ui-tshiskutamashut tshetshi ispitenimat aueshisha kie shishipa kie tshukui tshissenitamut. Eishinikaten nipina natuaishu shipu kie peskutinau ute tshentussinat.

Nte kaskutimatsheutshiuapits ni-mupistuaiants nish mak nist kaitipit auassit, issishueut niminuatenan epi-pampiniat ut katshipinist, ekusseiat, enitutikueiat, epepekatshimuiat, emetueiat, etuaiat, epepamuteiat nte minaskuat, mak emetueiat nte unuitimit, enituiat, kapiminast epushiat, mak neush epepampeituiat uta-panish, innutshuapit etaiat, (pitshiantshuap), katshipinishit mak atikut. Mak eueuepishunat, mitshetut eiapit essishuet auassit kassinu tshekuan niminuatenan nte nutshimit.

"Nimetuanan unuitimit, niuapekantshenan. Niminu-aten eutamantsheian, kie niminuenmau kun mak nuetapekantshen, ntekushin mistikut. Niminuaten uastentemanask, kapiminast kie skitu. Kie niminu-ataut utapaiaskut ntshen kepitsheshinutshi. Niminu-aten etuaian. Niminu-aten enipeikau atikussit. Niminuaten entutikueian kie entuineuian. Niminua-tenan etipatshimustakuiat." *Penute mak Kistinis utu-assimuau*

Nutshimit etaiaku, stissishuenan, aiat tshinistu-tatishunan, kie aiat-tshi-tshissenitenan tshinan eshipin, kanakatuentak assinu kie kassinu ueshishet. Nte nut-

shimit nimienu niashamuak tsheutshimau umishina-nikan. Muk ne-tshinashenan assit tshekuan uet nitaut-shit eshipimpin, kie tshiminikunan ne-shutshiun tshet-shi etu tapuetatishunak ne-tshekuan kassinu eniuimikak, miam nte unuitimit tshekuan etakuak. Metshinita metuatshenan nutshimiu mitshim nte nut-shimit. Muk ueskat stishinakushitan, tshitshue tshiuinakutatan nte uatshiak, kie kauepinashunanut ntemuk nte eitistepen tshauepiniak. Eku anutsh tshash pitshenik tshinistuatenan ishinakunishepan tshetshi nanikamak nta katshi uitshinaku nte nut-shimit. Nimieu tshetshi ishinakutaiak tshetshi uinaku-taiak nutshimit miam nte eshinakuak Utshimassit. Tshekui minu nakatuentenan nutshimit tshetshi ispitenitakuak. Etu anutsh tshimatenitenan tshetshi eka uinakutaiak assi. Tshika-ui-mamitunenimushunan tshekuan uatutamak, tshetshi eka tapuetuakut stuas-simit tshetshi eka uesham nipatat tshekuanu muk essi ispiniak tshekui nipatanan tshekuan, tshetshi eka piuenitamak.

Nte etaiak nutshimit mitshetuau tshiuapatenan uipats mitukapa, eukun ne-uetitaukunak uipats kaishiniuiak. Miste mitshen nte esk tshekuan eka uia-patamak. Nanikutini niuapatenan mistikua (peshuna) apastauakupan Innut mianikashutau, muk shash nenu nas uissitikua mistikua. Nimiskeian missin eku etenita-mat shash-au-kakeie petetat tatunuepun essi-umenu uitshit uen kie uentshe mana, tshekui-initshe uta uit-shikupan. Kie tekuatshinit kie mak napinits akeie-uit-shikupen, kie nipekupen atikua muatikuekupen-put uta-uatshit, kassinu niteitentenan.

Uet-tshi kuspinak nutshimit tante takun ne-kaupau-nantsh shuniau. Eukun ume peikushu, ne-tshekuan uatshinukunak nte Innuits tetshe apastakanu, kie tshiuitshi-nikunan, tshetshi minuat kau miam Innu itenitakushiak. Tshiuitshinikunan tshetshi minuat uap-atamak nte mushuat, tante kapiminast tshishikashu-nanu etau-ntak kie skitu, pimin kie nanikutini kutak eiapit tshiminikunan tshekuan. Nanikutini ne-uen niaketuatak kaupaunantsh atusseunu, uitshitussemeu nenu nitikunitshiskuessa, tshetshi papeik minat Innu kuespin nitukun miutaskua. Kassinu nte eitat Innut nutshimit, papeik minakanut takapitshenikea, tshetshi eimit nte Utshimassit kie tshetshi ntussenimanit etits. Eku tshekuanu eka menupinupitau uipat kue eimi-akanit, iakushitau kie mak nutepintau mitshiminu. Kaupaunantsh tshitshue nenu uitshinikut tshenut,

skidoos. As well, some elders say they can't go to the country when there are no aircraft to bring them.

"How would people feel if they had to travel in the country without using skidoos and without using a gun? The trip with aircraft is very short. By foot, we would probably have to set our tents up five times to get to our destination." *Shuash and Shanutis*

Some say it costs too much to go to nutshimit. But others say maybe we bring too much stuff when we go out, planeloads of it. Some people say they simply don't have the money they need to go to nutshimit, especially with a big family. They can't even buy groceries. People can't do without a lot of supplies, like sugar, flour, tea and butter. Some say it is like the government and its funding are breaking us up, breaking our ways. But others argue that if people today didn't have the Outpost Program, UIC, family allowances or social assistance, they would be really afraid to go to country. Their basic needs would not be taken care of. They need assistance to buy basic supplies. This was the generation young people were born into. They are used to these things.

"What's happened is that the government's way of thinking—that people depend on the services that we have here— has taken hold. Even if the services are not working for the people, people have still bought the idea. The dependency is there and it will be there for a long time. Services were supposed to better the lives of the Innu, but it has destroyed the spirit of going in the country by depending on these goods and services." *Kiti*

There are other problems in nutshimit. One is alcohol. Some people don't leave it behind in the village. It can cause serious accidents or other unexpected incidents or mishaps. Another problem for some of us is that we have not been practising our spirituality and are showing less respect to the animals. Some children are not learning nutshimit *atuseun* (work). Some say children are losing the culture because they are lazy and don't respect their parents any more. Some parents blame themselves for this. Some children don't want to stay in the country a long time and keep going back and forth. Sometimes they don't like to eat country food.

"Some young people say there is nothing there for them in nutshimit, so why should they go there?

Uiniam and Anis Katshinak making snowshoes /
Uiniam mak Miste-Anis nuthikuepants ashama, 1963

Then parents and their children are stuck in the community. Children are wanted in the country when their parents are going. Children should be good workers. There are lots of things that a child can do when he is in the country with his family, because other people are staying in the country too." *Penash*

In our workshops, the children said the things they don't like about nutshimit are being scared by low-level jets that make too much noise, missing a game of pool, swimming, falling in the water, berry picking, and times when the flies and insects are there, when their friends are not there or when their mom is not there. Some don't like fishing, are very scared in the boat and would like to be able to ride their bikes. Some don't like short skidoo rides; others don't like going on the skidoo at all. One child said he didn't like being left behind when everyone went on the boat. One said she didn't like going back to Davis Inlet.

Many of us worry that the knowledge of the elders is not being passed on. When the elders are gone, will people stop going to nutshimit? In the fall of 1994, Kaniuekutet, one of our most respected elders and teachers, died. This is a great loss for us. Some elders now can no longer go to nutshimit, people like Sam Napeu. He used to go. Now he is chronically ill and he can't. Elders like Tshenish are worried about their health; his eyesight is gone. Elders need help to go to nutshimit and sometimes they can't get it.

"Nobody would help me and get me the stuff I need. Like I need to have someone do the hunting for me because I have no spouse. Since my husband died, I was only in nutshimit last summer." *Utshimaskueu, elder*

RAY WEBBER PHOTO

utshen kakatshi-uapatak nte mushuat, uipats katshissenitak etenitakunits kie kamiste minuatak. Kutakuts Innuts issishueut etu tshipa minupinu etu mitshetit Innut kuespit nutshimit.

"Kaupaunantsh tshitshue enu-uitshinikut Innut tshetshi eka punits eapastat assinu. Etu tshipa-uimiste uapatenan assi, kie stuassiminut isshinakunu kie-uinuau tshetshi uapatats nutshimit, ui-kunenitakau kaishiniuits. Utauau kie uikanishuau, tshitshiskutamakut tsheishi nituiuits kie nte tsheituts nutshimit mushinau nutshimiu mitshim tshimitshinan. Kie auassit minuenitamut eka tsheskutamashutau. Matshiak nutshimiu, mitshim eku miskut metshitissi-mitshinan tautshiuapit mitshim."
Ustinitshishit

"Eku anutsh etu mitshetut kuespit Innut. Nipa minuentamuan etu mitshetit uentshi kuespit nutshimit, kie-tat nte nutshimit neu-pishuma kie mak petetat tatupishuma. Kie nipa-minuatamuan etu-mitshetit auassit uitshimats uikanishuau. Kie ume kaupaunantsh, nantim tshipa-ui-pimpinitakanu, tante auassit nte uitshimeut uikanishuau nutshimit, kie esk nte uinuau tshukuitauts nte nutshimit. Esk tshinashimuanan tshimushumpinuts kaishi pimutet uipats, esk metshunikuatimuanan. Ekun eshiniuiak ute." *Tamene*

"Minuau-e-tshitshue kaupaunants, nete uipats menita-en-tikunushipan, ume anutsh eshi-ui-tshiakanits uentshi kuespitau. Metapen kapiminast tshetshi upaunuets, muk pimutepan Innut, kie mamu kuspitshipin. Ishinakuakakue kapiminast tshetshi upaunuets kie ne-mitshim tautshiuapit essiuenutik, tshitshue eku tshipa minuatamupen Innuts, nastesh put-tut-nita-tshi nashipepan ute Utshimassit." *Meneshkuesh, kukuminash*

Tshekuan Eka Shuka Menupinits Nutshimit

"Uipats-nete mushinau minupinipin Innu nutshimit etat eku anutshish tshitshue mitshen tshekuan eka menupinits kie essi-animpinits nutshimit." *Manish, kukuminash*

"Uipats nete, mishiue uen nte tapan nutshimit kie mushinau minupinipen, muk tapue shauenanut ekuta animinupan. Nutepintau Innut mitshiminu, ekuta muk animentakunupen." *Ueniam, tshenu*

"Peik tshekuan tshekui minu tshissiten, tshetshi tain nutshimit, tshekui, minu tshisseniten tshekuan nutshimit etenitakuak tshetshi ut-pekassinushun. Eka sentamen nutshimiu atussuen, metsheketshi tshintuinushun, kie metsheketshi-tshi pekassinushun metsheketshi-tshi-tan nutshimit eka-tshi-ishamitshein kie stiskuem eka nitaussintshet. Kie tshekui mintshisseniten nte eshinakuak etain. Masten ne-etaian nutshimit mamu nutaun mak nikaun, shash peikunuepunutshe. Muk nipeikussinan ninan metaut nte kutakut Innut etautshit. Muk nin nutaun kie nikaun minu tshissentamupan nutshimiu atusseunu. Tshitshue nipa minuenten tshi-tshiskutamashunan nutaun kaishitshissentak nutshimit. Muk tante nikaun meshuka shash minueniu, eku nin meniketshi shash tshikuspin tante shash nikanist metshi kusput minuat." *Tamene*

Takun nte eiapit tshekuan eka menupinikuiak nutshimit, mitshetut ents Innut eshinakushit tante pesse etishiak, shash tshiuntanan kaishiniuiak, kie metshitispish kutshitanan, tshetshi tshiskutamashuiak stiniunu. Mitshetut Innuts essishuet, usham tshi-nispitetentamuanan nenu kakeshau eshiniut, nimiute nte muk Utshimassit etiak peikun nte eiapit nutshimit etaiak usham tshiui-kakeshau pimpinushunan. Eukun ne-eshikastankuiak tshekuan usham tshiui uetshinushunan. Eukun ume eka shuka minuaua etutamak, uipats nete tshinan tshutinamashunan tshekuan. Tshinan nte eshikunentamak stapastatan kie kassinu Innu utitshi apastapen ueshitat tshekuanu tsheitapastat kuespiak tshipimiskatan, Innu uta stapastatan, kie atimut stapatshiatan, kie tshutapetan. Eku anutsh kapiminast, kauasteitshest, katshipinist kie skitu. Passe Innu issishueut usham tshui utshimautshenimunan, nastesh metsheui mishiminan. Muk-ni-stet-takushipinan skitu eukun en-etuskakuiak tshekuan epimpin. Muk aiat metshekitshi shapishinan eka-ui-uskuistashunak. Kie eiapit nenu stapastauanan kakeshau eitapistat, takapitshenikan kie katshikaiashuet uastentamake. Menita issi-animinupan nte kuespinanut uipats. Anutsh u-essi-ekatakuak kaupaunantsh, passe Innut itenitamut, nas messi-tau uen tshipa kuspu nutshimit. Kutakut Innut issishueut usham Innu utshimaut miste mineut Innu tshekuanu kuespaunatau. Kutakut uentshi issishueut atu-tshi kusput Innut eka kunentak katakushisteshin kie skitu. Tshenut eiapit kuessishuet mentshi kuspinan-eka tat kapiminast, tshetshi itaunimit nutshimit.

Although people say Kaupaunantsh is a very important program, we see many problems with it as well, with the way it is run. The problem of dependency happens as well because of the way it is run. Too much money is spent because people are travelling back and forth on planes and helicopters. Sometimes people have a good excuse, like they are really sick, but people use many other excuses or pretend to be sick to go back to the village. Some say there are no incentives for people to remain longer. There is no education to teach us why it is important to stay.

> "I think we depend too much on the Outpost Program's charters. Back in the old days, there weren't any programs like we have today. The people used to carry their supplies on their backs when they travelled to nutshimit." *Matinin, elder*

People say that the money is misused in other ways too. When people are prepared to go in the country, many often receive all kinds of help from the Band Council to buy things for themselves—gas, skidoos, motor boats, tents and so on. Life is too easy. When the Outpost Program budget is overspent, people who want to go back to the country the following year are told there is no money left. Sometimes when the Band Council runs out of funding, there is not enough money to charter planes to bring people already in the country back to the village.

We need to be more straight about these problems. People have different opinions on who is to blame for all this mismanagement of the Outpost Program. Some people say it is the Band Council or chief that is to blame. They don't know where the money is going. They don't set limits on the planes and helicopters and then the money runs out. A few say that the Band Council are only helping themselves and their families. Many say that people are the problem, not the program. We should know better; the planes and helicopters are too expensive to be going back and forth. The Outpost Program will only work if people co-operate. What happens from overspending is that people can't go in the country the following year. It is not always the leaders' fault.

> "I think the people who want to go to nutshimit will go. What I think is that people are happy when the Band Council is supporting them. But other people feel left out. The Band Council doesn't look after

them. I think we only see the same people going to nutshimit. Why can't other people go? I think the people don't like that." *Manesh, elder*

Sometimes people have problems with the outpost co-ordinator and how he is doing his job. A number of people have complaints about the radio. One problem is that the bush radios are sometimes in bad shape and don't work well. There is a lot of bad-mouthing and making trouble that goes on with the radios.

> "In the last few years, we have been seeing more young people going into the country because we are taking a first step in helping them. We've never seen such a large amount of young people going in for a long time. We are providing the transportation they need to travel. It might not work at first. But as we progress, eventually young people will spend a lot more time in the country. The expansion of the Outpost Program is a step in bridging the gap between the elders and young people. Now young people are going in for a few days, they come back after a week or two. But eventually it will work itself out as more and more young people see what our elders are doing in the country. I think there is always going to be a price to pay. We have to spend money on aircraft and transportation to take people in the country. We have already paid a price in neglecting our elders and young people. There is no price too great in trying to create and build the relationship between the elders and the young people." *Kiti*

What Keeps People from Going to Nutshimit

If we are to encourage more people to go to nutshimit, we need to know what keeps them from going now. There are many pulls for us from the community. Some children don't want to go because the things they get in the community have become part of their needs. There is people's dependency on welfare cheques, or things like television, soap operas like "All My Children." We have bills and "car" (skidoo, ATV or boat) loans to pay off. Other influences include the store, the clinic, our houses and belongings, junk foods, bands, dances and bingo.

> "Some people don't want to go to nutshimit because they want to work. They have to pay for their loans, for hydro bills and telephone bills. Some people worry about this, others don't. When I told

"Tan-ma tshipa itenimut Innut kuspitshit eka apas-tat skitunu kie eka kunentat passikanu? Kapiminast kuespaunut nastesh mineush-tau. Eku pimutet Innu, put petetat tatauu tshipa uitshu eku patush tshipa takushinu uaitutet." *Shuash mak Shanutis*

Passe nisishueuts tshishue animin tshekuan uan-tuteashi nutshimish. Eku kutakuts isishueuts, tshishue tshimistetakunean tshekuan. Etuteaku nutshimish nas shakasineutashu kapiminast. Passe Innuts isishueuts mashuka nu ushuneaminan tshetshi eaiats tshekuan uakuspinashi. Entsh kepua mashetintuaui utu-asimuaua. Mitshiminu miste aiauts ni mitshiminu. Minispinu nanikutini kutuk Innu mitshiminu. Enu unuskauaia mak kashiuas, piminu, nipisha. Eku passe Innuts isishuets tsheutshimau nas pikunum mak nikam eshiniuau mak ne kainitinau uipats. Kutakuts esishuets katukuashi kakuspinant mak ustukuanisha mak uasishuneau shuneaua. Eku tshishue tshikakusta-muts tshetshi itutets nete nutshimits. Tshekesi takunu enu passe tshekuan uantapatshitatsh. Tshika minakanutsh tshekuanu tshesieats tshekuanu enkunu enu eshiniuts anush ustinitshutsh. Eshiniuts anush ustinitshutsh. Eku tshash enu inupunuts tshe espin-inukuts tshekuanu.

"Enu uishinishinakuash tshekuan, enu etenitak tsheutshimau enu uish miste etenitash uatshakanitsh Innuts. Kashuka menupunits uatshakantuaui passe Innuts. Takunu eshuitshakan auen mak mushinau tshikatakunu. Tshaka mista uitshakanipintsh Innuts minu puntakue, tshetshi miste uitshakanits muk. Kie miminupu mak pikunakanuts Innuts. Utininuau mak enu etutets ete nutshimish." *Kiti*

Takun nte kamenupints nte nutshimit enkun peik shitakunapun. Passe Innuts mitshinikatamuts ute Utshimassits, tshishue mishau esiushukunuetsh tshi-takunapun. Mak kutak tshekuan takun kamenupints. Enu mitshikutshitanan tshetshi kukuetshiunak uipits stiniunu. Mak Tshenish nakatuenimautsh aueshishitsh, mak passe auasits mishuka senitamuts nutshimish atuseunu. Mak issishueuts passe auasits tshash unitauts uipats kaishiniunanitsh make tshishue tshitimutsh auasits nastesh minututuets uikanishuaua mak passe ukamuauts mak utamuauts essishuets, ninan ntutenan uishekanakatueniminuts ntuasiminuts. Mak passe auassits mishuka minuenitamuts tshetshi neush tatsh nutshimit mak etataui, mushinau tshiut-

shiuepantutsh mak meshuka uimitshutsh nutshimish mitshiminu.

"Passe auasits isishueuts nastesh matakun tshekuan nte tshe tshitaiats nte nutshimish, tshekuan eku tsheuishstaiats nte nutshimish. Eku passe utamunuts mak ukuamuauts mak utuasimuaua. Kie etipits ute Utshimassits, nas uiuitsheuakanutsh auasits uikan-ishuauau uatshishipitshintaui. Tshika minu atusseuts nte tats nutshimish. Tshishue mishanu nutshimish atusseunu tshipa tshintatusseu auass tat. Mak mamu uikanisha etantshi mak mishiue mamu tats Innuts." *Penash*

Nematshis nte auassits eku nisishuents enu uishekaminuenitas tshetshitatsh nutshimish kusteuts enu katshipanishintshi kapiminashintshi, enu kemeste tsheuetakushinuani. Mak mitshenitamuts enu kanut-shikamutshi enu katshiskauakanuani, kapikashumu-nantsh, mak emushuts mak matshetintaui shitshimeua mak nte kaetantaui uikanishuaua mak uitsheuakanu-aua. Mak metshenitamuts tshetshi kussets mak nte tshetshi pipampinits utits tshishue ui-pipampantutsh utapanuaua passe mitshenitamuts pessish tshetshi-pimpatuts shuka neush, ui-pimpampatauts utapanissa. Peik auass isishuepan nastesh miniminueniten uakat-shimukunani pepampinantshi eku kutuk euass nisishueu nastesh minimunueniten tshetshi tshi-uepinan nte Utshimassits.

Passe tshinai stanimeniteian katshessenitamau enu uipats Innuts kaishiinants. Katatuaue tshenuts Innuts auinuau eskua tshika tauts a nte nutshimish anush. Esi takuatshish tshash tshiueanu peik tshitsheniminu mak tshikaskutimatsheminu Kaniuekutat tapue tshinan tshimiste unitashunan. Passe tshenuts tshash mitshin-tuteuts ete nutshimish. Mak Napeu mitshintuteu tshash uipats nutshimish tshash uipats akushu tante tshenuts tshitapam. Mak kutuk tshenu Tshenish, miste mishimenitam, enu tshash shuka muapatam. Tshishue uintuteuts tshenuts nutshimish muk matshi ituteuts.

"Nastesh auen miniuitshinuk uantuenitamani tshekuan mak uantuinikushinani. Mak mitau napem esi nipit napem. Muk peikua ntitashinatshe nut-shimish." *Utshimaskueu*

Innuts passe issishuets kaupaunantsh, tshishue misti ispitenitakun etutakant mak passe tshiuapatenan kamenupints mak eshpimpinitakantsh. Kimiste uit-shinuanu etenitakuash. En eshipimpinitakantshi

Miste-Pinip I needed to pay my loan, he told me I should have bought the skidoo with cash, not with a loan." *Tshatsh*

Alcohol keeps some people from going to nutshimit. They are too sick from drinking to go and live the life in nutshimit. For others, they don't like to leave their drinking buddies. For others, their addiction is too strong. They won't be able to drink out there without their home brew. Some people don't go to the country because they are scared of getting sick and having DTs.

Others say they can't go to the country because they have too many personal problems. Some people are scared to go. They think they will be homesick. Others worry that their houses will get vandalized if they leave them. Sometimes people don't get support from their friends, boyfriends, girlfriends or families to go. Laundry is hard work and there are no electrical appliances such as washing machines in nutshimit. Some people get bored. Some people fear unknown emergencies such as accidents could happen in nutshimit, or that they might get sick.

> "Some people say they don't want to go because there is nothing to do, but I know there is a lot of hard work to do. For the younger generation, it is a different story. There are no lights, no television, no power, nowhere to go at nights. They couldn't chase women. (In the country it's too dark; people are afraid!) People don't usually stay up late at night in the country. Parents will say to the kids that there is a lot to do tomorrow." *Etuetis*

Some people don't go to the country because they are scared to lose their jobs, or their wife or husband is working. We have to look after our responsibilities that keep us in the community. It is very hard for us to throw that away. Some of us say we can easily quit our jobs. Some of us have quit a few times already. And we are able to get them back when we return. We say if we have a good mind, we can handle it.

Sometimes people with permanent jobs can't afford to go to the country. They can't get on social assistance to take three months to go out. They're not on UIC. Where would that three months' of money come from? Social Services can't give them anything. People with jobs often can only go for a small number of days when they have holidays.

The school year is also a problem. A lot of people

Caribou / Atik, 1993

worry about their kids, because if they go to nutshimit, they will miss out on a lot of school and be set back a grade level. We worry they will never be able to finish. Some of us feel we have to send our kids to school even with the kinds of things they teach them there, and even if we have these ideas that we would like to go to nutshimit.

Food can be another problem, if you're not used to it or for younger people. They don't want to eat *nutshimit mitshem* (wild foods) because they are so used to eating foods in cans or chickens.

Recommendations for Nutshimit

There are many opinions about how long we need to spend in nutshimit. Some people say we should stay out there all the time, but others say we cannot turn back the clock. Some say we should spend half of our time in nutshimit and the other half in the community. And others say that it is up to each individual to decide when and for how long they want to go to nutshimit. Some suggest making changes so that the children don't miss so much school. Teachers should be able to live with people in the camps and teach the children.

For people who need to learn the skills of life in nutshimit, we should have workshops where they can find out what they need and what life in nutshimit is really like. The Band Council should set up such a program

PETER SIBBALD PHOTO

tshishue miste mestinikanu shuneau. Muk etshiutshiue piakanitsh kapiminashits mak kauauastantsheshits mak eiapits Innuts nakushitaui natauakanitsh. At eiapits kaiakushitaui passe Innuts senitamuts tshikauishtshiuepinuts uiakushikashuts eni. Passe Innuts issishueuts nastesh passe neush muitauts nte mak mitakun nte skutimashun tsheuish taiats.

"Nteniten nin, tshishue tshimisti-ispiteniteian enu kaupaunantsh kapiminashits, uipats nte nastesh mitakunipin tshekuan katauantshi nte uaian. Innuts uipats pimutepants mak uiushipants utapitshitaunuaua, uantutetuaui nte nutshimish." *Matinin* Passe Innuts esishuets tsheska nanikutini miste apatshitakanu shuneau. Etutetaui Innuts nutshimish, mak uaitutetau tshishue miste uitshiakanuts nte Innu Utshimauts enu pimina tshetshi e iats mak utapanuaua, mak apakuanu, mak ututuaua, mak kataustetshimuaua. Eshiniunatsh nastesh manimin, minestanakantshi shuneau kakuspinats, eku uantutetuaui passe Innuts eku mitakunu shuneaunu. Nankutini kaetukunitshi shuneanu Innu Utshimauts matshinataueuts Innua. Ete tshash ketantuaui nutshimish kuekut tante metekunu shuneau tshetshi natauakanitshi.

Tshika uish nas miste uskuistenan enua eshinakuashi tshekuaia. Passe Innuts eiash ntenitamuts, enu kamenupinits tshekuanu mak enu metshipinits tshekuanu nte kakuspinanitsh, tshika itamenimakanuts Innu utshimauts espinits tshekuanu, isishueuts Innuts misenitakanu espints shuneau. Nastesh memeatinamuts tshesinikauats kapiminashintshi mak kauauastantsheshintshi esinispeats eku minesipinits shuneaunu. Passe Innuts isishueuts muk utshimauts uitshieuts uikanishuaua mak uinuau uitshintuts. Eku passe isishuets meun tshekuan eshinakuash Innuts antsh tutamuts. Tshisenitenan essi animishitsh kapiminashits mak kauauastantshests tshetshi kau tshiuepinitsh. An kakuspinats tshipatshiminupanu uitshinueuts enuesh Innuts. An uineshapanitakantshi shuneau. Eku mitshi kusputs Innuts kutak pepunitshi. Meunu enu nanikutini etutak Innu utshimauts.

"Innuts uantutetaui nutshimish tshika ntuteuts mak ne Innuts minuenitamutsh, tapue passe Innuts miniuitshinikunan ntenitamuts. Nastesh minakatuenimukuts Innu utshimaua peikutau muk Innuts ituteuts nutshimish kuespunantshi, tshekuanu

kutakuts eash Innuts kauikusputshi passe Innuts ntenimauts mitshiminuenitamu tshentshi." *Manesh* Nanikutini passe Innuts miminuenitamuts enu eshitusentshi mak espinitantshi. Mak mushinau Innuts miminuenitamuts kamenupinitshi takapishenikea. Tshishue mushinau ntun inisishuanu nta takapishenikanish mak mushinau ntuanikamitunanu.

"Mishetupun tshash esi uapamauts ustinitshuts etats nutshimish tshash tante tshisenimaiats tante tsheuitshauts nastesh metshi nita uapamaiats. Essi mistetats nutshimitsh keuasiutshi auasits. Tshuitshaiats tante uisitats ete enu napitshitats pempinits tshekuanu. Nanikutini miminupanu eku manas mishuka minupinu eku etu tshipa kusputs entsh ustinitshuts etu minupunits. Eku nush mishuka neush tauts ustinitshuts etatui nutshimish nanikutini peik put nish meastakea tauts kuet minuats tshiuets. Senitats ustinitshuts eshitusenits nte uipits tshenua, eku ntenimauts tshikashuka tauts neka. Eskunte tshikauitshishikashunai tsheuish ntutshikakushinants. Tshishikashunaua esi upauits Innuts eapitshatsh kapiminashintshi mak nte uaitutets. Tshash tshimiste tshishika shunai esi kanakatuenimauts tshitsheniminuts mak stuasiminuts. Matakun tshekuan tshipa tshishikashunanu tshetshi mamu uitshintuts tshenuts mak ustinitshuts." *Kiti*

Tshekuanu Uesh Innuts Kaitutets Nutshimits
Tshika uin nas tutuaiats Innuts tshetshi mushinau tats nutshimits, tshipantusenita-muanan enu uishkauintutets. Takun tshekuan nanikanikunau uta utenats. Passe auassits muintuteuts tshash nutshimish, takunu tshekuanu mishue uetimikash nte utenatsh, takunu eapits Innuts ke uinuau uishiminupenitash esh uitshinikutsh, anu eshimakanitsh mak enu kashetshimakanitshi "Mishiue Ntuasiminaitsh" kishinikashunuani. Mak takunua etshishikashuts utapanuaua puk kie ututuaua mak pakushinantshets euashutaui shuneaunu mak kutuk tshekuanu esheshekanikunau, ataueutshiuap, ntukuntshuap, mak tshishinuau, stapitshitaunuai ntun mitshim, kanikamushits, kaniminantsh, mak pinku.

"Passe Innuts miuintuteuts nutshimish muk uiatuseuts, uitshishikashuts enua uastenimakanuaua mak kamituetishimaua passe enu animenitamuts mak passe mapitentamuts. Nuitamuapan enu Miste-

Tshenish and Tuamish / Tshenish mak Tuamish, 1989

CAMILLE FOUILLARD PHOTO

in nutshimit. Young people and children could go often to nutshimit where the elders could get back in action and teach them Innu ways. Elders could be hired to teach the culture. These programs have been undertaken in our communities before. There are elders who are willing to be instructors to teach these skills to young people. We could pay an elder in each camp. Nutshimit is a better place to hold these programs, because in the community there are too many distractions.

Many suggestions were made on ways we can encourage people to go out to the country and stay for longer periods of time. The Band Councils and the Innu Nation should get more involved in promoting this way of life. Job-sharing could help some young people go to the country. Some suggest that leaders meet with government to ease their restrictions or regulations on unemployment benefits, so people would not be penalized for quitting their jobs to go to nutshimit. People who work should be given a leave so they can go to the country without having to lose their jobs. Some people say that more funding for the Outpost Program would encourage more people to go to nutshimit. Many people mention incentives, like getting free things they need, could be a way to get more people interested in nutshimit. Like in Newfoundland, with the fishery, people lost their way of life because the fish are gone.

Now, with the package, they get money every week. This kind of program should apply here as well. We could pay people to go into the country, like a guaranteed annual income. Other communities have this kind of program that pays people to go to the country.

The people at Social Services could do more to support people going to nutshimit. People used to get three-month advances on their social assistance, but now some say they won't travel to the country because they only get monthly social assistance. This does not buy enough supplies for when they are in nutshimit, and sometimes they have a hard time finding food. The Unemployment Insurance could also help by not taking so long to straighten out all the paperwork for people when they come back from the bush and need their cheques.

Meetings need to be held before people go out to nutshimit so that there can be better planning of the Outpost Program. Then maybe we would find out what the problems are. We could make sure the store has the supplies we need. Fair guidelines and policies must be developed to deal with the abuse and overspending. We also need to have rules for what will happen if somebody abuses the program. Band Councils and Kaupaunantsh co-ordinators need to practise how to say "No" to the people. They can't make all the families happy and satisfied all the time. There should be strict control on the budget.

> "There should be an advertisement, like put up a notice around the village to let people know that the Outpost Program is happening and to give them a deadline. There should be a decision on what date the people will go or come. Reservations should be made for those who want to go. There should be an agreement for people to sign, which explains what date they want to go and what date they will be picked up on." *Innu peacekeepers*

Some people said the co-ordinator should be well qualified for the job. A number of people said the program is understaffed. The co-ordinator should have an assistant to help him out. In the long term, we should get our own aircraft. It would be a wise investment for the Outpost Program. People should also be encouraged to train as pilots.

To save money, people could use skidoos to travel to the country. It is easy and fast, and cheaper than

Pinip, nuitshishikashun kauashunan shuneau. Eku ntuk tshikisi euashunapen shuneau. Shuneau tshika apatshitaiapin tshetshi ian tshutapan." *Tshatsh*

Shitakunapun kustineu Innua tshetshi tantshi nutshimish, miste akushuts Innuts tshetshi tats nutshimish, passe muinikitaueuts kauitshiminimatsh uitsheuakanuaua. eku kutakuts tshishue tshash miste shutshimikinu esiminits, tshikasitshi minuts nu shitakunapunu nikatats, passe Innuts muintuteuts nutshimish kustamuts tshetshi miste akushits mak tshetshi utshipitukutsh.

Passe isishuets takun tshekuan uishkataiats nte nushimitsh, takunu tshekuanu uestaskakutsh enkunu enu kuestas. Kustumuts eapitsh tshetshi muestatas, kutukuts kustamuts tshetshi pishikanitshi uitshuaua kaetatuaui.

"Nastesh passe Innuts muitauts nte nutshimish ntenitamuts mitakun nte nastesh atuseun mak tshetutakantsh tshekuan, eku nin niseniten esi mishatsh atuseun nte nutshimish. Entsh ustinitshuts anush, enu nesishuets matauts ete uastepimakets mak kashetshimakanitsh nastesh minikuatu ntuteuts nte tepiskantshi. Mitshi nutshiniskueuts nte etipiskants, kuekut tante tepiskanu nte eku kuestatshitsh, tshishue tshetshinue nipaianu etaiantshi. Ukamuats mak utamuats iteutsni utauasimuaua, tshetshi tshetshnue nipantshi, tshishue tshika miste atusenau uapashe." *Etuetis*

Passe Innuts kustamuts tshetshi kuspit enu uish kustas tshetshi pikupeakanitsh etusetaui put kie unapemuaua put utiskuemuaua etusentaui. Mak takunu tshekuanu tsheknaka-tuenitas, etatuaui ute Utshimassit, tshishue miskuanu enu tshetshi uepinas auen. Pisse stesishuean manimin tshetshi punituseau. Mak kukukuts passe tshashi tshipunuts etatusets. Mak passe tshiutinimuts enu kau kaititusets katsh takushintuaui stesishuean, tshishue minuau tshimamitishi nenikanu uaapitshitaiaui.

Nanikutini pise Innuts mitshikusputs enu kamiste atusetuaui. Mak mitshi ashamakanuts mitshimitshimaua, tshetshi nistu pishuma tatsh nte neka mak mipimpinua ustukuanishumuaua. Tante tshipa utinam auen nist pishimua shuneanu tshetshi ntutet nte nutshimish. Mitshiminikuts nastesh tshekuanu mitshim utshimaua Innuts kutakuts meshantsh utatuseunuaua, tshishue pessish tashuts nutshimish ntupitaui.

Sheskutimashunants eapits anmenitakun, animenimeuts passe Innuts utuasimuaua, tshetshi kaskutimashuntaue mekuats etats nushmish. Kusteuts tshetshi aiashape-akanitshi mak tshetshi katshishitants kaskutimashuntshi. Tshinan pisse stenimaiats stuasiminu tshetshi skutimashuts, muk enu eshiskutimakanitsh nte mak etenitamau ke tshinai mak uantuteau nte nutshimit.

Mitshim eapits takun eanimak enu uamitshits mak uakamitshish. Auassits mak tshinau Innuts miui mitshuts enu nutshimit mitshiminu. Muk minuenitamuts tshetshi mitshits, mitshiminu nishekush katakunua mak tshikea.

Tshishue Mishen Tshekuan Tshika Uish Neush Tai Nte Nutshimit

Passe Innuts isishuets neush nte tshipataian nutshimit, kutukuts isishuets tshikatshitshi ashapatanan pishumukan. Pusk uta tshipasitai nte nutshimit mak pusk uta utenats. Eku mak passe uinuau Innuts tshika senitamuts uasitats nte nutshimit. Eku passe Innuts isishueuts tshipatshi aiatinenan, tshekasishuka miste pitamuts auasits skutimashuts. Kaskutimashet tshika tshitutam tshetshi uishat enu Inua ketanua-ni nutshimit. Eku ma tshipatshiskutamueuts ete auasa.

Auentshi uantusenitakau nutshimits atuseunu, tshipatshitutean tshetshi tutamak atuseun nte nutshimit, eku patush tshipaseniteain mak etenitakuash nte nutshimit, Innu Utshimau tshipatshitutam tshetshi takunits nutshimits atuseunu. Ete nteshe nutshimits, auasits mak ustinitshuts mushinau tshipatshimeuts tshenua etantuaui nutshimit, tshetshi skutimashuts uipits enitinanitsh. Tshenuts tshipa utinakanuts tsheshi skutimatshesh uipats kainitanitsh enua tshekuana tshipa minupinua minuatsh uta utenatsh. Tauts nte tshenuts uauskuuistas mak uaskutamuats auasa enu uipats skutimatsheunu. Tshipatshishikuakanuts enu skutimatshetau tshenuts. Nutshimit etu minuau tshetshi skutimanshunants, uipats kaishiniunantsh, mauats ute kistitananua tshishue mishau tshekuan tshipautimapatean.

Mishen tshekuan tshipa uish meskeian mak, tshipa uitamuanantsh ustinitshutsh tshika uishneush tauts nushimitsh, Innu Utshimauts mak Innu neshin tshipa uitshinueuts uatutakanitsh uenu tshekuanu uauitshinikushinantshi. Enkunu passe auasits tshipa uish uikusputs, passe Innuts itenitamuts utshimauts tshipa

charter planes. All we do is pack our gear and go into the barrens. Some people say there should be less use of machines. People used to use their physical strength when they went to nutshimit. Some say people should be given fewer supplies. If people have good-paying jobs, they could pay their own way.

Some people say we need to do research into our history in nutshimit to keep finding out who we really are as Innu. We should gather artifacts, do anthropological studies on our people. We should gather facts and get people on site in nutshimit to tell us what they know. We should go to the burial grounds of our ancestors. We can find out what these people did if we dig deep deep in the ground, like in archaeology.

TAKING CARE OF OUR SPIRITUALITY

In the People's Inquiry, we said we needed to make peace with the animal spirits. We have been working on this. Many of us have stopped being embarrassed about talking about these things. We've stopped listening to the church telling us these beliefs were evil. How could they say this religion was evil? It existed for thousands of years, far longer than the R.C. religion. We are beginning to respect and honour what our tshenut (elders) say about these sacred practices. They are the ones who can tell us how many animals we can kill, so we won't kill too many. We did not bother to listen to our elders and they stopped talking to us. They have started to speak again, and we must really listen. They have so much knowledge that we need to learn. We need to act fast on this. We have only a small number of elders in our community.

"To prepare for the mukushan, the meat must be scraped off the caribou bones, the bones must be crushed. The marrow must be saved from the bones and mixed with the mukushan. The bones are boiled with the fat, and the oil or grease must be taken out. The grease stays on the surface so it can be taken out by using a large spoon. Then you mix it with the marrow and let it freeze. According to Innu tradition, all this must be done very carefully as directed by an elder or the person in charge of the mukushan. The caribou broth must be in a cool place, or cooled in the snow. When there is grease left over on it, it can be eaten as a mini-mukushan, but also should be handled carefully and not wasted. Nothing must be wasted. Usually older people eat first at the mukushan, and then younger people.

Miste-Pinip, 1992

CAMILLE FOUILLARD PHOTO

"The drumming and singing is carried out by an elder, who is knowledgeable about the animals and their spirit world. This is a thanksgiving to the caribou spirit, a celebration of a successful hunt. The person can sing a song to communicate with the caribou spirit. The songs he sings are according to what he sees through the drum or his dreams. The songs are very important to an elder, and must be kept to himself until he is ready to give them away." *Shuash*

"I learned about our traditional medicines at the camp for the families and the kids who came back from Poundmakers. The things our elders were showing the other elders from Poundmakers were things I didn't know before. One elder was showing the plants they used for medicine. I also watched our elders in the sweat, seeing how they cleansed themselves. The younger people are learning stuff from the elders. That is happening now. We won't lose it all. The elders seem like they have started talking." *Epa*

Elders and hunters are talking about their dreams. Young people are dreaming about the drum, and when

tshiemeuts tsheutshimaua, tshetshi kashuka etenita-
minukuts enu kakustanakua mak tshetshi uetushuet.
Anta pempanits ustukuanish shuneau eku ma tsheka
skustinakanu auen uakuspitshi put kie tshetshi kauni-
tat utatuseun. Minuenitamuts passe nanikutini
maikantuaui tshekuanu mak tshekuaia enkunu enu
passe Innut, tshipauish minuenitamuts tshetshi ntutets
nte nutshimit ete ma nipunants, nutimeshets tshash
unitauts tshash mitanuau nimesha. Eku maiakanits
tshekuanu, minakanuts shuneanu eshikumpeik meastakea. Enkun ke tshipa tshi nishinakun ute tshipa
tshishikuakanu Innu uatatshi nutshimit. Nas ente
pempanitshi ushuneam tshipa itentakunu. Kutukuts
ete auentshi tutuekanitshen uish tat nte nutshimits.

Kaatuseshits nte mitshimutshimaua nas tshipa mist-
iuitsheutsh uatantshi nutshimits Innua. Tshiminakani-
pantsh nist pishuma auen mitshim shuneanu uatatshi
nte neka, eku tshash pisse muitauts nte nutshimish
tante kuekut muk peik pishuma ashamakanuts. Eku
nastesh minispanutsh tshetshi neustatsh, mak kaetaku-
nitshi nushmish mitshimuni. Ustukuanimisha auen
eapits tshipa tshinistipa minupununitakanua etatshi
auen nutshimit. Eku tshikasishuka mista tutakunua,
mitshinanikea at takushintshi mak tshe tshinistipa
tantshi utshikema.

Aianimuanipan pita esk ekakuspitaui Innuts, tshetshi ueueshitakantsh uakuspinantsh. Tshetshi min-
upintsh etu kuespunantshi. Mak tshipantusenitakanu
pita tshekuan kamenupints, eapits ataueutshiuapits,
tshipa tshishats takun tshekuan uantapatshitakansh
tshikaushitakanu meshinanikan. Tshetsh kamapiuen-
takan shuneau mak tshetshika ueshampintikants
shuneau uakuspinantshi tshipapenimakanu. Ke auen
kanetuta enu ueshitakanitsh mishinanikanu. Innuts
utshimauts mak kaupaunantsh katusesisits tshipaseni-
tamuts, tshipa teuts enu Innua "Mauats." Animan
tshetshi minuenitaiakan Innu mak utuassiminua mak
uinuau enitits, tshipa nakatuenitenan eku nas tshe
nesh mestanakan shuneau.

"Tshipa ikuaskuanikanu mishinanikan tshishats
uakuspitaui Innuts, mak nta tshesipinantsh. Tshipa
ishishuanu nte tshishuk uakuspaunakanitsh Innuts
mak ntshe uapushits. Tshipatshishatsh utinakanu
utetapuakan euen uakuspit. Tshipa mishinataushuts
auentshi uakuspits mak nta uanatankushits." *Innu
kamakunueshits*

Innuts passe isishuets tshipa utinakanu auen tshetshi minu atuset nete kaupaunantsh atuseunu. Mak
tshipa tanuau tsheuitshikut auenua eatuset esk nte
tshipa tshiteanan tshinan tshikapiminashi-minu. Eku
tshikasishuka mistemestenan shuneau. Tshepa uitamuakanuts etu Innuts tshetshi kapimpinita shiuts.

Etu uimeatinimau shuneaminu, utapanisa tshipa
apatshitakanua ui kuspinants. Nastesh manimin mak
tshishue tshipanua utapaea enu esi mista apitshakant
kapiminashits. Muk stet naunashunai uatshipi tshinaui
muk kuet stuteak—passe isishuets tsheksishuka mista
apatshitakunu pempints tshekuan, Innuts uinuau apit-
shitapants utitshiuaua uakuspitaui. Passe Innuts tshitshe mistiminakanuts tshekuanu uantutetuaui nutshimish nas minu tshishikuakanuts, Innuts passe
tshipa uitshishikashuts nte uakuspitaui.

Passe Innuts isishuets tshipatshitutenan tshetshi
ntusenitamak uipats tshekuan nte nutshimit. En tshetshi etu senitamak enniuiak, tshipa mamushatshuneai
uipats tshekuaia. Innuts uipats kaintutusets mak
tshenuts tshipa skutimakunaets, tshipa ninateian ete
uipats Innuts pemishinitsh nepitaui. Tshipa uitamaku-
naets Innuts eshinakunitsh nte uipats.

ENAKATUENINAMAU ESHEMAIAU

Kaushitakantsh ene mishinanikan stisishuenaipan,
tshetshi mintutuauts aueshishits stutuskatenan en esk.
Tshash tshimitshetinan katshinakuenimunak,
euauitakantshi tshekuan. Tshash tshipunan enituta-
mak emeun, kantukunak ene kamitshit utatuseun.
Tshekuan uish nisishuetau kamitshit enu utemeun
uipats enu uish eamashipants Innuts esk ente eka seni-
tas anutsh emeutshuap emeunu. Tshash tshisenitean
tshipa uish nitutenan mak tshetshi mintutamak enu
tshenut kaish uitamatauts enu uinuau eshe maiats.
Uinuau entsh eapits tshipa tshiuitamakunaiets
tshesinipanimak aueshisha eku tshikasi mistinipaiuts
aueshishitshi muitshuinitutu uaiaits tshenuts uatu-
mataui tshekuanu. Eku mitshiui tshash stutukunaits.
Eku tshash minuats tshetuts enkunu eku tshipaunitu-
tuaiats eku. Uinuau miste senitamuts tshekuan anu
uanaskutimashunak. Tshinistipa tshipa uituteian eku
tshash meshuka tauts tshenuts ute etaiak.

"Uaakantshi tshetshi mupimants nas pita
tshishikutishikanua uskea. Kuet pikuanikantshi
uskea kuet pikatankantshi tshetsh enpimin katshi
utetshi. Eku menakantsh en pimin, uesh nta takun

they are ready, they should come forward and take their place playing the drum. If you dream about it, you can play the drum. Some think our traditional spirituality will be hard to bring back, like with the shaking tent. Is there anyone who says they can do it? There are some elders who believe that the shaking tent could be revived. With other things, it won't be so hard, like how to respect the animals, how to build sweat lodges, the teachings in the legends, drumming and singing, the mukushan—those things that have not disappeared.

"There is an elder here that has dealt with the shaking tent. Only the shaman person who has experienced the shaking tent can talk about it. I have seen it performed but I have never experienced it. People here have experience using the drum, but they don't have a lot of songs of their own. If a person had a lot of songs to sing with the drum, he might be able to experience the shaking tent and know about it. A lot of white persons want to know about the shaking tent, but I don't know the answers. I have never seen a white person or the government performing the shaking tent. I cannot talk about these spiritual practices when the government is still trying to ruin us. I can only talk about the bones and the sweat lodges, about the caribou bones, how to take care of them. I don't know how many hundreds of years this has been done. I still carry on that tradition."
Kaniuekutat, elder

Our sacred practices help us find a way to hunt. In the past, when we ran out of animals to eat, we always used metusheun (shamanism). We had a spirit guiding our hunters. This spirit would help them know when to take their families in the country, how to take care of the animals and hang the bones in the trees. This spirit would be passed on from one person to another. The person who received this spirit would then be able to sing the songs and he would become a very good hunter. He would receive the knowledge he needed. The spirits talk to us through our dreams to tell us what we will get by hunting. Spirits and givers send messages in our dreams. People have what you call shadows, they are part of you—the spirits that you have when you are dreaming. They go travelling, almost like ghosts.

Some spiritual traditions are being revived. We now have sweat lodges again after many years of not having them. Some of us believe this is very important to the survival of our culture. Others fear that the way the sweat lodges are being done now is not our way, but the way of other First Nations. We used to use the sweat lodge to heal only the physical body. Can we allow our cultural practices to be influenced by the cultures of other First Nations? Should we only practise our ways as our ancestors did? Both elders and younger people have different opinions and answers to these questions.

"To preserve or revive our culture, we should have more sweat lodges, shaking tents and more advice from our elders, not from the other tribes across Canada." *Tepit*

"Back in those days, we only used the sweat lodge when somebody was ill, and we never used it in the evenings. But today in nutshimit, one time we were in the sweat and one of my sons was in there too. He spoke and shared and it really surprised me. He asked questions about life in nutshimit and how we feel today. And he complimented the beauty of nature where we live. He believes the sweat lodge has helped him whenever he is sick. He surprised me. That's why I feel different today about the sweat lodges. Back then, my grandfather only sang, and today everything is happening." *Shanutish*

"I feel strange about the sweat lodge they have today. It is not the same as the one that my grandfather performed. The ones they perform today is one they got from other people. The one we used to have was built inside a tent. The one they have today is done outside. That is not how the Innu sweat. Young people who are doing a lot of sweats, I feel like they are abusing the sweat lodge, because they can set it up anywhere." *Kaniuekutat, elder*

"What is happening here now is that people know we are a sick people in a spiritual sense. That is the reason why the young people go to the sweat lodge to be well again. I brought my three children in the sweat lodge over the weekend. It was their first time and they were afraid of it. But I saw a baby in the sweat lodge and he stayed all the way through." *Kiti*

Some people say we should start practising our spiritual ways in the community as well as in the country. For example, some of us have begun to take care of the bones and have been picking up the caribou bones off the ground in the village. We could also hang the wings

ni-pimin kuet meanikantsh miste emikuan napit-shakant. Kuet mamu astanakantsh pimin mak uina, kuet miskutitakantsh nash en mentutakanu mishiue tshekuan. Emin skutimatshet nte etat tshenu put kie kutuk auen anakatuenitak enu mukushanu. Uskea muskmin takastakanu nte tinakatsh put kie nte kun-ish eku etukuashi nta pessish pimin eku maneanikantshini tshetshi mitshinants esk etu. Nas en meatshitakanu nutshikakantshi uskea uamup-mantsh, nastesh minanuitakanu tshekuan, tshenuts mitshuts nistam kuet masten ustinitshuts.

"Kaniminantsh mak kanakamut mushinau tshenut tutamuts en menusenimat aueshisha. Enu uistutas naskumeuts enua utshimaminua katshiashamukuts aueshisha, nekumut enu auen tapiskut eimiatshi aueshisha utemeunish. Tshishue miste espiteni-takunu unikamun tshenu nekamutshi uin enu tshika nauenitum, esk eka minuet." *Shuash*

"Niseniten uipats etapitshitakantsh Innuts uipats untukunumuaua en uesh senitaman euapimikau auentshi etutas, mak euitamuats kutuka auasa. Minineniteapin enu uipats eshinakuashi Innu unutukunama patush uanapataman, mak pinetiman eshinakunikueni mak nuuapamaut eapits auentshi esh metishuts mak enu uish kauinakushits nteni-mauts auassits tshash tshishipanuts eskutimakuts tshenua tshika tshitshi unitanan mishiue mak tshash tshenut. Pitshenik aianimuets." *Epa*

Tshenuts mak kantuiuts tipatimuts upuamunuaua, mak ustinitshuts tshash tshipuateuts teuenikea. Eku nash tshash uitutakuaui eku tshipa utineuts teuenikea mak uinuau tshetshi nikamuts puatit ke muk tshin teuenike tshipa tshinikamun ke. Tshika miskuau tapue tshetshiminuatsh kastinimak ene uipats kaishemaiak en tapue tsheanimak kushapashikan ma nte tau auen stenimauau tshika kashiu tshetshi minuats tutak kushapashikanu. Tauts tapue passe tshenuts etenitats tshetshi minuats minupinits kushapashikanu. Mak enu kutukunu tshekuanu, anu tshetshi nakatuenimauts tshaueshishiminuts, mak tsheush ushitakants mtashan-shuap, mak eskutimashunants atinukaets, mak teuenike enikamunants, mak tshe neshasheantsh esk enu passe tshekuaia nukea etutakantshi.

"Tau uta peik tshenu nutshikash kushapashikanu, mak e meteut auen tshipatshiuauitam mak kesiut kushapashikanu. Auentshi pase senitamuts uinuau

unikamunuaua. Mak teuenikea mistisenitak auen nukumuna eku tshipatshitutam eapits kusha-pashikanu, mishetitshe kakeshau uasenita enu kushapashikanu. Muk minisenitamuan tshekuanu. Nastesh minita uapamau kakeshau put kie tsheut-shimau tshetshi nutshikash kushapashikanu. Mintshi uauiten tshekuan eshinakuats esk tsheutshimau uapikuntak muk enua mpatshiuauiten uskea mak aueshishitsh kasinakatuenimauts, nastesh minusen-iten etatu push eshiniunantsh muk esk tapue nakat-ueniten uipats kaitinantsh." *Kaniekutat*

Takun tapue tshekuan nanikutini uatshinukunak uantiuiunaui, uipats ete kaetatuaui aueshishish apat-shitakanipan kushapashikan, takunipan uatshinikut tshekuanu etuiutshi auen. Mak senimukuts tshekuanu tshetshi ntutets ete nutshimish mak tshetshi minuku-ats aueshisah nepatuaui mak tshetshi ekutats uskea nte mistikuts. Auen enu tsheshenitak etitak mintushi-unu eku uin miskuts tshipa nitauntuiuiu. Mak tshipa nikamu teuenikea. Nanikutini ste minikunai tshekuan nte uish tshipuamunatsh tsheish nutiunak. Mak ntshe stashakuts tshinuau in pueuatimini tshekuan. Mak pueuateti mentushiun nanikutini tshipa nispanuts tshipea.

Eshe meteunantshi pesish nukun, tshash eapits tukuea mitishantshuapa, uipats ete kakatikuashi, passe tshinai minuau ineshinakuash enkun tsheuish minuats kastinamak uipats stiniunu. Passe itenitamuts eash kispanua mak eash nishinakun tsheka tshekuan. Esh ushitakantsh mak ntapitshitakanipan nakushitshi auen nte uiats, tshika tapuetean a tshenishinakutaiau. Kutukuts Innuts uaiueshinakutats uinuau put kie tshi-nai tipan tshipa ishinakutaia tshinai ete uipats stin-iminuts katutamuake. Uinuau enu muk senitamuts tshipaisishuets, Innuts mak ustinitshuts.

"Etu uisenitamak tshinai uipats kaishiniunants mushinau put shipa kutshipintaia mtishantshuap put kie kushapashikan mak uinuau tshitsheniminutsh tshipaskutimakunaets, mauats nte kutuk uaiu Innu nte kamisits." *Tepit*

"Uipats ete muk nakushitshi auen apitshitatinakanu mtishantshuapi mak minita apitshitakanu uetakushitshi. Eku nte nush nutshimish peikuau nipisen mak peik nikus pisseu nuauitamakunan enu tshekuanu, eku nimiste miskatenimau. Uauitam enu tshekunu ute nutshimish mak etenitamutshish. Mak

Relocation meeting on site, Nutuashish / Kauiatikuants aianimuanipan nte Nutuashish, 1992

CAMILLE FOUILLARD PHOTO

of the goose outside on the branches instead of using them to sweep the dust like some women do in the community now. That is not the way to do it. Also we should hang the antlers on tree branches rather than leave them on the ground. We are not trophy hunters or weekend hunters. We should become Innu hunters again.

"I think we can learn about the culture in the community too. Now, it's impossible to hang the bones in the community. If we are told about it, we might. If when we were growing up, we were told to respect these things, we would. I'm learning now not to abuse the animals and the land, to respect the animal spirits. We can't abuse their land. We have to make it better for our children and the great-grandchildren we will have." *Nupi*

"We can teach our children about their spirituality. I don't think we will ever lose our traditions. Our spirituality can be taught anywhere. Innu people don't just live in the country; they also live in the village." *Katinin*

Some of us suggest we could hold drum dances, mukushan and other special events in the community. We could have culture teaching weeks, spiritual weeks for the elders and the whole community. We could have rituals in the community like other Natives where they offer tobacco to the elders. We need revival times, where people talk to each other more and more through home visits. Some people say we should develop these cultural programs ourselves because right now non-Innu organizations introduce programs about our culture rather than us doing it.

SELF-GOVERNMENT: ASSERTING OUR HUMAN RIGHTS

"Some of our children know what the government is doing to us, and they are fighting against it. Their children will take over this fight. They will try to see what the government is really doing. The things we have been doing, like protesting, blocking the runways, going to Ottawa, with these kinds of things we are showing our children how to be strong, how to fight for their rights." *Akatis*

Since the release of the People's Inquiry report, significant steps have been taken by the community to follow up on its recommendations and to assert our rights. One of the things we have tried to do is to involve the elders more in making decisions. Many of us say it is time to give our tshenut their rightful place. Governments created the Band Council and the Innu Nation so that one person, like the chief, could do the speaking for us. The Innu Nation is responsible for asserting political and land rights for the Innu of Sheshatshiu and Utshimassit. Its board has seven members from Utshimassit. It is also developing health, justice, social, education, environmental, economic and communications programs. At this time ten people work for the Innu Nation in Utshimassit. Our Band Council is staffed by sixteen people. It is responsible for providing community services, such as housing, water and sewer, garbage collection and recreation programs. It also administers the Outpost Program.

Some people complain that the Band Council and the Innu Nation only help some people, like their relatives, and not others. They don't see some people as their responsibility, even if they really need help. But the main problem with the Innu Nation and the Band Council is that governments recognize only these leaders and not the tshenut. Some say the tshenut are ignored when governments flash money to the younger generation. They say our leaders are money-chasing and become blindfolded by the dollar sign. Some of us believe these institutions don't work right for us. Some leaders admit they have made mistakes, but they say in their jobs, they are caught between both worlds.

"Sometimes I find it hard to deal with the elders because there is a lack of understanding of the white culture. One elder who goes to a lot of meetings outside keeps pounding us, the young leaders, that he wants to see the big boss—the government. He wants

enu esi minuashintsh nte nutshimit, nuitshinikunaua nte niten metishunani eakushinani nimiskatenimau katshi isisheuts. Enkun uish eash itenitaman anutsh mak mitishantshuap. Uipats nte muk nikamupan nimushupe eku nutsh tshash mishiue tshekuan initimikan." *Shanutish*

"Tshishue eash nteniten mitishantshuap anutsh eshinakutakantsh, meunu enu nishinakutapan nimushumpe ueshita, enu anutsh kushinakutautshi kutuka enua Innua ishinakutanua. En ninai napitshitaiats pitakamits nte Innutshuapits tutakanu. Eku uinuau ueuetimitsh ketshemetautshi meunu enu eshmitishut Innu nas ntenimauts ustinitshuts piuenitamuts ene esh mitishuts mak nastesh miminutauts." *Kaniuekutat*

"Tshekuan eshinakuash anush tshinai Innuts stakushinai ekase nitamak tshekuan. Enkunu enu uish pisets ustinitshut. Tshetshi minuats minushits nipitakapants nist ntuasimits nte mitishanish enkunu enu ueskats patikakau. Eku tshishue kustamuts eku nuapamau nte auasis peshisit nash tshishimitishu nineuinanitsh." *Kiti*

Tshipakutshitaia tsheskutimashunak nte mak ete uesh nutshimits. Tshash pise tshiseniteshinai tshenesh nakatuenitamak tshekuan mak uskea mak tshenesh nakatuenimauts pineshikits mak tshe tshiakutaik katshinipatamauki tshekuan, tshetshi minukutaiak. Meun eshinakuash tshekuan tshetshi mamashikantsh mak tshika akutaiets niunapamakuau esketsh. Tshinai ui kantuiuts meu tshinan kamamashikat ntuiunu.

"Tshipa eapitsh-senitean uipats ka uish iniunants uta kistitaiaua. Tshishue animin tshetshi akutakantshi uskea uta kitautshi Innuts uitamakunau etui eku put tshipa tshitutamuts. Uipats nte esk euasiuiak nuauitakunaipin tsheshi speuatimash tshekuan tshash peshish niseniten tshekuan kanishispeuaten assin. Aueshishits puk kie aueshish utipenimikushima mitshui piuenitenan assin. Nash tshipa minututanan tshetshi apashitats ente stuasiminuts mak utuasimuaua mak tshusiminuts." *Nupi*

"Tshipakustimuakanutsh ntenimauts auasits enu esh emantshi uipats Innua. Tshikatshi nita unitanan eshniunau nte uipats. Muk tapue meshuka tauts auentshi nutshimit. Tauts ute eapits utenatsh." *Katinin*

Ntenitamuts passe auentshi tshinan tipan tutean teuenike kaniminants mak tshetshi asheauk mak nte tshekuan uatutakantshi uta tshekuan Utshimassits tshikatutea ni tatumastakea tshetshi skutimashunau uipats kaitinants. Mak tatumastakea tshenuts mak mishiue auentshi tshipa mamutaia tshetshi nte nist tats tshenuts tshipaminakanutsh tshekuanu entsh eash Innu katutu-ueutshi utinimuaua. Tshipa tshi uitsh tishunai en muk tshetshi aianmueauk. Mak emupistatunak. Passe auentshi esishuets tshinaiu tshipa tshitu tashunai at eapits kauiuitshinikunak. Nanikutini eash asits tsheuish skutimakunai tshekuan tshinai u tshipaskutimashunaiapin.

Tshetshi Tipenimushunak, Tshinan Eshikunentamak Stepentamunu

Shash pesse auassit tshissenitamut etutatak tsheutshimau. Kie shash nenu mashikamuts uinuau kuessipennuau tshika mashitsheut mamishistitaui nas tshekui minu nitussenitamut etutatak tsheutshimau. Netshekuan kaishi-mashitsheiak, miam kanimaskutitsheiak, kapitepeitunantsh katueut kapiminashit, kie nete utauat, kanatshinima-skuetshiak eukun ume tshekuanu kassinu kaieitiak, tshitshiskutamuanut stuassiminuts tsheishi mashitshet tshetshi shutshit kie tan tshipa tutamut tsheutshi nistuapatekenet utipentamunuau.

Essi-unuipentan mishineke kantussentan Utshimassit espinits mamuetetau mishineke shash pessish tshitshipinu tshekuan kaui-ishiui-tshinushunanut. Tshetshi tshinan ssenitamak stipentamunu. Peik ne-tshekuan nantim kaui-ishi-kutshitaiak tshetshi tutamak eukun kaitenitamak tshenut nantim tshetshi, tat eianimuantshi kie tshekuan uatutakentshi. Uin nenu tsheutshimau tshiminepan Innu Nation kie Innu utshimau eku peik ne-muk Innu tshika petakushu eukun ne innutshimau stissishuenan, eku tshipaminanut tshenut, tshetshi minu nistuapamakut kie nte nikan tshipa iananuts Innu Nation uin-utatusseun nta tsheutshimat tshetshi uauitak tshekuanu eka menupinikuak kie assinu tshetshi uauitak tapiskut nenu atuskatam Utshimassit mak Sheshatshit. Ntshe pempintat Innu Nation, nishu-ashutat teshut ute Utshimassit. Shash-e-atuskateu ne-tshekuan eka menupinikuiak kamakunueshiu atusseun, kie ntshen kueueshianutshi Innut kie tshekuan eiapishat miam ne-etenitakuak auassit essi eka minupanits. Kie ne-

CAMILLE FOUILLARD PHOTO

Miste-Shishin ice-fishing / Miste-Shishin kusepan, 1992

to ask him why he doesn't want to help our people. We tell him what we know, how hard it is to deal with those people. We keep telling him that it wouldn't do any good. But he finds it hard to understand. If the government is not going to do anything to help us, the elder thinks they should tell us. We explain to elders that we need to protest and write letters. But to the elders, the government is like the trader. In those days, when Innu asked for things, they would get them. Today, the elders don't know the government structure." *Tshatsh, Innu Nation vice-president*

"The elders would like to see us deal with the ministers as nation-to-nation. They see us leaders as going out for meetings with the top people, but we only deal with the representatives that are being sent by the various ministers. They don't understand that. One of the hardest things that I find in being a leader is that I have a lot of responsibilities for the people. As a leader you have to live on both sides, both the Innu and the non-Native way. You have to follow the white man's way of living; you have to be able to understand their ways. You have to choose which path you will go for the people. Because people depend on you a lot, you want to take the steps towards what the people want, but the government also pressures me to do things their way. It is dividing the leaders, not in the sense that there is division amongst the leaders, but dividing us personally. I find this hard." *Kiti, Band Council chief*

But leaders are also recognizing that they want to include tshenut in real leadership roles. They are involving elders as consultants to the Innu Nation and the Band Council, as advisors around issues such as land claims. Elders go with the leaders to negotiation meetings with government as the ones who can show the governments that this is our land. The elders are also seen by the leaders as our wildlife officers. One elder is a real expert on the caribou. He knows more than Stuart Luttich, the wildlife biologist in Goose Bay. Some people have suggested that all the elders be gathered together to form an elders' committee. Other agencies, such as the school and Social Services, also need to get elders involved in their work and decision-making.

Our decisions should be based on the best information and advice available. We have made many political mistakes. Some people say leaders have to be able to take criticism and respect the opinion of others. They should do more to show young people what is good about being Innu. They should guide us to a path which leads to our destiny, not to any government. Another leadership problem is we need more planning, both short-term and long-term planning. We shouldn't jump at anything that everybody says because we don't know if it is the right thing for us.

Leaders need to work together as well as the various organizations. Elected and non-elected leaders need training in administration and the management of our own affairs. They need more education. They need to share more of the power with the people who elect them. People working on these problems with the different agencies, including the Band Council and the Innu Nation, shouldn't be there for the money. They need to be there to serve their people, not please their bosses. At the same time, people in the community also need to take responsibility to let the Band Council and the Innu Nation know what they want.

Some of us say that sometimes there is corruption in our band councils. We need to set up policies which meet the needs of the people. We should follow strict guidelines. Another suggestion was that the government should audit the councils to shake up the abusive behaviour so it will stop.

We have done a lot of research into different aspects of our lives and issues we need to address. We are making demands to the government. We want responses,

tshekuan uiapatamak pakunikan kie atusseuna kie tshetshi etu-minu-petakuats tshekuan eishiatussants. Anutsh-u-peikunueshut Innut etusset nte Innu Nation ute-Utshimassit. Eku nte Utshimassit Innutshimau peikunueshut ashu-ashutat etusset uentshi. Eukunts uinuau innutshimaut kassinu tshekuanu atuskatamut ute Utshimassit miam-ne mitshuapa, nipinu kie metshapunu, kauepinashunanunts kie kametuanun kie uinuau eiapit pimpintaut kaupaunantsh.

Kutets-ents Innut memenuenitamut eshi-pimpintshi Innu utshimau kie Innu Nation memeshue uitshieut, Innu iteuts, muk uikanishuau uitshieut eku-kuteka uenu nastesh metshitapameut issishueut Innuts. Nimieu ninan tshetshi ui-tshintshit kutakuts Innuts itenimeuts, at-ma-shuka tshitshue uauitshinikushitau Innut, mui-uitshiakanuts-ni. Muk- umuenu uets eka menupinits Innutshimaut mak Innu Nation, uinuau nenu muk nistunakut tsheutshimau eku nenu tshenu metshitapemeu nenu tsheutshimau. Kutekets Innut issishueuts, tshenut nastesh metshitapamakenuts tsheutshimau ueuashipitamunt shunianu umenu euassiun innutshimau. Kutakut Innuts ishishueuts, ntshe-Innu-utshimaut. Muk shunianu nashamut kie akukuepeshut nenu shuniau kemishinekenua. Kie tshinan tshessentenan ne-eka shuka menuat eshianimiunak. Kie Innu-utshimaut uitamueut Innu nenu tshessentak eka mentutak kie peteik, muk issishenut nte ninan ntatusseunats tetauts nta miam nimitshimushinan, nte tetshe Innut kie nte kakeshau.

"Nanikutini tshitshue nitanimenimauts tshenut essieka-shuka nistutak. Kakeshau eshiniun. Peik nte tshenu mushinau uishamakanu eianimuantshi nete uaiu, mushinau nitashikuatekunan ninan uetshimautshit, ui-uapameu nenu misteutshemau, tsheutshimau. Niui-uitamuau iteu tshekuanu uets eka uitshitak tshinan eniuak. Eku niminu-uitamuanan ninan eshitshentamutshit. Essi-animishit tsheutshimau tshetshi tapuetak uatamuakan tshekuanu. Kie niuitamuanan ume-tshenu, metsheketshi eiapits minupinu-ntanan muk metshi-nistutam. Itenitamut uinuau tshenut eka ua-uitshituakue tsheutshimau tshipa uitamakunu. Niminu uitamuanan-tshenut tshekui tutenan tshekuan tshetshi akuiak tsheutshimau, miam tshipa nimaskueitshenan, kie tshipa mishinitshenan tshetshi nist-matenimitak tsheutshimau. Muk anutsh tshenut itentemuts, tsheutshimau miam kantutauet uipats utshimaut eukun iteni-

takushitshe tsheutshimau itenimeuts. Miam-neteuipats netuentamuatau utshimau tshekuanu kueminikuts. Tshenut, messenimeut nenu anutsh eshipimpinit tsheutshimau." *Tshatsh, pitutshemau Innu Nation*

"Tshenut ntenimukunan nas-nenu tshitshue uetshimaun tshipa uapameut ntenimukunan. Miam ume ninan uetshimautshit niatshi-aianimuaiatshi nasnenu takut uetshimaun uapameuts nitenimukunan tshenut muk ents niuapamaiants, etishaukut utshimamuau, tshetshi uapimimits, eukunu nenu tshenut metshi nistutamuts. Peikushu tshekuan eianimentaman eutshimaunan eukun usham mitshenu eshi-aiatinikau Innuts. Uen eutshimauts tapiskut nte tshika ishe-tshitapaten nte Innits kie kakeshat. Tshekui minu nistutamuanan nenu kakeshau eshi-pimpinits. Uen einu-utshimaut tshekui minuanu nenu meskianu tsheui-ituteiat utenim, muk-e-tsheutshimau kie uin tshitshue ntaikeminuk tshetshi nenu nashemuk uin eshi-pimutet. Eukun uets animats uen einutshimaut ume ishinakun. Ui-katepan-epinut entsh utshimaut, muk nimiuts ents Innu-utshimaut tshetshi eneka nte tats, ne-muk itenitakun. Nenu Innut uaishi-uitshitau kie ne-tsheutshimau eiatapan nte tshui-ishi-pimpinikunu, eukun ne-etentakuak tshin nte uetshimauts, enika nte tshui ispituk, eukun ne-tshitshue eianimentaman." *Kiti, Innutshimau*

Ents-uetshimaut uentshi nistuapemeuts enu-tshenu, kie ui-uitshitussemeuts metshima nta etak kie nta Innu-utshimaut-eishitussets. Tshenuts, tshash mamu uitshitussemeut kie uitamuakanut tshekuanu ua-etinanun, kie kukuetshimukut Innu Nation kie innutshimau tshetshi uinuau uitamuat tshekuanu. Tshenut nta eiapits tauts assinu euauitekenets. Tshenuts tshimakenuts pushenantshi nte uaiu essinu euauitekenits uinuau tshi-minu uapatineuts kie tshi-uitamueuts tsheutshimau nenu innutsh tepentak assinu. Tshenuts eiapits ishi-tshitapamakenuts miam nas-nikan kamiste tshissenimat aueshisha. Peikusu nte tshenu nikantshessenimat atikua, etu uin ssenimetshe essi sseniman kastitikuet Stuart Luttich nte Kuspe (Goose Bay). Kutekets Innuts, issishuet kie itentamuts, tshenuts tshipa mamunanut kie tshipa tshiminakanuts tshetshi mamu atusset tsheniu-utshimaut tshipa ishinakatakenuts. Kutekets ents, uentshi kaitusset, mitshimitshimaut kie kaskutimatshet eiapit ui-uitshitussemeut tshenu tshetshi uauitshinikut.

because so many promises were made and none were kept. We think it is about time that governments make commitments and implement them. We will use all means of negotiation and non-violent protest to make sure they carry out their legal responsibilities and keep their promises.

Some of our attempts in the last year to get the necessary help and support from the government to combat the social problems we face have failed. In January 1993, when six of our youth were found sniffing in a cold shack, screaming that they wanted to die, leaders held a community meeting to decide how we should respond. From this, we prepared a seven-point plan called "Hearing the Voices" to present to government. The plan explained the steps needed to correct the situation. Some of these steps have been implemented, such as sending the children to an Alberta treatment centre and holding our own treatment program in nutshimit. But other important issues still remain outstanding, such as land rights, relocation and policing.

We had to take policing and justice matters into our own hands when the provincial government wouldn't listen to our concerns. First, they refused to recognize our five trained peacekeepers, but the Band Council hired the peacekeepers anyway. Our own police officers can relate to their people; they understand what people are going through. They are like social workers, and can do counselling if people need it. But the problem is that our peacekeepers still need office space and a holding cell. Sometimes their work is dangerous. Our woman constable was beat up one time because there was no place to put her assailant.

On December 16, 1993, we took another action to assert control over the justice system. We evicted the judge and his court from the community. We were saying that the whole justice system does not work for the Innu and does not meet our needs to heal. We should be the ones who judge our own people. Many of us feel that we should deal with the root causes of these problems through healing circles and treatment programs. Punishing people is not the answer. The province responded by laying charges against three women from the community, planning a military invasion of our community with a hundred armed R.C.M.P. and military in the summer, and getting the federal government to suspend all negotiations with us on land rights,

relocation and taking over control of the agencies in the community.

We should be able to have our own law enforcement and have our own laws. For example, if the Band Office developed by-laws, when somebody committed a crime, the Band could ask the family to go to nutshimit to help themselves. The judge could ask people who abuse their wives or kids to do community service, or to go to counselling or treatment. They could be involved in developing programs and policies to bring the suicide rate down. People who want to commit suicide could be sent to treatment or to the country. The tribal police should also be involved in dealing with sexual abuse and the Church. They should be part of a crime prevention committee to meet with priests who come to the community.

What right do governments have to assume they have jurisdiction over our lives, since Innu people have never signed any agreements or treaties? The federal government is not even following its own laws and legal responsibilities towards us as a First Nation. They should look at their own Charter of Rights and their Indian Act before they accuse us of breaking the law. This is a human rights issue.

The journey to self-determination is a very slow process, but we won't give up even if the government doesn't support us. With regard to other institutions in our community, a number of our young people have

Police and youth face off after judge is evicted from Utshimassit / Ueuespimitakanipan tshekamanuest mak kamakunueshits nte Utshimassit nta pishimusa, 1993

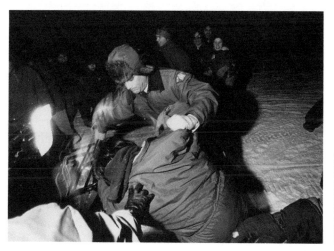

PETER SIBBALD PHOTO

Tshekuan uatutamak nast-eminuat mishineike kie nast-ne-menuuitamakuiak tshekuan tshipa utinenan. Mitshen tshekuan peteimak nte utat pets eishitusseiak. Kutekets Innut issishueuts, utshimauts tshipa-ui-menutenemuts metshuauinantau kie tshipa ispitenitamueuts nenu Innu essishuen. Tshipa kutshitauts tshetshi uitamuats, auassa tshekuan en-menuat ne-tshinan eshiniuiak. Tshipa minuuitamueut tante uaituteiak nimiute tsheutshimau tshenatak tshekaui ntuapatenan meskenu eminuat tshepmutenak tshetshi menupenak. Kutak tshekuan eka menupinits nte utshimaun eukun ume nantim tshishat ni-tshipa-ui-tshishatistanan tsheietinak nte nikan kie anutsh. Atut-si-muk-et kuaaskue-upiniutenan tshekuanu essishuetau uentshi tante meneshinakun tshetshi tutamak.

Utshimaut mamu tshipa-ui-atusseut kie ntshents kutekets kepimpintautshi atusseuna. Katakauanets kie eka takanekenets tshipa tshiskutamuakanuts tsheishi-pimpinushut kie etenitakunit nenu utatuskanuau, kie tshipa tshiskutamuakanut, tshetshi uinuau pempinushut. Kie etu tshipa miste tshiskutamashut, kie etu mamu tshipa-ui-uitshitussemeut nenu Innu katakaukuts. Kie uentshi ents etuskatak umenu tshekuanu eka menupunikuak, kie umenu uiauitshiaushits. Nenu atusseuna kenustautshi kie innutshimaut kie Innu Nation, uauitshiaushitau tshipa ui-nistutamut Innu nenu atuskueut, nimienu nenu muk shunianu tshetshi tshitapatak, Innua nenu ui-uitshieut, nimienu muk tshetshi-ui-minuentamiat utshimamuau. Kie uinuau Innuts uinuau nenu utatusseunuau tshetshi nukutat enu tshekuanu uaishi-uitshinikushit nte uts Innutshimauts kie nte-ut Innu Nation.

Kie nanikutini eiapits-ni-stissishuenan meshuka nte memenuanu nte Inu-utshimaut nanikutini usham-ni-miste apastakanu tshekuan. Tshipa tutakanu mishineke nenu tshipa ishi-pimpinut inutshemaut, tshipa takun ne meshineke, nenu tshipa, ishi-uitshi-akanut Innuts. Kie tshipa-ui nashenan-ne-meshineike etistest. Kie eiapit issishuanu tsheutshimau uin-tshipa nitussenimeu nenu innu utshimau eispinit nte uta-tusseunit, tshetshi eka minuat nenu ishi-animpinit Innu-utshimaut.

Mitshen shash tshekuan netussenitamat ne-eispinants nta eshiniunats kie kutaka tshekuia niui-minupentanan. Kie nipetakutanan nte tsheutshimat kie niui-petuanan tsheutshimau essishuet tante mitshenipan tshekuanu essishuet tsheutshimau tsheishi-uitshimit muk metekunu nastesh tshekuanu. Nitenimaian nastesh esk metshekuanu esk minueu, tshipa uitam kie nenu uauitshiakue Innu kie tshipa-ui nukutau. Mishiue nika-ishi-kutshianan nika petastimpistuanan kie kanimaskueitshanut, tshiam nimaskueitshanu, nimieu tshetshi mashintunanuts kie nimieu tshetshi pikuniken tshekuan, eukun ume tsheishi mashitsheiak tsheutshi petak tsheutshimau. Kie tshetshi mintak tshekuanu ne-kaissishuet tshetshi mintak.

Ne-passe kaishikutshitaiak tshetshi ishiuitshinikushinak nte tsheutshimaut kaui-mashikamak ne tshekuan eka menupinikuiak messi-ne-tutenan. Tshepishum 1993 eukun minuat mesteishinakuak tshekuan nte Utshimassit. Ashutat auassit miskuakenuts meameshepen pimina nte mitshuapishit. Kie tshitshue takanu kie iashikueut kie tepueuts, niui-nepanushu-nan issishueut itakanuts, eku mamu utshimaut aian-imueut tshetshi-ssentats tan tshipa tutamut essi animinits eshinakushit auassits. Ekuta uta-nitshitshipintan euauitamat tsheishitutamats kie nishu-ashutat tatenupen aianimuan mishinaneken ueshitaken, (tshetshi petakuak tshekuan) kie niminatan umenu tsheutshimau. Ume uatutamats, mishiue nta tshekuan uauitekenipen tshipa ishi-ueuestakenu ne-tshekuan eka menupiniuets. Tshash ne-pesse tshekuan nukunkauauitekents itishauakenipint. Auassit nete uaiu tshetshi uitshiakanits nete Alberta, apishipeutshuapit kie ninan nipimpintaian tshetshi uitshiakanits, uentshi nte nutshimit tetshe takun kauitshiakanit uentshi. Muk esk kutak tshekuan ne-meste itentakuats metshi tshitshipinu assin euauitekents kie, kaui-atukants, mak kamaku nueshiun-atusseun.

Ninan nekui-pempintanan kamukunueshiu atusseun kie kaueuestants. Tsheutshimau nastesh-ne-menetutakutan uatamutshit tshekuanu eka menuatamutshit essi-eka menupunutshit. Ueskat tsheutshimau mui-nistunueu nenu Innu kamakunueshen muk uinuau Innu-utshimaut utinepen tshetshi atussen nte Utshimassit. Ninan nikamakunueshimenan tshi-uitshitussemeut nenu Innu kie tshissenimeut Innu essi-pets animiun. Miam ne-tshekat kauitshiaushit itentakushut, tshi-eimieuts uenu eka menupinits, kie tshissenimeut tshipa ishi-uitshieuts. Muk-e-takunu eiapits tshekuanu uestupinikuts, mu-mishineikentshuaput kie metikunu nte tshipa makunauts uenu. Kie nanikutini kustikunu nenu utatusseunuau. Peik ne-iskueu Innu kamakunu-est mashikuakanishepan tante metikunu nte tshipa tshipaueu nenu miakunats.

Tanien, 1992

Hillary, 1992

been going out to get training, with the goal of eventually taking over these agencies. We have one certified teacher, and five people have been taking courses with the Teacher Education Program for Labrador. We have six teachers' aides and a principal's assistant. But we still have no one working for our community in the Curriculum Centre in Sheshatshiu. Eventually, we will run our own school.

Some people have started to get training in nursing, and one person in medicine. There is also a Community Health Representative who co-ordinates non-insured health benefits for us, like if someone has to go to Goose Bay to see a doctor, we might send a translator. We have two respite workers at the clinic. With regards to Social Services, we have four Innu people working in the Utshimassit office. Some of our workers are thinking about getting training as social workers. We don't make decisions about the programs or policies of Social Services. Our front-line workers will need to be put in positions where they can really help people be responsible for themselves.

We have also organized a number of community-based training programs. In Utshimassit, the Youth Leadership Development Program employs two young adults. There have been a few snags with the program, but the young people are making progress and will be able to take on leadership roles. The community also has a Youth Council.

Over the last five years, the Band Council, with the help of the MCC (Mennonite Central Committee), has run training programs for about fifty people to learn housing repairs and new housing construction. This is so we don't have to depend on people from outside

coming into the community and taking the jobs. We have been negotiating with the provincial government to take over its store. The first Innu business, a restaurant, opened last fall. This first attempt failed, but we will try again. In 1994, we opened a video store, and it continues to operate.

Many of us realize it will be hard to make changes, but we are trying to do it one day at a time. There are problems that we are just beginning to try to deal with. We are also getting help from the outside in our struggles.

Holding More Meetings

Over the last few years, our leaders have become more accountable. There are still problems with this, but it is better. For example, leaders hold more meetings to let people know what is going on. This is where people can tell the leaders what they want them to do. There is a lot more consultation going on between people and the leaders.

It was at one of these meetings that people told the leaders they didn't want outsiders coming in to fix their homes. They wanted to do it themselves. As well, after the crisis of gas sniffing in 1993, community meetings were held to try to figure out what to do with the children who needed help desperately. Another meeting in 1993 was held to address the ongoing problems of sniffing and alcohol abuse. It was decided to convert the nurses' residence into a safe house for women and children. But we couldn't run it with just volunteers, and we had to shut it down. There are still many issues we need to talk about, like the R.C. Church, Social Services, the police, government, the band councils,

Eku ne-pishimus 16, 1993 minuat takunupan tshekuan eshimashitsheiat, tshetshi ut-ninan pimpintaiat kaueuestaken. Ntenekatishinatan tshekamakunuest. Kie nenu uaueshiat Innu ute Utshimassit shash nte nitissishuetan umenu kakeshau eshiueueshiat Innu, nastesh nte mepeik Innu, metsheketshi nastesh uitshiniku umenu kakeshau kaueuestanits, eka tuteken ne-ninan uaishitshitshipiniats kie uaishipimpiniats. Nimitshetinan essishueiat kie etenitamat tshipa-ui-nutshikenan nete uets-ntautshik ume tshekuan eka menupinikuiak, kie tshika tutakanu tshetshi mamu eimitunants ne-kuaskapenanua ua-tshitunantshi. Emakunakants uen nimieu tsheuitshikunats. Miskut ntutakunan tsheutshimau nistinua neskueua miakunats ute Utshimassit, kie ashimakanisha, ute ui-petishaueu ute Utshimassit kukustikushiutshi kamakunueshit, mak ashimakanisha ute-ui-teneu napinetshe ute Utshimassit, kie ume kamisisit tsheutshimau (Newfoundland), nituentamueshepan utauat (Ottawa) tsheutshimau tshetshi kassinu nekeimints, assinu euauitakanits. Kie kaui-atukanints mak nenu kassinu uin tsheutshimau ui-pimpintau tshekuanu ute Utshimassit.

Neshenakun tshinan tshetshi pimpiniakut kamakunueshit, kie tshetshi takuak e-mishinaniken ua-ishitapueta-tishunak tshinan, ne-tshipa ishi-pimpinushunan kie tshipa itisteu ne-tshimishineikenu kie nantim tshipa-ui-nashenan etistet. Miam ume nika tipeikatshen, Innu-utshimauts tutats umishine-ikenuau nenu etenimat uenu tshipa ishinakatuenimeuts uen tshekuanu eka mentutak, ek nte nutshimit tshipa itishauakenu, tshetshi ui-minu-punushut. Ne-Innu utinakan miam tshekamakunuest tshetshi ishitusset ntshents uentshi kepiuenimeutshi utuassimuau kie utiskuemuau. Eku tshipa itekuts nenu Innu uetinakanits tshetshi tshekamakunueshiuts. Tshekitussenau nte Utshimassit, metshiketshi tshishikakunau, kie tshipa itikut, matshik nantuapamek uen tsheiemitak kie itutek nte kauitshiakanits Innuts. Kie tshipa-uauitshiaushiuts nte keui-uitshiakanutshi uentshi, eku tshipa nashukupenu miskut ne-kuinepanushutshi uentshi. Uentshi ents mushinau kuinepanushutshi nte tshipa itashanikenuts apishipeutshuapit kie mak nte nutshimits. Kie ntshen Innu kamakunueshit. Tshipa nutshikamut nenu eiapits kui-meshtu-tuakenui auassa kie nenu eimiutshuapinu. Tshipa-tauts nte kenakatuenitakanua tshekuan tshetshi eka minuat ustapen tshekuan kie

tshipa uapameuts kauapukueshin meshikan ute Utshimassit.

Tshekuanitshe-nenu uets issishuet tsheutshimau nin ntepenimauts Innuts, Innuts nastesh menita mishinaushut mishenekenu Innut tshetshi tepenimakanits, menita tutuakanuts tshetshi ukanumikuanits? Utaut tsheutshimau menashum nenu umishineneken etisten kie nenu tshipa ishiuitshiepan Innu First Nation. Tsheutshimau, utaut, tshipatshitapatam nenu umishinikan nenu uen kassinu uen eishiniut tshetshi tipenimushut kie nenu kutekenu umishinanikan Innu eshi-pimpiniakanit ute Kanata, esk eka issishuet kie eka itak, tshipikunenau ne-meshineike etistet ume tshekuan uataman ume itenitakun kassinu uen eishiniut tsheishi-tipeni-mushut.

Tshitshue tshimatnupenan tshetshi tshinan pimpininushunak, muk metsheketshi pestenimunan at-eka uitshintak tsheutshimau. Mitshen ute tshekuan tshatshipintaiak ute Utshimassit, shash mitshetut ustinitshut kie iskuessit niatshiskutamashut, atusseuna tshetshi-uinuau utinak kie tshetshi uinuau pempentauts nenu atusseuna. Peikussu Innu katshiskutamatshet nas uekanumit tshetshi tshiskutamatshet, mak petatat teshut tsheskutamashut nte katshiskuta mashunanunts, uen tshetshi katshiskutamatsheuts, ute Labrador. Eku ashutats teshut uiauitshiat katshiskutamatshen, mak peik pitu-tshimau katshiskutamatshet. Muk esk nte tshinan tshika pimpintanan kaskutimatsheutshiuap.

Kuteket uentshi shash tshiskutamashut tshetshi ntunishiskuessiut, kie ntukuna. Kie tauts ents shash niakatuapatat kie pempintats, nenu Innu keuitshiakanua eiakushit, miam nte mate uen pushiakan eiakushit eka kakeshaumits, tshika tshimeu uenu tsheiashuitamakuts, eukunu umenu utautsseunuau, tauts ents uiauitshiats uenu iakushin. Kie nishut nte eiapits uentshi etusset ntukuntshuapissit. Eku nta mitshimitshimau, neuts nta Innut etusset, kie passe ents kaitusset itenitamuts tshetshi natsheskutamushut, tshetshi etu-ssenitats etenitakunits mitshimitshimau atusseunu nimieu ninan uieuetishutamats ne atusseun kie nimieu ninan nustautshit nenu eshi-pimpiniakinet. Ntshen nikan etats tshekui uinuau utinamut nenu atusseuna. Etu tshetshi uitshiat Innu, etu tshetshi uitshinushun.

Mitsheia shash pempintaiat atusseuna tshetshi skutamuakanats Innuts. Ute Utshimassit ntshen ustinit-

forestry projects, the military, our dependencies and so on. We need to see what the most important issues are and begin addressing those first. We will need conferences for some of these.

"The leaders need feedback from the people, and should listen to our concerns. The Innu Nation and the Band Council should give us updates on what has to be done and what has been accomplished. Also, the different agencies should gather and update each other on what is being done." *Youth Leadership Council*

People have been trying hard to make these meetings work better. For example, there has been 100 per cent sobriety in people attending all the meetings for the relocation. We have never seen this before. This is a sign that people are taking the process seriously. Some suggest that children should also sit in on the meetings. They will listen to what is going on and they will understand and help out in the future. If one kid hears about these things, he will tell his friends, this one will tell another, and they will all gather around and help each other.

"If we could have one issue to talk about and just stick to it; that way we would be able to have the strength. We might eventually accomplish something if we focus on one issue at a time rather than issues piling up and ending up with so many difficulties." *Tshenish, elder*

There are different opinions about the usefulness of debating issues, although most people feel it is an important part of the process of working together. But sometimes some people only want their voice to be heard.

"When everyone has a different opinion, maybe the person who is in charge, like the chief, should go along with his or her say. The conflicts start when other board members are trying to say what should be done. When the person is trying to explain things, the board members don't want to listen to them. They tell them they have no right to speak. After, when the meeting is over, people say he is trying to control the meetings. Maybe they don't understand that we need to have one voice. Maybe when conflicts arise, the meeting should be cancelled and have a meeting the next day. Everybody should listen more and everyone should have a say." *Etuetis*

Stop Developments

Some people say leaders should stop every development on our land before these kill us all. We all need to work together on these issues. We should stand up for our rights and speak up against all the injustices that have been done to us. More women should speak out. We need to tell the white man and his governments to leave our land alone. We need to do this to protect the land, the plants and the animals. Developments are unhealthy on our lands. They ruin the territory that we depend on to continue our traditional way of life. Without any course of action, we are putting ourselves in danger, as well as the lives of our children and grandchildren. Governments must ask us if we agree before they start any big developments on our land.

Protests are a good way to get our voices heard. We need to use strong tactics, vocal speaking out against unwanted developments and in support of our rights. This can only strengthen us. We don't do protests to disrespect white people, but against their governments. This is a way to do public awareness, to help people from outside of Ntesinan know what is happening to us. We need to do this to get their support to help us fight governments. If other people understand our position, it will be good. We also need to lobby foreign governments on our human rights.

Some people say someday we will have to stop protesting and reach an agreement with governments on land claims. But some of us are worried about a land claims settlement. We worry that this will mean we have sold our land, that we will get more money and then more problems will occur. We were so nice in the past and took everything that was given to us by governments. We never thought about what this would do to us. We should think first before we accept anything now. We should not respect people like they are greater than we are. They are people too, just human beings.

Relocation

We are acting on the People's Inquiry recommendations to move forward with relocation in Nutuashish. We see this as a major step in regaining control of our lives. We have set up the Mushuau Innu Renewal Committee to plan relocation step by step. Meetings are held regularly where people, including elders and children, are consulted and can make choices.

shut kepempinushutshi nishinua nte uituassuau etuskeiat. Meshuka ne-minupinipan ueskats, muk anutsh aiats minupinuts kie shash tshekat ssenitamuts etenitakunits eutshimaunanits. Kie nte Utshimassit tauts ents eiapits ustinitshut pempininushut.

1993 mak 1994, etistet miste-etshitashun, Inu-utshimaut tshi-tshipintaut nenu Innu tshetshi tshiskutamuakenits, petetats tatunueshitshen Innuts tsheskutamuakanits, tshetshi mistikunapeuts nte mitshuapa ueshitakanits kie eueuestakanits. Ume-uet-tutaken tshetshi eka minuats itishimututshit nte uts uaiu kakeshaut, kie tshetshi ekaminuat utinak nenu atusseuna, eukun uets tshiskutamuakanits Innuts uinuau tshetshi ushitat mitshuapa. Kie uipats shash niuitamuanan tsheutshimau tshetshi utinamats tautshuap. Kie nas nistam Innu etshitshipintat uin tshetshi pimpinushut eukun shenikenipan mitshu-tshuap nte Utshimassit, muk memenupunu muk minuat nika kutshitaian, eku ne 1994 minuat, shenikanipan kaishetshimakanitsh tautshuap kie anutsh esk pimpinu.

Kassinu tshekat etishiak tshi-tshissenitenan animin tshetshi tshetshinue miskutinamak tshekuan muk tshika kutshitanan papeikutshishikau. Tante mitshen tshekuan eka menupinikuiak muk pitshenik shash tshinutshikenan. Kie mitshetut ents uentshi nte ut-uatshintakut ume essi-animiunak.

Etu Mitshetuau Aianimuanu

Meshuka nte mitshetupuna utats, tshenuts matentakushuts shash essi-uitshiaushit, muk esk meshuka nas minupinu, muk shash matenitakun essi minupinits. Umenika tipeikatshen tshenut shash ents kie uinuau aianimueut, tshetshi uitamuats Innu eshuapats, kie tshetshi uitamuats Innu tshekuanu eshi-matentats tshekuanu eka menupinits. Ekuta nta tshipa uitamueuts tshenu tshekuanu. Mishau shash tshekuan uatimatunants nte uts-Innuts mak nte uts-inutshimauts.

Peikuau ne-eianimuants, innutsh uitamueuts Innu-utshimau etenitak, menui-minuats uapamaiat. Kakeshaut nete uts-uaiu tshetshi mishikats ute tshetshi ueuestat mitshuapa kie ninan nika ushitaian iteuts. Kie ne-1993, katshi meste nutshikuat auassit pimina mushinau-ni-aianimuanu, uauitakanu tan-tshipa ishi-uitshianut ents uassit eshinakushit, tshitshue ishinakunu tshetshi uitshiakanits. Minuats ne-eianimuants 1993 uauitekenipan essi-miste mishat tshekuan eka

menupinikuiak pimin kie shitakenapun essi-nekatshikunak eku minuat issisishuanuipan tshetshi apastakanits nenu nitukunishiskuessit mitshuapinu kaipistak tshetshi kunenimakanits ents uentshi eka menupinits, iskueuts kie auassit. Muk ne-sheienimat mitshuap muk nte uen ua-atusset atussepen, metikunu shunianu tshetshi tshishikuakents, eku metshi-pimpinu. Tshipanikenu, ne-kaui-itapastakan, tshetshi nakatuenimanits uentshi eianimiuts. Esk nte mitshen tshekuan tsheuauitamats, eimiutshuap, mitshimitshimau, kamakunueshit, tsheutshimau, Innu-utshimaut, katshimikesenants. Ashamakeneshet, kie ne-tshinanketshui pimpinushunanua kie mitshen nte esk tshekuan tsheuauitaken. Ne-nistam tshekeui tshitapatenan tshekuan meste itenitakuak, eukun nistam tshenustaken. Mitshetuau tshitshue tshika animuanu ume tshekuan uauiteken, tan tshipa ishi-tutakanu.

"Innutsh tshipa uitamueuts Innu-utshimau tshekuanu kie Innu-utshimauts tshipa ui-netutuet Innu tshekuanu uatamakutau eka-menuatemen Innu Nation kie Innu-utshimaut tshipa uitamueuts Innu tshekuanu etutak kie tshekuanu nenu shash tshatshipintat, kie tshekuanu nenu tshash menupeintats kie nitshe kutekets kutshimaushutshi tshipa mamuituts, kie tshipa uauitamatut tshekuan etutak kie tshekuanu nenu shash tshatshipintats."
Ustinitshut utshimaut

Tshitshue-tshi-misteituskateu, essi-ui-minupin-takents eianimuatshi. Miam-ume tshitapatetau anutsh-u nastesh nte metau Innu tshetshi mateitak eianimuantshi, uiauitekentshi kaui-atukan, metauts nte nas kamateniteshet, menita eishinakunupen uipats eianimuantshi. Eku nas-nukun essi-ui-uitshinushut Innut. Kuteket Innut issishueut auassit nte eiapit tshipa uishamakanuts eianiamuantshi tshipa netutamut eissisishuanun kie tshipa nistutamut. Kie tshipa uitshiaushiut esk nte aisket. Peik uas petak nenu eissishuanun, eku tshetipatshimustuat uitsheuakea, eku nakutak uas, kutaka tshet uitamuat, eku tshet-mamuitut tshetshi ui-uitshituts mamu.

"Tshima peikust tshekuan uiauitamak, eukun nemushinau tshipa nustanan, eku etu tshipa shutshinan miskut. Kessi-neush teshikenan shash tshipa-etkastinenan tshekuan nutshikamak, peikust nepetima nustaiak tshekuan eku anutsh stishinakushinan usham miste ispanisteu ne-tshekuan nutshikamak eukun uets animinukunak." *Tshenish*

Although many of us are the first to admit that relocation will not be the solution to all our problems, it is a number-one priority for us right now. We know that we have to deal with the problems in the village here and leave them behind. We are trying to have a new beginning in our new village, a new life for the next generation. We will be able to live by our own laws in this new community we will build ourselves. But now we are waiting to see if the new federal government will finally assume its legal responsibilities regarding our case. Some of us believe the government should fund all of this relocation project, but we should still be the ones making all the decisions.

"I think when we relocate we should not rely on the white man. We should run ourselves. I really like the old ways and I think we should do it ourselves."
Patinik

Some of us think it will be like getting out of prison when we move. It will be like setting us free. But some people also worry that when we relocate, people won't want to go to the country as much, because they will be too busy looking after their new houses. They will be worried about their houses. Maybe when someone goes to the country, and sees his house has been broken into, he will be angry. The Band Council might get mad at the person if the house gets wrecked after they gave it to him. We have to do some planning to avoid these conflicts and to make sure people keep going to the barrens. Some people are more hopeful and say that when we move to the mainland we will be closer to the barrens. Our children will be able to concentrate more on going hunting and that kind of stuff. Maybe they won't bother with things like gas sniffing.

Many of us have a lot of hope for the future. We believe that in the next twenty years we can go a long way in solving the problems that plague our lives now. We will see more people helping people. Our new community will be healthy. We will have changed our lifestyles. There will be 100 per cent sobriety. We will be better parents and our children will get a better education. We will be strong and practising the traditions and culture of our ancestors. We will love one another.

We will not be able to go back to our traditions 100 per cent. We will be using some Innu ways and some non-Innu ways of living. There will be two paths for us. For example, there will be people in the country and others who will have careers. We want our kids to grow up to be nurses, teachers or doctors, but to understand the culture at the same time. We expect our lives will be more modernized. We will be using more modern machines, and less our traditional ways. But we will still be Innu, because we have never seen any First Nations community that has managed to become a healthy community living the white way.

"We are taking responsibility for what is happening, and responsibility for trying to solve it. People are starting to see hope for the future. We might have a few people that might not be involved. But people have reached rock bottom and they are starting to grow. There is no way we can go back to where we were. Our culture will be revived. Our people will be well. Hopefully, by that time people will go back to the country. We will become a model for other Native communities across Canada that have similar problems to us. We will be able to show other people how we have dealt with our problems." *Kiti*

Mitshetuit e-tshekuan ishinakun tshekuan tshipa eishi-mashikenan ne-tshekuan eka menupinikuiak, at-kepua passe-Innuts issishueut minuau etu mamu tshetshi uit-shitussemituiak kie mamu tshetshi nutshikamak tshekuan. Nanikutini kutekets Innuts, muk nenu uta-ianimuanuau ntuenitamut tshetshi petakunit, kie tshetshi ntu-tuakenets.

"Eianimuatshi mitshetuit ni-issishuanu tshekuan, eku peik ne-uen uetshimaut, put innutshimau tshipa-ui minutenemueu nenu uenu essishuen napeu put kie iskueu. Eku nta-uets eka-tshi menupinits-ni usham ents kanakatuapatak atusseuna usham nta uinauau, ui-ssentamut tshipa eitinanu. Innu at-ni uaminuuitatshe tshekuanu, ntshe kenakatuapata-mutshi atusseuna (board), nastesh nte menetuta-muts, kie nenu Innu eiminitsh. Kie itakenu naniku-tini Innu eimitshi nastesh nte meneshenakun tshet-shi aianimuein itakanu ni-Innu. Eku kastshi tshis-takentshi eianimuan, eku tshitshue ui-peikussu eian-imuet, etaken ni-Innu, at-ui aianimuetshi. Metshi nenu put nistutamutshen utshimaut tshekui-peiku-tanan u-stainimuanu, eka menupuntshi eian-imuantshi tshipa tshipanakenu eianimuants patush minuats uiapatshi tshipa aianimuanu. Mishiue uen tshipa-ui-nitutam kie mishiue uen ishinakunu tshet-shi eimits, uauitak tshekuanu." *Etuetis*

Nekaimuk Atusseun

Kutekets Innut issishueut Innu utshimaut tshipa-ui-nikeiniut atusseuna miami-shantshi, tshetshi eka tshi-tshepentshi, kie tsheka pikunakan assi esk eka nipanekunak kassinu etashiak. Mamu tshikaui uitshi-tussemitunan tshetshi shutshiak mashikamak tshekuan emishat. Nas mamu shipaui unikapustashunan, ume tshinan eshitipenimushunak kie shuka tshipa ani-muekatenan ne-kaispish pet-miste stimanikunak. Iskueuts eiapits tshipa mamuetamut. Tshipa uitamuanut kauapishit, kie nenu utsheutshimamuau tshet-shi enekatet nte tepentamuak assinu. Tshekui tutenan ume tshetshi tshispeuatamak assi-tepenita-mak, kie ntamuk nte assit netautshit kie ueshishets nastesh memenuau tshetshi tshitshepentakein atusseu-meshat ute tepenitamak assi. Nutam tshika pikunekenu assin kie tshika npatakanu kassinu tshekuan kie ne-kai-shipekassiuiak. Eka tshekuan takuak tsheishi mashit-shenak. Tshitshue tshika ustunakushinan kie tshekuni-anut stuassiminut kie tshussiminut. Nistam tshipa

kukuetshimukunu tsheutshimau tshetshi issishuueuak ehe kie mak mauat esk eka tshitshipintat emeshan atusseunu.

Enimaskueitshanut eukun eshi-minuats tshetshi petakushinak tshekui-apastan tshekuan eshut-shimekats kie tshetshi ui-shutshitakushiak tshetshi nekeimak eka menuatamak atuskan ute etaiak kie tshetshi ui-tshispeuatishunak. Ume-tutaman muk aiat-tshika shutshinan. Tshekui tutenan ume tshetshi uts-uitshikunak nte uaiu. Nimieu tsheut-nimaskuantsheiak tshetshi piuenimakut kakeshauts, muk tsheutshimau tshika nutshikuanu. Eukun ume mushe tshenukutaiak tshekuan tshetshi ut-uitshikunak nete uts-uaiu, tshika-uitshikunan petakuak eitiak tutamak-ume tshekemiskuanuts tsheuitshintakuts uentshi emashikuak tsheutshimau. Minunistutakaue kakeshaut eshimashitsheuak tshika uitshinikunuts miashikuak tsheutshimau. Kie ntshe nast-uaiu tsheutshimaut, tshekui-minu nistutamunakut eniuak kie tshinan.

Kutekets ents-Innut issishueut, tshekapunipinu nenu mushinau ketshenu tshikashunanua esk nte aiskat tshika ishinikaun, tshi-tapuetatishuiak kie nistu-apatak tsheutshimau, tshinan tepenita-muak assinu muk-e-tshinan tshimishimentenan tsheishinakuak tshikastinamak stassinu. Ne-uets mishimentamak, ne-tshika ishinakun miam eteuatsheiak assin tante tshika miste minikunan shuniau eku etu tsheka minupiniak. Ushamikat tshiminuentakushitan nte uipets, mishiue tshutinamuatan tsheutshimau mantak tshekuanu. Nastesh metshinita mamitunentenanakupen tshetu-takuiak ume manikuiak shuniau. Eku anutsh tshipa mamitunentenan esk eka tapuetamak kie esk eka uti-namak tshekuan kessi-eku minuat miste ispiteni-manuts kakeshaut mestutshimauts, tante unashut ents kie uinauau miam eshinakaushuak.

Kaui-Atukants

Tshinasheian ne-tshimishineikenu katutamak ne-kaishi uauitamak nte katutenkentsh tshimishinikenu eukun ne-anutsh ketshui atutshenanua nete natuashish. Shash tshitshue meste-nukun ne-uatutamak tshetshi tshinan pimpinushanak kie tshimiakenuts entsh uentshi tsheituskatat kui-atukanua, metnu muk atuskatamuts. Mushinau ni-aianimuanu, innutsh, tshenut, mak auassit eiapits uitamuakanuts, tshetshi uinauau ssentats uaitishutak.

Tshimitshetinan essishueiak at-tshiatukantshi nimieu

meshiue tshekuan tsheminupinits, kie nimieu e-
tsheuitshinikunak at-tshi atutsheiak, muk eukun e-nas
takut estaiak tshekuan anutsh. Kassinu etishinak
tshessentenan ekuta uta Utshimassit tshishat tsheui
enikatishinimak ne-tshekuan eka menupinikunak,
tshet-nekatamak ute atutsheiakue. Tshekui ussi-tshit-
shipinan nete tshi-atukantshe, tshetshi nas ueketshit-
shepenak, nenu minuat tshet-tatsh kutakuts auassit.
Tshinan tshekui tutenan tshimishinanikenu ne-uai-
shipimpinak tshi-atukantshe, etu tshekui min-
unakunushunan muk-e anutsh steshuapamanu Utauat
(Ottawa) tsheutshimau tsheshutinemukue kie
tsheisheui-tshiaushikue nenu eshinakushuak essi-eka-
menupenak. Tshekat mishiue etishinak stentenan,
tsheutshimau uin mishiue tshipa tshishikashu nenu
kui-atukanua muk tshinan mishiue tshekuan tshipa
ue-uetishutenan.

"Nin nitenten tshi-atukantshe, kessi-eku shuka mitshetut kakeshaut etuskatakut, tshinan tshipa-ui-
atuskashunan." *Patinik*

Kassinu etishinak miam nte uenuiak kamakuntu-
nantsh tsheitenimuiak tshi-atukantshe. Miam
iapikunekunaku tshika itenitakun, muk tsheketukun
eiapits tshekuan tsheka menupunikunak, metsheketshi
puts-ui-uapatamuts Innuts nutshimit, tante usham
tshika utemikamuts ussi-mitshuapetau, tshekameshe-
menitamut uitshuua-ua tshetshi pikunekentshi tatshe
Innu kuespit eku uapatatshe uitsh pikueikenets eku
tshetshuapit. Kie Innutshimau eiapits tshika tshuen-
imuku pikunekenets uitsh nenu kaminakants.
Tshishat-tshekui menunakunushunan tshetshi eka
takuat nte tshekuan minuats tshenutshikakunak, kie
shuka tshekeui-tutuanuts uentshi tshetshi eka punits
euapatats nutshimit. Kutekets Innuts tshitshue shut-
shenimut kie issishueut etu nte metshima tshika tanan
nte tetshe nutshimit. Kie stuassiminuts etu tshika
itenitamuts kie etu tshika menuatamuts tshetshi ntu-
iuits, kie nte kutekeuu tshekuanu uitutakaue. Metsheketshi shapenimeuts pimina tshetshi nutshikuats.

Tshimitshetinan tshitshue shutshenimunak, eteninta-
mak tshetshi menupeniak nte aiskatsh. Nas
stapuetashunan, tshi-nishunueputshi tshash tshitshue
uaiu tshika tanan kie tshash tshekemitshen tshekuan
tshetshi enikatishinamak ne-nutshikakunak anutsh.
Kie muk-aiatsh tshika mitshetuts Innuts tsheuitshin-
tut. Kie tshi-atukantshe etu-tshika minuau kie etu-
tshika minueniuts uentshi metshiketshi shuka takun

tshekuan uestuentamikuiak. Tshitshue etu tsheme-
nunakushinan eshiniunak, metsheketshi nastesh tau
uen tshenutshikak shitakenapunu. Kie ukaumauts
mak utaumaut. Etu tshika minushiut enakatuenimatsh
utuassimuau kie auassit etu tshika miste tshiskutamashut. Etu tshika shapinan etshiskutamashuiak ne-
ka-ishiniuiak kie nekants tshimushumpenants uteni-
unuau. Kie etu tshika shatshitunan.

Sentakun metsheketshi mishue kastinenan ne-
kaishiniuiak. Tshekui apatshitaian nenu Innu eshiniut
kie kakeshau eshiniuts. Tshika nishia meskenua
tshemitimeiak. Ume nikatipankatshen essishueian,
tshetshi nistutakuak. Tshekemitshetut Innuts tshetats
nutshimits kie tshekemitshetuts Innuts tshemiste
tshiskutamashut kie tsheishitusset nenu kaishitshisku-
tamashut tshipa-ui-tutuanaits stuassiminut, tshetshi
ntukunishiskuessiut kie mak tshetshi ntukunishiut
mamishistetau muk eiapit tshekui-ssentamut uteni-
unuau eshiniuits. Tshissenitakun tsheishinakushinak
miam ne-kakeshau tshekat tshika ishiniunan. Etu
tshika mitshen tshekuan tsheapastaiak nenu kakeshau
eitapastat etu tshika uetshinikunan tshekuan
tshetetemak, kie metsheketshi shuka meste-apastanan
e-tshinan kaishiniuiak. Muk peikun eiapits miam
Innut tsheitenitakushinak, tante esk metshinita uapa-
maiuts kutekets Innuts (First Nation) tshetshi minupi-
nushut e-apastauat kakeshau utiniunu.

"Tshinan tshika itamenimushunan ume-eshinakushi-
nak anutsh kie tshinan tshekui-atuska tenanan
tshekuan eka menupinikuiak. Kutekets Innuts,
tshitshue minuentamuts nte aiskat tsheishinakunits.
Tsheketauts ents Innuts tsheka uauitshinuet
tshekuanu tutakenits, ua-minupunishunants. Kie
tauts ents pesse Innuts nast nete nashuk, kie masten
nte nas tapents eku anutsh shash ents unaka-
punushut. Nastesh meneshinakun tshetshi tshiuenak
nete kaututenak, kie tshika papinu e-kau kaishiniu-
nak, kie tshika minueniut nas-steniminuts. Tshekuti-
tenan e-minuat tsheishinakuats, Innuts kau tshetshi
uets nte nutshimits. Eku tshenistuna kushinak eshi-
uitshinushunak kie tshekemitshetut kutekets Innuts
ute Kanata tsheui-nashastakuts kie tsheui-tutats
nenu eshiuitshinushuak, tatshentshi ute Innut
Kanata eshinakushit nenu miam eshi-stimatshiuak,
eukun ents tsheui-apastat umenu eshi-uitshinushuak
kie tshukuapatianuts kutekets Innuts eshi-tutamuak,
kie eshimashikamuak nenu tshekuanu eiakunukuak
kie metshipinikunak." *Kiti*

MISHINANEKAN ETISTETS A

ETATISHITS UENAPIMAKANTTS

Mishiue uinakanuts auentshi ents manuets utaianimuanuau tshetshi tutakanits umenu mishinanikanu. Nikamunu pise ushitapants. Tutamuts pise mishinanikea enu kukuetshimakanits. Eku kutakuts mamu aianimueuts. Kanishishi mishinanikea katutakantshi eukunts Innuts aianimuepants.

Manishan	Shimunish	Nitshet P.	Maki
Ricky A.	Tuamish	Shimun P.	Niskueu
Ipuan	Klanesh	Toma	Maniakat
Napain A.	Tepit	Tami	Manimukanet
Amanta	Napeu Nui	Nishapetish	Matshias
Pineshita	Tshimi	Mani	Nesheu
Manian A.	Shuashim	Shimun	Patinik
Melissa	Shuashimish	Atenin	Penash
Atonia	Tshan	Akat R.	Miste-Pinip
Tamene	Mak	Akat J. R.	Napain R.
Miste-Peashue	Manian	Antea	Ray
Miste-Sam	Ketastipineu	Anishenish	Imistinita
Katinin	Shenush	Kauinimishit	Romeo
Epa	Nishapet	Kashetan	Shaia
Roy	Tshenish	Kananin	Sham
Shane	Shanin	Miste-Shishin	Skat
Shuni	Kitis	Utshimaskueu	Nespastian
Paunin	Pien	Shenush	Stani
Pitshinia C.	Nitshet	Tan Manin	Stena
Shanutis	Susi	Tepi	Steve
Nishapet	Meneshkuesh	Tan	Tun
Shuash	Shapatesh	Eanipiskum	Tara
Shanet	Shamsen	Ema	Tenesh
Tsheni	Shunin	Miste-Nishapet	Tuma
Tshuna G.	Akatis	Nishapet R.	Penunik
Shushepmak	Anishish	Enik	Uani
Neisha	Puap	Etien	Tshimi
Mani Katini	Pnush	Peashue	Shunin S.
Mike G.	Teni	Kapinien	Stum
Pite	Etuetish	Kapia	Apeta
Nanishi	Tshakish	Tshatsh	Anmani
Tshatshish	Shamanin	Kenikue	Shunin T.
Shanime	Napeutik	Hillary	Etet
Shishinis	Tshani	Enk	Tshenu
Miste-Shushep	Kutshesh	Irene	Shapatesh T.
Miste-Matinin	Mata	Shakanin	Tshuaish T.
Ueniam	Maku	Shenum	Manish T.
Miste-Etuet	Robin	Tshu	Manishanut
Penu	Kuekuatsheu	Uinipapeu	Sheni
Tsheisen	Apen	Tshuaish	Nupi
Manuk	Brendas	Shutit	Munik
Maniaten	Kistinish	Shunin R.	Shimiu
Manteskueu	Tanien	Kiti	Patinishia
Ricky M.	Tanina	Len	
Samish	Tanen P.	Nian	
Tshipesh	Tuniti	Neshni	
Napeu	Tshimish	Lorraine	
Shustinish	Kaniuekutat	Lloyd	
Miste-Manian	Penute	Matininish	

APPENDIX A

LIST OF PARTICIPANTS

The following is a list of all the people who participated in the Gathering Voices People's Inquiry and the Royal Commission research project through interviews, kitchen and tent meetings, workshops, filling out questionnaires, or writing a song or a poem.

Mary Jane Andrew
Ricky Andrew
Yvonne Asta
Raphael Asta
Amanda Aylward
Brigetta Aylward
Mary Ann Aylward
Melissa Aylward
Antonia Benuen
Damien Benuen
Francis Benuen
Jan Benuen
Kathleen Benuen
Nympha Byrne
Roy Byrne
Shane Byren
Shunee Byrne
Pauline Collins
Virginia Collins
Charlotte Gregoire
Elizabeth Gregoire
George Gregoire
Janet Gregoire
Jerry Gregoire
Jonah Gregoire
Joseph Mark Gregoire
Lisa Gregoire
Marie Katherine Gregoire
Mike Gregoire
Peter Gregoire
Nancy Jack
George Jacobish
Germaine Jacobish
Cecile Katshinak
Joseph Katshinak
Madeline Katshinak
William Katshinak
Edward Mistenapeo
Henry Mistenapeo
Jason Mistenapeo
Manuk Mistenapeo
Mary Adele Mistenapeo
Mary G. Mistenapeo
Ricky Mistenapeo
Sam Mistenapeo
Tony Mistenapeo
Elizabeth Napeo
Sam Napeo
Justine Noah

Mary Ann Noah
Simon Noah
Thomas Noah
Clarence Nui
David Nui
Darryl Nui
Jimmy Nui
Joachim Nui (Jr.)
Joachim Nui (Sr.)
John Nui
Mark Nui
Mary Ann Nui
Mary Jane Nui
Charles Pasteen
Elizabeth Pasteen
James Pasteen
Janine Pasteen
Katie Pasteen
Peter Pasteen
Richard Pasteen
Susie Pasteen
Theresa Pasteen
John Baptiste Pastiwet
Samson Pastiwet
Julianne Pijogge
Agat Piwas
Alice Piwas
Bob Piwas
Bruce Piwas
Dennis Piwas
Edward Piwas
Jack Piwas
Jean Marie Piwas
Joe Piwas
Johnny Piwas
Kutshesh Piwas
Martha Piwas
Michael Piwas
Robin Piwas
Veryan Piwas
Aaron Poker
Brenda Poker
Christine Poker
Daniel Poker
Danina Poker
Darren Poker
Dorothy Poker
James Poker
John Poker

Prote Poker
Richard Poker
Simeon Poker
Thomas Poker
Tommy Poker
Elizabeth Pokue
Marie Pokue
Simon Pokue (D.I.)
Adeline Rich
Agathe Rich
Agathe (Jacobish) Rich
Aldea Rich
Angela Rich
Anna Rich
Annie Rich
Cajetan Rich
Caroline E. Rich
Caroline V. Rich
Cecile Rich
Charlotte Rich
Charles Rich
Dawn Marie Rich
Debbie Rich
Don Rich
Edward Rich
Emma Rich
Elizabeth Rich
Elizabeth Rich
Eric Rich
Etienne Rich
Francis Rich
Gabriel Rich
Garfield Rich
George Rich
Greg Rich
Hillary Rich
Hank Rich
Irene Rich
Jacqueline Rich
Jerome Rich
Joel Rich
Joseph Mark Rich
Joyce Rich
Judith Rich
Julianna Rich
Katie Rich
Len Rich
Leon Rich
Leslie Rich

Lorraine Rich
Lloyd Rich
Madeline Rich
Maggie Rich
Martina Rich
Mary Agatha Rich
Mary Margaret Rich
Mathias Rich
Nachelle Rich
Patrick Rich
Penash Rich
Philip Rich
Raphael Rich
Ray Rich
Rita Rich
Romeo Rich
Sara Rich
Sam Rich
Scott Rich
Sebastian Rich
Stanley Rich
Stella Rich
Steve Rich
Toon Rich
Tara Rich
Theresa Rich
Tom Rich
Veronica Rich
Wally Rich
Jimmy Saunders
Julianne Saunders
Storm Saunders
Alberta Toma
Anne Marie Toma
Julianne Toma
Edith Tshakapesh
Joachim Tshakapesh
John Baptiste Tshakapesh
Joyce Tshakapesh
Manish Tshakapesh
Mary Charlotte Tshakapesh
Shirley Tshakapesh
Ruby Tshakapesh
Simeon Tshakapesh
Monica White
Patricia Penunsi

MISHINANEKAN ETISTETS B

SHITAKUNAPUN NEPANUETS UTA INNUTS, UTSHIMASSIT

1965 espish Epishiminiskueu, 1992

Eshini-kashuts	Eniuts	Nepits	Niskueu kie Napeu	Etatu-puneshit
B.R.	—	26/3/73	napeu	amasheni-takanu
C.P.	—	17/4/73	napeu	amasheni-takanukanu
W.B.	16/2/74	8/8/74	napeu	auashish
P.N	23/7/74	2/1/75	napeu	auashish
P.P.	4/3/75	4/3/75	napeu	auashish
R.T.	29/5/75	14/7/75	napeu	auashish
W.K.	1901	2/3/76	napeu	75
E.R.	2/4/76	7/9/76	niskueu	auashish
M.R.	1904	21/11/77	niskueu	73
L.T.	1/7/76	28/8/77	napeu	auashish
A.P.	8/10/77	28/8/77	niskueu	auashish
J.P.	1942	28/8/77	niskueu	35
J.P.	—	28/8/77	niskueu	auashits
C.P.	—	28/8/77	napeu	12
J.P.	1967	28/8/77	napeu	10
S.P.	—	28/8/77	napeu	30's
M.N.	25/8/55	9/8/79	napeu	24
P.R.	—	2/3/81	napeu	amasheni-takanu
A.J.	5/2/66	2/4/83	niskueu	17
F.R.	9/4/47	15/4/83	napeu	36
M.T.	4/9/47	24/7/83	niskueu	36
A.T.	10/7/46	24/7/83	napeu	36
T.R.	22/12/36	7/9/84	napeu	48
A.R.	1961	1/7/85	niskueu	24
A.R.	9/4/72	26/4/86	niskueu	14
D.R.	8/2/32	14/6/86	napeu	54
A.M.	15/12/67	12/7/86	niskueu	19
A.T.	7/10/57	22/3/87	niskueu	30
B.P.	19/12/87	27/12/87	auashish	amasheni-takanu
W.P.	27/8/88	28/11/88	napeu	auashish
R.R.	1931	27/1/89	napeu	58
B.R.	4/6/89	4/6/89	niskueu	auashish
C.R.	1928	4/8/89	niskueu	61
M.A.	1920	30/9/89	niskueu	69
M.R.	1933	14/12/89	napeu	56
J.J.	1938	20/1/90	napeu	52
P.K.	1990	7/2/90	napeu	auashish
L.M.	1961	26/2/90	niskueu	29
M.K.	1939	16/3/90	niskueu	51
L.A.	1965	31/12/90	niskueu	25
P.K.	1938	14/4/91	napeu	53
M.R.	1983	14/2/92	niskueu	9
M.R.	1983	14/2/92	niskueu	9
W.R.	1988	14/2/92	niskueu	4
J.R.	1989	14/2/92	napeu	3
D.R.	1991	14/2/92	napeu	auashish
J.T.	1990	14/2/92	napeu	2

Uta 1965 nespish 1992, 66 niputs uentshi eku-47 ents nipanikut shitakenapunu. Ueskat meshineiken uen nepeikut shitakenapunu 1973 etistet atshitashun. Ekunu ene ashutat 6 nipipan auassit, eku petetat 5 ents shitakenapunu nta uts shet-shitinu uets nipits. Kie utshe nishunueshut-ashu-nist 23 nepits, esk eka nishunuepuneshit. Eku nistunueshut-ashu-neu 34 nepits esk eka neunuepuneshit 40. Eukunu ne-nepanikut nipinu shimunipen mak utiskuem mamu utuassim, 7 niputs uentshi peikunu nenu tshishikunu. Eku nashikupinu essi nipinantsh minuat nistupuna ispish. Nespish 1989 nte utat muk 17 teshut uentshi nepanikut shitakenapunu.

APPENDIX B

ALCOHOL-RELATED DEATHS OF INNU IN UTSHIMASSIT

1965–February 1992

Person's Initials	Date of Birth	Date of Death	Sex	Age
B.R.	—	26/3/73	male	unrecorded
C.P.	—	17/4/73	male	unrecorded
W.B.	16/2/74	8/8/74	male	infant
P.N	23/7/74	2/1/75	male	infant
P.P.	4/3/75	4/3/75	male	infant
R.T.	29/5/75	14/7/75	male	infant
W.K.	1901	2/3/76	male	75
E.R.	2/4/76	7/9/76	female	infant
M.R.	1904	21/11/77	female	73
L.T.	1/7/76	28/8/77	male	infant
A.P.	8/10/77	28/8/77	female	infant
J.P.	1942	28/8/77	female	35
J.P.	—	28/8/77	female	teen
C.P.	—	28/8/77	male	12
J.P.	1967	28/8/77	male	10
S.P.	—	28/8/77	male	35
M.N.	25/8/55	9/18/79	male	24
P.R.	—	2/3/81	male	unrecorded
A.J.	5/2/66	2/4/83	female	17
F.R.	9/4/47	15/4/83	male	36
M.T.	4/9/47	24/7/83	female	36
A.T.	10/7/46	24/7/83	male	36
T.R.	22/12/36	7/9/84	male	48
A.R.	1961	1/7/85	female	24
A.R.	9/4/72	26/4/86	female	14
D.R.	8/2/32	14/6/86	male	54
A.M.	15/12/67	12/7/86	female	19
A.T.	7/10/57	22/3/87	female	30
B.P.	19/12/87	27/12/87	unrecorded	infant
W.P.	27/8/88	28/11/88	male	infant
R.R.	1931	27/1/89	male	58
B.R.	4/6/89	4/6/89	female	infant
C.R.	1928	4/8/89	female	61
M.A.	1920	30/9/89	female	69
M.R.	1933	14/12/89	male	56
J.J.	1938	20/1/90	male	52
P.K.	1990	7/2/90	male	infant
L.M.	1961	26/2/90	female	29
M.K.	1939	16/3/90	female	51
L.A.	1965	31/12/90	male	25
P.K.	1938	14/4/91	male	53
M.R.	1983	14/2/92	female	9
M.R.	1983	14/2/92	female	9
W.R.	1988	14/2/92	female	4
J.R.	1989	14/2/92	male	3
D.R.	1991	14/2/92	male	infant
J.T.	1990	14/2/92	male	2

From 1965 to 1992, forty-seven (47) out of sixty-six (66) deaths were alcohol-related. The first recorded alcohol-related death was in 1973. Five of the six deaths recorded at this time were infant deaths. Twenty-three (23) of these deaths were people under twenty years of age. Thirty-four (32) were under forty years of age. Following the tragic drownings of the Poker family in 1979 where 7 people died, there was a decline in the number of deaths for the next three years. Since 1989, there have been seventeen (17) alcohol-related deaths in the community.

ESPISH MINANTS UTA UTSHIMASITS

Shitakunapun kie kaminastuskuets etatushits uta Utshimassit. Entushenima-kanits auentshi muku peik pupuna nispish epishiminskueu 15/91, nispish epishiminiskueu 15/92. Kastipet etutak mishinanikanu etshitapamat kie eiemiat 168 Innuts tatishuts kie 360 auashits.

Kaminits

A. 31 tatishuuts inuts mushinau eshukum tshishikaua kaminits.

B. 92 tatishuts inuts kaminits uts kaustupunits utatusheunuash, eakushit kie mishiue.

C. 30 tatishuts uapunitats shitakunapunu. Kutshitauts tshetshi punits kie nutshikamuts etutets naianimanitshi, uatshakanits.

D. 8 tatishuts kauishipets uipats punitauts eminits eka nastesh uitshakanits. Ekuts inuts kaui uitshakanits tshetshi punitats eustupunits eskua eminits.

E. Nishuashutash (7) tatishuuts kauishipetshi utuskuemaua put kie unapema. Ekun auen kakamint muku kauitshimat inua kamintshi.

Essi pupuash pitatatunu (50) tatishuuts inut nete kantutet kastipanits mitshuap tshetshi uitshinukushits. Tshekat mishiue apishipeuts. Nanikutini minuts tante ama uitshakanuts kie eshi eka minupinits uta utenats.

Kutuka Atshitashuna

Kastipets ntushenitamuts etutet enutshiakants shitakunapun. Ekun eshi petishinats tipatshimunu. Eskua etu ntuapatamuts tshetshi minakanits kutuka auenua. Ashinuapatamuts tshetshi itishamuakanits mishinanikea.

A. Mitshimithimau ishishueu tshekat mishiue nutshikamats Utshimasits tukun shitakunapun kie kamnastiskueshits. Eshi aspitshitaiats shuneau pupunush $677,000.00. Ekunu pishe napitshitaiats nete auashits kapushakanits kie nakituenimakanits nete Sheshatshiu.

B. Tshekamakunuest eshishueu tshekat mishiue euueshakau shitakunapunu tutakuuts.

C. Kamakunueshits eapits eshishueuts uta Utshimasits, 25 tatishuts tsheueushakanits, shitakunapunu etutakuts. Nishuashutash nutshikatut kie 15 pakunash tshekuanu. Peikuan eapits nete 1991 eshinakust. Eku auashits 43 tatishuts etatau pikunats tshekuaia nutshikats kaminastuskueshits.

ALCOHOL STATISTICS FOR UTSHIMASSIT, 1991-92

The numbers in this survey were compiled through observation, interviews and assessments by the Alcohol Program in Utshimassit over a period of one year, from February 15, 1991, to February 15, 1992. At the time of the survey there were 168 adults in this community and 360 children.

Alcohol Abuse

A. There are 31 chronic alcoholics in the community. These are people who drink every day or who are binge drinkers.

B. There are 92 problem abusers of alcohol. These are people for whom alcohol has begun to interfere with normal daily life, their responsibilities, their health and so on.

C. There are 30 recovering persons. These people have quit drinking and are actively working on not drinking again by going to A.A. meetings, doing counselling or other recovery methods.

D. There are 8 other persons who abused alcohol in the past and have quit drinking, but without support. Commonly known as "dry drunks," these are people who have made few changes in their lives and are still having many of the same problems they had when they were drinking.

E. There are 7 spouses of alcohol abusers. These are people who, although not drinkers, are married to alcohol abusers and experience very serious problems like their spouses.

Over the past year, approximately 50 Innu have received treatment for alcoholism, with approximately 70 per cent of these Innu maintaining sobriety. Relapse has occurred because of poor follow-up and basic living conditions in this community.

Other Important Numbers

The Alcohol Program is doing research on the costs of dealing with alcohol-related problems in the community. This is some of the information they have gathered so far. The following numbers have been provided to the Alcohol Program through letters from the various agencies. The program is still awaiting a number of responses to their requests for information.

A. The Regional Office of the Department of Social Services estimates that about 75-80 per cent of the cases they deal with in Davis Inlet are related to problems of alcohol and solvent abuse. Their total cost of operation for 1991-92 was $677,000. Of this total amount, over $200,000 was spent on the Child Welfare Program, the Youth Corrections Program and the group home in Sheshatshiu.

B. Provincial Court Judge James Igloliorte estimates that over 90 per cent of the court cases in Davis Inlet are a result of alcohol abuse.

C. The R.C.M.P. has on record for Davis Inlet in 1990, 25 reported Criminal Code cases where alcohol was involved. Seven of these were crimes against persons and 15 against property. In 1991, there were 22 reported Criminal Code cases where alcohol was involved. Seven of these were against persons and 15 were against property. With regards to children, there were 43 reported cases of crime which involved solvent abuse in 1990 and 66 reported cases in 1991.

3 3132 01151805 9